PARTNERSHIP RIGHTS, FREE MOVEMENT, AND EU LAW

This book considers the case for modernising partnership rights in EC family reunification law. Existing Community law guarantees immigration rights only to spouses, and yet there is a growing diversity of national laws on same-sex marriage, registered partnerships and recognition of cohabitation. The Community institutions which have recently framed new legislation seem to view this as a question that can be settled by political agreement with little or no outside constraint. The book challenges this assumption. The book outlines recent developments in national legal systems and traces the development of the recent Community legislation. Then, drawing on basic ECHR principles, the place of the ECHR in Community law, and basic Community law principles of free movement and discrimination, the book argues that the right of a migrant EU citizen to family reunification for a cohabiting partner is presumptively protected, and therefore justification for refusing to admit such partners must be provided. It also considers the possible justifications for marriage-only immigration policies and concludes that although possible, such justifications are far from certain to succeed in the ECJ. The discussion on immigration rights also tackles the important question of whether judicial activism is appropriate or whether there should be judicial deference to the legislative process recently completed. The book concludes with a wider discussion of the proper response of Community law to the increasing diversity of Member States family laws and policies beyond the field of immigration rights. The book will be of value not only to immigration lawyers, but also to those interested in partnership rights generally, as well as to a wider audience of EU lawyers, primarily academics but also graduate students and practitioners.

Volume 3 in the series Modern Studies in European Law

Modern Studies in European Law

Volume 3: Partnership Rights, Free Movement, and EU Law

Other titles in this series

1. Soft Law in European Community Law — *Linda Senden*
2. The Impact of European Rights on National Legal Systems — *Miriam Aziz*

Partnership Rights, Free Movement, and EU Law

HELEN TONER
The University of Warwick

·HART·
PUBLISHING
OXFORD AND PORTLAND OREGON
2004

Published in North America (US and Canada) by
Hart Publishing
c/o International Specialized Book Services
5804 NE Hassalo Street
Portland, Oregon
97213-3644
USA

Hart Publishing is a specialist legal publisher based in Oxford, England. To order further copies of this book or to request a list of other publications please write to:

Hart Publishing, Salters Boatyard, Folly Bridge, Abingdon Rd, Oxford, OX1 4LB Telephone: +44 (0)1865 245533 Fax: +44 (0)1865 794882
email: mail@hartpub.co.uk
WEBSITE: http//:www.hartpub.co.uk

British Library Cataloguing in Publication Data
Data Available

ISBN 1-84113-477-5 (hardback)

Typeset by Olympus Infotech Pvt Ltd, India
Printed and bound in Great Britain by
TJ International, Padstow, Cornwall

Acknowledgments

This book is based on a DPhil thesis submitted to the Faculty of Law at Oxford University in 2003. My first acknowledgment has to be of my supervisors: Professors Paul Craig, who supervised the project from its beginnings in EU citizenship, and Elspeth Guild who kindly agreed, among her numerous other commitments elsewhere, to act as an additional external supervisor as my work moved more and more towards immigration law. They provided expert guidance and patient encouragement, were generous in sharing their wide knowledge and experience during the writing of my thesis, and have also been most generous in their continued interest in the subsequent progress of my work since then. I am also grateful to my examiners, Professors Stephen Weatherill and Robert Wintemute, who subjected my thesis to the customary thorough and expert but also remarkably prompt examination, and provided many helpful suggestions and comments. I have been very fortunate to have benefited from such a range of expert knowledge and experience both in my supervision and examination.

Gráinne de Búrca also deserves a word of thanks for her patient responses to my regular questions when I first arrived at Somerville in 1997 and for continued advice and encouragement from a distance in Florence. Steve Peers' regular emails have been an invaluable source of information, documents and references, and the ILPA EC Law Subcommittee continues to be a welcoming and lively forum for regular discussions of Community immigration law from which I have learned much. Nick Bamforth and Mark Bell read part or all of the manuscript at various stages, and I am also grateful to Rob Wintemute, Mark Bell, and Kees Waaldijk in particular for passing on helpful information about the development of same-sex partnership laws to keep the material up to date. Anastasia Iliopoulou shared my interest in EU Citizenship during her year as a visiting research student in Oxford, and it was a great pleasure to find ourselves in agreement on almost everything—except the proper time for a lunch break! Our continued academic collaboration and friendship is a great inspiration.

I am pleased to acknowledge the support of the Arts and Humanities Research Board for this project. Somerville, Queen's and the Oxford Law Faculty have all provided additional financial support for the research and/or various trips abroad, and have provided excellent environments in which to work. It has been a particular pleasure to work alongside Nick Bamforth, Dan Sarooshi, Jeroen Kortmann, and Samantha Besson at Queen's. A brief word of acknowledgment is also due to the students of EC law who have tolerated my particular interest in EU citizenship, residence rights, and migration law, and also to the Bodleian Law Library staff for their assistance with more obscure materials.

Finally, and most importantly, my greatest thanks are due to my parents—without whom this would never have been started, much less finished. For their unconditional and loving support over many years, and more particularly for learning much more than they ever wanted to know about proper forms of legal citations, same-sex marriages, and EC immigration law while this project was being completed, I am deeply grateful.

Contents

Table of Cases

European Court of Justice

European Court of Human Rights

Other Courts

Table of Legislation

Directives

Regulations

National Legislation

Introduction

THE BACKGROUND: EXISTING COMMUNITY IMMIGRATION LAW AND THE DIVERSITY OF NATIONAL LAW — A BRIEF OVERVIEW

Community law currently restricts *guaranteed* immigration rights to married partners (possibly only opposite-sex spouses) of migrant EU citizens, ie those living in another Member State of the European Union (EU). Beyond this, immigration rights for unmarried partners, same-sex partners, and those with legal recognition or registration of their partnership other than a marriage, are left to the Member States to decide. This mainly affects bi-national couples where one partner is a Third Country National ('TCN'). Couples who are both EU citizens are in a far better position, both having independent rights of residence throughout the EU subject to the requirement of financial means to avoid being an unreasonable burden on the State (which could be provided by one working partner for the other) and health insurance. Community law also lacks general competence to act in the field of substantive family law in the sense of adopting measures to harmonise rules on who can marry, the introduction of other forms of registered partnerships, and the legal rights and obligations attaching to marriage or other registered partnerships or simply to cohabiting couples.

This however sits alongside a diversity of approaches to family law, and the legal recognition of partnerships in domestic laws, both within the EU and elsewhere. There is an increasing trend towards recognition of same-sex partnerships, and this has prompted the introduction of non-marital registered partnerships of various sorts, even though some of these also include the possibility of registration of heterosexual relationships. Most strikingly, The Netherlands in 2001 was the first state to break the heterosexual monopoly on marriage by its legislation opening civil marriage to same-sex couples and Belgian law has now followed suit. At the time of writing Canadian law is in the process of confirming a similar development, and the issue is becoming one of the most high profile and controversial domestic issues in US politics. There is also a growing trend towards recognition of and protection of 'de facto' family life between unmarried couples, whether same-sex or opposite-sex. Turning to the specific question of immigration law, marriage is losing its uniquely privileged place as the only form of long-term, stable, conjugal relationship giving rise to immigration rights for a partner. Increasingly, although again not universally, registered partnerships and cohabiting relationships (same-sex, opposite-sex, or both) may also give rise to immigration rights for a non-national partner.

SCOPE OF THE BOOK

In the light of this complex legal background, the aim of this book is to examine, analyse and evaluate the case for modernising partnership rights in EC family reunification law to include those other than heterosexual married couples. In doing so the focus will be on the position of *couples* rather than wider issues concerning other family members such as parents, children, and other relatives. The focus will also be on *immigration* (and indeed *admission* rather than *resisting expulsion* of those already legally resident) rather than other rights, thus excluding specific comprehensive consideration of the range of other rights, benefits and obligations that Community law or national law might grant or impose. The only limited exception to this is that I consider that the accompanying partner should also be permitted to work, although the extensive consideration and defence of this particular proposition is not part of the book.

It will be seen that many of those involved in the EC legislative process do not consider the response to this particular problem to be significantly constrained by external legal factors. They view it as a matter primarily for political agreement, and consider that individual Member States wishing to maintain marriage-only immigration polices in relation to migrant EU citizens are, in principle, free to do so. The particular focus of this book will be to challenge this assumption. Basic legal principles exist which not only act as normative values underpinning the development of Community law, but impose constraints on the legality of Member State or Community action which are ultimately legally enforceable. It will be argued that these principles are clearly applicable to partners' immigration rights and lead to the inevitable conclusion that the right of the migrant EU citizen to be accompanied by a partner is presumptively protected under Community law.

Two normative assumptions are made and a focus adopted on particular a category of couples that must be made explicit and explained at the outset.

1 Desirability of Residence Rights

First, the importance of family reunification is assumed from the outset—this can hardly be understated. Cholewinski notes:

> Reuniting migrant workers with their families living in their countries of origin is recognized to be essential for the migrants' well-being and their

> social adaptation to the receiving country. Prolonged separation and isolation lead to hardships and stress affecting both the migrants and the families left behind and prevent them from leading a normal life. The large numbers of migrant workers cut off from social relations and living on the fringe of the receiving community create many well-known psychological problems that, in turn, largely determine community attitudes towards migrant workers.[1]
>
> Family reunion is clearly an important social entitlement. Individuals cannot enjoy their basic rights unless protection is exended to the social context in which they find themselves. The family, however broadly defined, constitutes the closest attachment human beings possess. Such attachments effectively define who we really are. This truism is in line with modern communitarian thought, which considers an individual, detached from family, friends, and community, as 'a person wholly without character, without moral depth.' The right of migrant workers to reunite with their families is essential not only to their own well-being and to the welfare of their families, but also, as argued in Chapter 3, because it contributes to the social stability in both receiving and sending countries.[2]

Carens continues along the same lines of thinking, emphasising that liberal democratic states are indeed constrained in their immigration policies to admit immediate family members because 'People clearly have a deep and vital interest in being able to live with their immediate family members' and suggesting that this cannot be satisfied by permitting individuals to exit to live elsewhere with those family members because of the continuing interest they have in remaining where they have settled roots.[3] His arguments point towards a general obligation to respect the choice of residence of the bi-national family.[4]

Meilander also takes a similar view, even though as Carens notes he is more generally a defender of state discretion in immigration control and in the particular work in question sets out to defend as a general principle state control over admissions. Nonetheless he sets family members of settled residents apart as one group which there is a general duty to admit:

> We are bound to our family members through a more richly complex web of relationships, a mixture of love and dependence, than we share with any other people. These relationships give rise to an especially intense feelings of mutual affection and concern. To deprive someone of these relationships is to deprive him of his richest and most significant bonds with other human beings. That is something we should only do in rare circumstances. ….

[1] R Cholewinski, *Migrant Workers in International Human Rights Law* (OUP, Oxford, 1997) 117, quoting the ILO Report VII (i) *Migrant Workers* (ILO, Geneva, 1973) 27.
[2] Cholewinski (n 1) 332.
[3] J Carens, 'Who Should Get In? The Ethics of Immigration Admissions' 2003 (17) *Ethics and International Affairs* 95. Thanks to Dallal Stevens.
[4] He is however more reticent about whether he considers states should be *constrained* to recognise, for example, same-sex, unmarried, or polygamous relationships when they do not fit with the host society's views of family life.

> Because the family bond is of such vital importance, it is not something that governments should ask residents to relinquish....[5]

I assume these considerations apply equally to those conjugal couples who are not in opposite-sex marriages. These considerations of protecting the social context of migrants, the problems encountered when detaching the individual from the ties of family, friends and community, the mutual interdependence of relationships and the problems arising out of disruptions to such relationships may be applied equally to all conjugal relationships. Likewise the rather more pragmatic concern of ensuring successful integration into the host state and its society is equally valid. The forcible separation by immigration law of cohabiting couples—and a fortiori, couples who are legally married or registered partners under domestic law of another state—is problematic for all of these reasons. As AG Geelhoed in the recent case of *Baumbast* notes,[6] current family reunification law and policy in the EU was drawn up more than 20 years ago and thus there is a risk of undesirable lacunae in the legal protection offered as a result of social developments during this time. This is undoubtedly one of them. I readily admit that the normative justification for family reunification of unmarried couples is stronger in the case of those in same-sex relationships who cannot marry, and for those in non-marital legally registered partnerships. And yet the separation of couples who are legally free to do so but who do not (yet) wish to marry or register their partnership still seems problematic.

As to the question of normative justification for intervention through Community law to secure this aim, no a priori assumptions about this are made at this early stage. However, throughout the book various foundational legal principles central to Community law will be examined, particularly equality, respect for family and private life, and free movement. In examining these legal principles, associated normative justifications will also emerge, and it will be suggested that the case in favour not only of immigration rights, but of Community law regulation and protection of these immigration rights is compelling.

2 Scepticism about Development of a 'European Community Family Law'

Secondly, it is assumed that the extent to which there is a Community family law and policy is and should be limited. The question of residence rights for family members is one of, if not the primary core area in which EU law

[5] P Meilaender, *Towards a Theory of Immigration* Palgrave (Macmillan, New York, 2001) 182. Again however, he does not tackle the question of defining the family and admission of non-marital partners.
[6] Case C-413/99 *Baumbast & R v SSHD*.

has traditionally operated in the 'family law' field broadly conceived. And yet the Community's activities elsewhere in the field of family law and policy have been gathering pace. In particular, there have been non-binding policy declarations and Communications,[7] and the provisions under Title IV of the Treaty lend themselves to the suggestion that they may provide competence in matters of judicial co-operation in civil matters relating to family law. This has been followed more recently by measures in the field of private international law, in particular recognition and enforcement of judgments,[8] and most recently the draft Constitutional Treaty expressly envisages expressing competence to deal with matters of family law with a cross-border dimension (Article III-165 of the draft Treaty Establishing a Constitution for Europe). There is also a growing academic interest in the question of how far unification or harmonisation of family law may be possible or desirable in Europe, including a lively interest in the way the EU itself and its institutions and lawmaking processes can or should be involved in any such activity. Indeed a Commission on European Family Law[9] was established in 2001 to provide an intellectual focus for this activity, and there is a fast-growing literature on the subject.[10]

This work however proceeds from an assumption that the Community itself does not have and should not immediately aspire to develop, any kind of general competence in the field of family law in the sense of

[7] European Parliament Resolution on Family Policy in the EEC [1983] OJ C184/116, Communication from the Commission on Family Policies COM(1989)363.

[8] Council Regulation 1347/2000 of 29 May 2000 on Jurisdiction and the Recognition of Judgments in Matrimionial Matters and in Matters of Parental Responsibility for Children of Both Spouses [2000] OJ L160/19: see P McLeavy, 'The Brussels II Regulation: How the European Community has Moved into Family Law' (2002) 51 *ICLQ* 883. This Reg was replaced in 2003 by Council Regulation 2201/2003 of 27 November 2003 Concerning Jurisdiction and the Reognition and Enforcement of Judgments in Matrimonial Matters and Matters of Parental Responsibility [2003] OJ L338/1. Originally confined to children of both spouses the new Reg goes further than this implicitly recognising a wider range of family forms.

[9] See their website, *www.law.uu.nl/priv/cefl/*.

[10] The available literature has expanded considerably even since the thesis on which this book was based was completed at the end of 2002. D Martiny, 'Is Unification of Family Law Feasible or even Desirable?' in A Hartkamp et al (eds), *Towards a European Civil Code* (Kluwer, The Hague, 1998); A Verbeke, 'Perspectives for an International Marital Contract' (2001) 8 *MJ* 189; C McGlynn, 'The Europeanisation of Family Law' (2001) 13 *CFLQ* 35; C McGlynn, 'A Family Law for the European Union?' in J Shaw (ed), *Social Law and Policy in an Evolving EU* (Hart Publishing, Oxford, 2001); M Antokolskaia, 'The Harmonisation of Family Law: New and Old Dilemmas' (2003) *ERPL* 28; H Stalford, 'Old Problems, New Solutions? — EU Regulation of Cross-National Child Maintenance' (2003) 15(3) *CFLQ* 269; H Stalford, 'Regulating Family Life in Post-Amsterdam Europe' (2003) 28 *ELRev* 39; N Lowe, 'The Growing Influence of the European Union on International Family Law' (2003) *CLP* 439; E Caracciolo Di Torella and A Masselot, 'Under Construction: EU Family Law' (2004) 29 *ELRev* 33. See also particularly the most helpful volume K Boele-Woelki (ed), *Perspectives for the Unification and Harmonisation of Family Law in Europe* (Intersentia, Antwerp, 2003).

wholesale harmonisation of domestic law concepts of marriage, partnership, cohabitation or the consequent rights and obligations. I am inclined to share McGlynn's scepticism on this point.[11] She expresses concerns about the dominant concept of family that currently exists in EU law, the 'model European family' being the heterosexual married couple, with the husband as the main breadwinner. Her fear is that any measures taken by the EU in the field of family law based on this model will reinforce this dominant ideology and continue to exclude and disadvantage families that do not conform to it. The argument presented in this book would of course present no concerns for someone adopting this view. However, similar concerns although from a different perspective may equally be expressed by those who would advocate that a degree of legal protection and privilege for the married or similarly registered same-sex couple is perfectly legitimate, or by those who resist the suggestion that same-sex relationships should be recognised at all. Regardless of one's stance on these questions,[12] there has to be a real concern about the extent to which the EU is the appropriate forum in which to address these issues. Whether or not one's preferred vision of the family is one of the traditional married heterosexual couple or an altogether more liberal, egalitarian and 'Utopian'[13] vision which would embrace other alternative family forms, the necessity and desirability of EU law developing any substantial family law and policy onto which any particular visions of the family may be projected must be open to question. This is not to suggest that some degree of regulation may not be appropriate and welcome in relation to particular issues, particularly those with a clear and obvious cross-border or transnational dimension. I do not assume this, but merely that particular aspects of Community intervention in family law and policy should be justified—as should any particular form of the 'family' which is projected onto such EU family law and policy. It may well be that in time, steps taken to address issues with cross-border implications will prove to be a potent force for greater harmonisation of domestic family laws.[14] However, this is likely to be in the longer term, and the extent to which it

[11] McGlynn, n 10 above. See also C McGlynn, 'Challenging the European Harmonisation of Family Law: Perspectives on "the Family"' in K Boele-Woelki (ed), *Perspectives for the Unification and Harmonisation of Family Law in Europe.*

[12] I consider that second concern relating specifically to same-sex couples is unfounded, but that the first, to provide a distinctive legal framework for long-term committed partnerships which have been duly formalised in law, is a plausible and potentially valid one.

[13] McGlynn (n 10).

[14] Dethloff considers that harmonisation of rules of civil procedure and conflicts of laws may not be enough to address the issues adequately: N Dethloff, 'Arguments for the Unification and Harmonisation of Family Law in Europe' in K Boele-Woelki (ed), *Perspectives for the Unification and Harmonisation of Family Law in Europe* (Intersentia, Antwerp, 2003).

would be appropriate for the Community itself to be involved in such further 'spillover' harmonisation is contestable.

3 Resolving these Apparently Contradictory Assumptions

It may be seen therefore that the particular subject under scrutiny sits somewhat uneasily between these two normative assumptions. Preserving Member State autonomy in family immigration law will mean compromising the normative assumption that the autonomy, dignity and free movement of couples who cannot or chose not to fit themselves within the dominant ideology of the heterosexual married couple should be protected by ensuring immigration rights at the very least. Yet advocating that Community law should effectively force Member States into the adoption of immigration rights for such couples is undoubtedly an intrusion into an aspect of Member State family law and policy and may inevitably beg the question 'if this, what next?' The resolution of this dilemma will be at the heart of this study.

4 The Focus on Unmarried Couples

The paradigm of the unmarried couple, whether same-sex or opposite-sex, is adopted throughout. Thus, although the way Community law and the Member States deal with claims for residence rights made by TCN partners in same-sex marriages and registered partnerships will necessarily involve some consideration of transnational recognition of same-sex marriages and registered partnerships,[15] this is not the primary focus of this study. I focus mainly on the possibilities of harmonisation at the level of granting immigration rights to all cohabiting partners in stable relationships rather than seeking a solution based solely on mutual recognition of same-sex marriages and registered partnerships.

This approach is taken for several reasons. First, if the recognition of immigration rights depends on the recognition of a same-sex marriage as a valid marital relationship or on the recognition that resgistered partnership rights may be portable from state to state, these are primarily issues of private international law. Although the regulation of questions of private international law in relation to family status in EU law would be

[15] For a consideration of this including some consideration of private intenational law see H D'Oliviera, 'Freedom of Movement of Spouses and Registered Partners in the European Union' in K Siehr and J Bassedow (eds), *Private Law in the International Arena: From National Conflict Rules Towards Harmonization and Unification* (TMC Asser Press, The Hague, 2000).

an interesting topic, they are outside the scope of this particular work which mainly concerns immigration law. If on the other hand it can be suggested that *all TCN partners* regardless of sexual orientation and legal status of the partnership ought to be granted immigration rights, this less easily opens up the possibility of the regulation of private international family law through Community law. Even though I would not myself necessarily object to some moves in this direction, some might be sceptical and therefore I consider any argument for immigration rights to be stronger without specific reliance on it. Further, although I do not regard retention of *some* distinctive legal incidents of marriage or similar same-sex registered partnership as undesirable nor impermissible, I do take the view that immigration rights should not be limited in this way. Finally, if immigration rights are tied to the existence of legal partnership registration, a significant number of same-sex couples living in states where such legislation has not yet been introduced will fall outside the scope of the protection offered, and this would create undesirable and arbitrary discrimination in the enjoyment of family reunification rights.

The paradigm is also that of the *conjugal couple*—in the sense of the couple who have a mutually interdependent, stable, usually cohabiting and sexual, relationship. I thus exclude from specific consideration polygamous marriages[16] or other multiple partners and non-conjugal relationships.[17] This is not because I consider these issues to be insignificant or unimportant, but to confine the scope of this study within manageable limits. Of course some of the principles explored and conclusions reached could be applied to such relationships but I leave that aside for the present.

5 The Focus on Member State Nationals

I also start from the paradigm of the couple consisting of at least one migrant EU citizen. I do this because this is the current extent of

[16] As Wintemute points out, R Wintemute, 'Partnership Rights as Human Rights', Oxford Amnesty Lecture 2002 (OUP, Oxford, forthcoming), polygamy is a different question from the recognition of same-sex relationships and same-sex marriages, and if there is in the future a sustained campaign for widespread systematic recognition of polygamous relationships or legalisation of polygamy that issue can be addressed on its merits. Views on how far the two issues are or are not comparable vary—see eg D Chambers, 'Polygamy and Same-sex Marriage' (1997) 27(1) *Hofstra Law Review;* M Strassberg 'Distinctions of Form and Substance: Monogamy, Polygamy, and Same-sex Marriage' (1997) 75 *NCL Rev* 1501.

[17] There are those who contest the primacy of the conjugal couple and consider either that rights and benefits should be individualised or that an individual should be able to designate a beneficiary other than a conjugal partner. On this subject generally see B Crossman and B Ryder, 'What is Marriage-like Like? The Irrelevance of Conjugality' (2001) 18 *CJFL,* and and the report produced by the Law Commission of Canada, *Beyond Conjugality* (Law Commission of Canada, Ottawa, 2001).

Community family reunification law. It is of course possible—indeed highly likely—that in the future the scope of this area of Community law will expand. A Directive has now been agreed to deal with the position of some legally resident TCNs and addressing family reunification rights through Community law for those non-migrant EU citizens in 'internal' situations is also now on the agenda.[18] My main concern however throughout the bulk of the book will be with basic principles of Community law as they currently apply to migrant EU citizens with TCN partners—although in the final chapter in reviewing and evaluating the different arguments I will consider the degree to which these principles could be adapted to the situations of non-migrant EU citizens and TCNs as Community law begins to regulate the situation of these individuals in relation to family reunification.

STRUCTURE OF THE BOOK

Chapter 1 will introduce the diversity of different national laws on partnership regulation and partners' immigration rights. Chapter 2 will set out the current state of Community law and outline the recent development of new Community legislation. Chapters 3 and 4 will examine the way in which human rights principles might constrain immigration policies of Member States and the Community in this respect, particularly focusing on the European Convention on Human Rights (ECHR) (chapter 3) and its place in Community law (chapter 4). The principles of respect for private and family life (Article 8 ECHR) and non-discrimination in the enjoyment of other Convention rights (Article 14 ECHR) will be central to this discussion. Chapters 5 and 6 will examine other Community law principles—discrimination on the grounds of nationality and other grounds (ch 6) and going beyond discrimination, the concept of obstacles to free movement (ch 5). In chapters 3–6, I shall be primarily concerned to show that the restriction of immigration rights to married partners is presumptively an interference with protected rights, which must therefore be justified, leaving discussion of the question of justification itself to a later chapter.

Chapter 7 will consider the extent to which such justifications are convincing. A brief consideration of the policy issues involved, and the approach to justification of interference with protected rights used by the European Court of Justice (ECJ) in particular, will reveal that justification of a married partners only immigration policy is, although possible, far from

[18] See ch 2 below.

certain to succeed in the ECJ or before any well-informed policy-maker seeking to ensure compliance with these basic principles of Community law.

Chapter 8 will conclude with a consideration of the implications of these different conceptual approaches in securing modernisation of partnership rights in current EC family reunification law while at the same time (1) minimising undesirable spill-over effects in other areas of family law; (2) articulating a clear and coherent basis for beginning to map the proper boundaries of the EU's ambitions in the family law field; and (3) being adaptable beyond EU migrants to include others also—ie, TCNs and those in 'purely internal' situations as and when Community law regulates family reunification in these situations.

1

Diversity in National Law

THIS CHAPTER WILL illustrate the diversity of relevant national law and practice. It is primarily descriptive rather than analytical or normative, setting out the legal and factual background for the rest of the discussion. In selecting the specific countries mentioned, the illustration of this diversity and the range of different approaches was the main criterion. The focus is largely on EU Member States but where there are developments of significance elsewhere (particularly when they appear in English language literature) these are also mentioned.

Part 1 examines the degree to which legal recognition is made available to, or indeed imposed upon, couples in stable conjugal (usually cohabiting) relationships, addressing in particular (although not exclusively) the status of same-sex couples and the high-profile debate over same-sex marriage. Part 2 examines the diversity of immigration policies of states, and the extent to which the heterosexual married couple is no longer the 'model' or 'traditional' form of conjugal partnership for which *immigration* rights may be preserved in the case of bi-national couples. Finally, Part 3 considers briefly the question of transnational recognition of foreign marriages and registered partnerships in private international law.

This area of law is extremely fast-moving and controversial. Legislative change and litigation are proceeding in a number of jurisdictions,[1] and this chapter cannot be totally comprehensive. If the reader appreciates anything from this chapter it will be the fast, even 'explosive' pace of change in this area in recent years.

[1] Where relevant, pending cases and legislation are indicated. This chapter draws in particular on R Wintemute and M Andenas (eds), *Legal Recognition of Same-sex Partnerships* (Hart Publishing, Oxford, 2001); Y Merin *Equality for Same-sex Couples, the Legal Recognition of Gay Partnerships in Europe and the United States* (University of Chicago Press, Chicago, 2002); W Eskridge, *Equality Practice—Civil Unions and the Future of Gay Rights* (Routledge, New York, 2002).

PART ONE — DIFFERENT APPROACHES TO LEGAL REGULATION OF PARTNERSHIPS

Introduction

Beyond the immediate observation that all states recognise heterosexual marriage but attach a range of different legal consequences to it,[2] six different legal approaches may be identified to the recognition and regulation of conjugal relationships:[3]

1 Marriage may be opened to same-sex couples.
2 Registered partnerships or civil unions may be established, usually open only to same-sex couples and granting all or almost all of the rights and obligations of marriage.
3 Less extensive registered partnerships may be provided, involving fewer rights and obligations involved and less clearly comparable to marriage.
4 Municipal registers without legal effect, and domestic partnership registers primarily aimed at providing employment benefits may exist.
5 Heterosexual marriage only may be the only form of legal recognition or registration of conjugal relationships.
6 Any of these approaches can also be combined with a varying degree of recognition of unmarried cohabitants flowing not from the legal registration of the partnership, but from the mere fact of the relationship, and/or the cohabitation of the couple.

1.1 Same-sex Marriage

1.1.1 The History of Marriage and Why Gays Now Feel They 'Belong' in Civil Marriage[4]

It would be impossible to embark on a history of marriage at this point. Nevertheless, inclusion within civil marriage (the distinction between civil and religious marriage should be emphasised at the outset—very few if any would advocate requiring religious institutions to change their views of religious marriage or to celebrate same-sex marriages if this

[2] On diversity, uniformity and change in family law generally see C Hamilton and K Standley (eds), *Family Law in Europe* (Butterworths, London, 1995), and the literature cited above (Introduction, n 10).
[3] Similar classifications are used by Merin and Eskridge, *ibid*.
[4] Along with others, I generally use the term 'gay' to refer to lesbian, gay and bisexual individuals inclined to form relationships with those of the same gender, and 'same-sex' or 'opposite-sex' to refer to marriage and other partnerships between two persons.

would be against their religious doctrines) is now high on the agenda of gay rights campaigners, and is provoking much academic writing, as well as vigorous public debate. It is useful to separate the normative and constitutional arguments involved, although unsurprisingly some writing brings the two together.[5]

Many of the reasons that gays now feel they belong in marriage, normatively, socially, and constitutionally, are linked to the changing concept of marriage itself.[6] It should be noted, however, that support for same-sex marriage in the gay community, although perhaps now more widespread than ever, is not and certainly was not always unanimous.[7] Many feel uneasy about joining an institution that they see as inherently traditional, sexist and oppressive, not nececsesarily ideally suited to the needs of gay couples, and which will marginalise non-married same-sex couples and single gay individuals. Some also consider that there are more immediate issues of concern to the gay community. However, the idea of same-sex marriage (or as a step along the way, comprehensive registered partnerships or civil unions) is gaining support among the gay community. Particularly in situations where gays are (relatively) free to live their lives free of harassment, prosecution and open discrimination, it is an attractive option. It short-cuts numerous fights over particular rights for same-sex couples, whether over housing rights, 'spousal support', immigration, social benefits, or any of the other legal rights that still attach to marriage in various legal systems. As Graff points out, it provides ready-made answers to a range of situations that couples find themselves in, both during and after their relationships. It also has a powerful symbolic significance, signalling society's acceptance of the relationship. Although in the past criticism of same-sex marriage has come from *both* sides, it now comes more often (although still not exlcusively) from conservative traditionalists favouring heterosexual marriage than from radical 'sexual dissidents' in the gay community.

[5] For an overview of the debate see W Eskridge, 'The Ideological Structure of the Same-sex Marriage Debate' in Wintemute and Andenas (n 1). Wolfson, Strasser, Eskridge and Merin are among the most prominent advocates of same-sex marriage: M Strasser, *Legally Wed: Same-sex Marriage and the Constitution* (Cornell University Press, Ithaca, 1997); M Strasser, *The Challenge of Same-sex Marriage* (Praeger, Westport, CT, 1999); Eskridge (n 1); W Eskridge, *The Case for Same-sex Marriage: From Sexual Liberty to Civilised Commitment* (Free Press, New York, 1996) and Merin (n 1).

[6] See Merin (n 1) especially ch1; E Graff, *What is Marriage For?* (Beacon Press, Boston, 1999).

[7] See P Ettelbrick, 'Since when is Marriage a Path to Liberation?' (Fall 1989) 6 *OUT/LOOK*, reprinted in W Eskridge, *Sexuality Gender and Law* (Foundation Press, Westbury NY, 1997); N Duclos, 'Some Complicating Thoughts on Same-sex Marriage' (1991) 1 *Law & Sexuality* 31; N Polikoff, 'We Will Get What We Ask For: Why Legalising Gay and Lesbian Marriage Will Not "Dismantle the Legal Structure of Gender in Every Marriage"' (1993) 79 *Virginia L Rev* 1535; K Norrie, 'Marriage is for Heterosexuals—May the Rest of Us be Spared from It' (2000) 12 *CFLQ* 363. See also the different views set out in the first section of Wintemute and Andenas (n 1).

1.1.2 Normative Arguments

One approach is functional, inquiring into the nature and purpose of marriage in contemporary Western society, and arguing that these functions may be fulfilled just as well by same-sex couples. Graff traces the history of marriage and its purposes.[8] She discusses six main purposes of marriage—'money, sex, babies, kin, order, and heart'—and concludes that all of the purposes of marriage in contemporary Western society may be fulfilled by same-sex couples. Over the last few hundred years, marriage has been freed of its nature as an economic bargain between families intended to produce legitimate heirs and to form (depending on the social class of the couple), either alliances between family groups or a working business partnership, ofter with gender-specific roles. It has become, more and more, in contemporary Western cultures and societies, characterised as a public manifestation of a unitive, companionate, affectionate, and sexual relationship between the couple, as well as a powerful way to ensure stability and long-term care by both parents for any children born of the union. In contemporary Western culture, affection and affinity is now widely[9] expected to be, and usually is, the prime reason motivating marriage choices. Marriage surrounds the couples who enter into it with legal protections and societal expectations or norms which support the pairing during its lifetime, and the survivor after death or divorce, and it is argued that same-sex couples need and deserve the option of obtaining such protection through marriage in the same way as heterosexual couples. Now that these changes have taken place, same-sex couples assert that they 'belong' as married couples just as heterosexuals do, because they are just as capable of forming economically interdependent and mutually supportive relationships, having loving and faithful sexual bonds, raising children, and providing links between wider family groups.

This approach is closely related to one based on liberal equality stressing the normative case against discrimination based on sexual orientation and in favour of the same options of recognition being available to longstanding same-sex partnerships.

It is also true that marriage laws signal powerfully society's approval of some unions and disapproval of others—the most obvious example being the widespread bans on interracial marriage in the US enacted in the 1800s and only gradually swept away by legislation during the twentieth century and eventually declared unconstitutional by the US

[8] Graff (n 6).

[9] Although admittedly not exclusively, as the tradition of the arranged marriage still persists particularly among Asian communities settled in Western countries. However, anecdotal evidence certainly suggests that increasingly young couples for whom a marriage is arranged will wish to get to know each other before finally agreeing to the match.

Supreme Court in the case of *Loving v Virginia*.[10] This social approval conferred by marriage is one reason why the idea of same-sex marriage has gained such popularity among gay rights lobbyists recently,[11] although the conferral of such social approval is less often advanced as an independent normative reason *why* same-sex couples should be allowed to marry.

1.1.3 *Constitutional Arguments*

To engage in successful litigation, these normative arguments must be fitted into the particular framework of constitutional protection available to the applicants. The constitutional arguments involved tend to cluster around claims of protection against sex or sexual orientation discrimination, or the fundamental right to marry the partner of one's choice (see particularly below the discussion of the situation in the US and Canada).

1.1.4 *The Case Against Same-sex Marriage*

This may be addressed by both a definitional and normative approach. It is argued by some that marriage is by its current definition heterosexual and therefore either does not currently include same-sex couples or, more radically, can never be altered to include them (definitional), and that it would be a bad thing to alter this definition to allow same-sex marriage (normative). These objections seem to be motivated by similar convictions that same-sex relationships are not and should not be treated as equal to heterosexual relationships, and that marriage is the preferable location for childrearing.[12]

1.1.5 *The Netherlands Leads the Way*

The Netherlands was the first state to enable same-sex couples to marry. The Dutch law on same-sex civil marriage came into effect on 1 April 2001, and within nine months more than two thousand same-sex couples

[10] *Loving v Virginia* 388 US1 87 SCt (187) (1967).

[11] However, those who maintain that homosexual conduct is immoral and should not be sanctioned or approved of by the law use this same argument to insist that same sex couples should not be allowed to marry.

[12] George, Wardle and Finnis are among those articulating these views: R George and G Bradley, 'Marriage and the Liberal Imagination' (1995) 84 *Geo LJ* 301; R George, *In Defense of Natural Law* (OUP, Oxford, 1999); L Wardle, 'Multiply and Replenish: Considering Same-sex Marriage in the Light of State Interests in Marital Procreation' 24 *Harvard JLPP* 771; J Finnis, 'Law, Morality and Sexual Orientation' (1993–94) 69 *Notre Dame Law Review* 1049; J Finnis, 'The Good of Marriage and the Morality of Sexual Relations: Some Philosophical and Historical Observations' (1997) 42 *Am J Jurisprudence*.

married. The road towards this radical step has been admirably charted elsewhere.[13] However, a few key points may be highlighted.

1.1.6 Judicial Restraint and Slow Legislative Action

Attempts to raise this issue in The Netherlands all failed, and no case reached the European Court of Human Rights (ECtHR). The cases heard in the ECtHR have all concerned the recognition of a new gender after reassignment surgery, rather than same-sex marriage as such,[14] but even in this context they show an adherence to a 'common understanding' of marriage as a heterosexual relationship.

The legislative reform came after a series of small steps. First came decriminalisation of homosexual activities (1811), prohibition of discrimination on the grounds of sexual orientation (1983, 1992, 1994), and the initial creation of informal municipal registers of partnerships, followed by a comprehensive registered partnership law (1998). These went alongside the increasing social acceptance of homosexuality and of same-sex partnerships. Legal recognition of same-sex partnerships and eventually marriage was pursued by gay rights groups and gained increasing public support. The government then had to decide how to respond to this pressure. Initially it was opposed to same-sex marriage, and a registered partnership law was introduced in 1998, despite a report recommending (by a majority) civil same-sex marriage in 1997.[15] This however did not silence those calling for civil same-sex marriage. A Bill was introduced in July 1999, passed in December 2000, and came into effect in April 2001.

1.1.7 The Response in Europe

It is striking that, even though the first legislation introducing same-sex marriage has appeared at the heart of Europe and of the EC, the response so far has been relatively quiet.[16] It raises two interesting questions: whether it will either prompt similar legislative activity in

[13] C Waaldijk, 'Small Change: How the Road to Same-sex Marriage Got Paved in the Netherlands' in R Wintemute and M Andenas (n 1); N Maxwell, 'Opening Civil Marriages to Same-gender Couples: a Netherlands-United States Comparison' (2001) 18 *Arizona Journal of International and Comparative Law* 141; Merin (n 1) ch 4; Eskridge (n 1).

[14] The only exception to this is *C & LM v UK* Application 14753/89. Same-sex sex marriage was raised as a subsidiary issue in an immigration case. The Commission declared the marriage complaint inadmissible on the basis of its consideration of the nature of marriage in the transsexual cases.

[15] *Commissie Inzake Openstelling van het Burgerlijk voor Personen van Hetzelfde Geslacht—Rapport* (Ministry of Justice, The Hague, 1997), commonly known as the *Kortmann Committee Report*.

[16] *The Harvard Law Review* notes that 'this type of backlash [in particular constitutional amendments to reverse rulings requiring same-sex marriage] has not occurred in any of the European countries that legalised same-sex unions', *Harvard Law Review* 'Developments in the Law—the

other states, and/or any kind of specific legislative action to regulate the legal effect of these arrangements in other states, whether to require or prevent their recognition.

Same-sex marriage and partnerships have certainly been taken more seriously elsewhere in Europe since the Dutch law was passed. Belgium has led the way,[17] passing legislation in February 2003.[18] However, the Dutch marriage law does not stand alone—it is only one part of a series of ongoing legal changes taking place in Europe, many of which predate the marriage law itself. It is difficult to untangle all the strands of these changes and to attribute or suggest simple causative links. I shall return briefly to the question of transnational recognition of marriages later.

1.1.8 The United States

The debate on same-sex marriage has raged throughout the US in the 1990s.[19] Marriage and family law is a state matter, not federal, so it is within the competence of each individual state to regulate this issue, subject to state or federal constitutional requirements—which have been hotly contested in the field of marriage and partnership rights. States are generally free to allow same-sex couples to marry, to prohibit them from marrying, and to regulate the extent to which they recognise marriages from other states. In early cases, applications for marriage licenses by same-sex couples were refused,[20] but some of the judicial challenges seeking same-sex marriage in the early 1990s were strikingly more successful than they had been 20 years earlier,[21] and than they had been in The Netherlands at about the same time. Several state courts used their

Law of Marriage and Family. II—Inching Down the Aisle: Differing Paths Toward the Legalisation of Same-sex Marriage in the United States and Europe' (2003) 116 *Harvard L Rev* 1996, 2013.

[17] Press Releases, 22 June 2001, 7 December 2001, January 2002, Belgian Federal Ministry of Justice Website, *http//194.7.188.126/justice/index_fr.htm*. *Loi du 13 février 2003 ouvrant le mariage à des personnes de même sexe et modifiant certaines dispositions du Code civil*, Moniteur Belge 28.2.2003 p 9880.

[18] Email from Kees Waaldijk 3 Feb 2003. The law was initially limited in its scope to nationals of countries whose law allows same-sex marriage, thus presently only Belgians and Dutch. The problems that arise from this restriction will be alluded to later. It is to be welcomed that the restriction was removed in early 2004—*Circulaire remplacant la circulaire relative à la loi du 13 février 2003 ouvrant le marriage à des personnes de même sexe et modifiant certaines dispositions du Code civil*, 27.1.04 published in the Moniteur Belge 27.01.2004.

[19] N Maxwell (n 13); Eskridge (n 1) 86, contrasting the legislative-driven route to registered partnership in Europe with the court-driven quest for same-sex marriage in the United States.

[20] Although note *Adams v Howerton* 673 F 2d 1036 (US Ct of Apps (9th Cir) 1982), certiorari denied 458 US 1111 1982. The couple obtained a marriage licence and married in Colorado. They then tried to obtain residence rights for the Australian partner. The couple had moved to California and the case was brought there. It was held both that the marriage was not valid under Colorado law, and that Federal immigration law imposed an autonomous definition of marriage and spouse, which would exclude same-sex partners, even if legally married under state law.

[21] There was a wave of cases, all unsuccessful, in the 1970s.

state constitutions to declare the denial of marriage to same-sex couples to be presumptively unlawful, taking a more activist view of the role of the judiciary in this matter than in Europe. There are four landmark cases—*Baehr v Lewin*[22] (Hawaii); *Brause v Bureau of Vital Statistics*[23] (Alaska); *Baker v State of Vermont*,[24] and most recently *Goodridge v Department of Public Health* (Massachusetts).[25]

Several rather different approaches have been taken.[26] The first case to succeed was in Hawaii, *Baehr v Lewin*. Denial of marriage licences to same-sex couples was judged to be prima facie discriminatory on the grounds of sex.[27] The state subsequently failed to provide a convincing justification for this discrimination when the case was remitted for consideration of that issue. Before the state's appeal on this point could finally be heard, the state legislature enacted an amendment to the Constitution to confirm the legality of restricting marriage to same-sex couples.[28] The Superior Court of Alaska, in *Brause v Bureau of Vital Statistics*, proceeded mainly on the rather different basis that the right to have one's choice of life partner recognised (and recognised as a spouse) was a fundamental right that it was presumptively unlawful to deny to same-sex couples. Again however the Alaskan Constitution was amended after a referendum, to define marriage as a relationship between a man and a woman. Other courts were more cautious and rejected similar claims. This is attributable to the fact that the US is somewhat behind Canada and most EU states in the sequence of standard steps identified by Waaldijk[29] (decriminalisation, prohibition of sexual orientation discrimination, partnership recognition) that pave the way for same-sex marriage.[30] A different approach was taken by the Supreme Court of

[22] *Baehr v Lewin* 74 Haw 645 452 P.2d 44 (Hawaii Supreme Ct 1993).

[23] *Brause v Bureau of Vital Statistics* 3 AN-950562 CI (Alaska Superior Ct Feb 1998).

[24] *Baker v State of Vermont* 170 Vt 194 (Vermont Supreme Ct 1999).

[25] *Goodridge v Department of Public Health*, Massachusetts Superior Court, transcript available on website *www.same-sexmarriage.ca* and *www.glad.org*, also reported at 440 Mass 309; 798 NE 2d 961.

[26] On the different reasoning in the judgments see the *Harvard Law Review* (n 16), 2017.

[27] This is an adaptation of the argument that discrimination on the grounds of sexual orientation is also and at the same time discrimination on the ground of sex. See R Wintemute, 'Recognising New Kinds of Direct Sex Discrimination: Transsexualism, Sexual Orientation and Dress Codes' (1997) 60 *MLR* 334, and A Koppelman, 'The Miscegenation Analogy in Europe, or, Lisa Grant Meets Adolf Hitler' in R Wintemute and M Andenas (n 1).

[28] The question of whether the marriage licences had to be granted was therefore declared moot in the end by the Supreme Court.

[29] Waadlijk (n 13).

[30] Merin (n 1) concludes that 'Until *Hardwick* is resolved [*Bowers v Hardwick* 487 US 186 SCt 2841, upholding the constitutionality of criminalising same-sex sodomy], sodomy laws are abolished, antidiscrimination legislation is adopted, and broad recognition of gay partnerships is provided, same-sex marriage is not feasible in the United States, either at the federal level or in most States …'. Note however that this has now happened—*Bowers* was overruled by the Supreme Court in *Lawrence v Texas*, 26 June 2003 reference 539 US 558, 125 SCt 2472. Despite this, same-sex marriage cases continue to fail—see eg most recently *Standhardt v Arizona* 77P.3d 451 410 Ariz Adv Rep 25, holding that the overruling of *Bowers v Hardwick* by *Lawrence v Texas* did not call into question the constitutionality of the Arizona prohibition on same-sex marriage.

Vermont, in 1999. In *Baker v State of Vermont*, instead of suggesting that same-sex marriage was required under the Vermont Constitution, it held that it was contrary to the 'Common Benefit' clause of the Constitution of Vermont[31] to deny the legal incidents of marriage (in arranging private affairs, and in dealing with third parties and state authorities) to same-sex couples. Thus, although it was not a total victory for the marriage campaigners, the decision in *Baker* was not far short of this, even though it has no effect on the effects of marriage regulated by federal law.

1.1.9 The Goodridge *Case*

The most recent case is that of *Goodridge v Department of Public Health* from the Massachusetts Superior Court. The Court considered applications from a group of same-sex couples wishing to marry, and on 18 November 2003 ruled in favour of the couples under the Massachusetts Constitution. It was not however immediately apparent whether this required marriage or whether civil unions would suffice. The Massachusetts Supreme Court confirmed in a second ruling that indeed marriage not just civil unions were required.[32] It did however allow time (140 days) for the legislature to bring in legislation. Marriage licences will be issued from May 2004, and any constitutional amendment to reverse the judgment will take longer to secure—by which time no doubt many marriages will have taken place with the full legitimacy of a ruling from the State's highest court—and once they have it will be difficult to reverse the effect of these rulings by subsequent constitutional amendment.[33] It is undoubtedly a groundbreaking decision, even thought it is no real authority in any other state, being based on the Massachusetts State Consistution.

1.1.10 The Californian Experience

There was another attempt to raise the issue early in 2004 in California. The mayor of San Fransico decided to instruct registrars to grant licences to same-sex couples, considering that refusal to do so was unconstitutional. This was greeted warmly in the large gay community

[31] Ch 1 Article 7 of the Constitution of Vermont: 'The government is, or ought to be, instituted for the common benefit, protection, and security of the people, nation, or community, and not for the particular emolument or advantage of any single person, family, or set of persons who are a part only of that community.'

[32] Opinions of the Justices to the Senate SJC-09163, 4.2.2004. Transcript available at *www.glad.org*, also reported at 440 Mass 1201; 802 NE 2d 565.

[33] At the time of writing the Massachusetts legislature voted to move a constitutional amendment to reverse the ruling, and Governor Romney announced he would apply for a further stay of the judgment in the meantime until that process is complete—which could be as late as 2006 by the time approval is sought in a referendum ballot. However, marriages went ahead in may 2004. Nonetheless, problems continue as out-of-state residents are not being permitted to marry and a further legal challenge is underway on this issue. See *www.glad.org*.

in the city and beyond, and for a number of days couples queued to get their licences and to go through civil marriage ceremonies. It became a highly policticised issue, with newly elected Governor Schwarzenegger instructing the State's Attorney General to seek injunctions to prevent these marriages proceeding. Eventually they were halted but the issue looks set to provoke high profile litigation concerning the validity of the marriages and whether the mayor's instruction to grant licences to same-sex couples should be reinstated.[34]

1.1.11 Legislative Response — (Anti) Same-sex Marriage Statutes and Constitutional Amendments

The response to this litigation was far more swift and hostile in the US than it has been in Europe.[35] Many states intervened to ensure that judicial challenges would not succeed, some with consitutitional amendments effectively overruling judicial decisions that same-sex marriage was or might be required under the state constitution.[36] Legislative moves towards same-sex marriage have been made,[37] but nowhere have these moves yet been successful. Action also followed swiftly to ensure that same-sex marriages would not be *recognised* if they travelled from a state where they were permitted. I shall return to this and discuss the legislative response in a later section.

1.1.12 Legislative Response — Civil Unions

As we have seen, *Baker v State of Vermont* required the inclusion of same-sex couples in the *legal benefits and obligations* of a marital-type status, without explicitly requiring same-sex marriage. In response the state legislature considered the issue at length, including the option of marriage. There was a vigorous public debate capturing the attention of all Vermonters.[38] Eventually, a 'Civil Unions' statute was introduced, providing for same-sex civil unions with legal effects equivalent to marriage under Vermont state law. The question of what, if any, effects this kind of partnership may have in another state is hotly debated.[39]

[34] See the news items on the website of the Human Rights Campaign, *www.hrc.org*.

[35] Perhaps bearing out the fears of some gay rights groups that initially refused to back the claim in Hawaii, fearing it was too soon to pursue a new wave of marriage cases.

[36] Thirty-six states have explicit statutes prohibiting same-sex marriage.

[37] Same-sex marriage Bills have been introduced in New York and Rhode Island, but neither has been passed at the time of writing. GayLawNews, *www.gaylawnet.com*, 1 March 2000.

[38] Merin (n 1) ch 7.5 and Eskridge (n 1) ch 2.

[39] First considered in *Burns v Burns* (253 Ga App 6000 560 SE 2Ed 47) annotated by K Eyer (2002) 20 *Yale Law and Policy Review* 297. The Court decided that the relationship was not a 'marriage' and that even if it were (1) there would be no obligation on it to recognise the marriage and (2) it would be against public policy in Georgia to do so. See now also

1.1.13 *Canada*

In Canada, a similar pattern is emerging of judicial challenges, legislative discussion, and public debate.[40] The Law Commission of Canada has been engaged on a comprehensive review of the law in this area,[41] and recommended that this change be introduced. There have been three recent cases—in Ontario,[42] British Columbia,[43] and Quebec[44]—in which same-sex couples have sought to have their unions recognised as marriages, along with legislative responses, both provincial and federal. In British Columbia the case failed,[45] in Ontario and Quebec the claims succeeded,[46] but these judgments were stayed for two years to allow the government time to address the situation. All three judgments were appealed, all three appeals upheld the couples' right to marry.[47] Since these judgments, same-sex couples have been able to marry in register offices in these provinces. A definitive legislative response from the government is awaited although it does intend to bring in legislation confirming same-sex marriage.[48]

Rosengarten v Downes 19 Sep 2002 (Mass Supreme Ct) (261 Conn. 936: 806 A.2d 1066), in which the Connecticut Supreme Court denied jurisdiction to dissolve a civil union; and *Saluccov v Allredge* (17 Mass L.Rep 498) in which the Essex Probate and Family Court allowed an uncontested request to dissolve a Vermont civil union (in a case where neither was resident in Vermont, thus precluding dissolution there); and *Langan v St Vincent's Hospital* 10 April 2003 (765 N.Y.S. 2d 411) in which the Supreme Court of New York concluded that a dececased civil union partner was to be regarded as a 'spouse' for the purposes of the New York wrongful death statute.

[40] The Equal Marriage for Same-sex Couples website, *www.samesexmarriage.ca*, is a useful source of recent information on the fast-changing legal situation in Canada.
[41] Canadian Law Commission Report *Beyond Conjugality*, available with other materials at *www.lcc.gc.ca*.
[42] *Halpern v AG Canada* 2002 Ont Sup CJ Lexis 1417 12 July 2002, transcript available at *www.samesexmarriage.ca*.
[43] *Egale Canada v AG Canada & others* 2002 BCD Civ J 967 [2002] BCD Civ 50.60.50.30-01 December 2001, transcript available at *www.samesexmarriage.ca*.
[44] *Hendricks & Leboeuf v Procureur General de Quebec* Cour Supérieur de Quebec No 500-05-059656-007 6 September 2002, transcript available at *www.samesexmarriage.ca*.
[45] The Court concluded that denial of marriage to same-sex couples was discrimination *on the grounds of sexual orientation* under the Canadian Charter of Rights and Freedoms, but that this discrimination was justified and therefore saved by s 1 of the Charter.
[46] Holding that it was discriminatory under the Charter and lacked convincing justification.
[47] *Halpern v Canada (Attorney General)* 65 O.R (3rd) 161, *Egale Canada* 228 DLR (4th) 416, both ordering immediate issuing of marriage licences. *Hendricks & Lebouf v Procureur General de Quebec*, 19 March 2004, transcript available online at *www.samesexmarriage.ca* or *www.jugements.qc.ca* reported at 238 D.L.R. (4th) 577.
[48] The federal government announced on 17 June 2003, that it would not appeal these cases but would introduce legislation for same-sex marriage. However it has referred to the Surpeme Court of Canada several questions about the proposed draft Bill—see the Department of Justice website *http.canada.justice.gc.ca*. The Reference is due to be heard in October 2004, followed by legislation if the answer, as expected, confirms the federal jurisdicition to legislate and that the restriction of marriage to opposite-sex couples violates the Canadian Charter of Rights and Freedoms. Thanks to Rob Wintemute for this information.

1.2 Registered Partnerships — A Nordic 'Same-sex Marriage'?

An alternative approach has been taken in other states. Denmark was the first in 1989, but since then Sweden, Norway, Iceland, Greenland, and Finland have all enacted almost identical legislation providing for non–marital registered partnerships. Although this kind of legislation originated in these Nordic countries, it has begun to spread further afield. The Netherlands, Vermont, and Quebec, have all adopted similar legislation, although the federal nature of Canada and the US means that these legislative provisions are unable to provide the same comprehensive package of legal rights and obligations.[49]

1.2.1 The Basic Presumption of Equality of Legal Effect

The Nordic laws all follow very similar patterns. They provide that same-sex couples may register their partnership. It is therefore *not* usually a generally applicable alternative to marriage open to all, including heterosexual couples who for some reason do not wish to or cannot marry.[50] For this reason, the basic presumption is that the rights and obligations involved should be modelled on marriage. The legislation itself is often simple, turning on a basic provision[51] that the partnership, once created, is assumed unless otherwise specifically provided to have the same effect in law as a marriage.

1.2.2 The Exceptions

If the initial presumption is that the legal consequences of the partnership will be the same as marriage, how and why are *specific* issues targeted for special treatment? Two areas are typically seen to justify a cautious approach. The first is assisted conception, adoption, parenting and filiation of children,[52] although these restrictions are slowly being

[49] On the federal/provincial question in Canada in relation to marriage, see the report by Egale Canada for the Law Commission on the Law Commission's website (n 41). On the origins of the federal jurisdiction over marriage and divorce see F Jordan, 'The Federal Divorce Act (1968) and the Constitution' (1968) 14 *McGill LJ* 209. Thanks to Hamish Carr.

[50] The Netherlands and Quebec are exceptional in opening registered partnership and civil unions to opposite-sex couples. Other states considered it unnecessary because heterosexual couples could marry.

[51] S 3.1 of the Danish Act, s 3 of the Norwegian Act, ch 3 s 1 of the Swedish Act, s 5 of the Icelandic Act, ch 3 of the Finnish Act, all reproduced in English translation in Merin (n 1) Appendix A.

[52] It has been noted that European states are more cautious about granting same-sex individuals and couples parental rights, but more generous and progressive in developing partnership rights, with the US granting greater parental rights but being more cautious in developing partnership rights. See N Polikoff, 'Recognising Partners but not Parents/Recognising Parents but not Partners. Gay and Lesbian Family Law in Europe and the US' (2000) 17 *NY Law School Journal of Human Rights* 711.

removed. The second is the personal scope of the legislation. Given the sensitivity of the issues concerned, some states[53] wish to insist on a close connection with the country, by one (or even both) of the partners, before the registration will be permitted, to avoid so-called 'partnership tourism'. Most of the Nordic laws began by requiring one party to be a national and resident, but are now being amended to provide (1) for partnerships to be registered between two residents whatever their nationality, and (2) for the nationality of other states which have similar registered partnership legislation to be treated in the same way as the nationality of that state, allowing a resident national of that state to enter into a partnership with a non-resident non-national.[54]

1.2.3 A Form of Marriage?

The close relationship that these arrangements bear to marriages in their legal effects may be clearly seen in the public (and legal) reaction to them. Although I take the view that they are not marriages and need not necessarily be dealt with straightforwardly under the legal regime for recognition of foreign marriages, the opposite view is sometimes expressed. In *D & Sweden v Council*,[55] the argument that the applicant was a 'married' man for the purposes of the Staff Regulation was advanced in the ECJ, even though it did not succeed. The question of whether the Vermont civil unions could be treated as marriages elsewhere remains controversial; although the couple involved in the first two cases in which the status of such partnerships was tested outside the original jurisdiction failed to obtain any legal recognition of the partnership, one court has now declared that the term 'spouse' has to be interpreted to include a partner joined by civil union.[56] This reaction is not just a technical legal one pursued in courts. Lobbying against such legislation[57]

[53] See Merin (n 1). Note however that the Vermont law on civil unions does not include this kind of requirement. Several authors note the high number of out of state unions, up to 80%: Eyer (n 39), Merin (n 1) 210 and Eskridge (n 1) 82. It is therefore not surprising that the first case considering the question of recognition of the civil unions, *Burns v Burns*, (n 39) involved two women who had travelled from Georgia rather than a Vermont couple who had subsequently moved.

[54] See Merin (n 1) 265 and A Sloane, 'A Rose by Any Other Name: Marriage and the Danish Registered Partnership Act' (1997) 5 *Cardozo Journal of International and Comparative Law* 189.

[55] Cases C-122 and 125/99P *D & Sweden v Council* [2001] ECR I-4319.

[56] *Burns v Burns* (n 39). The Court even denied that the partner was a second degree relative. See now also *Rosengarten v Downes* in which the Connecticut Supreme Court denied jurisdiction to dissolve a civil union, and *Langan v St Vincent's Hospital* in which the Supreme Court of New York concluded that a deceased civil union partner was to be regarded as a 'spouse' for the purposes of the New York wrongful death statute (n 39).

[57] Advocates of civil unions are more careful to distinguish between the two to avoid raising prejudice or hostility against those who would accept similar rights for same-sex couples but be uneasy at calling such relationships marriages.

often proceeds on the basis (inter alia) that the legislator is in the process of creating a 'gay marriage' law, and reaction to it (more evenly distributed among opponents and supporters) is often in similar terms. Media reports sometimes create unhelpful confusion between these two issues,[58] and although they are more clearly distinguished in academic writing, both confusion and more considered difference of opinion is sometimes also found.[59] Most of these arguments suggest that, because these partnerships are functionally so very similar to marriage, they should be seen as such. This may be so, but the symbolism remains, and the initial judicial reactions indicate that arguments such as this are vulnerable. Some legal effects may still attach to these relationships, but the reality is that they are unlikely to be treated straight-forwardly as marriages by many courts in the near future.[60]

1.3 'Marriage-lite '— Diluting the Rights and Obligations of Marriage

A further, slightly different, approach is found in the legislation passed in France[61] and Belgium.[62] The legislation now in force in Germany,[63]

[58] The BBC website's declaration that Germany had introduced same-sex marriage ('Germany Legalises Gay Marriage' 1 August 2001) and similar comments following the government's announcement of its intention to proceed with registered partnership legislation ('Gay "marriages": what would change?' 6 December 2002). Municipal registers are sometimes reported as same-sex 'marriages' even though they have no legal effect. See also the cover of the ILGA-Europe Newsletter of May 2002 proudly proclaiming that a board member of the organisation was 'Just Married in Finland'.

[59] Eg A Brownstein, 'Why Same-sex Spouses should be Granted Preferential Immigration Status: Revaluating *Adams v Howerton*' (1994) 16 *Loyola LA Int and Comp L J* 763, who states that 'although no US state permits same-sex marriages, they are recognised by some foreign countries, including Denmark and Norway'; A Sloane (n 54); E Brumby, 'What Is in a Name: Why the European Same-sex Partnership Acts Create a Valid Marital Relationship' (1999) 28 *Georgia J Int and Comp Law* 145.

[60] The most likely situation where this might happen would be in a host state which has no registered partnership but permits same-sex marriage—there might be a good case there for recognition of a same-sex registered partnership as a marriage.

[61] PACS—Pacte Civil de Solidarité (Journal Officiel de la Republique Francaise 16 Nov 1999 16959): C Richards, 'The Legal Recognition of Same-Sex Couples: the French Perspective' (2002) 51 *ICLQ* 305; D Borillo, 'The Pacte Civil de Solidarité in France: Midway between Marriage and Cohabitation' in Wintemute and Andenas (n 1); chapters in J Rubellin-Devichi, *Des Concubinages—Droit Interne, Droit International, Droit Comparé: Etudes Offertes à Jaqueline Rubellin-Devichi* (Litec, Paris, 2002); X Tracol, 'The Pacte Civil de Solidarité (PACS)' in K Boele-Woelke and A Fuchs (eds), *Legal Recognition of Same-sex Couples in Europe* (Intersentia, Antwerp, 2003).

[62] Legislation providing for statutory cohabitation has been introduced: O De Schutter and A Weyembergh, '"Statutory Cohabitation" under Belgian Law: a Step towards Same-sex Marriage?' in Wintemute and Andenas (n 1).

[63] Lebensparnerschaften—[Life Partners Act] BGBI.2001 I 226: R Schimmel and S Heun, 'The Legal Situation of Same-sex Couples in Germany—an Overview' in Wintemute and Andenas (n 1); N Dethloff,' Germany—The Registered Partnerships Act of 2001' in A Bainham (ed), ISFL 2002 171; K Thorn 'The New German Law on Same-sex Partnerships' K Boele-Woelke and A Fuchs (eds), *Legal Recognition of Same-sex Couples in Europe*.

regions of Spain,[64] and proposals put forward for discussion in the UK in 2002,[65] also have more affinity with this rather weaker form of partnership than with the stronger Nordic model. These partnerships vary between themselves far more than do the Nordic registered partnerships, and it is therefore more difficult to make broad generalisations with any great degree of accuracy. However, the following brief observations may be made by way of introduction.

These laws often have their origins (at least in part) in campaigns for legal recognition of same-sex relationships.[66] However, they differ from the previous approach in some important respects, perhaps as a consequence of the different, and rather less gay-friendly, political or constitutional[67] atmosphere in which they were developed. One key difference is the inclusion of opposite-sex couples within the scope of the legislation. France and Belgium take this approach, as would the two Bills proposed in the UK in 2002, (although now the current proposal will create a strong marriage-like status only for same-sex couples)[68] but the German Life Partnerships Act is somewhat unusual in being clearly distinct from marriage in its legal effects yet still restricted to same-sex couples. The consequence of this is that the tendency to *start* from the 'perfect assimilation' approach outlined above is less marked. There is a greater perceived need to distinguish these partnerships from marriage in their legal effects and not just in name, and partnership registrations tend to have a less clear impact on the civil status of the partners, the unions not barring a subsequent marriage, which then dissolves the previous partnership.[69]

[64] Catalonia, Valencia, Aragon, Navarra, N Perez Canovas, 'Spain: The Heterosexual State Refuses to Disappear' in Wintemute and Andenas (n 1). See F Jaurena I Salas, 'The Law on Stable Unions of Couples in the Catalonia Autonomous Region of Spain' in R Wintemute and M Andenas (n 1).

[65] Relationships (Civil Registration) Bill (Bill 34 of 2001/2) introduced by Jane Griffiths MP and Civil Partnerships Bill (HL Bill 41 of 2001/2) introduced by Lord Lester. See House of Commons Library Research Paper 02/17 *The Relationships (Civil Registration) Bill and the Civil Partnerships Bill.*

[66] Jane Griffiths' Relationships Bill is an interesting example that does not fit this pattern exactly. She had significant input and assistance from Stonewall (one of the largest mainstream Gay rights lobby groups in the UK) in drawing up her Bill, even though she included, and always intended to include, heterosexual couples as well as same-sex couples. Her interest in the issue was started by a bereaved heterosexual partner. Interview with Jane Griffiths, 4 December 2001, see also *www.janegriffithsmp.org.*

[67] The debate in Germany is influenced by the constitutional protection of the family and thus marriage.

[68] Civil Partnerships Bill 2004, introduced in the House of Lords 31 March 2004. It has been amended during its passage on this point, allowing certain categories of family member to register. The Government did not support this amendment and apparently on this point refuses to certify compliance with Convention rights under the Human Rights Act. (Information as of September 2004).

[69] The situation in Germany is quite complex. Seemingly, a life partnership may not be created during the existence of a marriage of one of the parties, but the existence of a life partnership presents no impediment to marriage nor does it provide reason to dissolve a marriage—N Dethloff (n 63) 173, criticising this and suggesting that it is an 'astonishing oversight'.

The approach in drawing up this kind of legislation is therefore not to ask which effects of marriage would be specifically unsuitable or unacceptable, whether legally or politically, to attach to a same-sex relationship. It is to pick out those particular legal consequences of the relationship that *are* to be granted to those who register. In doing this, the approaches vary,[70] and there is often intense discussion about what rights and benefits to attach to the status.[71] Any decision not to restrict the partnership option to same-sex couples means that any financial, social, or legal benefit will be open not just to the small percentage of same-sex couples, but to opposite-sex couples too, without buying into the complete package of rights and, perhaps more significantly, obligations of marriage. Another issue that gives rise to concern (although by no means absent in public and academic discourse concerning same-sex marriage or partnerships) is the possibility of undermining heterosexual marriage by providing an alternative but 'diluted' option to heterosexual couples.[72]

Immigration rights for a non-national partner are sometimes included in exactly the same way as for marriage,[73] sometimes recognised to a lesser degree,[74] and could be excluded altogether.[75] Sometimes it is a subject of discussion and debate—the German Life Partnerships Act did not originally provide for a residence permit for the partner but was amended to do so before it was passed,[76] and the two Bills brought forward in the UK in 2002 took different views, and seem to foreshadow a debate on this

[70] Table in Merin (n 1) 125. Some effects are in brackets indicating that they are granted in some states but not others. Even here however I consider that he does not fully convey the complexity of and differences between the different legislations adopted.

[71] Chs on France, Belgium, Catalonia and Germany in Wintemute and Andenas (n 1), and also generally Merin (n 1). The very different Bills proposed by Jane Griffiths and Lord Lester (n 65) also provide an interesting comparison—and have resulted in a team of civil servants being commissioned to study and report on the question. The introduction of these Bills was undoubtedly merely the start of what will be a long process of negotiation and discussion.

[72] This argument—and that heterosexual couples should marry if they want explicit legal recognition of their relationship—seems to have prevailed in the consultation paper published by the British government in 2003.

[73] Eg the Relationships Bill proposed by Jane Griffiths (n 65), German Life Partners Act (n 63), Civil Partnerships Bill (2004) is intended to have this effect.

[74] The French PACS legislation (n 61) has consequences for the immigration rights of a non-national partner, but these are discretionary, as a factor proving links with France relevant to granting a residence permit, not more or less automatic as would be the case for a married couple.

[75] This is somewhat more unusual. However, if *both* partners have to be lawfully resident in the state in order to register, the issue of immigration rights is not crucial. If the state or region concerned has no jurisdiction over immigration law (such as in Vermont, Quebec, and regions of Spain), the question is out of their control. An interesting contrast between the two Bills in 2002 before the UK Parliament (n 65) is that one (the Relationships Bill) did include provision for immigration and settlement rights for a non-national partner but the other (the Civil Partnerships Bill) did not.

[76] Merin (n 1) 145/7.

precise question. I would agree with Merin that 'in an ideal system, "cohabitation-plus" (his term for these arrangements) would also entail rights to enter the host state to be with one's partner.' On the evidence so far, states which have taken this approach in domestic law have been relatively close to this ideal. Where immigration rights are not granted on very much the same basis as marriage, there is either a lack of jurisdiction to grant such rights (as in regional legislation in Spain, or in Vermont or Quebec) or a lesser discretionary approach is taken (as in France).

1.4 Domestic Partner Benefits and Registrations

The weakest forms of partnership recognition are those that involve municipal registers and employer domestic partner benefit plans. Municipal or city registers often have limited or no legal effect. Domestic partner benefits are most common in the US,[77] where healthcare insurance is often a significant part of the remuneration package offered to employees. One example of this is the partnership registration scheme that the Community institutions make available to their staff officials. Cohabiting couples may register their partners who are then entitled to a range of facilities, although not to the most important financial advantages available to married staff officials. Neither of these involve the same kind of comprehensive legal recognition or regulation as the other options previously discussed, and I shall not pursue them further here.

1.5 The 'Traditional' Approach, Preserving Heterosexual Marriage as Unique

Currently, the UK,[78] Ireland, Italy, Portugal,[79] and Greece are among the EU states in this category.[80] Spain would have to be included as a whole

[77] A Leonard, 'Legal Recognition of Same-sex Partnerships under US State or Local Law' in Wintemute and Andenas (n 1).
[78] Although this is about to change as the government published a consultation paper in 2003, *Civil Partnership—A Framework for the Legal Recognition of Same-Sex Couples* (Women & Equality Unit/HMSO, 2003), followed by a Bill introduced in the House of Lords in 2004.
[79] Although Portugal has now introduced legislation regulating same-sex relationships, and Merin (n 1) includes it in his chapter on 'same-sex partnerships in other European countries' with France Belgium and Germany, it seems far closer to the model of cohabitation regulation. I therefore include Portugal as a country that preserves the heterosexual and exclusive nature of marriage as the only form of legally registered partnership but also as one which regulates, at least to a limited extent, cohabitation. Two Bills were introduced in 2001—one replacing and expanding the 1999 legislation on (heterosexual) cohabitation with more extensive provisions also applicable to same-sex couples: S Oliveira Pais, 'De Facto Relationships and Same-sex Relationships in Portugal' 2002 *ISFL* 337, 354.
[80] Although as noted above, none of them have enacted specific statutes intended to deny recognition to foreign same-sex marriages, many of these states would assume that recognition would be denied under existing law anyway—*Kortmann Committee Report* (n 15).

despite legislation in some regions and plans to introduce a bill for same-sex since the election of a new government in 2004.[81] This was until recently a minority of EU Member States, although not yet overwhelmingly small—but the balance has changed with the accession of ten new Member States in 2004.[82] Beyond the EU however, this remains a far more common position, and indeed on a truly global scale it predominates. This, as Wintemute points out,[83] is hardly surprising in the situation where criminal penalties, sometimes severe, for same-gender sexual activity remain widespread and where democracy and human rights are sadly all too often absent or fragile, reducing opportunities for gays and lesbians (and sympathetic heterosexuals) to organise, and reducing the opportunity for successful recourse to human rights arguments in legal and public discourse. There may also be a tradition of strong religious influence on public life and political discourse. Social and legal acceptance of homosexual activity, unmarried cohabitation, or a general principle of non-discrimination on the grounds of sexual orientation have still to be established, and legal recognition of non-marital and/or same-sex partnerships or same-sex marriage are a distant and remote prospect at present.

1.6 Cohabitation as an Independent Source of Rights and Obligations

There is also an unmistakeable trend in the last 30 or 40 years towards greater social and legal recognition of unmarried partnerships and families, together with an increasing prevalence of such forms of family living.[84] The legal recognition of such relationships is by no means uniform but there is increasing acceptance that at least *some* of the basic legal rights and obligations of marriage ought also to be granted to stable cohabiting couples.[85] Sometimes this includes same-sex couples,[86] sometimes not,[87] and sometimes benefits are granted only or largely to

[81] N Perez Canovas (n 64).
[82] See B Hardt in 3(2) ILGA-Europe Newsletter.
[83] R Wintemute, 'Partnership Rights as Human Rights', Oxford Amnesty Lecture, March 2002 (OUP, Oxford, forthcoming).
[84] See the section on statistics, below.
[85] For an examination of the development of statutory regulation of cohabitation and an attempt to explain influences on this process see D Bradley, 'Unmarried Cohabitation in West-European Jurisdictions' (2001) 15 *IJLPF* 22. See also K Kiernan, 'The Rise of Cohabitation and Childbearing Outside Marriage in Western Europe' (2001) 15 *IJLPF* 1.
[86] Canada, Portugal and Hungary are examples of this.
[87] The French Conseil D'Etat was notorious for construing protection for 'concubins' or cohabitants to exclude same-sex couples: see D Borillo in Wintemute and Andenas (n 1); Rubellin-Devichi (n 61); Richards (n 61), and De Schutter and Weyembergh (n 62) note that the increasing tolerance of cohabitation in Belgian law prior to the 2000 legislation rarely benefited same-sex couples.

same-sex couples because they are unable to marry.[88] Issues addressed include tenancy succession rights, access to and responsibility for children, healthcare and social security benefits, post-relationship 'spousal support' and division of property (particularly the formerly co-occupied home), provision for inheritance on death, damages for wrongful death, protection from domestic violence, as well as immigration rights. A comprehensive survey is impossible here,[89] but it is an increasingly common phenomenon. Norway, Sweden, The Netherlands and France have introduced forms of statutory regulation of cohabitation; Belgian law had become more tolerant of heterosexual cohabitation even before the legislation in 2000 on statutory cohabitation, and 'de facto relationships' or 'common law marriage' reforms have been introduced in Portugal and Hungary. Beyond Europe, similar reforms have been undertaken in Canada, some jurisdictions in Australia, and New Zealand. Some states in the US also recognise unmarried cohabitation to a limited degree but same-sex couples do not always benefit from this recognition.[90]

There are four major policy debates involved:[91]

1 There is a vigorous and interesting policy debate about the extent to which marriage is morally preferable or in any way an objectively 'better' form of family life for children, for the economic situation of the couple, and for their physical and mental health.[92] The extent to which the State can and should legally privilege the form of family life it considers better or best also remains contested and fluid, different States forming their own views in different ways and at different speeds.

[88] This was the case until recently in the UK in respect of immigration law, the concession later introduced into the immigration rules for some years only being applicable to those who cannot legally marry which are overwhelmingly same-sex couples.

[89] Wintemute and Andenas (n 1) contains some information on the general regulation of cohabitation as well as same-sex partnerships. See also, on the situation in Canada, Z Wu, *Cohabitation—an Alternative Form of Family Living* (OUP, Oxford, 2000); on the UK, P Morgan, *Marriage-lite: The Rise of Cohabitation* (Institute for the Study of Civil Society, London, 2000) and A Barlow, *Cohabitants and the Law* (Butterworths, London, 2001); A Barlow and G James, 'Regulating Marriage and Cohabitation in 21st Century Britain' (2004) 67 *MLR* 143; and generally, R Probert and A Barlow, 'Displacing Marriage—Diversification and Harmonisation Within Europe (2002) 12 *CFLQ* 153; J Rubellin-Devichi (n 61), the symposia papers published in (2000) 17(1) *Canadian Journal of Family Law* and (2001) 15(1) *International Journal of Law Policy and the Family* (including Kiernan and Bradley n 85 above) and the Canadian Law Commission Report, *Beyond Conjugality* (Law Commission of Canada, Ottawa, 2001), with accompanying preparatory research reports, available on the Law Commission's website, *http.www.lccgc.ca/en.*

[90] Wintemute and Andenas (n 1) contains chapters on all these countries.

[91] For an overview of the debate see J Lewis, 'Debates and Issues Regarding Marriage and Cohabitation in the British and American Literature' (2001) 15 *IJLPF* 159.

[92] For this view, see L Waite and M Gallagher, *The Case for Marriage* (Broadway Books, New York, 2001).

2 Some choose not to 'buy into' the package of marital rights and obligations, even when they are legally free to do so, and it is sometimes argued that this choice should be respected. This conflicts with the understandable desire to do justice to the parties (and sometimes the children involved)—sometimes when the situation is irreversible (death or breakup of the relationship). It also marginalises the possibility that there may be a 'weaker' party who would welcome the legal protection of marriage, but is unable to secure agreement or unwilling to press the point on a reluctant partner. States vary in the extent to which they (1) create a 'minimum' set of rights and obligations from cohabitation and (2) if they do, whether they make this a minimum standard which cannot be avoided even by specific action to 'contract out' of these consequences.

3 Equality between cohabiting opposite-sex and same-sex couples may be problematic. In Canada, judicial decisions such as *Egan v Canada*[93] and *M v H*[94] address this point pursuant to the Canadian Charter of Rights and Freedoms,[95] in both cases concluding that the exclusion of same-sex couples from benefits granted to opposite-sex cohabitants violated the equality provision in the Charter but coming to different conclusions on the question of justification.[96] *Karner v Austria*[97] establishes now in the ECHR a presumption of equality between cohabiting but unmarried same-sex and opposite-sex couples. Once benefits are extended to same-sex couples because they cannot marry, this then raises the question of whether and to what extent opposite-sex couples who can marry but choose not to are being unjustifiably discriminated against.

4 If there is no registered partnership or marriage available to same-sex couples, the inherent discrimination against such couples when marriage is privileged is increasingly seen as problematic. *Levin v Yeshiva University*[98] used this argument to challenge a marriage-only policy for student housing. In the specific context

[93] *Egan v Canada* [1995] 2 SCR 513.
[94] *M v H* [1999] 2 SCR 3.
[95] These have been followed by a challenge to discrimination in favour of marriage by a heterosexual woman—*Walsh v Bona* (2000) 186 DLR (4th) 50, rejected by the Canadian Supreme Court—[2002] SCR 325. See also the pending case before the ECHR, *MW v UK* Application 11313/02.
[96] *Egan v Canada* (n 93) involved public funds through an old age pension and the discrimination was held justifiable. In contrast, *M v H* (n 94) concerned 'spousal support' after the end of the relationship. This involved no immediate and direct cost to the public and, since the plaintiff was able to obtain support from her ex-partner, would arguably avoid later recourse to public funds. The discrimination was not justifiable.
[97] *Karner v Austria* Application 40016/98, Judgment of 24 July 2003.
[98] *Levin v Yeshiva University* 96 NY 2d 484 754 NE2d 1099 730 NYS 2d 15 (Ct App NY).

of immigration rights, the *National Coalition* case in South Africa[99] is an example of how this kind of reasoning could proceed, concluding that the restriction of immigration rights to married couples discriminated against same-sex couples.

1.7 Statistics

1.7.1 Gay Individuals and Same-sex Relationships

All the evidence shows that the proportion of individuals predominantly or exclusively attracted to form same-sex partnerships is low. As Carey notes[100] estimates vary between approximately 3 and 10 per cent of the population, and the UK Government Consultation Report on Civil Partnerships[101] assumed 5 per cent. Nevertheless, in the EU as a whole, even such a relatively small percentage means a large number of individuals and couples.

1.7.2 The Rise of Cohabitation

There is a complex picture of the prevalence and duration of cohabitation.[102] Many suggest there are two distinct kinds of cohabitation—cohabitation as a prelude to marriage, and long-term cohabitation as an alternative to marriage. To this might be added cohabitation as a response to unexpected pregnancy.

Statistics vary considerably between generations, with young persons more likely to be cohabiting than the older generations. There is also considerable variation between the different EU Member States. These statistics reflect the fact that social approval and tolerance of non-marital cohabitation also varies across countries and age groups. Estimates vary between 1 and 3 per cent of all couples in Greece, Italy, Spain and Portugal, to 70 or 73 per cent of couples aged under 30 in Sweden, and close to or more than 60 per cent of couples in this age group in Denmark, Finland and the Netherlands. As a whole in the EU, approximately 8 per cent of couples cohabit, but in the under-30 age group, the EU average is about 30 per cent.[103] These statistics are for couples, however, and do

[99] *National Coalition for Gay and Lesbian Equality v Minister for Home Affairs* 1999(3) BCLR 280, 2001(1) BCLR 99.
[100] N Carey, 'From Obloquy to Equality: in the Shadow of Abnormal Situations' (2001) 20 *YEL* 79, 104 refering to several sources.
[101] (n 78).
[102] K Kiernan, 'Cohabitation in Western Europe' (1999) 96 *Population Trends* 25; see also Editorial Note, 'The European Picture of Cohabitation' [2001] *International Family Law* 168.
[103] Editorial Note, 'The European Picture of Cohabitation' (n 102); Eurostat, *Eurostat Yearbook 2002* (Eurostat/European Commission, Brussels, 2003) 34 (data from 1997).

not show how many individuals have formed couples rather than living alone, with friends or parents. If statistics for those in unmarried cohabiting partnerships as a percentage of the under-30 group are taken, Denmark is highest with 30 per cent of under-30s cohabiting:[104]

> The household structure among young people is affected by the incidence of marriage and cohabitation. At EU level, marriage is becoming less common (5.1 marriages per 1000 population in 1999, compared with 6.3 in 1980 and 7.9 in 1960) while the number of consensual unions is increasing: 8 per cent of all couples are living in an unmarried cohabitation, and 31 per cent are doing so when considering the 16–29 age group (1996 data). In this age group, large differences appear between northern and southern Member States in the shares of young people living in a couple (more than 40 per cent in Denmark and Finland, around 15 per cent only in Spain and Italy) and in the proportion of consensual unions among couples (Italy and Spain show below 10 per cent, and Nordic countries above 60 per cent). These behaviours are correlated with the median age of leaving the parental home. It means that, in the Member States where people leave the parental home at a younger age, it is more probable that they start a consensual union rather than marry. However, in the southern Member States where young people stay longer at the parental home, if they leave it, it is more probable that they get married.[105]

1.7.3 *Registered Partnerships*

The number of registered partnerships in Europe was estimated at about 10,000 in 2000,[106] although the French 'PACS' (Pacte Civil de Solidarité) has added a significant number, over 65,000 couples.[107] There is a difference between those registered partnerships only open to same-sex couples, and those also open to heterosexuals. There is clearly a far greater pool of potential couples to whom the latter partnership option is relevant, as illustrated by the statistics from France. It is hardly surprising that registration schemes open only to same-sex couples operate with far fewer figures than (heterosexual) marriage or partnerships. Nevertheless, most homosexuals support the idea[108] and many are open to the possibility of registering if and when they form a long-term stable partnership. There may also be a 'pent up' demand to formalise existing same-sex relationships which may create a 'peak' of initial demand,

[104] Statistics for married/cohabiting/other categories are found in Eurostat, *Social Situation in the EU 2001* (Eurostat/European Commission Brussels 2001) 117 Annex 2.
[105] *Social Situation in the EU 2001* (104) 26.
[106] Eskridge (n 1) 95.
[107] Email from Marie Digoix, November 2002: Information from the French Ministry of Justice. See also X Tracol (n 61).
[108] See the comments of Barbara Roche in her speech to the TUC Gay Lesbian & Bisexual Conference, transcript online at *www.tuc.org.uk/equality/tuc-5200-f0.cfm*, that over 90% of gays and lesbians supported partnership recognition, and most would consider partnership registration themselves.

which will later drop off. It does however seem clear from the French statistics that there is some demand for, or rather interest in, a heterosexual non-marital cohabitation arrangement where it is introduced. This could be because of (anti)-religious or other principled objections to marriage, or because couples see it as a 'trial marriage'. Statistics on the prevalence of marriage, registered partnerships and cohabitation across nationalities are difficult to come by.[109] However, Dethloff estimates that 15 per cent of marriages involve different nationalities (although the figures are higher in some countries than others) and suggests that the statisctics in other kinds of cohabiting relationships may be similar.[110]

1.7.4 Migration Statistics

Family reunification is the largest source of primary immigration into the EU and has been since the economic slump in the 1970s resulted in the drastic reduction of opportunities for legal economic migration. Overall, the demographic picture that emerges is that the largest group of non-nationals living in Member States are indeed TCNs, being overall two-thirds of the non-national population—the numbers of EU citizens living in other Member States is relatively low. The traditional concern of Community law with migrant EU citizens focuses on what is in fact a small proportion of the EU population.[111] Nonetheless, it does mean that there are significant numbers of TCNs within the EU who may wish to move with their partners, so it is not just immigration from outside the EU that raises the issue of partners' immigration rights.

PART TWO — DIFFERING APPROACHES TO FAMILY REUNIFICATION

Introduction — Admission of Aliens in International Law

The modern nation state guards its sovereignty over the admission, residence and expulsion of aliens jealously. Non-nationals traditionally have little or no claim to any *legal right* to enter or remain in a state's territory. However, this is overly simplistic and does not reflect the reality of modern international law. Fourlanos[112] and Plender[113] illustrate the extent to which the 'relative sovereignty' of states in the matter of admission of

[109] See J Murphy, 'The Recognition of Same-Sex Families in Britain: the Role of Private International Law' (2002) 16 IJLPF 181, 185 and (n 34).
[110] N Dethloff, 'Arguments For the Unification and Harmonisation of Family Law in Europe' in K Boele-Woelki (ed), *Perspectives for the Unification and Harmonisation of Family Law in Europe* (Intersentia, Antwerp, 2003) 35 at p 37.
[111] Eurostat Yearbook, *Social Situation in the EU* (n 104).
[112] G Fourlanos, *Sovereignty and the Ingress of Aliens* (Almqvist and Wiksell, Stockholm, 1986).
[113] R Plender, *International Migration Law* (2nd edn Nijhoff Dordrecht 1988). Plender deals in detail with Family Reunification in Ch 11.

aliens is curtailed by international law, and Plender comments that (in the second edition of the volme in question) 'less space is devoted to dispelling the notion that the control of nationality and migration fall within the reserved domain. The qualifications to that assertion are now so clear that they speak for themselves.'[114] State sovereignty in matters relating to the admission and expulsion of aliens can now only be described as subject to significant qualifications, including family reunification.[115]

In relation to the precise definition of the family, international law is less helpful and adheres to minimal standards. Generally, the relevant international and European instruments define the family as spouse and minor dependent children,[116] and any extended definition, particularly in relation to partners other than one opposite-sex spouse, is adopted by choice not by obligation. Fourlanos suggests that:

> Still, the only duty incumbent upon a State according to international law is to respect family unity; a State is not obliged by this law to apply a particular family concept on its territory which is not accepted by its domestic legal order. ... Individuals wishing to be reunited with their families abroad should, therefore, reckon with the possibility of not being recognized as family members for reasons of strictly regional relevance: international law should not have much to say in such a situation.[117]

Introduction — Approaches to Family Reunification in Domestic Laws

The approaches outlined above to legal recognition of partnerships may also be combined with varying approaches to family reunification

[114] *Ibid*, Preface, xiv.

[115] Fourlanos (n 112) ch 3; Plender *ibid* ch 11. See further L Sohn and T Buergenthal, *The Movement of Persons Across Borders* (ASIL, Washington DC, 1992) Governing Rule 8 dealing with Family Unity. Cholewinski notes, however, that this is 'one area where rights clash with state sovereign interests in the immigration field, with the result that these grand and noble phrases concerning the protection of families have effectively been little more than hortatory statements which seem to have had minimal practical effect'—R Cholewinski, *Migrant Workers in International Human Rights Law* (OUP, Oxford, 1997) 70. See also E Guild, *Immigration Law in the European Community* (Kluwer, The Hague, 2001) 1.

[116] Cholewinski, *ibid*, 335; R Cholewinski, 'The Protection of the Right of Economic Migrants to Family Reunion in Europe' (1994) 43 *ICLQ* 568. See also G Lahav, 'International versus National Constraints in Family-reunification Migration Policy' (1997) 3 *Global Governance* 349; S Starr and L Brilmayer, 'Family Separation as a Violation of International Law' (2003) 21 *Berkeley J Int Law* 213 discussing immigration law among other issues.

[117] Fourlanos (n 112) 92–3. See further on the difficulties of recognition of polygamous marriages, Starr and Brilmayer, *ibid* although they argue in favour of a general (although not unlimited) right of family unity or intergrity but suggesting that polygamous relationships need not be recognised, at least *prospectively*, by states in their immigration laws.

rights for partners in immigration law, and there is no necessary correlation between the two.[118] This is to a large extent (although not exclusively) an area of concern for same-sex couples. An opposite-sex couple may not consider marriage purely in order to obtain tax concessions, pension rights, inheritance rights, and so on, although no doubt the practical, legal and financial benefits of marriage may have some influence on the general aspiration to marry and the particular decision to formalise a serious relationship into a marriage.[119] However, if faced with the option of separating, abandoning their plans to live in the location of their choice, or marrying, marriage is often an attractive option and many will take it. It is largely same-sex couples who have been and largely remain unable to comply with 'marriage-only' family settlement rules, and thus the question is and traditionally has been of greatest concern to them.[120]

2.1 The Importance of Being Married

Community legislation is very generous in relation to spouses, effectively giving rise to a presumption of entitlement to residence that can only be rebutted in particular circumstances.[121] The ECJ has also interpreted this legislation widely and generously. Decisions such as *Commission v Germany*,[122] *Carpenter*[123] and *MRAX*[124] demonstrate its willingness to strike down immigration policies which unduly interfere with the enjoyment of these rights. Measures condemned include strict insistence

[118] The odd and interesting combinations that may occur may be illustrated by the following (1) the UK, currently without partnership recognition, has since 1997 had immigration rights for same-sex partners, (2) the PACS in France has equivocal significance in immigration law, (3) some lawful residents may be precluded from entering into the Nordic Registered Partnerships and therefore be unable to benefit from the consequent immigration rights and (4) equating immigration rights of registered partners with those of married couples will only be as beneficial as the rights accorded to married couples. In this respect it is notable that Denmark, in the vanguard of registered partnership laws, has recently introduced what can only be described as rather draconian restrictions on residence rights of foreign national spouses.

[119] Although note M Hibbs, C Berton and J Beswick 'Why Marry?' [2001] *Family Law* 197 surveying reasons given for marriage in a group of engaged couples in England. Many were not aware of the impact that marriage would have on their legal rights and obligations. See also Barlow and James (n 89).

[120] The effect of the US immigration laws in particular (which still do not permit sponsorship of a same-sex partner) is well-documented in the immigration section of the Partners Task force for Gay and Lesbian Couples, *www.buddybuddy.com*.

[121] Eg, proven fraud, objections on the basis of public policy security or health, availability of suitable housing or (limited) financial grounds in the case of those who are *not* economically active.

[122] Case 249/86 *Commission v Germany: Re Housing of Migrant Workers* [1989] ECR 1263.

[123] Case C-60/00 *Carpenter v SSHD* [2002] 2 CMLR 64.

[124] *MRAX* (n 121).

on the adequacy of housing throughout the family member's residence (*Commission v Germany*); deportation of a spouse who had married while illegally resident in order to comply with entry formalities (*Carpenter, MRAX*); expulsion (albeit temporary) of applicants who entered illegally or whose visa has expired (*MRAX*), and even strict insistence on valid visas or particular forms of identification at borders (*MRAX*). The ECJ has also taken a strict view of expulsion of EU citizens and family members.[125] The disparity between these generous rules and more restrictive national policies has given rise to a well-established if comparatively rare phenomenon of couples migrating to other EU states to secure more favourable treatment under Community law and later returning to their state of origin,[126] although some inroads may recently been made into this principle by the case of *Akrich*.[127]

Even in domestic law, however, all EU states have a general policy to admit spouses. It is conceptually possible to envisage an immigration regime which attached no significance whatsoever to marriage or family relationships, leaving a non-national spouse to seek residence rights independently of any relationship—but no EU country does so.[128] Less

[125] Council Directive 64/221 of 25 February 1964 on the Coordination of Special Measures Concerning the Movement and Residence of Foreign Nationals which are Justified on Grounds of Public Policy, Public Security or Public Health [1963/64] OJ (Sp Ed) 117 and the case law concerning its provisions. See P Craig and G de Búrca, *EU Law* (3rd edn, OUP, Oxford, 2002) ch 19; the Commission's *Communication on the Application of Directive 64/221* COM(1999) 372, and E Guild 'Security of Residence and Expulsion of Foreigners: European Community Law' in E Guild and P Minderhoud (eds), *Security of Residence and Expulsion: Protection of Aliens in Europe* (Kluwer, The Hague, 2001).

[126] R Guttman, 'Discrimination against Own Nationals: a Brief Look at European and German Immigration Law' (1995) 9 *INLP* 97, and in the ECHR *Choudhry v UK* Application 27949/95. See also the comments by B Ingoldsby in N Hyland (ed) The Free Movement of Worker Within the European Union (Irish Centre for European Law, Dublin, 1999) on the situation of British nationals who find it necessary to take an extended 'working holiday' in Dublin before returning to the UK.

[127] Case C-109/01 *Akrich v SSHD*. The Court indicates that those not already lawfully resident in one EU Member State cannot use Reg 1612/68 to travel elsewhere as a spouse. It is not clear whether this is confined to the *Surinder Singh* situation where the couple wish to return to the state of origin of one of them, whether it is confined to denying the benefits of Reg 1612/68 to clandestine illegal entrants to the EU, whether it is confined to the situation where the marriage takes place in the Member State of origin of the EU citizen while the spouse is there irregularly, or whether it has broader application, making initial passage through national immigration law to legal residence somewhere in EU territory *always* a precondition of benefiting from Reg 1612/68—a drastic suggestion, one that was not canvassed by the parties in argument before the Court, and not one to be favoured. Anecdotally, there is some evidence that the traditional understanding is still persisting in practice, and no amendment to the forthcoming Directive has been made to clarify the issue. Many thanks to Elspeth Guild, Nick Rollason, Nicola Rogers, Steve Peers, Don Flynn and the rest of the ILPA EC Subcommittee for an interesting and spirited discussion of the implications of the case.

[128] Such an immigration regime might well contravene Art 8 ECHR if it allowed no possibility of settlement—see ch 2.

favourable regimes than that prevailing in Community law may be adopted, making the presumption of residence on marriage rather more easy to rebut, or limiting it in certain circumstances:[129]

1 Recognition and validation of marriage certificates from abroad may prove time-consuming and be subjected to cumbersome administrative procedures. The alternative of entry to the host state in order to marry there may itself be problematic.
2 Rules often exist to avoid fraud and marriages of convenience,[130] or to deter those faced with deportation who might see marriage as a simple way to regularise their situation. These rules are adaptations of rules denying residence if fraud is actually proven, but can be far more proactive and intrusive. Residence can be and is denied to couples who are not fraudulent at all.[131]
3 There may be different rules and regulations for those whose settlement or residence status is not permanent.[132]
4 Financial conditions may be attached to entry of a spouse, or financial commitments from a 'sponsoring' family member may be required to ensure that no claim is made on public benefits, at least for some time after settlement.
5 Those in polygamous marriages generally find that only one spouse is recognised for immigration purposes.[133]

[129] For the compatibility of such policies with the ECHR, see ch 3. For the position in UK law, see *Macdonald's Immigration Law and Practice* (5th edn, Butterworths, London, 2001) ch 11. For a comparison of UK, French, Dutch and EU law, see M Wijers, MA Thesis, Nijmegen. See also the highly restrictive recent developments in Denmark: Copenhagen Post, *http://chpost.periskop.dk/*, 24 Jan 2002 'The Government's New Immigration and Integration Proposals' and 12 July 2002 'Spouses Turn towards Sweden for Residency Hope', 23 October 2003 'Immigration Law at Odds with Global Conventions, Experts Say', and 17 October 2003 'Groups: Immigration Law at Odds with Global Conventions', and reports on the BBC News website on 27/11/2001, 05/02/2002, 31/05/2002 and 24/06/2002. See also generally for a wideranging survey, the different Country Reports in J Niessen and S Yongmi (eds), *EU and US Approaches to the management of immigration: Comparative perspectives* (Migration Policy Group Brussels 2003).

[130] Eg, inquiries of the couple to verify the genuine nature of the relationship at the time of application, and to verify that the marriage is still subsisting at a later stage when leave to remain is renewed or made permanent.

[131] The 'primary purpose' rule in force for some time in the UK is a prime example of this. S Sachdeva, *The Primary Purpose Rule in British Immigration Law* (Trentham Books, Stoke on Trent, 1993).

[132] See eg the Dutch rules in Case 59/85 *Netherlands v Reed* [1986] ECR 1283, the UK rules in Case C-356/98 *Arben Kaba v SSHD* [2001] ECR I-2623, and the traditional reluctance to permit family reunification for temporary 'guestworkers'.

[133] Until recently France had a policy of accepting more than one wife but has now reversed that policy, even to the extent of having retrospective application to those already admitted with serious consequences for the families involved. See particularly S Starr and L Brilmayer (above n 116).

2.2 Registered Partnerships and Immigration Laws

The existence of a registered partnership may have one of a number of consequences, from total equality with marriage to no consequences at all. The trend however is to grant immigration rights. Where the state has adopted a strong 'marriage-like' same-sex registered partnership, the usual position is to grant immigration rights, unless the legislature lacks jurisdiction over immigration.[134] One problem encountered with such partnerships is the initial trend to restrict them to those who have a connection with the country. As we have seen, if this connection is by nationality, it is at first often only nationals of the state performing the registration that may use the law (and only if resident). Limited concessions have been made to allow nationals of other like-minded states to do so. If the connection is not by way of nationality but residence, then both partners may have to have residence, which makes the position of some bi-national couples problematic. Those who wish to use the partnerships to formalise a genuine relationship to acquire residence rights for a partner may still not be able to do so. Nevertheless this will not always be an insuperable obstacle as these countries are often in any event among the more liberal regimes that do allow cohabitants to immigrate. Alternatively the partnership may be one of a number of factors to be taken into account in assessing the connection with the host state. France is an example of this, as a PACS with a French national or resident is not necessarily conclusive, but in determining the application for residence, links with France are relevant and the PACS may be used in this context.[135]

2.3 Cohabitation and Immigration Law

A stable de facto relationship may be assimilated to marriage for the purposes of immigration law. Different methods of proof and inquiry may be adopted in different states in order to establish the duration and stability of the relationship. The Netherlands is an example of a jurisdiction that has adopted this approach,[136] as is the UK initially for those who could not marry (largely same-sex couples) and now more generally,[137] and

[134] Section 1.2 above.
[135] See D Borillo, C Richards, X Tracol (n 61). See also newspaper report, P Krémer, 'La Marche des Fiertés Homosexuelles sous le Signe de la Vigilance' *Le Monde* 30 June 2002 10.
[136] This dates as far back as *Netherlands v Reed* (n 132).
[137] See generally *MacDonalds Immigration Law and Practice* (n 129) ch 11. The Immigration Rules (HC 395) were changed in 2003 to delete the requirement, carried over from an extra-statutory concession introduced in 1997 that the parties be unable to marry legally in the UK. See the Immigration Rules reproduced in Butterworths Immigration Law Service at para B[667] [681]ff on entry and leave to remain as an unmarried partner.

some other EU states also operate such policies.[138] These rules may distinguish between same-sex and opposite sex couples—either in favour of 'traditional' opposite-sex partnerships[139] or indeed in favour of same-sex partnerships as a result of the inability of such couples to marry.[140] It is also common for humanitarian grounds to be invoked albeit in a potentially inconsistent manner,[141] or for non-statutory concessions to operate either as an alternative to or a prelude to the adoption of a more formal rule. A number of states permit sponsoring or settlement of same-sex partners:[142] within the EU, Belgium, Denmark, Finland, France, the Netherlands, Sweden and the United Kingdom do so, as well as Australia, Canada, Iceland, New Zealand, Norway and South Africa outside the EU.

PART THREE — RECOGNITION OF FOREIGN FAMILY RELATIONSHIPS

This section will consider briefly the recognition of marriages and registered partnerships in states other than that in which they were registered.

3.1 Transnational Recognition of Marriages

Problems with the recognition of foreign marriages usually arise when different cultural and legal concepts of marriage clash—over issues of age, consanguinuity, polygamy, divorce, recognition of sex-changes, and now same-sex marriages.

[138] See K Lundstrom, 'Family Life and the Freedom of Movement of Workers in the European Union' (1996) 10 *IJLPF* 250, 276. She cites Belgium, France, Ireland, Luxembourg and Portugal as states where heterosexual partners may not immigrate unless they are married. See also C Waaldijk, 'The Legal Situation in the Member States' in C Waaldijk and A Clapham (eds), *Homosexuality: A Community Law Issue* (Martinus Nijhoff, The Hague, 1993). Greece, Spain and Portugal are also among the most vocal opponents of residence rights for unmarried partners in the EU legislative process—see ch 2.

[139] As the UK did at one time, discriminating also on the basis of sex. Sexual orientation discrimination would now quite possibly be contrary to Arts 8 and 14 ECHR, after *Da Silva v Portugal* Application 33290/96 (2001) 31 EHRR 47 1055. See the discussion of this in ch 3.

[140] As the UK did until very recently, and as the US might if the campaign for the Permanent Partners Immigration Bill succeeds—see the HRC website and the website of the Lesbian and Gay Immigration Rights Taskforce.

[141] Couples in Canada in particular have had recourse to 'humanitarian and compassionate' grounds for entry pending the introduction of formal regulations. See D Cresswell, *Lesbians, Gay Men, and Canadian Law* (Edward Montgomery, 1996) 567; W Van der Meide, 'Who Guards the Borders of Canada's "Gay" Community' (2001) 19 *Windsor Yearbook of Access to Justice* 39.

[142] Information from the Partners Task Force for Gay & Lesbian Couples, *www.buddybuddy.com* as of 2002.

3.1.1 *Recognising Same-sex Marriages in Europe*

The response has been slow and low-key, both in individual Member States and in EC law itself. To my knowledge, no EU state has enacted any specific legislation to ensure that these marriages either will or will not be recognised,[143] although a considerable degree of scepticism may be expected on the basis of existing legislation or principles of private international law. The public reaction has also been somewhat muted, perhaps better described as rather more curious and/or amused that a 'sister state' in the EU should take this step, rather than be openly hostile.

In 1997 the Kortmann Committee examined the issue as part of its wider ranging report discussing the issues involved in same-sex civil marriage as a precursor to the legislative change discussed above.[144] The minority opposed to same-sex marriage considered that the problems of international recognition were greater, and posed more significant problems than the majority thought. In responding to the survey, a few states (Denmark, Romania,[145] Slovakia, Turkey (subject to a public policy proviso), and Sweden) considered that the marriage would possibly or probably be recognised, a majority (Germany, England, Greece, Hungary, Italy, Liechtenstien, Portugal, Scotland, Spain, and Switzerland) thought not, and some were unable to give any answer as the question was hypothetical (Norway).[146] Much will depend on the attitude of the judiciary, with public policy exceptions often available to allow discretion to deny recognition.[147] So far, very few cases have arisen. The first was, paradoxically, in Belgium, which does now allow same-sex marriage. Nonetheless, the authorities refused to recognise the marriage of two men which took place in the Netherlands, because one of them is a Portuguese-Brazilan national (the other being Dutch).[148] Neither Portuguese nor Brazilian law permits

[143] Note however the provisions of the UK Civil Partnerships Bill: cls 152–58 and sch 14 contain provisions for recognition of overseas partnerships but include same-sex marriages from Belgium and the Netherlands which would mean these marriages would be recognised as civil partnerships which might have the effect of precluding their recognition *as marriages*.

[144] *Kortmann Committee Report* (n 15). I am grateful to Jeroen Kortmann for translating the relevant section of the report from the original Dutch.

[145] But not if one partner was Romanian.

[146] One of the few reported cases to consider this was in Switzerland, in which a Danish marriage involving a post-operative transsexual was treated as a same-sex marriage and denied recognition, see F Baur, 'At the End of the Fairy Tale, Will Heidi Stay Single? Same-sex Partnerships in Switzerland' in R Wintemute and M Andenas (eds), *Legal Recognition of Same-sex Partnerships* (Hart Publishing, Oxford, 2001). BGE II 264, 3 March 1993.

[147] Eg, in the UK, unless it was denied that it was a marriage altogether (unlikely but possible if the history of recognition of polygamous marriages is followed), a same-sex marriage between two individuals domiciled in the Netherlands at the time of the marriage would presumptively be recognised unless it was judged to be against public policy. See Murphy (n 109).

[148] Email from Kees Waaldijk.

same-sex marriage, and thus the marriage would not have be permitted at the time[149]—or apparently recognised either—in Belgium. The second case[150] is from Austria, and involves a couple married in the Netherlands one of whom was American (the other being German). The Austrian authorities were unwilling to recognise this as a valid marriage and the case is pending before the Austrian Constitutional Court, with some suggestion that it might eventually proceed to the ECtHR or the ECJ.[151]

3.1.2 Reaction from the European Community Institutions

A number of parliamentary questions have been asked to raise the issue.[152] The Commission's views seem slightly inconsistent. Commissioner Kinnock replied[153] that the term 'spouse' extends in principle to include same-sex spouses, and confirmed that the Commission would raise the matter with national authorities if any of its own staff members were affected by a refusal to admit a spouse. Commissioner Vittorino replied a month later that the Netherlands law,

> while it can have affect in its own territory, does not have the consequence of extending the notion of 'spouse' under Article 10 of Regulation 1612/68 or of imposing on other Member States an extended definition of spouse.[154]

Subsequently, in the Proposal COM(2001) 257[155] regarding the residence rights of Member State nationals, the word 'spouse' is used without any qualification or explanation in relation to same-sex spouses. In the subsequent discussions, the question has been raised and discussed. There is some residual uncertainty about whether 'spouse' can or must be interpreted to include same-sex spouses, and some disagreement over whether any clarification should be included, either to confirm or reject any obligation to include same-sex spouses.[156]

[149] The law has since been changed—see n 18.
[150] ILGA-Europe Newsletter 3(4) December 2003, 14 'No Free Movement for Same-sex Spouses?'.
[151] As of December 2003. No further information is available on this case at the time of writing.
[152] Question E-3261/01 by Joke Swiebel (13 November 2001), Questions E-3211/01 and P-2438/01 by Kathalijne Buitenweg (9 November and 29 August 2001), and Questions E-1830/01 and E-1829/01 by Lousewies van der Laan (12 and 22 June 2001).
[153] 7 Feb 2002, reply to question E-3211/01. Cf Commissioner Kinnock's Reply to Question P-2348/01, 15 October 2001.
[154] 12 March 2002, reply to question E-3261/00.
[155] Proposal for a European Parliament and Council Directive on the Right of Citizens of the Union and their Family Members to Move and Reside Freely Throughout the Territory of the Member States COM(2001) 257 [2001] OJ C270/150.
[156] See ch 2.

3.1.3 *Recognising Same-sex Marriages in the US*

There has been more legislative activity, public debate and scholarly writing on this issue in the US than in Europe. When state courts in Hawaii and Alaska began to deliver judgments in favour of same-sex marriage under the state constitutions, attention also turned to the possibility that if permitted in one state, such marriages would inevitably travel and seek recognition in other states, and many states responded by including specific provisions to prevent *recognition* of same-sex marriages celebrated elsewhere.[157] Action also followed swiftly at the federal level. In a controversial move,[158] Congress passed in 1996 the Defence of Marriage Act[159] (known as DOMA). This regulates the validity of same-sex unions as marriages for all federal law purposes, including immigration. It clearly states that same-sex partnerships shall not be recognised as marriages and that states shall not be obliged under federal law or (purportedly) the US Constitution to recognise same-sex marriages celebrated elsewhere. Two initiatives have been brought before Congress—one to underline the propriety of state rather than Federal regulation of marriage.[160] Most recently, a resolution which would add an amendment to the Constitution relating to marriage has been introduced:[161]

> Marriage in the United States shall consist only of the union of a man and a woman. Neither this Constitution nor the Constitution of any State, nor state or federal law, shall be construed to require that marital status or the legal incidents thereof be conferred on unmarried couples or groups.

The response to this remains to be seen, but there is already concern being expressed about the amendment.[162] The passage of a measure such as this would be highly controversial, with couples marrying already in some provinces in Canada and the federal government intending ultimately to confirm same-sex marriage nationwide, the recent decisions of the Superior Court in Massachusetts, and the high-profile but ultimately (for the present) short-lived attempt by the mayor of San Francisco to permit same-sex marriages in the city, it has more than ever become a divisive and heated debate. It has also now become an issue in the Presidential election campaign of 2004,[163] with George Bush lending his support to the federal constitutional amendment in the absence of state legislation to ensure that marriage remains, within the US, exclusively heterosexual. The very real

[157] See the information on the website of the Human Rights Campaign *www.hrc.org*.
[158] There has been an enormous literature on DOMA. A search of the Combined Law Reviews library on Lexis for 'DOMA' (March 2004) returned 372 items.
[159] 28 USCA 1738C (1996).
[160] State Regulation of Marriage is Appropriate Act, H.R 270, Jan 30, 2001.
[161] See the website for the Alliance for Marriage, *www.allianceformarriage.org*.
[162] Human Rights Campaign Website (n 157).
[163] Statement by President George Bush on 24 Feb 2004, see also notes of press conferences on 24 and 25 Feb 2004 on the White House website *www.whitehouse.gov/news*.

possibility of marriage in Massachusetts and the possibility for couples to marry in Ontario means that the question of recognition is now a very live one indeed. The first case concerning DOMA has only recently been decided and the timing and context of the first significant challenge may be important.[163a] Indeed, an NGO heavily involved in campaigning for immigration rights for partners has warned of the danger of couples domiciled in the US and facing immigration problems marrying in Canada, and have suggested that this situation would not make the best test case, certainly until one state within the US recognises same-sex marriage.[164]

There has also been a lively academic debate about inter-state recognition of same-sex marriage, focused around several issues in US private international and constitutional law.[165] The first is the application of the 'public policy' doctrine—whether recognition of a same-sex marriage would be contrary to public policy in a forum which does not permit celebration of such marriages itself. A second challenges the constitutionality of the exception. The third is the possibility that denying recognition to same-sex marriages would violate the demands of 'equal protection' for gays.[166] The fourth issue is the 'full faith and credit' clause of the US Constitution—whether this would mandate recognition of a sister-state marriage, and whether the provision of DOMA section 2 which explicitly empowers states to refuse to do so is permissible. Finally, Strasser has suggested an argument based on *Saenz v Rowe* and the privileges and immunities clause of the US Constitution.[167]

3.1.4 Why the Difference?

There are no doubt complex explanations for the difference between the European and American response to same-sex marriages—ie, the low key, albeit cautious and somewhat sceptical response to the reality of the Netherlands law, and the swift, hostile legislative response to the *possibility* of same-sex marriages in Hawaii and Alaska.[168] I offer the

[163a] In *re: Lee Kando and Ann Kando* (Debtor) No 03–51312 2004 Bankr. Lexis 1233 (US Bankruptcy Court for Western District of Washington). The Court dismissed the objections to the constitutionality of DOMA.

[164] See the advisory warning on the website of the Lesbian and Gay Immigration Rights Taskforce.

[165] Most recently see Harvard Law Review, 'Developments in the Law—the Law of Marriage and Family: III—Consitutional Constraints on Interstate Same-sex Marriage Recognition (2003) 116 *Harvard L Rev* 1997, 2028; A Koppelman, 'Same-sex Relationships, Choice of Law, and Public Policy' (1998) 76 Tex L Rev 921; S Fruehwald, 'Choice of Law and Same-sex Marriage' (1999) 51 *Fla L Rev* 799; and see the variety of papers in the *Quinnipiac Law Review* in 1996 and the *Creighton Law Review* in 1998.

[166] *Romer v Evans* 517 US 620 116 SCt 1620 is sometimes used to suggest that *Bowers v Hardwick* (n 30) is not an insuperable obstacle to this approach.

[167] M Strasser, 'The Privileges of National Citizenship: On *Saenz*, Same-sex Couples, and the Right to Travel' (2000) 52 *Rutgers Law Review* 554.

[168] For some further reflections on the differences between the US and Europe in respect of same-sex marriage and relationships see Harvard Law Review (n 16).

following thoughts, which lead me to conclude that the difference is not at all surprising:

1 European states, human rights standards, and even now Community law (to a degree, and after a slow start) are further along the sequence of 'standard steps' towards recognition of same-sex partnerships than US law,[169] with registered partnerships in several states now. Those in the US may also have felt more strongly that same-sex marriage was being forced upon them by litigation rather than being democratically debated and legislated as in the Netherlands and Belgium.
2 Americans are more mobile between states than Europeans. The possibility of marrying away from one's state of residence, domicile, or origin, and of subsequently changing domicile from one state to another, is perhaps somewhat greater in the US.
3 There is an obvious difference between the much tighter federal structure of the US and the much looser association of independent sovereign states that is the EU. Perhaps there is a greater assumption that a US sister state *ought* to recognise a marriage than there is in the EU.[170]
4 These last two may be the reason for the third, legal, difference. There is seemingly something of difference in the way validity of marriages in private international law is treated, with European states more usually following the pattern of personal law (either of nationality[171] or pre-nuptial domicile) and US states more generally following the pattern of the *lex loci celebrationis* to determine substantive validity of the marriage in terms of capacity to marry, as well as issues of formality.[172] As Wardle points out, an approach founded on the place of celebration more easily permits 'suitcase marriages' having little connection with state of celebration and perhaps not able to be celebrated in the state of domicile or residence of one or both parties, to claim recognition elswhere.
5 It is also quite possible that the difference in the media may play some role. The US has an identifiable 'national' media, potentially bringing issues such as same-sex marriage into the public domain nationwide in a way that simply does not happen

[169] K Waaldijk (n 13).
[170] Although Europeans and Americans (leaving aside the same-sex issue) would all have a very high expectation that their marriage would be recognised in another state.
[171] Although note the difficulties this will present, as illustrated by the repercussions of the Belgian law.
[172] See L Wardle, 'International Marriage Recognition—A World Dilemma' in N Lowe and G Douglas, *Families Across Frontiers* (Martinus Nijhoff, The Hague, 1996), D Henrich, 'Family Law Across Frontiers: Facts, Conflicts, Trends' in N Lowe and G Douglas *Families Across Frontiers* (Martinus Nijhoff, the Hague, 1996).

throughout the EU. The tone of some of the coverage may have been relevant, with some open statements by gay rights lobbyists that couples should try to spread same-sex marriage nationwide by marrying in Hawaii and seeking recognition in their home states. Differences in language may also play a part, in that discussion in one EU state, whether in the media or in academic literature, is less likely to be linguistically accessible to those in other Member States.

3.2 Transnational Recognition of Registered Partnerships

A different issue is presented by the mobile registered partnership.[173] It is not likely that these arrangements would routinely be recognised as marriages, but beyond this the outcome remains uncertain.[174] Some statutes have specific provisions,[175] and the Nordic countries recognise generally each other's partnerships.[176] These would provide relatively clear solutions to most problems. Elsewhere, much will depend on whether the host state has its own domestic registered partnership law, and if it does how closely the two laws match in providing similar rights and obligations. It would seem distinctly unsatisfactory to deny a particular right to a couple who would have such rights under both the partnership law of the state where they registered (if they had stayed there) and of the state in which they currently live (if they had registered there) simply because they have in the meantime moved. The most difficult situation will be where a registered partnership seeks recognition of some kind in a state where there is no similar domestic law. It is perhaps unlikely that the relationship will be seen as a marriage,[177] but other terms,

[173] There is now a small but growing literature on the implications of registered partnerships in private international law—see K Siehr, 'Family Unions in Private International Law' (2003) *NILR* 419; I Sumner, 'Registered Partnerships and Private International Law: Great Britain and the Netherlands Compared' (Conference paper, publication forthcoming).

[174] See *Burns v Burns* (n 39), *D & Sweden v Council* (n 51) and further cases cited at (n 39).

[175] Eg, the German Life Partnerships Act (n 63)—K Thorn, 'The German Conflict of Laws Rules on Registered Partnership' in K Boele-Woelki and A Fuchs (eds), *Legal Recognition of Same-sex Couples in Europe* (Intersentia, Antwerp, 2003); Civil Partnerships Bill (2004) cls 152–8 and sch 14 specifying various partnerships including Vermont Civil Unions (but not Quebec), French PACS, German Life Partnerships and Belgian Statutory Co-habitation including Dutch and Belgian same-sex marriage. Recognition would however be restricted to same-sex couples even when the foreign legislation allows opposite-sex couples to register. Thus on migrating to the UK the same-sex registered couple would be better off than the opposite-sex registered but not married couple.

[176] M Jänterä-Jareborg, 'Registered Partnerships in Private International Law: the Scandanavian Approach' in K Boele-Woelki and A Fuchs (eds), *Legal Recognition of Same-sex Couples in Europe* (Intersentia, Antwerp, 2003).

[177] Except perhaps for the purposes of contracting a subsequent marriage.

(even terms such as 'spouse' where this is not already confined only to married couples), 'family member' or 'relative' might well be construed to include a registered partner.[178] If trying to claim some right that is not available to cohabitants in the host state, but *would be* available under the partnership law under which they were registered, and to a married couple in the host state, it is not clear what solution would be adopted.

3.3 The Impact of the ECHR

This question has not yet been considered fully by the ECHR. There are two issues that it has considered however, that are of some relevance:

1. Rules refusing residence for more than one spouse are routinely applied and have been held not to violate Article 8 ECHR.
2. It has been held in the past that Articles 12 and 8 ECHR do not require transsexuals to be permitted to marry in their assumed gender. The question of what happens when a marriage such as this, legally and validly celebrated in one state, travels to another which would not permit it to be celebrated, has not yet been considered fully by the ECtHR, although[179] after the latest case *Goodwin v UK*,[180] in which it was held that the UK was in breach of the ECHR by not allowing marriage in the new gender, this may become a moot point. The point has seemingly been raised in Switzerland, the Swiss court concluded that it was a 'same-sex' marriage and that recognising it would violate Swiss public policy. This was not considered to be a violation of Article 8 ECHR.[181]

States' obligations under Article 8 ECHR in relation to registered partnerships from other states are unclear. It seems possible that it would be seen to be an *interference*, or *lack of respect* not to recognise the family life recognised by the partnership in some way. The crucial question will be the precise extent of the margin of appreciation under Article 8(2) ECHR, and the extent to which the ECtHR is prepared to accept that such action is justified. This seems entirely possible if there is no registered partnership law in the host state, but the argument seems much less convincing where there is such a similar partnership law. At the time of writing, however, no contested case has been reported, and the ECtHR has not yet had any opportunity to comment.

[178] See *Langan v St Vincent's Hospital* (n 39).
[179] The question is touched upon in *Sheffield & Horsham v UK* Application 22865/93 (1998) 27 EHRR 163 but there is no conclusion on the matter, either under UK law of the ECHR.
[180] *Goodwin v UK* Application 29857/95 (2002) 35 EHRR 18.
[181] BGE 119 II 264, 3 March 1993.

CONCLUSIONS OF CHAPTER ONE

Through a mixture of litigation and legislation, the unique position of marriage as the only legally recognised form of conjugal cohabiting partnership, and as the only way to obtain residence rights for a partner, have both been challenged in recent years. Cohabitation in general is increasingly recognised, non-marital registered partnerships of various kinds have been introduced, and same-sex couples can marry in the Netherlands, Belgium, and parts of Canada, with a heated debate raging in various states in the US and Massachusetts being the first state to grant valid marriage licences. However, there is no uniform consensus—states adopt different positions, and such developments rarely take place without extensive public debate.

In domestic immigration law, marriage is generally accepted as a legitimate ground for settlement, but a variety of administrative formalities, restrictions, and limitations are imposed on the rights of non-national spouses. Registered partnerships usually give rise to immigration rights of some sort in the domestic law concerned, but the position of these couples—and of same-sex spouses when they travel abroad and seek residence rights elsewhere—is far more difficult and uncertain. Fewer states recognise the claims of cohabiting couples to settle together, although the demands of same-sex couples have led to some change in this area.

2

Legislative Reform in EC Law

INTRODUCTION

THIS CHAPTER WILL examine the development of rules on family reunification in Community law, with particular emphasis on the definition of the family and whether it includes partners other than the 'traditional' heterosexual married spouse.[1] Part 1 will examine the position of migrant EU citizens. Part 2 will examine the position of legally resident TCNs, both (briefly) under specific Association Agreements, and more generally under the Proposals that are currently being discussed to exercise the Community's competence in immigration matters under Title IV EC, and Part 3 will examine the situation of EU citizens resident in their state of origin.

THE CURRENT LAW

Migrant EU citizens are entitled to bring with them their spouse, subject to having available adequate housing. This definition stems initially from Regulation 1612/68,[2] although it has been adopted without significant alteration in later legislation.[3] The only significant difference is that economically inactive EU citizens are subject to a requirement to have sufficient means and medical insurance for the spouse. 'Spouse' currently means exactly this and nothing more: registered partners[4] and

[1] For a more comprehensive description and analysis of the EU family reunification law and policy in the light of international human rights norms, see S Van Der Velde *The EU Right to Family Reunification in the Context of International Human Rights Protection* (PhD Thesis, EUI Florence, 2003).

[2] Council Regulation 1612/68 of 15 October 1968 on the Freedom of Movement for Workers within the Community [1968/9] OJ Sp Ed (II) 475, Art 10(1), repeating the previous transitional provision dating from 1964.

[3] Council Directive 1973/148 of 21 May 1973 on the Abolition of Restrictions on Movement and Residence within the Community for Nationals of Member States with regard to Establishment and the Provision of Services [1973] OJ L172/14; Council Directive 90/364 of 28 June 1990 on the Right of Residence [1990] OJ L180/26; Council Directive 90/364 of 28 June 1990 on the Right of Residence for Employees and Those who Have Ceased their Occupational Activity [1990] OJ L180/28 and Council Directive 1993/96 of 29 October 1993 on the Right of Residence for Students [1993] OJ L317/59.

[4] Cases C-122 and C-125/99P *D & Sweden v Council* [2001] ECR I-4319.

cohabitants[5] are excluded.[6] In *Netherlands v Reed*,[7] the ECJ held that a residence permit for an unmarried partner was a 'social advantage' within the meaning of Article 7(2) of Regulation 1612/68. It cannot therefore be denied to migrant EU workers if it is granted to the host state's own nationals, nor granted on a basis which discriminates indirectly against migrant workers from other Member States. Nonetheless, the prevailing consensus is that this does not confer any right where the domestic host state law does not yet recognise immigration rights for cohabitants.[8]

Now, all legally resident EU Citizens can use *Reed*[9] to require the host Member State to extend the same family reunification rights in relation to partners available to its own nationals. The benefit is likely to be seen as within the material scope of the Treaty for such individuals as well as being a social advantage for a worker. This has not yet been confirmed by any case in the ECJ, but it seems a sound assumption to make after cases such as *Martínez Sala* and *Grzelczyk*[10] in which the status of lawfully resident EU citizen is used as a link to ensure the guarantee of equal treatment under Article 12 EC. The only possible exception to this is that the position of workseekers is uncertain.[11]

[5] Case 59/85 *Netherlands v Reed* [1986] ECR 1283. See also Case T-65/92 *Arauxo-Dumay v Commission* [1993] ECR II-597.

[6] The only excecption is couples that include one partner who has undergone gender reassignment and who are prevented from marrying in breach of the ECHR, could probably use the Case C-117/01 *KB v NHS Pensions Agency* to challenge the exclusion of the partner pending change of national legislation to permit the gender reassignment to be recognised and the couple to marry in conformity with the ECHR.

[7] Above (n 5).

[8] To this effect, see G Barrett, 'Family Matters: European Community Law and Third Country National Family Members' (2003) 40 *CMLRev* 369.

[9] Above (n 7).

[10] *Martínez Sala* (n 11) and Case C-184/99 *Grzelczyk v Centre Public d'Aide Sociale d'Ottignies/Louvain-La-Neuve* [2001] ECR I-6193.

[11] Case C-370/89 *Ex p Antonissen* [1992] ECR I-745 establishes that workseekers have rights to enter and remain temporarily in the host state to look for work. However, in Case 316/85 *Centre Public d'aide sociale de Courcelles v Lebon* [1987] ECR 2811 it was held that workseekers' rights were limited and in particular that Art 7(2) of Reg 1612/68 did not apply, but it has been suggested that this principle must now be open to question in the light of later cases, particularly Case C-85/96 *Martínez Sala v Friestaat Bayern* [1998] ECR I-2692—M Dougan, 'The Workseeker as Citizen' (2001) 4 *CYELS* 1503. Whether workseekers enjoy family residence rights under Art 10 of Reg 1612/68 is not clear, although note the comments of AG Juiz-Jarabo Clolomer in Case C-138/02 *Collins* denying that *Martínez Sala* has overruled *Lebon*, and excluding workseekers from Arts 7 *et seq* of Reg 1612/68—seemingly (although this point is obiter) including family rights in Arts 10 *et seq*. The ECJ in *Collins* is more positive, indicating in para 32 that the restrictive concept of worker (ie, excluding a workseeker) only applies to certain parts of the Regulation (Title II of part I) and that in other parts of the Regulation (which include the provisions dealing with family reunification) the term must be given a broader meaning. Although not explicitly ruling on the point of family reunification, it would seem that the Court might well be inclined to include a wider concept of worker, including a workseeker, to the family reunification provisions. It is unlikely that anything in the new Directive would change this.

The Commission officials who drafted the latest Proposal[12] on the rights of EU citizens take this view and incorporated in the initial version a requirement of equal treatment with the host state's own nationals in relation to all Community migrants, not just workers. The difficulty with this approach, however, welcome though it is, is that the substantive and procedural protection available under Community law would not necessarily be available to protect individual's rights modelled on national law which are sometimes less advantageous.[13]

Workers under Regulation 1612/68 may also benefit from the provisions of Article 10(2) which provides that the Member State must 'facilitate' the admission of other members of the family who are dependent on or living under the same roof as the worker. Directive 73/148 contains a similar provision in Article 1(2). However, both 'family member' and 'facilitation' remain highly uncertain concepts, and the first attempt to rely on this provision[14] failed on the basis that it created no directly effective right for the worker's same-sex partner. Although regrettable (particularly that the case was not referred to the ECJ) the outcome is probably correct with respect to 'facilitation' not giving rise to directly effective rights.[15] The concept of a directly effective right has certainly been expanded since the early days of *Van Gend en Loos*[16]—however, it is dubious whether the term 'facilitate' is sufficiently clear, precise and unambiguous to enable any court to give effect to it as a directly effective right of entry. It is not entirely clear whether the judge also intended to exclude a longstanding same-sex partner from the category of 'family member' but it is suggested that such a conclusion would be erroneous.

These Regulations however only apply to *migrant* EU citizens, not to those in a purely internal situation because they are not exercising Treaty rights. The two limited exceptions to this are those who have exercised their Treaty rights and subsequently returned to their state of origin (*Surinder Singh*)[17] and after *Carpenter*[18] those who remain in their state of origin but travel to and provide services in other Member States as a significant part of their business.

[12] Proposal for a European Parliament and Council Directive on the Right of Citizens of the Union and their Family Members to Move and Reside Freely Throughout the Territory of the Member States COM(2001) 257 [2001] OJ C270/150.
[13] See eg *McCollum v SSHD* [2001] EWHC Admin 40 [2001] Admin Ct Digest 58 where Community law was used (although unsucessfully) to try to avoid particular restrictions in the UK rules on same-sex partners.
[14] *McCollum, ibid.*
[15] O De Schutter, 'Le Droit au Regroupement Familial au Croisement des Ordres Juridiques Européens' (1996) 90 *RDE* 531, 536.
[16] Case 26/62 *Van Gend en Loos v Nederlandse Administratie der Belastingen* [1963] ECR 1.
[17] Case C-370/90 *Ex Parte Surinder Singh* [1992] ECR I-4265.
[18] Case C-60/00 *Carpenter v SSHD* [2002] 2 CMLR 64.

This was the situation prior to *Akrich*[19]—it was thought that any migrant worker could use Community law to assert a right of residence for a spouse subject to the public policy exceptions contained in Directive 64/221. In *Akrich*, the main question raised was whether the couple—who had gone to Dublin on legal advice, anticipating a return to the UK after about six months with the benefit of Community law rights, pursuant to *Surinder Singh*—were or were not abusing their rights with the consequence that the UK authoritites were not required to recognise the Community law dimension of the case. AG Geelhoed suggests a radical rethinking of the traditionally understood scope of Community law rights. He suggests a distinction between migration within the EU and first legal entry into the EU, and suggests that Regulation 1612/68 may not be available to those seeking first entry to the territory of the EU, but only to those already legally resident somewhere within the EU to move elsewhere with their EU citizen/worker spouse. This is certainly a strange and unorthodox interpretation of the Regulation. It is not supported by the text nor the longstanding practice of Member State authorities, migrants and their legal advisers, it is difficult to reconcile with other recent judgments of the ECJ concerning the situation of TCN family members with irregular immigration status,[20] and it is particularly troubling as none of the parties had any opportunity to comment on the suggestion before the AG's Opinion. The Court of Justice appears to pick up a similar theme in its judgment. However, the judgment has been met with some criticism and concern and it is not clear what the future implications of this will be. It may be that it will be confined to the situation of attempting to return to the Member State of origin, to marriages contracted in the state of origin rather than the host state or elsewhere, or will be confined to those who are actually unlawfully resident but not a bar to using Regulation 1612/68 for first entry into the EU from lawful residence in a third country.

PART ONE — MIGRANT COMMUNITY NATIONALS

There are two questions of interest here. The first is the attempts that have been made to integrate the position articulated in *Reed*[21] (or some similar proposition based on equal treatment of migrants) into the legislative scheme. The second is the attempt to broaden the definition of the family to include unmarried partners in the category of family members with secure residence rights. I shall follow both points chronologically since 1989. There are four stages of discussion—first, proposed amendment of Regulation 1612/68 in 1989/90; secondly, enactment of the general

[19] Case C-109/01 *Akrich v SSHD* Judgment of 23/09/2003.
[20] *Carpenter* (n 18) above and Case C-549/99 *MRAX v Belgian State*.
[21] Above (n 5).

residence rights directives in 1990 and 1993; thirdly, renewed attempts to amend Regulation 1612/68 in 1998 and finally, the drafting and discussion of the new consolidatory EU Citizens Directive.

1.1 Early Developments and Proposals

1.1.1 Amendments to Article 10(1)a of Regulation 1612/68

Proposals were put forward by the Commission to amend Regulation 1612/68 in 1989 and 1990.[22] During the consultation process,[23] the words 'or any other person with similar status under the system of the host country' were added after 'spouse' in Article 10(1)a, giving such partners a right to enter. There are however two problems with this provision. It does nothing to *require* the host state to recognise a relationship as equivalent to marriage, merely to grant the benefit of such recognition to migrant workers and their unmarried partners if they already do so. In this respect (ie, requiring only equal treatment if this is provided in national law) it does not go any further than *Reed*.[24] However, it does not specify for what purposes the relationship should be regarded as having 'similar status', and for this reason seems rather unclear. There are four possibilities:

1 It could mean any relationship treated in the same way as marriage by the host state for some, perhaps any, purpose. This would be a very broad reading, enabling any significant recognition of the equality of marital and non-marital partnerships, perhaps only subject to a kind of 'de minimis' exception, to be used to argue that the Member State should be required to extend this recognition to the field of immigration law.

2 It could mean those relationships *generally* regarded as having similar status to marriage. This could be if the state had a system of registered partnerships, or a general provision or principle that cohabiting couples were to be treated in the same way as married couples. This would be a far more restrictive reading, requiring either a formal substitute for marriage or a general recognition of cohabiting couples. The former would be unduly narrow, the latter would cause problems if there were differing criteria for recognition of de facto partnerships for different purposes.

[22] Proposal for a Council Regulation to Amend Regulation 1612/68 COM(88) 815 [1989] OJ C100/06; Amended Proposal for a Council Regulation to Amend Regulation 1612/68 COM(90) 108 [1990] OJ C119/05.

[23] Between COM(88) 815 which does not contain this amendment and COM(90) 108 which does.

[24] Above (n 5).

3 Another reading would stick to the principle in *Reed*,[25] following the host state's immigration law. Legal certainty would prevail as there would only be one criterion. It would be relatively simple to determine in any given case both what rule should be applied and whether admission of the partner was required. This would of course do nothing to alter the substance of Community law.

4 Finally, an intermediate view could be taken, that one should examine whether the state and its legal system recognises the relationship as equivalent to marriage in significant ways for a substantial number (although not necessarily an overwhelming majority) of purposes. It might be possible to recognise that the *balance* of that particular legal system points in favour of recognising the equivalence of such a relationship to marriage. This would then arguably require the state to treat it in such a way for immigration purposes under Regulation 1612/68, even if under a stricter reading of *Reed* there might be no obligation to do so because this equivalence has not yet been recognised in immigration law. This more balanced and subtle approach would enable restrictive immigration law and policy to be challenged substantively, not only to ensure equal treatment of migrant EU citizens.[26] However, it would present real difficulties of legal certainty both in relation to fixing exact criteria for recognition of unmarried partnerships (if different criteria were used for different purposes), and in determining whether recognition of the equivalence of married and unmarried partnerships was sufficiently significant and widespread to require extension to immigration law without explicit statutory provision.

The Proposal itself gives little clue to the intent, beyond that it clearly stops short of providing a *uniform right* for unmarried partners to enter with migrant workers. It seems likely however that the drafters of these measures did not necessarily consider that they were doing anything more than extending explicit statutory recognition to the principle in *Reed*.[27]

1.1.2 Addition of Article 10(1)c to Regulation 1612/68 — 'Other' Family Members

Under these proposals a new Article 10(1)c would have been added to give 'any other member of the family dependent on or living under the roof of the worker or the spouse in the country whence they come' a *right*

[25] Above (n 5).
[26] In this respect only argument 2 above seems similar.
[27] Above (n 5).

to install themselves and the present Article (10)2 would be removed. This would avoid the unresolved problem of interpreting the obligation to 'facilitate' entry of such family members. Nevertheless, it would for this very reason highlight the interpretation of who is a 'family member'. This might be relatively easy in some situations, such as relations by blood or marriage more distant than children or parents—for example uncles/aunts, nephews/nieces, cousins etc. But given the stronger *right* for such individuals to enter and install themselves with the migrant worker, the more contentious issues addressed in this book would be bound to arise if such a Proposal was adopted.

Had this Proposal been approved with this amendment, it could easily be argued that unmarried and registered partners, whether same-sex or heterosexual, should be seen as 'family members'. Nevertheless, these arguments might be vulnerable given the strongly implied (almost express) exclusion by the legislature of cohabitants from Article 10(1)a. A requirement to admit unmarried partners could easily have been inserted, and it could be contended that it would *not* be legitimate for the ECJ to engage in this kind of reasoning when the legislature has refused to act. Nevertheless, these arguments are, I would suggest, unfounded. Given the fact that these 'family members' would *clearly* be given a directly effective right of residence, it would be for the ECJ to interpret this in its normal way. The Community legislature *may not* have wished to *require* the Member State to assimilate unmarried partners to spouses. Yet in using the language of 'family members', interpretation to incude cohabitees seems an obvious possibility.[28] It could convincingly be argued that any legislature using such terms was or should have been well aware of the potential for creative interpretation, even if the prevailing climate in the ECJ seems not to be favourable to such a move presently.

1.1.3 The 1990 Directives and the Economically Inactive

There was throughout the late 1970s and 1980s extensive discussion of the possibility of enacting directives to extend residence rights beyond the economically active to all EU Member State nationals.[29] A Commission Proposal was brought forward in 1979[30] and discussed extensively, but never adopted, and O'Leary describes this as 'one of the most celebrated

[28] Perhaps the inevitability of such questions arising might have influenced the reluctance to adopt this Proposal alongside concerns about the possibility of Member States being required to admit other more distant family members.

[29] S O'Leary, *The Evolving Concept of Community Citizenship* (Kluwer, The Hague, 1996) ch 4 and H Taschner, 'Free Movement of Students, Retired Persons and Other European Citizens —a Difficult Legislative Process' in H Schermers et al (eds), *Free Movement of Persons in Europe* (Martinus Nijhoff, Dordrecht, 1993).

[30] Proposal for a Council Directive on a Right of Residence for Nationals of a Member State in the Territory of Another Member State [1979] OJ C207/14.

examples of Community inertia involving a piece of proposed legislation.'[31] Eventually a new set of three Commission Proposals was brought forward in 1989,[32] dealing separately with students, retired persons and other Member State nationals generally. They all contained the same spouse-only rule from Regulation 1612/68.

There was some discussion about the definition of the family but this largely focused on ascending and descending relatives rather than unmarried partners. Taschner however comments that:

> The notion of family used in Community law is based on the traditional instrument to create such a community of life, the marriage. But how about 'modern' families, communities of life without marriage? If a man and a woman[33] one not being a EC national, live together for decades and now wish—having more than sufficient means—to move to another Member State, does the 'spouse' being a non-EC National have a right of residence to be derived from that of the companion? The answer is no, unless the ECJ someday interprets 'spouse' to include life companion. But it must be said that renouncing marriage to be the creating factor of a 'family' and allowing any less stronger link of human relationship as the basis for the genuine right of residence would open many doors to abuse.[34]

There was however some discussion of the matter in the European Parliament. In the Report on the Students Proposal, amendments were proposed.[35] The seventh recital would read:

> Spouse or cohabiting partner where the latter is recognised by law or administrative practice either in the Member State of origin or in the host country.

The text of Article 1(1) was amended accordingly to read:

> Spouse or cohabiting partner where the latter is recognised by law or administrative provision either in the Member State of origin or in the host country.[36]

[31] O'Leary (n 29) 111.

[32] Proposal for a Council Directive on the Right of Residence for Students, Proposal for a Council Directive on the Right of Residence for Employees and Self-Employed Persons who have Ceased their Occupational Activity, Proposal for a Council Directive on the Right of Residence COM(1989) 275 [1989] OJ C191/2-5.

[33] Note that Taschner does not seem to envisage 'communities of life' between same-sex couples.

[34] Tashchner (n 29) 435.

[35] Report of the Committee on Youth, Culture, Education the Media and Sport on Proposal COM(1989) 275 on the Right of Residence for Students. Document A3-77/89, PE134.304/fin.

[36] This would at least allow exportation of residence rights for an unmarried partner from a country where they are recognised to one where they are not, although this proposal still does not require a general recognition of unmarried couples in all circumstances. The TCN

In the accompanying explanatory statement this is not expanded upon, although the Legal Service Opinion is rather more forthcoming. It suggests that:

> The definition of the family in the proposal for a directive seems too limited, because only spouses and dependent children are included. Other patterns of social behaviour have to be considered among students, such as unmarried couples living together. The amendment proposed by the Committee on Legal Affairs is in accordance with a concept of the family already current in several Member States.
>
> The definition of the family (Article 2(1)[37] subparagraph 1) is too narrow and no longer corresponds to reality. Care must be taken to ensure that existing relationships in the country of origin are not broken up because the student is going to study in another Member State. Consequently this amendment gives a somewhat wider interpretation of the term 'family', as do the amendments to the directives on the general right of residence and the right of residence for retired persons.

The amendment itself suggests that the family member be defined as:

> ... and of members of his family as defined in Article 10(1) and (2) of Regulation 1612/68, including any person with whom the student is already cohabiting in the Member State of origin.

These suggestions were not taken up and all three Proposals were eventually passed and became directives in 1990 and 1993 respectively without any mention of cohabiting partners other than spouses.

1.1.4 *The High Level Panel*

In 1997 a High Level Panel was asked to examine the position in relation to free movement of persons generally. It made a number of comments on other matters, but in relation to unmarried couples stopped short of recommending any immediate change. It contented itself with observation in the following terms:

who sought to accompany his or her partner from a state where they had independent residence rights but not residence rights as a partner, would not be able to rely on this provision but the TCN coming from a country where unmarried partners rights were recognised would be able to do so.

[37] This should actually read Art 1(1).

> Beyond this affirmation, [this is a reference to the Judgment in *Reed*] attention is drawn to the fact that the 'family group' is undergoing rapid change, and that growing numbers of people, often with children, form de facto couples. In view of the possible need to take account of these changes in community legislation, it would be useful to carry out a study intended to identify the criteria which, in the Member States, provide for non-married couples to be treated in the same way as married couples, as well as the extent to which this similation applies.[38]

Such a study has yet to be carried out by on or behalf of the Commission, although they have access to reports compiled elsewhere.[39] Far stronger words are contained in paragraph 4(c) of the same report. Here, it is suggested that:

> Other practices denounced as discriminatory by certain people reflect 'societal problems', especially as regards personal and family status, whose solution is clearly a matter exclusively, or at least primarily, for the Member States. Undoubtedly, the differences in attitude which the Member States show in this respect for their own moral, political and social reasons may result in restrictions on entry or residence for certain persons, or involve refusal of various advantages, eg in social or tax matters; but it is not for the Community to push for a levelling of such practices under the pretext of free movement. It must be pointed out here that all the relevant chapters of the EC Treaty contain reservations relating to public policy which there is no question of circumventing in order to promote freedom of movement.

The flaw in this analysis is to equate immigration and residence rights with other 'social and tax advantages' to which the partners may or may not be entitled when they settle in the host state. One of the main threads of argument running through this book is that such a distinction can and should be made. The report fails to do so, and even fails to address the question. For this reason its view seems inadequate. In particular it is also, with respect, misguided to suggest that regulation of the immigration rights of partners would be 'under the pretext of' free movement. One might be able to consider that regulation of the availability to unmarried partners of *other social benefits*, or insistence on *complete equality*

[38] Report of the High Level Panel on Free Movement of Persons.
[39] Email from France Mochel of the Commission, 6 April 2001. A similar but more wide-ranging report was requested by the Council's Committee on Civil Law Matters (Council Document 13017/01), which 'would like the Commission to be asked to conduct a study identifying differences between national laws with regard to family law issues which could undermine the principle of free movement of persons, and to submit the results to the Council not later than 30 June 2003.' I am grateful to Ian Sumner for drawing my attention to this document.

between married and unmarried couples would be 'under the pretext of' free movement—but this cannot be said of the possibility of Community regulation of the *immigration rights* of unmarried partners of Community migrants. If this were so, Regulation 1612/68 and other similar measures relating to family reunification could also be seen as being 'under the pretext of' free movement. Given that family life now exists in many forms other than the 'traditional' marriage, it is no less necessary or possible to provide residence rights for these family members in 2004 in order to facilitate free movement than it was in 1964 and 1968 to provide residence rights for the wife (as it usually was then) and children of the migrant worker.

1.1.5 1998 Proposal to Amend Regulation 1612/68

Another Proposal to amend Regulation 1612/68 was produced in 1998.[40] Article 10 would now read:

> 1 The following shall, irrespective of their nationality, have the right to install themselves with a worker who is a national of one Member State and employed in another Member State.
>
> a) His spouse or any person corresponding to a spouse under the legislation of the host Member State, and their descendants.
>
> b) Relatives in the ascending line of the worker and his spouse.
>
> c) Any other member of the family of the worker or that of his spouse who is dependent on the worker or is living under his roof in the Member State whence he comes.

Unlike the previous Proposals in 1988 and 1990, Article 10(2) remained, providing that the State should 'facilitate' the entry of other 'family members'.

Similar concerns arise in respect of this wording, which is essentially the same as in 1990. The explicit recognition of the position of non-married conjugal partners is welcome, but these proposed amendments would be no better than those proposed in 1989 and 1990. The reluctance to place Member States under any *obligation* to treat unmarried partners, however long and enduring the relationship, as corresponding to spouses and therefore having the same immigration rights, continues. The uncertainty surrounding the concept of 'other family members' remains, this time exacerbated by the seemingly unnecessary retention of Article 10(2). These Proposals were never acted upon or even discussed seriously by the Council.

[40] Proposal for a Council Regulation to Amend Regulation 1612/68 COM(1998) 394 [1998] OJ C344/9.

1.2 An EU Citizens Directive?

There has been discussion for some time about the possibility and desirability of consolidation of the measures dealing with the residence rights of Member State nationals in the light of their status as EU citizens and the introduction of Article 18 EC. A Proposal to complete this task was presented by the Commission in May 2001.[41] It contains proposals to eliminate some of the differences between categories of residents, measures to reduce the administrative formalities for all,[42] and most controversially, contains what is described (largely accurately) as a permanent residence status,[43] removing the remaining power of Member States to expel EU citizens and their family members who have been lawfully resident for more than four years. In addition, it clearly offered an opportunity to rethink and modernise the definition of 'family member', and to move decisively away from the existing 'married couples only—unless the host state wishes' model of partnership. This Proposal supersedes all previous documents and will now be the focus of the next part of the discussion, tracing its development from the first Proposal in 2001 through various discussions and amendments before the final text was agreed early in 2004.

1.2.1 Proposal — COM(2001) 257

The Proposal is disappointing on this question of modernising the concept of the 'family.' The Commission's draft aims to preserve a large degree of discretion for Member States. It follows a pattern similar to those discussed above, including the unmarried partner, but only if the host Member State assimilates such couples to the position of married couples. Article 2 provides that the 'family member' for this Directive means the spouse, or:

> The unmarried partner, if the legislation of the host Member State treats unmarried couples as equivalent to married couples and in accordance with the conditions laid down in any such legislation.

Certainly, a degree of discretion and flexibility was intended in this wording—in particular the possibility of using existing equal treatment in *other areas of law* as the basis for a claim that equal treatment in *immigration*

[41] COM(2001) 257 (n 12).
[42] Chs II and III.
[43] Ch IV establishing the right of permanent residence, and Ch VI concerning expulsions.

law might be required under the Directive.[44] It is however equally clear that the discretion of a Member State not to permit settlement of unmarried couples is to be preserved.The same criticisms can be made of this as of earlier similar drafts. It is also notable that although the prevalence of registered partnerships of various kinds has increased dramatically over the last few years since previous Proposals were published, this was not taken into account.

The prime reason for this caution is political pragmatism on the part of the Commission. The officials involved in drafting the document were clearly of the opinion that any further extension of the concept of family member would be politically unacceptable to certain Member States. Despite this pragmatism, however, they seemed willing to take on board the possibility and desirability of such change if agreement could be reached in the Council, even if not persuaded of the case being made in this book that such change is in fact necessary.[45]

There are two other provisions of note in the Proposal. The obligation derived from Article 10(2) of Regulation 1612/68 to 'facilitate' entry of 'other family members' is retained in a simplified form (dependants or members of the household of the union citizen) and now extended from workers to all migrant EU citizens. The Proposal also contains in Article 4 a general 'non-discrimination' clause, and of crucial importance is the prohibition of sexual orientation discrimination. It seems obvious that this has implications for Member States who do not grant same-sex couples any possibility of immigration rights in their implementation of the Directive, but few involved in discussing the Proposal seem to accept this logic.

There are several fora in which a Proposal such as this will be discussed, the most important being the Council and Parliament. I shall first examine these two most important discussions, followed by other less influential sources of views and opinions, namely other EU institutions (Economic and Social Committee—ECOSOC; Committee of the Regions—COR) and external NGO lobbying. In scrutinising the progress of the Proposal, it is important to note the legislative procedure used, as this influences the institutional dynamics of the discussions, and the relative positions of power of the different institutions. The procedure used is co-decision with Parliament. The voting procedure to be used was initially unanimity in the Council, although the Treaty of Nice altered this to Qualified Majority Voting (QMV) after its entry into force in February 2003. Parliament is thus

[44] Discussion with Alain Bruin and other Commission officials in December 2001. See also the Commission's comments on the suggestion of one or more delegations that the assimilation of unmarried and married partners should be specifically tied to immigration law. The Commission considered this too narrow—Council Document 10572/02, p 11.
[45] Meeting in December 2001 with Commission officials on behalf of ILPA.

in a strong position, potentially able to block the legislation entirely on an issue about which it feels sufficiently strongly. The unanimity procedure initially gave a very strong hand to Member States wishing to block progress or object to particular issues, but the final vote will now inevitably be taken under QMV. However, accession of new Member States drew ever closer during the negotiations, complicating the 'arithmetic' of obtaining a qualified majority vote in the Council even further. Undoubtedly the prospect of postponing the final decision until a stage when 25 states would vote on it had an effect on the closing months of the negotiations and may have been a significant factor in closing a final deal between the Council and Parliament to avoid deadlock and to ensure that the package as a whole is not sunk at the last minute by one or two points on which complete agreement is not possible.

1.2.2 Discussions in Council

The proposal had a first reading in November and December 2001,[46] and a second reading in February, March, April and June 2002,[47] in the Working Party on Free Movement of Persons. The exact content of the discussions is somewhat difficult to extract from the documentation that is publicly available, beyond that the definition of 'family member' was perceived as problematic. However, a few further observations may be made. It is striking that no delegation seems to have questioned the omission of registered partnerships from Article 2(2)a, alongside spouses with a right to enter, although this issue was raised by Sweden in the discussion of the Family Reunification Directive.[48] The question of same-sex spouses was raised,[49] and different solutions suggested. Some delegations were uneasy about any obligation to admit 'homosexual spouses' if they did not have provision for this in their own laws.[50] Suggestions were even made that the definition of spouse should explicitly be referred to national law, or that the 'heterosexual' spouse should be dealt with in Article 2(2)a and the 'homosexual' spouse in Article 2(2)b removing any obligation to admit. The Commission and several Member States preferred the latter option. The concept of assimilation or equal treatment of unmarried couples in Article 2(2)b was also the subject of some discussion and criticism on the basis that it needed further specification, and one or more delegations preferred the wording of the Family

[46] Council Document 15380/01.
[47] Council Document 10572/02.
[48] See discussion below section 2.2.
[49] It is not clear whether this only applies to *married couples* or whether marriage-like registered partnerships are intended to be included as 'spouses'. The former seems more likely.
[50] It is not clear whether this means their own marriage laws, or their own conflict of laws rules relating to recognition of marriages, or immigration laws.

Reunification Directive.[51] The Commission was unwilling to restrict the concept of assimilation by reference to immigration law only, but indicated that it would consider alternative more precise wording. One or more delegations questioned whether the equality clause contained in Article 4 of the Directive would have any impact on the concept of family member contained in Article 2, and whether it 'might entail an obligation to alter the civil code.' The Commission considered that it did not alter current law. The cautious approach of the Commission seems to have been based on sound reading of the attitudes of Member States to these issues. Some were clearly reluctant to accept any concept of family other than the heterosexual married couple and used to the full their initially strong bargaining position. This is perhaps to be expected. More disappointing, however, was that even those states whose laws do have a considerably wider concept of family seem to have been reluctant to speak out strongly on the issue.

1.2.3 *Views of the European Parliament*

The Committee on Citizens' Rights and Freedoms (the 'LIBE' Committee) was the lead committee preparing the report, and initially appointed Ana Palacio as rapporteur. It is clear from available information[52] that the question of how to define the family was a live one and very much part of the debate. Palacio was apparently willing to take these views on board and make what might be seen as a 'progressive' recommendation in her report. She was interested in an approach based on 'mutual recognition',[53] at its simplest probably meaning that a host Member State would be obliged to recognise immigration rights for those in registered partnerhips from another Member State. Although welcome, several cautionary comments may be made:

1 It does not deal with couples currently resident in a Member State with no registered partnership.
2 It does nothing for couples moving from outside the EU.
3 It might not do anything for those unwilling for whatever reason to register or formalise their relationship.

[51] Given the timing of the discussions, this is almost certainly a reference to the first Amended Proposal—COM(2000) 624 [2000] OJ C62/99 not the subsequent Amended Proposal COM(2002) 225 [2002] OJ C203/136 in which admission of unmarried partners is entirely at the discretion of the Member States.

[52] See the discussion of the free movement campaign in the ILGA-Europe Newsletters, and the LIBE Committee Working Document of 14 March 2002, Document PE 311.026.

[53] Personal communication from Mark Bell, expert commenting on the Proposal for ILGA-Europe, at conference in Turin, June 2002, see also ILGA-Europe Newsletters.

4 It also does not seem to assist in the limited way of enabling in a general way a lawfully resident TCN in one Member State to move with a partner to another Member State, as it envisages mutual recognition of the partnership for the limited purpose of immigration law, rather than mutual recognition or transferability of the residence status of the partner as such.

Discussion continued throughout the summer and autumn of 2002.[54] It is clear that the issue of registered partnerships and unmarried couples was a significant part of the agenda. Palacio repeated her concern to pursue a form of mutual recognition. Some (Baroness Ludford, Joke Swiebel) spoke forcefully in favour of legal rights for registered and unmarried partners. No conclusion was reached but a timetable was drawn up which included a meeting with the Danish Presidency of the Council on 5 July, a draft report in September and a discussion of that report in the Parliament in October. The tone of the discussion indicates that there were considerably divergent views on the question, with some support for granting explicit legal rights to legally registered or recognised partnerships, but less support for and more concern about any move to include unmarried partners. It also indicates that the basis of discussion seems to be a search for political consensus on the question, with little recognition or discussion of the possibility that some or all of these changes might be required by legally enforceable principles of Community law.

In July 2002 Palacio was appointed as Foreign Minister in Spain, and this resulted in some delay. Giacomo Santini was appointed rapporteur to succeed her, and a very conservative draft report was eventually produced in November 2002.[55] Relying on the ECJ case of *D & Sweden*,[56] the draft suggested amending the Proposal to make clear that only heterosexual spouses are to benefit from its provisions, and there was no attempt to include registered partners. The wording relating to unmarried partners is altered to provide for admission of an unmarried partner if the host state recognises *de facto couples*, although the gist remains the same. Santini himself was clearly against extending the scope of the Proposal. However, other more generous amendments were proposed[57] and approved at a LIBE Committee meeting in January 2003.[58] In particular

[54] I am grateful to Mette Vadstrup, Information Officer at ILGA-Europe, for assisting me with a note of the discussion—email of 26 June 2002, on file with author.
[55] Draft Report of the LIBE Committee on the Proposal COM(2001) 257 Document PE3 19.238, 25 November 2002.
[56] Above (n 4).
[57] Meeting Document, LIBE Committee, 9 December 2002, PE 319.238/47–103, amendments 53–8.
[58] Press release, LIBE Committee, 21 January.

these amendments would include same-sex spouses and registered partners as well as umarried partners if the legislation of the *home or host* state recognises them.[59] A more generous amendment along the lines argued for here (ie, unmarried partners in stable long-term relationships to be admitted together with a non-exhaustive list of factors relevant to determining the existence of the relationship) was proposed by Gianni Vattimo[60] but not accepted. It is interesting and heartening that the draft report was rejected in favour of more progressive suggestions in the LIBE Committee. The report was adopted in plenary session in February 2003. (Since then, the Commission has amended its Proposal to take account of the views of the EP, but the wider concept of the family is one of the most significant issues on which it could not accept the EP's views).[61]

1.2.4 *Other Institutions*

ECOSOC[62] and the COR[63] welcome the Proposal, and comment favourably on the limited extension of family member beyond married couples. No specific mention is made of the possibility of extending the definition of the family further than it is already in the Proposal, or of any difficulties foreseen by the Committee in the application and implementation of the Proposal as it stands.

1.2.5 *External Lobbying*

There has been considerable lobbying from external sources on the content of this Proposal. Two sources in particular are worth mentioning, ILGA-Europe,[64] and ILPA.[65] Both favour a wider definition of the family, although unsurprisingly, ILGA's submissions focus more centrally on the position of lesbian and gay families. As the process progressed,[66] it

[59] Amendment 53, accepted. The reference to home or host state would be useful for those wishing to move from a state where unmarried couples were recognised to one where they were not, but will provoke more opposition from sceptical Member States in the Council.
[60] Amendment 56, rejected.
[61] Amended Proposal Proposal for a European Parliament and Council Directive on the Right of Citizens of the Union and their Family Members to Move and Reside Freely throughout the Territory of the Member States COM(2003) 199.
[62] Opinion of the Economic and Social Committee on Proposal COM(2001) 257 [2002] OJ C149/46.
[63] Opinion of the Committee of the Regions on Proposal COM(2001) 257 [2002] OJ C192/17.
[64] See the ILGA-Europe Position Paper on the Proposal, and the comments in the ILGA-Europe newsletter (2002 2(4) p 8, 2002 2(3) p 4) on the progress of the lobbying campaign. These are available on the ILGA-Europe website, *www.ilga-europe.org*.
[65] The UK-based Immigration Law Practitioners Association. See the scoreboard on this Proposal, available on the ILPA website, *www.ilpa.org.uk*, complied by the author and others.
[66] (2002) 2(4) ILGA-Europe Newsletter 8, November 2002.

appears that ILGA-Europe grew more pessimistic about the prospects of securing the inclusion of all same-sex partners in the Directive and concentrated on 'mutual recognition' to secure if possible the inclusion of registered partners migrating from states in which such legislation exists.

1.2.6 *Towards the Final Agreement*

As noted above, in mid-2003 the Commission adopted an Amended Proposal[67] and the Council adopted its common position in December 2003. It is a disappointing compromise. The common position provides that:

> Article 2
>
> 2 Family Member means
> (a) The spouse
> (b) The partner with whom the Union Citizen has contracted a registered partnership, on the basis of the legislation of a Member State, if the legislation of the host Member State treats registered partnerships as equivalent to marriage and in accordance with the conditions laid down in the relevant legislation of the host Member State.
>
> Article 3
>
> 2 Without prejudice to any right of free movement and residence the persons concerned may have in their own right, the host Member State shall, in accordance with its national legislation, facilitate entry and residence for the following persons
> (a) Any other family members …
> (b) The partner with whom the Union Citizen has a durable relationship, duly attested.
>
> The host Member State shall undertake an extensive examination of the persons' circumstances and shall justify any denial of entry or residence to these persons.

In particular, there is no clarification of the position of same-sex spouses, no *obligation* to permit entry of a registered partner unless the host state has such an arrangement already (recognises registered partnership as equivalent to marriage), and the position of other couples in stable relationships is confined to the obligation to 'facilitate' entry—the possibility

[67] COM(2003) 199.

of a clear obligation to admit such partners if the host state recognises unmarried couples in some way is gone.

There are a number of points to be made here. The refusal to acknowledge the existence of same-sex marriage is regrettable and leaves the question for the courts to address—but at least it is better than an explicit denial that 'spouse' includes same-sex spouses which had been discussed. The concession to Member States that the registered partner is entitled to enter only if the host state recognises registered partnership 'as equivalent to marriage' poses two difficulties. First, it does nothing in the situation where the host state does not have registered partnership—the very situation where it is most likely that protection from Community law will be needed, as in states with registered partnership rights already established couples are less likely to face difficulties. This obligation also now seems to exclude registered partnerships from outside the EU.[68] Secondly, it does little to clarify when this obligation will apply. It seems clear enough that the 'strong' registered partnerships will be sufficient to trigger this obligation—but it remains unclear, for example, whether the German or French partnership laws or the various kinds of statutory cohabitation will be seen as 'equivalent' to marriage and thus triggering this obligation. Finally, although it is welcome to see the situation of *all* stable (cohabiting) couples addressed directly, and to have express confirmation that the obligation to *facilitate* entry applies to these couples, it is far from an ideal solution. It has already been seen that in traditional terms it seems unlikely that this kind of statutory language in a Directive or Regulation would easily be construed to grant directly effective rights to individuals, and although the final paragraph of Article 3 may strengthen the argument in favour of direct effect, it still remains vulnerable. It seems that it would not be permissible to have a blanket policy of non-admission, but equally clear that on the face of the legislation, a general blanket policy of admission of all such partners does not seem to have been envisaged as part of this obligation. How Member States apply this will be critical—the way they formulate and adopt criteria, the transparency of the process and consistency of decision-making, whether the obligation will be interpreted to be of particular assistance to those legally unable to marry or formalise their relationship rather than to those who can but choose not to, will all be of importance. Given the obligation at the least to 'facilitate' entry, and the lack of clarity about what exactly this might mean, the basic principles of Community law such as equality, free movement and respect for family and private life to be disussed in subsequent chapters may well have a continuing and vital role in settling these questions.

[68] Contrast COM(2003) 199, which simply refers to registered partnerships not registered partnerships according to the legislation of a Member State.

1.2.7 Conclusion

There was much at stake in these discussions. ILGA-Europe notes:

> A major directive such as this is extremely rare—the previous Directive has been in force since the 1960s. So there will probably not be another opportunity to bring about these changes for many years. Therefore, we face an historic opportunity to bring about major changes in recognition of same-sex partners and their families for immigration purposes across a high proportion of Europe.[69]

It is quite true that there is much at stake, but it seems overly pessimistic to comment that 'there will probably not be another opportunity ... for many years.' My argument is that Community law contains a number of principles that could be used, inter alia, to mount a challenge in court against a marriage-only immigration policy. Successful litigation could then prompt further legislative action. However, it is certainly true that there was an unrivalled opportunity to make these changes through the legislative process that has come to a rather disappointing conclusion. As ILGA-Europe notes, one of the most striking things about the process of discussion of this Directive was the welcome prominence given to discussion of the question of marriage and partnership and the position of same-sex couples in particular. However, the result is a compromise and close attention will have to be paid to the transposition and application of the terms of the Directive in individual cases.

PART TWO — LEGALLY RESIDENT TCNS

2.1 The Initial Lack of Competence and its Subsequent Development

2.1.1 Initial Calls for Action and Development of Association Agreements

There have been sustained calls for action to improve the situation of TCNs who are legally resident in the EU Member States.[70] One of the major problems with this was the issue of competence. The regulation of

[69] (2002) 2(1) ILGA-Europe Newsletter 3.

[70] On the development of the legal status of TCNs in Community law see H Staples, *The Legal Status of Third Country Nationals in the European Union* (Kluwer, The Hague, 1999); E Guild, *Immigration Law in the European Community* (Kluwer, The Hague, 2001); E Guild and C Harlow (eds), *Implementing Amsterdam* (Hart Publishing, Oxford, 2001); B Melis, *Negotiating Europe's Immigration Frontiers* (Kluwer, The Hague, 2001); S Peers, 'Towards Equality—Actual and Potential Rights of Third Country Nationals in the European Union' (1996) 33 *CMLRev* 7, and the papers in the special issue of the *Journal of Ethnic and Migration Studies* (1998) 24(2) *JEMS*.

the legal status of TCNs began as an essential tool to further the mobility of Member State nationals. It was therefore confined to those TCNs having a family link to a migrant Member State national. Indeed at the time, those Member State nationals who were not economically active (non-working spouses and children) had no independent residence rights. The inclusion of family members in Regulation 1612/68 was therefore of particular importance to Member State nationals, although TCNs also benefited from it. Association agreements with particular states or groups of states have also provided opportunities for Community action to regulate the status of nationals of these states and their families, although on a less advantageous basis than the provisions applicable to Member State nationals.[71] In particular, these agreements have had a very limited role in protecting the rights of migrants from the associated states to family reunification. For example, the Turkey Agreement and implementing Decision 1/80, one of the most longstanding and most favourable, gives rights to the family members (of continued residence and access to the labour market) only once the host state has authorised family reunification according to national law and procedure.[72] None of the other agreements go beyond this, whether with Central and Eastern European or the Maghreb countries. The only exception to this is the situation of nationals of EEA countries and Switzerland, who are assimilated to EU citizens. Otherwise, the actual admission of family members remains in the discretion of the Member States.[73] Beyond this, TCNs are excluded from the protection of Community law and any moves to alter this position were constrained by the lack of legal competence.

2.1.2 *The Development of Competence — Towards Amsterdam*

The first major step towards general competence and a coherent basis for action on TCNs was taken in Maastricht. This was based in the 'Third Pillar' and dealt with by intergovernmental co-operation rather than the traditional Community method. A non-binding resolution was agreed in 1993,[74] using the term spouse, although this predates the Maastricht Treaty. Before long the next IGC was underway, which eventually resulted in the Treaty of Amsterdam. Among other things, this moved

[71] Guild (n 70) chs 3-6 and Staples (n 70) ch 7.

[72] Case C-351/95 *Kadiman v Friestaat Bayern* [1997] ECR I-2133 para 31; Case C-327/91 *Kus v Landeshaupstadt Wiesbaden* [1992] ECR I-6781 para 25, also Guild (n 70) ch 5.

[73] On this see further G Barrett (n 8); S Van Der Velde, *The EU Right to Family Reunification in the Context of International Human Rights Protection* (PhD Thesis, EUI Florence, 2003), esp ch 5.

[74] Resolution on the Harmonisation of National Policies on Family Reunificaiton, SN 2828/1/93 REV 1. Never published but reproduced in R Plender, *Basic Documents on International Migration Law* (Kluwer, The Hague, 1997) 487.

issues of immigration and asylum law into the Community Treaty. A new Title IV of the EC Treaty was drawn up (Articles 61–69 EC), giving the Community competence to enact certain measures in these areas—although the UK, Ireland and Denmark negotiated opt-outs and will not be bound by such decisions. Since 1999 the issue of how and when this competence will be exercised has been high on the agenda. The prospects for developing measures to tackle more generally the rights of TCNs are being studied and measures are slowly being developed—including general proposals to regulate the legal status of long-term resident TCNs, giving them greater mobility around the EU. The development of these measures is an issue of significant importance and interest, but for the present I shall concentrate on the development of family reunification rights of legally resident TCNs.[75]

2.2 The Use of this New Competence — A Family Reunification Directive?

In December 1999, the Commission adopted a proposal for a Family Reunification Directive,[76] based on Article 63 EC. The consultation process began in February 2000. ECOSOC was consulted and gave its opinion in May 2000.[77] Parliament was also consulted,[78] approving the Proposal subject to amendments in September 2000. The Commission has amended its Proposal twice, in October 2000[79] and May 2002.[80] The legislative process used for this Proposal was different from that used in the EU Citizens Directive, with consultation of Parliament (rather than co-decision) and no move to QMV.

2.2.1 The First Proposal and Early Discussions

In its personal scope the initial Proposal was quite generous, although it has gone through some changes and restrictions in the process of

[75] The concept of family member is also touched on in some of the other Directives—see discussion in M Bell, 'We Are Family? Same-sex Partners and EU Migration Law' (2002) 9 *MJ* 335; L Papadopoulou, 'In(di)visible Citizens(hip): Same-sex Partners in European Union Immigration Law'(2002) *YEL* 229.

[76] Proposal for a Council Directive on the Right to Family Reunification COM(1999) 638 [2000] OJ 116/66.

[77] Opinion of the Economic and Social Committee on the 'Proposal for a Council Directive on the Right to Family Reunification' [2000] OJ C204/40.

[78] Committee on Citizens' Freedoms and Rights, Justice and Home Affairs adopted a report on 13 July 2000, document A5-201/2000, incorporating Opinion of the Legal Affairs and Internal Market Committee.

[79] COM(2000) 624 (n 51).

[80] COM(2002) 225 (n 51).

discussion.[81] Those legal residents on permits of more than one year are included, as are recognised refugees regardless of the duration of the permit. Asylum-seekers and those benefiting from temporary protection are excluded.

As to the definition of the spouse, the Proposal would give residence rights to the spouse, or:

> … An unmarried partner living in a durable relationship with the Applicant, if the legislation of the Member States concerned treats the situation of unmarried couples as corresponding to that of married couples.

In the event of a polygamous marriage the Proposal would preclude the admission of more than one spouse and the children of that one spouse.

The ECOSOC Opinion comments that:

> In the Committee's view, the concept of 'corresponding to' should be interpreted in the light of the Article 2(e) mentioned in the previous point (forming or preserving the family unit) and Article 7(5) (the best interests of the children). What counts is that the non-married couples are free to live together, support each other, secure legal recognition for, raise and educate their children, and exercise the rights and duties of parents. Restrictive interpretations are therefore to be avoided, and for that reason, the Committee calls upon the Commission to monitor the transposal of the Directive into National Legislation and report back as provided under Article 18.[82]

This highlights the problems referred to earlier, concerning the proposed amendments to Regulation 1612/68.[83] It seems clear that ECOSOC's opinion would take the final approach. It certainly does not envisage that unmarried couples need be recognised by the law for all purposes, and it does not seem to envisage that recognition for immigration purposes (as is seemingly required by *Reed*)[84] is strictly necessary. The implication here is that the Directive might be interpreted, if the Member State affords various other kinds of legal recognition to unmarried couples, in such a way as to require the authorities then to extend this kind of treatment into immigration law and permit the entry of unmarried partners. It suggests that the overriding guiding principle should be avoidance of restrictive interpretations. This approach is laudable in its flexibility, and in its sentiments that 'broad interpretations' are to be favoured. However, I have

[81] See the changing wording of Art 3 through the different drafts of the Proposal.
[82] Para 3.2. There is here an interesting discrepancy between this and its Opinion on COM(2001) 257 (n 62), which does not seem objectively justified by the different provisions contained in the two Proposals.
[83] Above section 1.1.1.
[84] Above (n 5).

already noted above the difficulties that this would cause in terms of legal certainty. The better way to avoid narrow interpretations and restrictive practices by Member States has to be an alteration of the proposal.

The European Parliament discussion of this proposal also considered the definition of the family. The rapporteur initially appointed, Ewa Klampt, produced a draft Report on 1 May 2000.[85] One of the striking features of this report is the emphasis on what the author terms the 'nuclear family', in particular, the married couple. She proposed several amendments to eliminate even the limited recognition of reunification envisaged —ie, where the legislation of the host state treats the unmarried couples as corresponding to married couples. However, after the Committee had considered the draft in July 2000, voted on the amendments, and adopted the draft legislative resolution, Klampt requested that her name be removed from the report, and it was finally submitted in the name of the Committee chairman, Graham Watson. In the final report,[86] all the amendments deleting the limited reference to unmarried partners are removed—although no strengthening of the Proposal is suggested, and the limitations on the obligation to admit unmarried partners remain unchallenged. The report was then adopted by Parliament.[87]

2.2.2 *Amended Proposals*

The initial Proposal has been amended twice,[88] and significantly weakened in response to Member State concerns.[89] The personal scope of the Proposal has been limited, in particular the TCN with a legal residence permit will have to show a reasonable prospect of gaining permanent residence status before enjoying the benefit of its provisions. No significant progress was made on the definition of partners. The first amended Proposal in 2000 used exactly the same wording as the initial Proposal, and in fact in the most recent Proposal in 2002, there is a retrograde step. The Commission explained tersely that:

> Given the diversity in national legislation concerning those enjoying the right to family reunification, it does not seem possible for the moment to extend the obligation to allow entry and residence beyond the spouse and minor children. There is therefore a possibility but not an obligation, as regards relatives in the ascending line, dependent adult children and unmarried partners.

[85] Meeting document for the meeting of the LIBE committee on 6 June 2000.
[86] Report of the LIBE Committee on Proposal COM(1999) 638 PE//285892, A5/2000/201.
[87] OJ [2001] C135/178.
[88] Above (n 51).
[89] So much so that the European Co-ordination for the rights of foreigners to family life NGO no longer supports it—Press release 17.6.2002, *http://members.aol.com/coordeurop/indexce.html*.

> The rules applicable to unmarried partners are similar to those for relatives in the ascending line and adult children described above. The third paragraph distinguishes between unmarried partners, who must be in a long term stable relationship with the applicant, and registered partners, to whom this condition does not apply precisely because the partnership is registered. Entry and residence are extended to their unmarried minor children, including adopted children.

The Proposal itself as amended states in Article 4 that:

> 1 The Member States shall authorise the entry of … the applicant's spouse.
>
> 3 Member States may, by law or regulation, authorise the entry and residence, pursuant to this Directive and subject to compliance with the conditions laid down in Chapter IV, of the unmarried partner, being a third country national, with whom the applicant is in a duly attested stable relationship, or of a third country national who is bound to the applicant by a registered partnership in accordance with Article 5(2), and the unmarried minor children, including adopted children, of such persons.

The restrictions on polygamous spouses and their offspring remain, and there is an added provision in the amended Proposal that the Member States may require the applicant and his or her spouse to be of a minimum age before admission.

The Commission produces little explanation for this reversal of the previous limited recognition of unmarried partners, other than a simple statement that agreement 'does not seem possible' at the present time. Such concession to the intransigence of Member States is disappointing, if perhaps inevitable. The consequence of this is that discrimination against TCNs may be perpetuated, as they will not even be guaranteed the same treatment as the host state's own nationals. The unmarried couple will remain reliant on national law or the ECHR to protect their rights. Both of these are of concern—the first in the light of the Tampere Conclusions and the commitment to develop rights for TCNs comparable to those of EU Citizens,[90] and the second in the light of the EC's clear commitment to human rights and the ECHR. It is perhaps of greatest concern that this Proposal, like all the others which exclude unmarried partners totally or leave the issue to the discretion of the Member States, may well permit breaches of the standards required by Articles 8 and 14 ECHR. This is the case most obviously in relation to couples with children who may continue to have battles to obtain residence for a second parent or step-parent, and in

[90] Conclusions of the European Council in Tampere, October 1999.

relation to same-sex couples, but is also arguably the case more generally.[91] Once again pragmatism prevails over principle and protection of the individual and the family, and reality fails to live up to rhetoric.

2.2.3 Discussions in Council

The depth of some Member States' hostility to the details of this Proposal is revealed by the subsequent discussions of the text after the second amendments from the Commission.[92] The suggestion of the Swedish delegation to grant registered partners the same rights as spouses, although supported by two others, was clearly opposed by a majority of delegations. Spain, Greece and Portugal were still hostile to the limited possibility of Member States being expressly *permitted* to admit unmarried partners, being concerned that this should not force Member States who did not have such rules to admit migrants and their partners from states which did.[93]

2.2.4 And in the Parliament

A draft report from the LIBE Committee[94] on the most recent proposal suggested[95] reintroducing express mention of unmarried partners but maintaining the basic position that their admission would be discretionary unless the host state already treats them as having equivalent status. The report was adopted in April 2003 after a lively debate in the Parliament.[96]

2.2.5 The Final Text — and Beyond?

Political agreement was reached on the final text of the Directive in February 2003 and it has now been adopted.[97] No move was made to

[91] See the more detailed discussion of this issue in ch 3.

[92] Council Working documents 10857/02 and 11787/02, recording discussions held in the summer of 2002. I am grateful to Steve Peers for drawing my attention to the full version of working document 10857/02 on the internet, unusually revealing the identity of the delegations making particular points. Other Council working documents referred to are partially accessible with the identity of delegations deleted.

[93] Council Document 10857/02 p 8. See also Council Document 14272/02 noting that a recital had ben agreed to suggest that this Dir would be without prejudice to the possibility of other Member States granting family reunification to those whose admission was not required under this Dir, particularly unmarried partners, although four delegations maintained scrutiny reservations on this point. This reservation is confirmed in the most recent Council Document 5881/03 p 8.

[94] Draft Report of the LIBE Committee on Proposal COM(2002) 225 on the Right to Family Reunification, Document PE319.245.

[95] Amendment 10 concerning Recital 11, Amendment 22 concerning Art 4(1)a.

[96] Debate on Tuesday 8 April, report adopted Wednesday 9 April.

[97] Council Directive 2003/86/EC of 22 September 2003 on the Right to Family Reunification [2003] OJ L251/12.

accommodate the views of the European Parliament, and the definition of partnership remains tied to marriage and otherwise in the discretion of the Member States.[98] The Parliament has now taken advice from its legal service and has commenced an action for annulment of parts of Directive on the basis of infringement of fundamental rights.[99] However, this focuses on the position of children and potential delays in applications[100]—the position of couples is not one of the elements of the Directive that is being challenged.

PART THREE — EU CITIZENS IN INTERNAL SITUATIONS

Community law has traditionally held back from regulating the legal position of the national of a Member State within that state,[101] subject to the judicially-developed proviso that the migrant who has used his or her free movement rights then returned to his state of origin can be assimilated to position of the migrant still exercising the right in another country. This concept of non-intervention in the 'wholly internal situation' also applies to the Community rules on family reunification—indeed this is one of the classic cases in which this principle appears in sharp relief.[102]

[98] Art 4(1) refers to the spouse, Art 4(3) makes clear that partners in stable relationships *may* be admitted, Art 5(2) lays down guidelines for examination of the application including evidence of the family relationship. 'When examining an application concerning the unmarried partners of the sponsor, Member States shall consider, as evidence of the family relationship factors such as a common child, previous cohabitation, reglistration of the partnership and any other reliable means of proof.' Recital 10 states that 'It is for the Member State to decide whether they wish to authorise family reunification for relative in the direct ascending line, adult unmarried children, unmarried or registered partners as well as in the event of a polygamous marriage, minor children of a further spouse and the sponsor. Where a Member State authorises family reunification of these persons, this is without prejudice of the possibility, for Member States which do not recognise the existence of family ties in the cases covered by this provision, of not granting to the said persons the treatment of family members with regard to the right to reside in another Member State, as defined by the relevant EC legislation.' This is a reference to the Long Term Residents Directive (Council Directive 2003/109/EC of 25 November 2003 Concerning the Status of Third Country Nationals Who are Long Term Residents [2004] OJ L16/44 which authorises the family members of long term resident TCNs already admitted in the first state to join them when the use their right to move to a second EU Member State – the family that has a *right* to do so is only that in Art 4(1), ie here, the spouse, even if the first state is more generous and *does* admit registered or unmarried partners. Those individuals admitted as family members in one state but outside Art 4(1) would have to wait for their own long-term resident status rather than moving as family members.

[99] Case C-540/03, [2004] OJ C-47/21. See further the discussion in 4(1) ILGA-Europe Newsletter (March 2004).

[100] The precise objection is to *the last subparagraph of* Art 4(1), Art 4(6), both concerning children and Art 8 concerning waiting periods.

[101] There is a considerable literature on this. Most recently, see N Nic Shuibhne, 'Free Movement of Persons and the Wholly Internal Rule—Time to Move On?' (2002) 39 *CMLRev* 731, and for a judicial defence of the traditional Community law view, see the Opinion of AG Léger in Case C-192/99 *Ex p Manjit Kaur* [2001] ECR I-1237.

[102] Cases 35 and 36/82 *Morson & Jhanjhan v Netherlands* [1982] ECR 3723; Case C-370/90 *Ex p Surinder Singh* [1992] ECR I-4265.

This pattern may be seen most recently in *Carpenter*,[103] in which the Philippine wife of a British national who had never lived or worked abroad sought to claim residence rights under Community law. One of the main questions in the case was whether Community law was applicable to the applicant's situation. The ECJ held that the relevant Directive (73/148) did not apply to the applicant's situation as this concerned Member State nationals in states *other than* that of their nationality,[104] but that Article 49 EC itself could act as the basis for the right of residence of the spouse, as the applicant was indeed providing services in other Member States although he was living in and established in the UK. This provided a way out of the 'internal situation' difficulty that would otherwise have been encountered. The current debate on this matter centres around the significance of EU Citizenship and Article 18 EC to this approach, and whether these mean that the reluctance of Community law to touch 'internal situations' may no longer apply. The traditional approach was confirmed by the ECJ in *Uecker & Jaquet*,[105] and by AG Léger in *Kaur*.[106] The opinion in *Kaur* reaffirms this both in relation to what might be called 'secondary incidents' whereby Community law refuses to protect certain derivative rights of the non-migrant individual, but also considers for the first time in detail[107] the basic right of the individual to reside in his or her state of nationality. *Carpenter*[108] makes some inroad into this, but any major change will in all likelihood have to come about through legislation.[109] *Akrich* may be seen in part—in so far as it suggests diluting the previously held orthodoxy that Regulation 1612/68 represented a clear and precise set of family reunification rights available to *all* spouses of migrant EU citizens regardless of previous lawful residence—as a response to this.

Such legislation may however be on its way at some stage. The first two drafts[110] of the Family Reunification Proposal would apply the new rules also to EU citizens in their state of origin and not otherwise protected by Community law. This would be a major development, although why it is included in the Title IV Proposal on TCNs rather than under the consolidatory provision on EU citizens' residence rights' is unclear. The legal basis of this seems rather questionable, as Nic Shuibhne points out,[111] noting that Article 18 EC seems to provide a sounder legal basis

[103] Above (n 18).
[104] Para 36.
[105] Cases C-64 and 65/96 *Uecker & Jaquet v Land Nordrhein-Westfalen* [1997] ECR I-3171.
[106] *Ex p Manjit Kaur* (n 101).
[107] The point is raised briefly in *Ex p Surinder Singh* (n 102).
[108] *Carpenter* (n 18).
[109] On the choice of legislative vs judicial means of tacking the issue of Community law's reluctance to intervene in 'internal situations' in the context of free movement of persons, see Nic Shuibhne (n 101).
[110] COM(1999) 638 (n 76) and COM(2000) 624 (n 51).
[111] Nic Shuibhne (n 101).

than Title IV. However logical and compelling this argument might be, there may be a more pragmatic subtext. Perhaps adopting this measure under Title IV would be less overtly disruptive to the principle of the 'internal situation' than would adopting it under Article 18 EC.[112] The provision was removed in 2002.[113] The Commission still expresses its intention to proceed with this project, but at a later stage, once the streamlining and consolidation of the rights of EU Citizens and their families is completed, but there is no specific timetable. Reaching agreement over family reunification rules for resident TCNs and streamlining and improving the residence rights of migrant EU Citizens are sufficiently complex projects in themselves without adding the issue of 'domestic' immigration law. The Commission also links the issue with the consolidation of the legal rights of EU Citizens, hinting (although not clarifying expressly) that any future Proposal on this might be adopted under Article 18 EC rather than Title IV.

CONCLUSIONS OF CHAPTER TWO

Community legislation does not at present *require* a Member State to admit a TCN partner of a migrant EU citizen, other than a spouse in the strict sense of husband and wife joined in a legal marriage. This concept of the family was first drafted in 1964, repeated in 1968, and has been adopted in subsequent legislation. The only limited exception to this is the obligation not to discriminate against migrant EU citizens—who must be granted the benefit of any more extensive provision of national law. The possibility of amending this legislation has been discussed on several occasions, but there is little political agreement on adopting any extended definition of the family, even in response to the rapid growth of non-marital registered partnerships and cohabitation. This is so even in the recently agreed Citizens Directive, which had provided an ideal opportunity to do so. Many of those discussing the question viewed it as something to be settled by political agreement, and seem reluctant to accept that commitments to higher constitutional values—such as fundamental rights or the free movement of persons—might *require* action to be taken. The compromise reached to speed through the Directive in advance of enlargement in May 2004 is dissapointing. It leaves many questions unanswered, and will inevitably be the subject of litigation to

[112] By this I mean that proceeding with a measure like this under Art 18 might be seen to have more far reaching effects on the 'internal situation' rule, in that it might be seen as an acceptance in general terms that such non-migrant citizens come within the personal scope of Community law in a way that enacting specific regulations for their family members under the competence in Title IV might not be.
[113] COM(2002) 225 (n 51).

clarify the extent of the obligations contained in it. In the meantime, however, it still leaves scope for Member States who do not wish to permit entry for those other than opposite-sex spouses to continue to do so, or at the very least to maintain a range of restrictive policies and practices which may make entry and residence difficult to secure.

Currently, Community legislation on family reunification only applies to migrant EU citizens. There is now a Directive relating to certain long-term resident TCNs and rather more vaguely, there are plans to address the situation of non-migrant EU citizens. However, the concept of family adopted for the TCN Family Reunification Directive is even narrower than that applicable in the new EU Citizens Directive, and gives rise to the unpalatable possibility of different standards being applied to migrant EU citizens and those covered by the TCNs Directive—clearly incompatible with the spirit of the Tampere conclusions and the commitment to developing rights for TCNs comparable to those of EU citizens.

3

The ECHR Perspective

INTRODUCTION

THIS CHAPTER ADDRESSES the extent to which the European Convention on Human Rights (ECHR) requires Contracting States to permit settlement of family members, particularly partners. The reason for focusing so narrowly on this source of fundamental rights protection is simple. It is the major regional European human rights instrument. All the individual Member States are parties to it, and it has had, and retains, an important role in the development of Community law concepts of fundamental rights. The Community, in developing its own Charter of Fundamental Rights, has borrowed extensively from the ECHR; in particular the provisions of the Charter dealing with respect for family and private life and discrimination follow the pattern of the corresponding ECHR rights closely.

Articles 8 and 14 ECHR are crucial, indicating that the Contracting States must respect and not unjustifiably interfere with the individual's family and private life and must refrain from discrimination in the enjoyment of other Convention rights:

> **Article 8**
> (1) Everyone has the right to respect for his private and family life, his home and his correspondence.
> (2) There shall be no interference by a public authority with the exercise of this right except such as is in accordance with the law and necessary in a democratic society in the interests of national security, public safety or the economic well-being of the country, for the prevention of disorder or crime, or for the protection of the rights and freedoms of others
>
> **Article 14**
> The enjoyment of the rights and freedoms set forth in this Convention shall be secured without discrimination on any grounds such as sex, race, colour, language, religion, political or other opinion, national or social origin association with a national minority, property, birth or any other status

Three particular questions will be addressed:

1 The first is the definition of family. Who enjoys the protection of Article 8 ECHR? In particular, are 'non-traditional' couples considered to be family under Article 8 ECHR?
2 The second is the extent to which Article 8 ECHR may oblige a Contracting State to admit a family member of a settled resident. This will involve particular consideration of *positive* obligations to permit entry and settlement rather than the *negative* obligation to refrain from expelling individuals who are already lawfully resident. I will also consider here the extent to which certain private relationships which are not 'family' relationships may be protected by Article 8 ECHR in the context of immigration law.
3 The third major question is the relevance of Article 14 ECHR and the extent to which this may prohibit discrimination between different family units or cohabiting couples.[1]

PART ONE — WHAT IS FAMILY LIFE?

1.1 The Paradigm of the Married Couple

The married couple is clearly included in the meaning of the term 'family life', even if they have not yet lived together and are in the process of establishing their joint family life.[2] The only exception is likely to be if the marriage is one of convenience, a 'sham' marriage.[3] Two problematic points remain. The first is with the limited consequences in immigration law under Article 8 ECHR of being a 'family', discussed further below. The second is whether and to what extent a marriage, validly contracted in another Contracting State or elsewhere, can be denied recognition in a state where that particular marriage would not be permitted, discussed briefly above in chapter 1.

[1] Protocol 12 on Discrimination introduces a new freestanding equality right: G Moon, 'The Draft Discrimination Protocol to the ECHR: A Progress Report' [2002] 1 *EHRLR* 49; 'European Equality Rights' [2002] *Legal Action* (April) 26; U Khaliq, 'Protocol 12 to the ECHR: A Step Forward or a Step Too Far?' [2001] *PL* 457; C McCafferty, 'General Prohibition on Discrimination: the New Protocol to the Human Rights Convention' *IFL* July 2001 78; U O'Hare, 'Enhancing European Equality Rights: a New Regional Framework' (2001) 8 *MJ* 133. This has not yet come into force—10 ratifications are required and as at March 2003 there are only 6—the status may be followed at the website of the Council of Europe *www.coe.int*. In any event there is usually a sufficient link to Art 8 to engage the application of Art 14 where family reunification rights are concerned, I shall not discuss this further.
[2] *Abdulaziz, Cabales & Balkandali v UK* Series A No 94 (1985) 7 EHRR 471.
[3] G Cvetic, 'Immigration Cases in Strasbourg: the Right to Family Life under Article 8 ECHR' (1987) 36 *ICLQ* 647; *Macdonald's Immigration Law and Practice* (5th edn, Butterworths, London, 2001) paras 8.57 and 11.45.

1.2 Opposite-sex Unmarried Partnerships as Protected 'Family Life'

Despite the paradigm of the married couple the ECtHR has insisted that factual reality rather than legal formality is the focus of the inquiry. This extends to a general conclusion that cohabiting herterosexual couples may enjoy 'family life' together under Article 8 ECHR.[4] The European Commission on Human Rights (ECommHR) also stated for example[5] that the position of unmarried heterosexual couples may be 'assimilated to the married family', and both the ECommHR and the ECtHR have considered the position of an unmarried couple (albeit with a child) in an immigration matter to concern family life.[6]

The relationship will be particularly likely to fall within the scope of 'family life' if it is longstanding, if the couple have taken the opportunity to cohabit or raise children together, if they have joint financial affairs and/or are financially interdependent, and so on.[7] Extramarital relationships existing concurrently with ongoing marriages may be treated more harshly than non-marital relationships.[8] A period of cohabitation is important but not totally decisive.[9] The stability of the relationship and the intention of the parties are the crucial matters. It has been suggested that context and purpose for which it is being asserted may affect the assessment of whether or not there is family life under Article 8 ECHR.[10] It is also fair to say that the ECtHR and ECommHR acknowledge that the

[4] *Marckx v Belgium* Series A No 31 (1979) 2 EHRR 330; *X, Y & Z v UK* Application 21830/93 (1997) 24 EHRR 143; *Kroon v Netherlands* Series A No 297-C (1994) 19 EHRR 263; *Keegan v Ireland* Series A No 290 (1994) 18 EHRR 342; also *Nyland v Finland* Application 27110/95; *Elsholtz v Germany* Application 25735/94.

[5] *S v UK* Application 11716/85 (1986) 47 DR 274.

[6] *Solomon v Netherlands* Application 44328/98, no violation was found. See also *Yildiz v Austria* Application 37295/97 concerning a cohabiting couple married under Islamic law for several years before a civil marriage took place. Although not a classic de facto family life case, the ECtHR accepts that there is family life between the couple, talking of the applicant's 'life-partner' and child, despite the fact that the civil marriage had not yet taken place at the relevant time.

[7] Eg, *X, Y & Z v United Kingdom* (n 4). Family life was accepted to exist between a post-operative female-to-male transsexual and his female partner who had had children by artificial insemination. All outward appearances were of a 'traditional family', despite the legal bar to the couple marrying.

[8] For example *X & Y v Switzerland*, Applications 7289/75 and 7349/76 1977 Yb ECHR 372, 408. One applicant was married and usually lived with his wife and legitimate children, but had children by another woman. The Commission was prepared to accept the existence of family life between the father and his illegitimate children but classified the extra-marital relationship with their mother as private life not family life. This may well indicate a rather stricter view of *extra-marital* (ie adulterous) relationships than *non-marital* relationships where neither party is married to and living with another.

[9] R Clayton and H Tomlinson, *The Law of Human Rights* (OUP, Oxford, 2000) 13.93–13.95.

[10] P Duffy, 'The Protection of Privacy, Family Life and Other Rights Under Article 8 of the European Convention on Human Rights' (1982) 1 *YEL* 191. Duffy suggests a difference between cases involving immigration and domestic cases.

ECHR is a living instrument that must develop over time, and their attitude to the family and related matters seems to have evolved somewhat over time.

For the purposes of this discussion, this is not the most problematic situation. Most established opposite-sex couples wishing to migrate together will find little or no problem establishing the existence of 'family life' protected by Article 8 ECHR. It is also possible that the ECJ would recognise the ECtHR jurisprudence which recognises 'de facto' family life between heterosexual couples.[11] This is not to say that this issue would never arise and would never be problematic. How long a couple have to be together before they are regarded as enjoying 'family life' could occasionally be a problem, and there may be issues concerning couples who have not yet lived together, but wish to make the transition to cohabitation at the same time as migrating from one state to another. How to define a couple in a stable relationship (exactly what evidence would be needed, and what duration of relationship would be required) would have to be approached in the light of the ECtHR jurisprudence mentioned above.

Yet acceptance of 'family life' does not secure admission of the non-national family member to the Contracting State. The more important question would be the consequences of the couple having family life and degree to which interference with 'de facto' family life through immigration laws would be permitted. Further, the inclusion of stable unmarried couples in the concept of 'family' does not necessarily mean that Contracting States are under any *general* obligation to treat married and unmarried couples equally. Particularly in relation to issues described as 'special protection' or 'particular assistance', some distinction between married and unmarried couples in order to protect the 'traditional' family is held to be permissible. This, unfortunately, severely limits the practical implications of the acceptance *in theory* of the ECHR that the unmarried couple enjoy family life. I shall return to discuss these issues more fully later.

1.3 Same-sex Couples as Families, or their Relationships as a Protected Aspect of Private Life[12]

The ECtHR has however so far refused to countenance the suggestion that a same-sex couple might be a 'family' for the purposes of Article 8. Indeed

[11] To this effect, Case C-65/98 *Eyup v Landesgeschaftsstelle des Arbeitsmarktservice Vorarlberg* [2000] ECR I-4747, and hints in the Opinion of Advocate General Stix-Hackl in Case C-459/99 *MRAX v Belgian State*. See also the comments of AG Ruiz-Jarabo Colomer in Case C-117/01 *KB v NHS Pensions Agency*.

[12] See generally, R Wintemute, 'Strasbourg to the Rescue? Same-sex Partners and Parents under the Convention' in R Wintemute and M Andenas (eds), *Legal Recognition of Same-sex Partnerships* (Hart Publishing, Oxford, 2001); R Wintemute, *Sexual Orientation and Human*

initially, in the early days of the Convention, it refused to accept that the concept of 'respect for private life' could protect the individual against the imposition of criminal penalties for homosexual acts, but this has now changed. The criminalisation of homosexual activities between consenting adults is now recognised to be a breach of Article 8 ECHR.[13] This is one illustration of a more general principle that certain constraints on or interferences with same-sex relationships can be seen as violations of Article 8 ECHR 'respect for private life', in the absence of justification and 'necessity in a democratic society.' This principle is now well established in the ECtHR.

However, in a number of cases the ECommHR emphasised its view that the 'family' is founded on heterosexual not homosexual unions. In particular, of relevance to our problem are a number of cases concerning refusal of entry or leave to remain to same-sex partners where the exclusion of same-sex relationships from the concept of 'family life' is stressed.[14] This can also be illustrated vividly by the case of *X, Y and Z v UK*[15] in which a post-operative transsexual sought recognition as the father his partner's children conceived by artificial insemination. One of the reasons that the ECtHR was willing to accept that there was 'family' life was the 'appearance' of a normal family founded on a heterosexual union. This seemed to fit more acceptably into their concept of family than the obviously same-sex couple, even though the interference was held to be justified. For now, the 'family' remains distinctively heterosexual and same-sex couples must fall back on the potentially less helpful concept of private life.

1.3.1 Da Silva Mouta *and* Fretté — *Towards the Gay 'Family' in the ECHR*

The case of *Salguiero da Silva Mouta*[16] could however indicate the emergence of a different attitude to this point. The ECtHR establishes clearly that sexual orientation is one of the 'like' grounds of discrimination covered by Article 14 ECHR. This basic principle is also followed in *Fretté v France*[17] although on the facts of the case the claim (relating to refusal of the French authorities to authorise a single gay man to adopt a child)

Rights (OUP, Oxford, 1995); C Forder, 'The Anti-discrimination Principle as an Instrument of Change in Family Law' (1998) 45 *NILR* 29; P Van Dijk, 'The Treatment of Homosexuals under the European Convention on Human Rights' in K Waaldijk and A Clapham (eds), *Homosexuality: A European Community Issue* (Martinus Nijhoff, Dordreecht, 1993).

[13] *Dudgeon v UK* Series A No 45 (1981) 4 EHRR 149; *Norris v Ireland* Series A No 142 (1988) 13 EHRR 186; *Modinos v Cyprus* Series A No 259 (1993) 16 EHRR 485.

[14] *WJ & DP v UK* Application 12513/86; *C & LM v UK* Application 14753/89 and *ZB v UK* Application 16106/90.

[15] *X, Y & Z v UK* (n 4).

[16] *Da Silva Mouta v Portugal* Application 33290/96 (2001) 31 EHRR 47.

[17] *Fretté v France* Application 36515/97. The claim did not succeed for other reasons.

failed. This means that in general unjustified discrimination on these grounds in the enjoyment of other Convention rights will be in breach of Article 14 ECHR (see further on this part 3 below). Most recently, the Court also held in *Karner v Austria*[18] that Article 14 ECHR protects against discrimination against same-sex *partnerships* as well as *individuals* (at least in the situation where a distinction is made between unmarried opposite-sex and same-sex partnerships). In the light of these decisions, the ECtHR's insistence that a same-sex couple cannot enjoy 'family life' together cannot be sustainable for much longer. It would be self-contradictory for the ECtHR to reject as prima facie 'not acceptable' any distinction made by a Contracting State in enjoyment of Convention rights based on sexual orientation, while itself preserving this distinction between unmarried heterosexual and homosexual couples in the concept of family life.

There are precedents in domestic law for this kind of interpretation of the concept of 'family', particularly *Fitzpatrick*[19] in which the UK House of Lords accepted that a cohabiting same-sex couple could be members of each other's family for the purposes of statutory succession to a tenancy of their joint rented home. Later, the Court of Appeal[20] even used Article 14 ECHR to overturn the House of Lords' remaining reservation (that the phrase 'living as his or her wife or husband' implied a heterosexual relationship). However, these are domestic law cases, not overwhelmingly persuasive for the ECtHR, let alone anything like a legally binding precedent. Nevertheless, the current attitude of the ECtHR seems relatively favourable to gay individuals and same-sex families and it would be unsurprising and very welcome for it to follow in this direction. The question has not yet been considered fully by the ECtHR, although the cases of *Craig*[21] and *Mata Estevez*[22] are of interest. *Craig* involved a lesbian couple in which one partner (C) was prohibited by a court order (which had been consented to by her partner L) from visiting L when L's children were staying with her during contact visits. The applicant contended that this restriction on her visiting with her partner was an interference with the couple's private and family life. The ECtHR declared the application inadmissible, although its judgment, perhaps deliberately, proceeds on the basis that *even if there were family life between the couple* the interference would be justified. This is a subtle but potentially significant development,

[18] *Karner v Austria* Application 40016/98 Judgment of 24 July 2003. The English Court of Appeal had already taken this view in *Ghaidan v Mendoza* [2002] EWCA Civ 1533 [2002] 4 All ER 1162. The ruling has been upheld by the House of Lords [2004] UK HL30 [2004] 3 All ER 411.
[19] *Fitzpatrick v Sterling Housing Association* [2001] 1 AC 27.
[20] *Ghaidan v Mendoza* (n 18).
[21] *Craig v UK* Application 45396/99.
[22] *Mata Estevez v Spain* Application 55601/00. Thanks to Rob Wintemute for drawing my attention to this case.

as in all previous cases the ECommHR was quick to point out that the same-sex couples were not to be considered to have family life together under Article 8 ECHR. *Mata Estevez* is a far less favourable case, repeating the earlier negative conclusions of the ECommHR, but after the conclusions of the ECtHR in *Karner*, it seems now to be something of an isolated aberration.

1.3.2 *The Continuing Significance of Recognition of Same-sex Couples as Family*

The ECtHR accepts in principle that interference with same-sex relationships may constitute interference with private life, and the ECommHR accepted that refusal of settlement to same-sex partners does raise issues of 'private life' pursuant to Article 8 ECHR. It might therefore be considered that the foregoing discussion of their position regarding 'family life' is of limited relevance. It is undoubtedly a less important issue than if the 'private life' question had not been decided in the way it had some years ago. Nevertheless, it may retain some significance, for three reasons:

1 As we will see, the protection of relationships accepted to be part of 'family life' is more extensive than those accepted to be part of 'private life' only. There is therefore possibly some real benefit to be gained in the acceptance of same-sex relationships as protected 'family life', as their treatment under the concept of private life has thus far been distinctly unsatisfactory.
2 The denial of the status of 'family' to the same-sex couple permits more easily the use of the argument that protection of the 'traditional family' is an objective and reasonable ground to differentiate the same-sex couple from the opposite-sex couple. It does not necessarily mean that the argument could not persist, but it makes it less likely.
3 The existing structure of EC Regulations and Directives does in fact give *some* room for argument that if either the same-sex couple or the unmarried couple are 'members of the family' of a migrant worker, they may benefit from some special consideration even if not from directly effective rights.[23] Clearly the argument that the same-sex couple are 'family members' under the Community law regulations is not ruled out by the current ECtHR stance.[24] But if the ECtHR does conclude that 'family life'

[23] Council Regulation 1612/68 of 15 October 1968 on Freedom of Movement for Workers within the Community [1968/9] OJ Sp Ed (II) 475, Art 10(2) provides that the host state 'shall facilitate' the entry of certain 'members of the family' of the migrant not covered by Art 10(1). On the interpretation of this provision, see discussion in ch 2 above.
[24] Eg, the similar decision in *Fitzpatrick* (n 19).

includes same-sex couples, the argument that they ought to be treated as 'members of the family' where EC legislation uses such a vague terms becomes stronger. This is no longer such an important issue in relation to immigration rights with the passing of the new EU Citizens Directive which specificially confirms that the obligation to 'facilitate' entry and residence of partners applies to all couples in stable relationships, but it may have some relevance in other contexts in the future.

1.4 Registered Partnerships

There is no case law from the ECtHR on the status of registered partnerships, so the following observations are speculative. It is highly likely that the couple living together in such a relationship would be seen to have 'family life'. This is certainly so in relation to opposite-sex couples. There is no reason why the relationship capable of being 'family life', if it is sufficiently stable and lasting, would be excluded because of its legal registration. At the very least, it would be cogent evidence of the necessary stability and commitment in the relationship. As to same-sex couples, similar conclusions may be suggested. The legal registration of the partnership should not in any way prejudice the couple. On the contrary, it can only work to their advantage, providing evidence of the stability of the relationship in question and the future intent of the parties. Further, even if the argument relating to the family life of the unmarried and unregistered same-sex couple is not, or not *yet*, accepted, the legal registration of the relationship might persuade the ECtHR to depart, in at least this limited way, from the previous stance of the ECommHR on this issue and to accept the existence of family life between registered partners. The main contentious question would be the consequences of this and the extent of the 'margin of appreciation' open to Contracting States in the way they treat such families. Two crucial questions will be whether and to what extent a refusal to recognise or give some legal effect to a registered partnership entered into in another state will be an unjustified interference with family life, and if a decision to introduce same-sex partnership registration is taken, the extent to which Article 14 ECHR will affect this situation.[25]

[25] Would it be a violation of Art 14 ECHR to provide registered partnership for gay couples with significantly fewer rights and obligations than marriage? Would registered partnership for same-sex couples only discriminate against heterosexual couples who do not wish to marry? This argument does not seem attractive if the aim is to provide a same-sex marriage in all but name, but if the same-sex registered partnership is significantly different from marriage it could be an issue.

1.5 Same-sex Marriages

A similar speculative approach has to be taken to the status of same-sex marriages. It seems clear enough that Article 12 ECHR does not yet require Contracting States to permit celebration of same-sex marriages within their own jurisdiction.[26] However, the application of Article 8 ECHR to a migrating same-sex married couple away from the state in which they have married is an entirely different matter. It would seem undeniable that they have 'family life', and that they may avail themselves of the protection of Article 8 ECHR when in another Contracting State. The crucial question will be the consequences of Article 8 ECHR and in particular whether this requires the host State to recognise the validity of the marriage. This view can be supported by considering that valid[27] foreign polygamous marriages have not been considered incapable of giving rise to family life, either in general terms or on the particular facts of the case. On the contrary, when the issue has been considered by the ECommHR, it has always seemed to accept that these are family relationships within Article 8 ECHR, albeit ones that may be interfered with by refusing recognition for particular purposes on the grounds of public policy, in order to maintain the monogamous nature of marriage.[28] It seems likely that similar arguments will be raised by Contracting States that are unwilling to accept a homosexual partnership as a marriage even if it has been legally and validly celebrated as such abroad, and again the margin of appreciation will be critical here. The Belgian and Austrian cases referred to earlier[29] may provide the first test of the transnational validity of such marriages.

1.6 Conclusion — 'Family Life'

Although the paradigm of the heterosexual married couple remains strong, the ECtHR is often willing to recognise 'de facto' family life

[26] No case has yet been brought before the ECtHR regarding same-sex marriage. But the heterosexual nature of marriage is implicit in the rulings relating to transsexuals (*Rees v UK* Series A No 106 (1986) 9 EHRR 56; *Cossey v UK* Series A No 184 (1990) 13 EHRR 622, and *Sheffield & Horsham v UK* Application 22865/93 (1998) 27 EHRR 163) to the effect that marriage can be denied to a post-operative transsexual in his/her new gender. This point is made even more clearly by the ECommHR in *C & LM v UK* Application 14753/89 in which same-sex marriage was raised as a subsidiary issue in an immigration case mainly concerning the deportation of a same-sex partner. The most recent consideration of transsexuals, *Goodwin v UK* Application 28957/95 (2002) 35 EHRR 18 and *I v UK* Application 25680/94 [2002] 2 FLR 518 does not change this. The ECtHR accepts that the new gender must be *recognised*, not (yet) that marriage must be made entirely *gender-neutral*. See R Probert, 'The Right to Marry and the Impact of the Human Rights Act 1998' [2003] IFL 29.

[27] Valid under the law of the place of celebration and of domicile of the parties.

[28] Dealt with further below, section 3.4.5.

[29] See ch 1.

between stable unmarried heterosexual couples, and may also be on its way to doing so with same-sex couples. If this is the case, then same-sex marriages and registered partnerships should also suffice to create family life between the couples concerned.

PART TWO — IMMIGRATION CONTROL AND ARTICLE 8 ECHR

Introduction

The ECHR contains no provision specifically dealing with migration or immigration. Subject to international obligations, Contracting States remain free to regulate the immigration and expulsion of non-nationals from their territory—but the ECHR itself is one of these international obligations which may constrain states' decisions and policies in this area. In particular, Articles 2 and 3 ECHR prevent return to the risk of extra-judicial killing, torture or inhuman and degrading treatment,[30] and Article 8 ECHR may prevent unjustified interference with the family or private life of the individual by expulsion or exclusion from territory in which close family members reside.[31]

The current attitude of the ECtHR to Article 8 in immigration cases will be discussed in four sections. First, section 2.1 will consider cases in which policies refusing settlement to family members—particularly married couples—are challenged. Then in section 2.2, the case law suggesting that Article 8 ECHR offers greater protection against expulsion than opportunites for admission will be addressed, and section 2.3 will address the tension between two approaches ('connections' approach vs 'elsewhere' approach) and the still quite recent but discernable tendency to adopt a

[30] *Chahal v UK* 1996-V 1831 (1996) 23 EHRR 413.

[31] There is an extensive literature on this, inter alia, H Lambert, 'The European Court of Human Rights and the Right of Refugees and Other Persons in Need of Protection to Family Reunion' (1999) 11 *IJRL* 427; C Anderfuhren-Wayne,'Family Unity in Immigration and Refugee Matters' (1996) 8 *IJRL*; E Courouge, 'Le Respect de la Vie Familiale: des Etrangers et Article 8 CEDH' (1997) 13 *Revue Francaise de Droit Administratif* 318; H Storey, 'Right to Family Life and Immigration Case Law at Strasbourg' (1990) 39 *ICLQ* 328; A Sherlock, 'Deportation of Aliens and Art 8 ECHR' (1998) 23 *ELRev* 70; Cvetic (n 3); R Cholewinski, 'Strasbourg's 'Hidden Agenda?' The Protection of Second-generation Migrants from Expulsion under Art 8 of the *ECHR*' (1994) 12 *Netherlands Quarterly of International Law*, and D Seddon, 'Families, Dependants, Relationships' in *A Guide to the Human Rights Act*, Butterworths Immigration Law Service Special Bulletin (Butterworths, London, 1999); K Groenendijk et al (eds), *Security of Residence and Long-term Migrants: A Comparative Study of Law and Practice in European Countries* (Council of Europe, Strasbourg, 1998); E Guild and P Minderhoud (eds), *Security of Residence and Expulsion—Protection of Aliens in Europe* (Kluwer, The Hague, 2001); N Rogers, 'Immigration and the European Convention on Human Rights: Are New Principles Emerging?' [2003] *EHRLR* 53; N Blake and R Hussain, *Immigration Asylum and Human Rights* (OUP/Blackstone, Oxford, 2003) esp ch 4.

stricter view of when a family may reasonably be expected to settle elsewhere. Finally, in section 2.4, settlement of same-sex partners as a protected aspect of private life will be addressed. The aim of this review is to test the strength of the argument that Article 8 ECHR alone might require admission of non-marital partners.

2.1 Immigration Policies and Family Members

2.1.1 Abdulaziz

In the early 1980s, the non-national husband of a woman settled in the UK was subject to stricter entry rules than the wife of a man settled in the UK. Three women sought admission for their husbands and were refused. They challenged this refusal in the ECtHR in the leading case of *Abdulaziz, Cabales and Balkandali*.[32] The principles articulated here are the origin of all the later jurisprudence, so the case deserves some close attention at an early stage of this discussion.

The ECtHR confirms that the immigration regulations of the Contracting states, and how they exercise them, are in principle subject to scrutiny under Article 8 ECHR. Yet it also concludes that Article 8 ECHR does not give rise to a presumption that the state must allow free choice of family or matrimonial residence by admitting the non-national spouse. The applicants suggest that,

> The dilemma either of moving abroad or being separated from one's spouse is inconsistent with this principle [the obligation of the State to respect private and family life].[33]

The ECtHR however insists that this is not the case:

> The duty imposed by Article 8 cannot be considered as extending to a general obligation on the part of a Contracting State to respect the choice by married couples of the country of their matrimonial residence and to accept the non-national spouses for settlement in that country.[34]

The ECtHR also asserts that the applicants,

> … have not shown that there were obstacles to establishing family life in their own or their husbands' home countries or that there were special reasons why that could not be expected of them.[35]

[32] *Abdulaziz* (n 2).
[33] Para 66.
[34] Para 68.
[35] *Ibid* 68.

This implies that there is some onus of proof on the applicant to show that family life could not reasonably be enjoyed elsewhere. The ECtHR also suggests that in all cases the couples were or should have been aware of the rules when they married, opening up the possibility of a distinction between those who migrate and then seek entry for their already established families, and those who seek leave to remain or entry for partners in newly begun relationships. The only possibility was that the rules discriminated on the grounds of sex, race or birth, and only the first of these complaints was upheld. As regards its general attitude to immigration policies, the ECtHR makes the following comments, quite clearly setting a course of judicial deference to national policies and a wide margin of appreciation:

> However, especially as far as those positive obligations are concerned, the nation's requirements will vary considerably from case to case. Accordingly, this is an area in which the Contracting Parties enjoy a wide margin of appreciation in determining the steps to be taken to ensure compliance with the Convention with due regard to the needs and resources of the Community and of individuals. … In particular, in the area now under consideration, the extent of a State's obligation to admit to its territory relatives of settled immigrants will vary according to the particular circumstances of the persons involved. Moreover, the Court cannot ignore the fact that the present case is not only concerned with family life but also with immigration and that, as a matter of well-established international law and subject to its treaty obligations, a State has the right to control the entry of non-nationals into its territory.[36]

2.1.2 *The Legacy of* Abdulaziz

Other subsequent cases concerning general immigration policies have repeated the basic approach set out in *Abdulaziz*. Contracting States are generally free to apply policies denying entry to second or subsequent wives in polygamous marriages and their children,[37] and to maintain policies which do not automatically grant settlement rights to spouses and other family members, including children.[38] States often have policies making entry of spouses or other family members conditional on the

[36] Para 67.
[37] *Bibi* Application 19628/92; *El Abasse* Application 4561/89 and *M & OM* Application 12139/86. Cf admissibility decision in *Alam v UK* Application 2991/66, son seeking admission to join father, also *ML v State Secretary of Justice* 13 Nov 1979 Rechtspraak Vreemdelingenrecht (1979 no 32) (1980) 21 NYBIL 308, and *BBIB v Netherlands* 28 Feb 1980 (1982) 23 NYBIL 349.
[38] But see *Sen v Netherlands* Application 31465/96 and dissenting judgments in *Ahmut v Netherlands* 1996-VI 2017 (1996) EHRR 62 and *Gül v Switzerland* Application 23218/94 1996-I 159 (1996) 22 EHRR 93.

existence of adequate accommodation and/or funds for the support of the additional family members, and there is no suggestion that these are incompatible with Article 8 ECHR.[39] Policies which as a general rule deny immediate settlement on the basis of a marriage contracted after a deportation order has been served or an expulsion decision made are considered to be compatible with Article 8 ECHR.[40] Finally, policies authorising the refusal of continued residence or of deportation on the grounds of criminal behaviour are also considered and have been upheld, although the application of the principle of proportionality in such cases remains difficult and disputes continue to arise in individual cases as to the proportionality of the State's interference with family life in response to a threat to public order by criminal behaviour of non-nationals.[41]

2.1.3 *The example of DP3/96*

The UK policy statement DP3/96[42] is an instructive example. This policy (and the similar but more generous preceding policy, DP2/93)[43] provide guidance in the case of an illegal entrant or overstayer who relies on family ties—particularly marriage—to resist deportation.[44] DP3/96 states that marriage will not normally constitute grounds for permitting the applicant to remain where entered into after deportation proceedings have been initiated, and will only generally be considered grounds for permission to remain if it predates the enforcement action by two years.[45]

These policies and other similar ones[46] have already been considered by both the ECtHR[47] and far more extensively by the UK courts.[48] It has never been considered that the existence of the policy in general terms is unlawful,[49] and the circumstances in which the individual decision on

[39] Cholewinski notes that none of these policies have been considered in the ECtHR — R Cholewinski, *Migrant Workers in International Human Rights Law* (OUP, Oxford, 1997) 343.
[40] *Choudhry v UK* Application 27949/95; *Solomon v Netherlands* Application 44328/98.
[41] Individual applications of these policies gives rise to difficulty. *Al-Nashif v Bulgaria* Application 50936/99 (2002) 35 EHRR CD 76 is unusual in condemning the entire procedure as not being according to law rather than the individual decision.
[42] DP3/96, reproduced in *Butterworths Immigration Law Service* (Butterworths London) D [551].
[43] DP2/93, reproduced in *Butterworths Immigration Law Service* (n 42) D [501].
[44] Generally *Macdonald's Immigration Law and Practice* (n 3) para 11.59 page 438.
[45] What happens when the marriage predates the enforcement action by less than two years is not entirely clear—see *Ex p Mahmood* [2001] 1 WLR 840.
[46] Eg *Solomon v Netherlands* (n 40) and in the ECJ Case C-459/99 *MRAX v Belgian State.*
[47] *Choudhry; Solomon* (n 40); *Poku* Application 26985/95; *Ajayi* Application 27663/95.
[48] Lexis searches on England and Wales reported and unreported cases database (12.07.2002) revealed 17 references to DP3/96, and 68 references to DP2/93. In particular, *Ex p Gangadeen* [1998] Imm AR 106; *Ex p Ahmed* [1999] Imm AR 22, although these cases also involved children. Most recently, *Ex p Mahmood* (n 45) in which the policy itself was not directly challenged, rather the failure to recognise the applicant's case as one involving 'exceptional circumstances' and *Ex p Isiko* [2001] Imm AR 291.
[49] Eg *Ex p Isiko* (n 48) para 6; *Ex p Ahmed & Patel* [1998] INLR 570, 577 Lord Woolf.

removal of a spouse can be challenged successfully are limited.[50] In the words of Scheimann LJ in *ex parte Isiko* (speaking specifically in the context of DP3/96), building on the case of *Abdulaziz*:[51]

> It is clear that the European Court of Human Rights has recognised that many factors play a part in immigration policy, that those factors are likely to differ between one country and another, that the state has a right to control entry of non-nationals, and that the elected government of the country concerned is entitled to lay down and enforce a general policy which does not offend the principle of proportionality.[52]
>
> It is clear that the mere fact that the presence of an individual and his family in this country will not in itself constitute a threat to one of the interests enumerated in Art 8(2) of the Convention does not prevent a decision to enforce a lawful immigration policy which applies in the individual's case from being lawful.[53]

2.1.4 The Limits of the Margin of Discretion in Policy Making

In all of these situations rational and at least potentially defensible reasons behind the refusal of immigration rights may be identified. In the first case polygamous marriages are not permitted in Contracting States, and indeed bigamy is a specific criminal offence. Given such penal measures to prevent the celebration of such marriages within these jurisdictions, it is hardly surprising or manifestly irrational that the validity of bigamous and polygamous marriages contracted abroad may be seen to raise issues of public policy. Likewise, states will wish to discourage individuals who are threatened with deportation from seeing marriage as an automatic and immediate solution to their problems. If it were so, perhaps the temptation to enter into sham marriages would be too great, and there is a reluctance to allow concessions to those who have violated immigration controls. Policies that permit deportation of or non-renewal of residence of foreign spouses on the basis of public order or security following serious criminal offences also have an obvious rationale. In all these cases, the issue is not whether there is a legitimate aim, but whether the policy is proportionate, both generally and in particular cases.

Beyond this, the limits of what Article 8 ECHR requires in the context of immigration law are not clearly drawn. In particular, although it seems highly likely, it is not clear beyond doubt whether a Contracting State is

[50] *Ex p Hashim* (CO/2052/99 12 June 2000 unreported Lexis transcript) in which it was held to be disproportionate to expect the applicant to return to Brazil to apply for entry clearance seems exceptional.
[51] Above (n 2).
[52] *Ex p Isiko* (n 48) para 14.
[53] *Ex p Isiko* (n 48) para 36.

required to adopt *some* kind of policy permitting settlement of close family members. For example, would a policy denying marriage altogether as a lawful ground for settlement of a non-national spouse be compatible with Article 8 ECHR? This seems unlikely, unless the state had a very liberal entry policy, amounting to an open borders policy, to permit settlement anyway. On a less draconian note, might rationing residence permits for spouses so that only a randomly chosen and very limited number of such applications were successful, or a policy imposing a 5, 10, or 15 year waiting period on all applicants, or an unreasonably high level of financial resources before settlement was permitted, be compatible with Article 8 ECHR?[54] The questions above are all hypothetical.

More realistically, Denmark has just completed the passage of highly restrictive new legislation.[55] Among other things it would attach financial conditions and an impose age of at least 24 before any resident could expect a residence permit for a spouse.[56] Whether these conditions will be compatible with Article 8 ECHR remains to be seen. No doubt the analysis would proceed initially in the same way as in all these other cases, with the assertion that the refusal of settlement was an interference with family life that had to be justified. The final stages of the analysis might however proceed differently. It is not clear whether a mere assertion of sovereignty and control over immigration would be enough to save these policies, or whether a further and more clearly articulated justification would be required. *Abdulaziz*[57] is perhaps as close as one can get to this, and the attitude of the ECtHR is negative on this point, suggesting a relatively wide margin of appreciation. On the contrary, as we have seen above, the ECtHR is quite emphatic that general immigration policies may be maintained. The only reason why the refusal of settlement was incompatible with Article 8 ECHR in *Abdulaziz* was the element of sex discrimination.

The most recent judgment to come anywhere near a conclusion that the entire policy concerned is a breach of Article 8 ECHR is *Al-Nashif v*

[54] Cholewinski notes that the conditions commonly applied to family members have not been considered in the ECtHR (n 39). A rare case is *X v UK* Application 7048/75 9 D & R 42 where a newly married wife waited six months for entry clearance. The application was declared inadmissible.

[55] *Copenhagen Post, http://cphpost.dk/*, 24 Jan 2002, 'The Government's New Immigration and Integration Proposals' and 12 July 2002, 'Spouses Turn towards Sweden for Residency Hope' and reports on the BBC News website on 27/11/2001, 05/02/2002, 31/05/2002 and 24/06/2002. Note the further reports in October 2003 suggesting that NGOs have questioned the compatibility of these new rules with international obligations—23 October 2003, 'Immigration Law at Odds with Global Conventions, Experts Say', and 17 October 2003, 'Groups: Immigration Law at Odds with Global Conventions'.

[56] It seems to be accepted by all concerned that these requirements would not be compatible with EC law. They do not apply to migrant EU citizens and the Swedish Government have expressed concern that Danes will move to Sweden in order to take advantage of more favourable EC law settlement rights for their partners.

[57] Above (n 2).

Bulgaria.[58] This concerned the deportation of an individual on the grounds of national security. The Bulgarian legislation on such issues did not provide for an appeal against such a decision and this was held by the ECtHR not to satisfy the requirements of the restriction being 'provided by law'. The ECtHR did not have to go as far as determining whether the policy struck a fair balance between the different interests in question.

2.2 Negative and Positive Obligations under Article 8 ECHR — Deportations and Admissions

The obligation under Article 8 ECHR, as under other Articles of the ECHR,[59] may be both negative and positive. The negative obligation may be seen as an obligation not to take a particular action which will interfere with family life, the positive obligation being to put in place positive structures and laws or procedures to permit family life to be established and conducted privately. Broadly speaking, this may be seen to operate in immigration matters by drawing a distinction between deportation or exclusion of those already in the territory, and admission of those who are resident elsewhere wishing to settle in the host state.

2.2.1 *The Origin of this Distinction* — Abdulaziz

It is clear from the extracts quoted above that the ECtHR placed some emphasis on the fact that the applications were for admission rather than trying to resist deportation. It was not in fact until later that the case law concerning the balancing of the public interest in deporting criminals with the competing demands of respect for their private lives and family ties in the Host State began. *Abdulaziz*[60] therefore has to be seen as one of the primary sources of the emerging distinction, such as it is, between entry and deportation, even though the question is only mentioned briefly.

2.2.2 *The Next Cases* — Gül, Ahmut *and* Nsona

While there are a number of cases in which Article 8 ECHR has been used to prevent deportation, with varying degrees of success,[61] the ECtHR

[58] *Al-Nashif v Bulgaria* (n 41).
[59] On positive obligations generally, K Starmer, 'Positive Obligations under the Convention' in J Jowell and J Cooper (eds), *Understanding Human Rights Principles* (Hart Publishing, Oxford, 2001) and K Starmer, *European Human Rights Law* (Legal Action Group, London, 1999) ch 5.
[60] Above (n 2).
[61] On this, K Groenendijk et al (eds) (n 31); E Guild and P Minderhoud (n 31), and generally the other literature cited above (n 31).

does seem to have developed *Abdulaziz*[62] in the direction of being more reluctant to admit a *positive* obligation to permit immigration and settlement than to refrain from deportation of those already settled.[63] Primarily, this is developed in cases where the existing links with, and family life that have been developed in, the host state are considered. To the extent that there is an emphasis on removing an individual from an existing, stable family setting in the host state, understandably the family which has been living together elsewhere, or has been separated for some time before the application is made for entry, will be in a more difficult position.

Gül,[64] *Ahmut*[65] and *Nsona*[66] are leading cases in which claims for settlement of children have been rejected, and are the foundation of this stricter approach to admission than expulsion. This is certainly so, but it is perhaps unwise to read too much into these cases, mainly because of the paucity of cases involved in which admission rather than expulsion is in question. In all these the conclusion was that there had been no breach of Article 8 ECHR—but even here, the ECtHR admits that the boundaries of positive and negative obligations are not clearly drawn and that the applicable principles are similar. In *Gül* and *Ahmut* it was considered that there was a reasonable prospect of settling the family in the state of origin, and in *Nsona* a crucial factor was the applicant's fraud. Many of the cases involving plural wives and their children[67] are also admission rather than expulsion cases.

More recently, further admissibility decisions continue this trend.[68] The precise status of these decisions is somewhat difficult—on the one hand they are admissibility decisions and therefore perhaps not entitled to the same weight as final decisions as to whether or not there has been a violation of the Convention. On the other hand, they are now given by chambers of the ECtHR rather than the ECommHR—and the decision is not simply that there is no violation, but that there is no appearance of violation and that the case is *manifestly* ill-founded and inadmissible. It has to be concluded that the dichotomy between expulsion and admission cases exists, but the precise extent to which it is applied in practice is difficult to pin down.

[62] Above (n 2).
[63] Peers sugests that there is an almost unlimited discretion in relation to admission but a complex balancing act when expulsion is involved—S Peers, 'The European Court of Justice and the European Court of Human Rights: Comparative Approaches' in E Orucu (ed), *Judicial Comparativism in Human Rights Cases* (BIICL 2003) citing P Van Dijk, 'Protection of Integrated Aliens Against Expulsion under the European Convention' in E Guild and P Minderhoud (n 31).
[64] *Gül v Switzerland* (n 38).
[65] *Ahmut v Netherlands* (n 38)
[66] *Nsona v Netherlands* (2001) 32 EHRR 9.
[67] Section 3.4.5 below.
[68] *Kwakye-Nti v Netherlands* Application 31519/96; *Selim v Cyprus* Application 47293/99, and *Mensah v Netherlands* Application 47042/99.

It is also questionable whether exactly the same balancing exercise is called for in each case, given the absence of a *general obligation* to admit even the closest family members. It would be one thing to have the same or very similar approach to admission and expulsion of spouses/partners and minor children—if this approach starts from the general proposition that settlement of close family members was a general obligation. But if this is *not* the case then a different approach is called for to respect the 'acquired rights' of the individual and the right to stay and enjoy family life and ties already established in the host state.[69] This approach may be supported by consideration of the dissenting judgments of Judge Martens in *Gül* and *Ahmut*. These are among the clearest calls in the ECtHR for a unified approach to settlement and admission—and they contain the clearest articulation to be found in the ECtHR that Article 8 ECHR may impose a *general obligation* on Contracting States not to permit immigration laws to disrupt family life between particular categories of close family members, particularly young children in need of the care of their parents lawfully settled in the host state.

Thus, as long as the ECtHR distances itself from any concept of a 'general obligation' to permit settlement and continued residence of even the very closest family members, a distinction between settlement and expulsion cases seems unavoidable to deal with the cases fairly. The fundamental weakness in the ECtHR approach is not so much the distinction between positive and negative obligations (to the extent that such exists) but the unwillingness to admit, even as to the closest of relatives of settled residents, any 'general' obligation to permit family life to exist or continue on Contracting State's territory.

2.2.3 *A More Liberal Approach?* Sen *and* Boultif

The cases of *Boultif*[70] and *Sen*[71] however may represent a considerable shift in the ECtHR's willingness to accept positive obligations to admit family members for settlement.[72] *Boultif* is not a classic admission case and has much in common with expulsion cases. However, it may also be seen to have more in common with the admission cases than many of the expulsion cases do, as the applicant was applying from outside Switzerland complaining of a refusal to renew his residence permit, and had spent a relatively short period of time in Switzerland.[73] It is clear from

[69] On this, K Groenendijk et al (n 31); E Guild and P Minderhoud (n 31) and P McFadden, 'The Right to Stay' (1996) 29 *Vanderbilt Journal of Transnational Law* 1.
[70] *Boultif v Switzerland* Application 54273/00 (2001) 33 EHRR 50.
[71] *Sen v Netherlands* (n 38).
[72] See Rogers, (n 31) and Blake and Hussain (n 31).
[73] He entered in December 1992 as a visitor, married in March 1993, committed the alleged offence in April 1994, was tried in 1995—and sentenced in January 1997.

the circumstances of the case that the concern to protect long-established residence stretching over many years, even decades, was not at its strongest. Despite the additional circumstance of the criminal offence, the ECtHR considered that the balance had not been struck fairly between all the interests involved—particularly because it would be unreasonable for the Swiss wife to accompany her husband to Algeria.

Sen is far more clearly an admission case and therefore merits fuller discussion. Turkish national Zeki Sen had come to The Netherlands to join his parents at the age of 12, in 1977. In 1982 he married a Turkish woman in Turkey, and they started a family in 1983. The first child was left in Turkey with the mother's relatives when the mother joined Mr Sen in The Netherlands in 1986, and another child was born in 1990. In 1992 the parents sought a residence permit for their first child to join them. There had apparently been some disagreement over the issue as well as some marital difficulties between the couple which they said explained their decision to leave their first child in Turkey in 1986. It was therefore only in 1992 that the wife agreed that the elder daughter should come to the Netherlands. Before the final decision rejecting the application was made in 1995, a third child was born in 1994. Although at first it was doubted by the authorities in the Netherlands that the first child was still part of her parents' 'family' for the purposes of Article 8 ECHR this was conceded before the ECtHR. The government however continued to rely on *Ahmut*[74] to suggest that there was no obligation to admit the first child.

The main point of distinction fixed on by the ECtHR in *Sen*, in distinction to *Ahmut*, was that the two other children had been born and educated in The Netherlands. It was therefore unreasonable to expect the family to return to Turkey to enjoy family life there, and the decision of the parents to leave their first child in Turkey temporarily should not be seen as irrevocable. This emphasis on the unreasonableness of return to Turkey fits into a pattern of recent cases (discussed below) and may be considered to be part of a stricter approach on this point that is emerging from the ECtHR in all cases. It is however particularly interesting to note that for the first time in an admission case, the ECtHR considers that the balance favours remaining in the host state rather than relocating family life elsewhere, even though it does not refer explicitly to the guidance given a matter of months earlier in *Boultif*.

It is of course also significant and welcome that the ECtHR repeats that Article 8 ECHR may impose obligations on a state to admit as well as to refrain from expelling. However, the obligation is still far from a *general* one. The ECtHR still fixes on the reasonableness or not of the family regrouping in another country, and it is only a dissenting minority judgment of Judge Tulkens in *Sen* that comes close to recognising a *general*

[74] Above (n 38).

right of entry even of minor dependent children to join parents settled in the host state. It is difficult to say whether *Sen* marks a clear break from an earlier stricter approach to admission or whether the case is better seen as part of the general trend to scrutinise more strictly host states' assertions that family reunification may reasonably be expected elsewhere. Further cases clearly concerning admissions will have to be decided to clarify this point, and there have been none of major significance since *Sen*.[75]

2.3 The (Diminishing?) Importance of being able to Settle the Family Elsewhere

We have seen from *Abdulaziz*[76] that the ECtHR has from an early stage noted the possibility that couples could settle elsewhere.[77] It has considered that this could prevent a host state from being under any obligation to permit family reunification on its territory. This approach has been subject to well-founded criticism.[78] If both states involved take this view, how is such a dispute to be resolved? This approach would of course not be helpful as the basis for coherent and consistent policy on migration of mixed nationality couples.[79] In principle, it also seems unsatisfactory to suggest that the ECHR only requires protection against the violation or non-enjoyment of a right *anywhere in the world* rather than requiring protection against violation or non-enjoyment of that right *within the territory of that state*.[80] Nevertheless, this approach been applied in a number of cases. It has, as Storey and Anderfuhren-Wayne note,[81] had some competition from an approach more clearly based on connections with the host state, and has seemingly been applied more restrictively to

[75] The most recent case of *Yildiz* (n 6) like *Boultif* (n 70) has far more in common with expulsion cases than admission cases. Many of the decided cases since *Sen* have been expulsion cases. The cases of *JM v Netherlands* Application 38047/97 and *Adnane v Netherlands* 50568/99 (both declared inadmissible, both involved admission of children) were decided shortly before *Sen*. The subsequent case of *Ebrahim v Netherlands* Application 51986/00 (judgment of 18.3.2003) did not cite *Sen* (but did cite *Gul* and *Ahmut*)—it involved an older child who at the time when the ECtHR gave judgment was 20 years old, could thus be expected to provide for himself in Lebanon, had significant ties with Lebanon, and had earlier voluntarily departed from The Netherlands to return to Lebanon. The latest similar case involves much younger but adopted child *Singh v UK* Application 60148/00, declared admissible on 3 September 2003, judgment has not yet been given.

[76] Above (n 2).

[77] As we have seen *Abdulaziz* (n 2) seems to suggest that this is a matter for the Applicants to prove. Other cases concerning married couples include *Solomon* and *Choudhry* (n 40). The cases concerning same-sex couples referred to above (n 14) take a very harsh view on this, but this may be a manifestation of the difference between 'private life' and 'family life'. I shall return to this point later.

[78] Eg Storey (n 31), Cvetic (n 3).

[79] Cvetic (n 3).

[80] Storey (n 31) 337; Anderfuhren-Wayne (n 31).

[81] Storey (n 31); Anderfuhren-Wayne (n 31).

cases of settlement than expulsion. Nevertheless, it has remained a persistent and striking feature of the case law, and has presented significant obstacles to the success of complaints in the ECtHR. However, the most recent cases, *Sen*,[82] *Boultif*[83] and *Amrollahi v Denmark*[84] seem to indicate something of a new direction on this issue. It may be that the much criticised tendency of the ECtHR to expect couples and families to settle elsewhere may be diminishing, even if the ECtHR has not yet considered it possible to dispense with it entirely, even in limited categories of cases.

In *Boultif*, the ECtHR notes that it has not had extensive opportunity to consider the situation where there are significant obstacles to the migration of the couple to the state of origin of the non-national spouse to continue their family life there. It notes that it,

> Has only to a limited extent decided cases where the main obstacle to expulsion is the difficulties for the spouses to stay together and in particular for a spouse and/or children to live in the other's country of origin. It is therefore called upon to establish guiding principles in order to examine whether the measure was necessary in a democratic society.[85]

This it proceeds to do as follows:

> In assessing the relevant criteria in such a case, the Court will consider the nature and seriousness of the offence committed by the applicant; the length of the applicant's stay in the country from which he is going to be expelled; the time elapsed since the offence was committed as well as the applicant's conduct in that period; the nationalities of the various persons concerned; the applicant's family situation, such as the length of the marriage; and other factors expressing the effectiveness of a couple's family life; whether the spouse knew of the offence at the time when he or she entered into a family relationship; and whether there are children in the marriage, and if so, their age. Not least, the Court will also consider the seriousness of the difficulties which the spouse is likely to encounter in the country of origin, though the mere fact that a person might face certain difficulties in accompanying her or his spouse cannot in itself exclude an expulsion.[86]

It went on to find that there had been a violation of Article 8 ECHR. It considered that the threat to public policy was, comparatively speaking, only moderate. Although the husband had committed a serious offence of violent armed robbery, he had not re-offended since 1994, had retrained as a waiter and painter, had found work since his release, and had a

[82] *Sen v Netherlands* (n 38).
[83] *Boultif v Switzerland* (n 70).
[84] *Amrollahi v Denmark* Application 36811/00.
[85] Para 48.
[86] Para 48.

contract prepared for future gainful employment, conditional on his residence permit being renewed. Rehabilitation and reintegration into society was seemingly progressing quite well. One may indeed question whether there was anything else that the applicant could have done to demonstrate that he was no longer a threat to the public order and security of Switzerland. On the other hand, the Swiss wife did not speak Arabic, although she had established a degree of communication with her mother-in-law in French. She was employed in Switzerland, economically independent of her husband, had never lived abroad and had not visited Algeria. The ECtHR considered that there would be significant practical obstacles to her moving to Algeria with her husband, and that it would be unreasonable to expect her to do so.

The ECtHR considered that, when the interests of Switzerland were balanced with the degree of interference in the family life of the couple and the unreasonableness of the expectation that the wife might move to Algeria, the refusal of continued residence was not justified. The case does seem to indicate a new direction, and a greater willingness to take seriously applicant couples' complaints that they cannot reasonably be expected to migrate together elsewhere, particularly to the state of origin of the non-national spouse. It is however notable that the ECtHR still insists that some difficulties in the spouse settling abroad will not necessarily exclude an expulsion. To that extent it is not fair to describe this case as supporting an absolute right to remain or settle with a spouse even if there are difficulties in settling elsewhere. It is even further from any *general obligation* to respect family life by permitting settlement or continued residence of spouses, if there is indeed a reasonable possibility of settlement elsewhere.[87]

The approach taken in *Boultif* was repeated again in *Amrollahi*[88] and in *Yildiz*.[89] In *Amrollahi*, the ECtHR considered that the family (a Danish woman, her children by her Iranian husband and her daughter by another man) of a convicted drug importer could not be expected to follow the applicant to Iran if he were deported. *Yildiz* is a similar case, although it concerned less serious criminal offences. The interesting thing about this case is that the ECtHR seems to place more of a burden on the State to show that (or at least consider whether) it would be reasonable for the family to relocate elsewhere. This is a welcome move away from the suggestion in

[87] Note the paradoxical result of this analysis in relation to EU citizens, who of course under the EC Treaty have a right to settle in any EU Member State. The fact that such a possibility exists in law (with the exception perhaps of situations in which there was an unreasonable language barrier) might be taken as a reasonable possibility of settlement elsewhere. For a case in which the couple took advantage of the more generous family reunification rights under EC law, settling in Dublin pending an anticipated return to the UK, see *Choudhry* (n 40).

[88] Above (n 84).

[89] Above (n 6).

Abdulaziz that the applicants must show it would be unreasonable for them to settle elsewhere. It is also perhaps significant that that it considers this not in relation to a spouse of the nationality of the expelling state, but in relation to a second generation immigrant spouse of the same nationality (Turkish living in Austria). It is possible that these two particular cases reflect a concern that Western (or Westernised) women should not be expected to move to Islamic countries.[90] However, together with *Sen*, they may also demonstrate a more robust approach to the scrutiny of immigration decisions generally—and in particular to the general assertion often made that families may reasonably be expected to reunite elsewhere.

Further applications have been made, some citing *Boultif*, some not. The outcomes vary, some being inadmissible,[91] some cases resulting in findings of violation,[92] some resulting in findings of no violation.[93] Even though the factors that influence the Court are perhaps articulated more clearly now, the tendency towards somewhat unpredictable (arguably sometimes inconsistent and contradictory) judgments from the ECtHR, and the 'elsewhere' approach, has not yet been eliminated.[94]

2.4 Private Life and Immigration under Article 8 ECHR

The next question is the extent to which the protection of *private life* may affect immigration law. This is most important in the situation of same-sex couples. It has been suggested in dissenting judgments in particular[95] that the interference with private life that may follow from the deportation of a long-term resident may be unjustified, regardless of family ties. This is, however, beside the point here as we are considering

[90] I am grateful to Nick Rollason for this suggestion. *Yildiz* (n 6) and *Sen* (n 71) do not fit perfectly with this suggestion, involving wives of the same nationality, but of course this may not be the Court's only concern. Strong links with the host state may exist even where the wife is of the same nationality as the foreign husband, and there may also be a reluctance to send back to countries of their parents' origin children born and raised in the host state who may after all have dual nationality including that of the host state.

[91] Recent applications held inadmissible include *Rahmani v France* Application 74109/01; *Brahimi v France* Application 64357/01; *Musa v Germany* Application 22813/02; *Antate v France* 48211/99 and *Boudahef v Switzerland* Application 140222/02.

[92] Recent applications where there was a violation include *Yilamz v Austria* Application 52853/99 and *Jacupovic v Austria* Application 367557/97 and *Mokrani v France* Application 52206/99.

[93] A recent application where there was no violation is *Benhebba v France* Application 53441/99.

[94] See especially in relation to potential separation of couples, *Kaya v Netherlands* Application 44947/98 6 Nov 2001, in which the Court considered there were 'no insurmountable or significant obstacles for her (the applicant's wife) to settle with him in Turkey.'

[95] Schermers in *Lamguinadiz v UK* Series A No 258-C (1994) 17 EHRR 213. See also judgments of Judge Martens, Wildhaber, Morellina and De Meyer, and the judgment of the Court in *C v Belgium* Application 21794/93—see Rogers (n 31 above).

(1) cohabiting couples not general social surroundings and (2) admission rather than deportation of a long-term resident. The main issue is the extent to which the concept of private life has been able to protect bi-national same-sex couples from interference with their relationships. *X & Y v UK*[96] is the first case in which the ECommHR considered the question.

2.4.1 *The first ECommHR decision* — X & Y v UK

The ECommHR reasons as follows. A same-sex couple do not have a relationship protected by the concept of 'family life' within the meaning of Article 8 ECHR. This is 'despite the modern evolution of attitudes towards homosexuality.' However, 'certain restraints on homosexual relationships' can constitute a violation of the right to respect for private life within Article 8 ECHR. *Dudgeon*[97] (one of the leading cases on criminal penalites for gay sex) is cited in support of this. The refusal of a residence permit for the same-sex partner is however not a violation of Article 8 ECHR. The ECommHR gives several reasons for this.

It notes that there is no absolute right under Article 8 ECHR to choose the location of the family's residence, and applies this reasoning to same-sex partnerships. As to the particular facts of the case, it notes that the UK authorities have given careful consideration to all the issues, the applicants are both professionally mobile (they had both apparently worked abroad previously), and it has not been shown that they would be unable to live together anywhere other than the UK, or that the link with the UK is 'an essential part of the relationship.' This is despite the fact that the two had in fact gone to Malaysia (the country of origin of the other partner) when they decided to live together, but the British partner had only been granted limited residence and had not been granted permission to work. It is apparent that the couple were in fear of ill-treatment and even prosecution (homosexual acts being an offence under Malaysian law) if they returned to Malaysia. This, and the other same-sex couples cases discussed below, are particularly harsh examples of the application of the 'elsewhere' principle. As to discrimination and Article 14 ECHR, two points are made. First, because the same-sex couple do not enjoy 'family life' together under Article 8 ECHR, it is not possible to compare them to a couple who are treated as 'family' under the immigration law of the UK. Second, the only proper comparator is said to be a female same-sex couple. This couple of course would face exactly the same problems as the male same-sex couple so the ECommHR determines that there

[96] *X & Y v UK* Application 9369/81 (1983) 32 DR 220.
[97] *Dudgeon v UK* (n 13).

is no discriminatory interference with private life.[98] I shall return to discuss discrimination in more detail later.

2.4.2 *Further ECommHR Decisions*

Despite this unpromising start, same-sex couples have continued to use the ECHR to challenge immigration decisions, in particular to prevent deportations.[99] In all these cases, the ECommHR refuses to recognise any general right of settlement for same-sex partners as part of the Contracting State's obligation to respect the couple's 'private life'. This in itself is perhaps not surprising given the attitude to family life of married couples. The ECommHR refuses to consider the long stay of the partner, potential destitution and poverty of the mother and child on deportation, and de facto parental relationship of a young child with the British partner (ie, not the birth mother) as exceptional circumstances. Nor is the criminalisation of homosexual conduct in the state of origin of the other partner any reason to depart from the general view that private life may be interfered with by the deportation of that partner. It still maintains that, in theory, the inability of the couple to continue their private life elsewhere *might* make deportation a violation of Article 8 ECHR, yet in none of these cases does it seem to take seriously the practical obstacles to the couple moving elsewhere. If none of these cases present instances where the ECommHR could find 'exceptional circumstances' that might justify the applicant's case that deportation would be a violation of Article 8 ECHR, it is hard indeed to imagine what would. These cases are all the more unsatisfactory in that the arguments are dismissed as 'manifestly unfounded', without the fuller discussion and more detailed scrutiny that might have been possible if the case had gone to the ECtHR. However, given that the ECtHR has, in *Boultif*,[100] embarked on a closer scrutiny of the real possibilities for married couples to live together elsewhere, it is certainly possible that this approach might be extended to cases involving unmarried couples, whether same-sex or opposite-sex, in the future. And given the new direction with respect to sexual orientation discrimination in *Da Silva Mouta* and *Karner* the outcome of these particular cases in relation to same-sex couples might well be different.

[98] Whether this approach will survive *Da Silva Mouta* (n 16) and *Karner* (n 18) is doubtful. The argument that the proper comparator should be a heterosexual couple becomes now significantly more compelling.

[99] *WJ & DP v UK* 12513/86; *C & LM v UK* 14753/89 and *ZB v UK* Application 16106/90.

[100] Above (n 70).

2.4.3 *Parallels with 'Family Life'?*

In the first case concerning immigration rights of same sex couples,[101] The ECommHR expressly drew a parallel with its approach to the protection of 'family life' under Article 8 ECHR. It also followed *Abdulaziz*[102] in suggesting that it is for the applicants to show that their private life could not be carried on elsewhere, rather than for the State to show a specific reasonable and possible alternative location. Yet elsewhere in the later cases,[103] a harsher view seems to appear. In *WJ & DP*,[104] it is suggested that 'the non-appearance of settlement rights in pursuance of stable, private relationships other than family relationships is not a violation of Article 8.' The analysis proceeds on the basis that the deportation of the individual who has been settled for a time in the State is not in itself a violation of Article 8 ECHR. More interestingly, a distinction seems to emerge between private relationships and family relationships. It is suggested that in relation to the latter, in order to find a violation of Article 8 ECHR, 'exceptional circumstances' would have to be shown—which they have not been. Although it is certainly the case that there is no general obligation to allow settlement of partners or spouses under the Convention, it is at least questionable whether 'exceptional circumstances' need be shown to demonstrate a violation of Article 8 ECHR in relation to *family* life—especially in a deportation case.[105] *C & LM*[106] follows up this latter and more restrictive view, citing *Chandra v UK*[107] and looking for 'exceptional circumstances' before concluding that there are none and therefore that there is no violation of Article 8 ECHR.

In *ZB*,[108] the same pattern emerges, but seems to go further. The Commission indicates firstly that a lawful deportation or extradition will not in itself mean that the inevitable disruption of the individual's private life amounts to a violation of Article 8 ECHR. But it then simply asserts that 'accordingly, in so far as the applicant complains of the effect that the deportation will have on his relationship with Mr R, the Commission finds that there has been no lack of respect for private life within the meaning of Article 8 of the Convention.' This is arguably the most unsatisfactory of all the cases. The circumstances are among the most compelling as return to the partner's state of origin, Cyprus, would have exposed

[101] *X & Y v UK* (n 96).
[102] Above (n 2).
[103] In *WJ & DP; C & LM*, and *ZB* (n 99).
[104] Above (n 14).
[105] Discussion above sections 2.1–2.3. Although some of the decisions, particularly in relation to admissions, may be seen as harsh, the overall picture of the case law cannot fairly be described as requiring 'exceptional circumstances', and certainly not in the most recent cases, nor in deportation cases. This phrase is not used in the Judgments.
[106] Above (n 14).
[107] *Chandra v UK* Application 10427/83 (1986) 47 DR 88.
[108] Above (n 14).

them to the possibility of criminal penalties for homosexual offences and almost certain deportation of the British partner. It is not clear why there are not 'exceptional circumstances'. The ECommHR merely asserts that it has not been shown that the risk of prosecution is 'high'. It also says that it must attach significant weight to the reasons for his deportation, namely violation of immigration law.[109] The more surprising and troubling aspect of this particular case is that the ECommHR barely mentions the possibility that an interference with a private relationship could, even in exceptional circumstances, result in a violation of Article 8 ECHR. It merely asserts that interference with private relationships does not in principle give rise to a violation of Article 8 ECHR, given the right of the Contracting State to impose immigration controls. Its next (unsupported) assertion is that 'in so far as the applicant complains of the effect that the deportation will have on his relationship with Mr R, there has been no lack of respect for private life.' If and in so far as this seems to indicate an abandonment of even the consideration of whether there are 'exceptional circumstances', this decision seems to move the attitude of the ECommHR in relation to private life some distance away from its attitude to family life.[110] It seems therefore that the obligation to respect private life would not even help a cohabiting same-sex couple to seek entry and settlement for the non-national partner to the same degree as might be expected if they were a married couple.

2.4.4 *A More Receptive Approach under National Law?*

National courts applying these provisions have however recently begun to be more sympathetic to same-sex couples. Although to my knowledge there have been no successful challenges to the lack of a general policy permitting entry of same-sex partners under private and family life principles in domestic courts,[111] there have been a few cases in which individual decisions have been successfully challenged. The French Conseil d'Etat in *Marrousitch*[112] and the English High Court in *Hashim*,[113]

[109] Although it is questionable whether this is a proper consideration in terms of the 'exceptional circumstances' relating to the relationship between the parties.
[110] It could be suggested that the consideration of the illegality of homosexual activities in Cyprus was consideration of whether there 'exceptional circumstances', but it is not clear that the ECtHR viewed it in these terms.
[111] Such as has happened in South Africa in *National Coalition for Gay and Lesbian Equality v Minister for Home Affairs* 1999 (3) BCLR 280, 2001(1) BCLR 99. It is quite possible however that the background of Arts 8 and 14 ECHR combined may have been behind the development of regulations and concessions allowing settlement of same-sex partners without litigation.
[112] Annotated by R Errera [2000] *PL* 731.
[113] *R v SSHD ex p Hashim* (unreported CO/2052/99, 12 June 2000 Lexis transcript). See also *SSHD v Z* [2001] EWCA Civ 952 [2002] Imm AR 560 in which the rejection of claim that deportation would interfere with a relationship in the UK was overturned by the CA because it had not been examined properly.

as well as the Swiss courts[114] have declared individual decisions to remove foreign same-sex partners to be in breach of Article 8 ECHR. It is particularly interesting that *Hashim* is later referred to as a '*marriage*' case (by the judge in another similar deportation case involving a married couple *Ex p Mahmood*).[115] This seems not entirely unjustified as in *Hashim* there is little relevance attached to the fact that case concerns a same-sex couple rather than husband and wife and it concerned a rule (that entry clearance should be obtained from abroad) that was the same for spouses and same-sex partners. It would certainly be very welcome for the ECtHR to follow this lead if and when any further cases come before it.

2.5 Conclusion — Article 8 ECHR and Immigration Law

The ECtHR and ECommHR jurisprudence on family reunification centred on Article 8 ECHR alone can hardly be described as flawless. I shall take up in the next chapter the specific question of whether it is an appropriate model for Community law to follow. However, it also has intrinsic weaknesses. In relation to individual decisions it lacks consistency, and in relation to general policies, it leaves a significant margin of appreciation open to the Contracting States—arguably too broad when it comes to cohabiting couples (even when they are married) and minor dependent children. Both weaknesses seem to flow from two of the underlying assumptions of the ECtHR—(1) that however close the family relationship there can be no 'general obligation' to permit settlement or continued residence of a non-national, and (2) that the reasonable possibility of residence elsewhere has to be considered and may be decisive. A challenge to a married partners only settlement policy founded purely on Article 8 ECHR would be vulnerable to failure.[116] The alternative is a claim based on Article 14 and 8 ECHR together that a policy distinguishing between different kinds of families (married, unmarried, hetero/homosexual, registered partners) is discriminatory, and this will be the focus of the next section of the discussion.

[114] The position in the Swiss courts is somewhat inconsistent: F Baur, 'At the End of the Fairy Tale, Will Heidi Stay Single? Same-sex Partnerships in Switzerland' in R Wintemute and M Andenas (eds), *Legal Recognition of Same-sex Partnerships* (Hart Publishing, Oxford, 2001) 538. As early as 1992 the Federal Supreme Court did indeed permit the continued residence of the partner, but more recently a decision of the Government Council of the Canton of Zurich not to permit the partner to stay was upheld by the Federal Supreme Court, (BGE 126 II 425) which considered that the interference involved in the private life of the couple was permissible under Art 8(2) ECHR. Thanks to Samantha Besson for assistance with these cases and references.

[115] *Ex p Mahmood* [2001] 1 WLR 840.

[116] Expulsion might be different.

PART THREE — DISCRIMINATION UNDER ARTICLE 14 ECHR

3.1 The General Approach

The analysis of discrimination under Article 14 ECHR[117] proceeds in the following four stages, although the reasoning of the ECtHR and Commission sometimes fails to separate the issues clearly:

1. It must be shown that the situation in question falls within the broad scope of one of the other ECHR rights, although it is not necessary to show a breach of any of the other Articles independently.
2. It must be shown that the applicant is in a comparable situation to another individual or group and has been treated differently in relation to the enjoyment of the right in question.
3. It then falls to the defendant state to show a reasonable and objective justification for the difference in treatment. This is sometimes described as the necessity to show that the difference in treatment pursues a legitimate aim.
4. Finally, it falls to the defendant state to show that the means used in pursuit of the legitimate aim are proportionate.

3.2 Interference with Enjoyment of the ECHR Rights

Distinctions on prohibited grounds in family reunification rules might contravene Article 14 ECHR: an example involving sex discrimination is *Abdulaziz*.[118] Thus the issue (which sometimes arises)[119] as to whether there is sufficient connection to the rights contained elsewhere in the Convention (here Article 8 ECHR) is easily settled. I shall therefore not dwell on this further but move on to the issues of comparability, justification, and proportionality which are of crucial importance to the current problem.

[117] Clayton and Tomlinson (n 9) ch 17. In relation to sexual orientation and family status in particular see also R Wintemute (n 12); R Wintemute, 'Strasbourg to the Rescue? Same-sex Partners and Parents under the Convention' in R Wintemute and M Andenas (n 114); C Forder (n 12); and S Livingstone, 'Article 14 and the Prevention of Discrimination in the European Court of Human Rights' (1997) 1 *EHRLR* 463.
[118] Above (n 2).
[119] Some judges denied the applicant's claim in *Fretté v France* (n 17) on the rather dubious basis that Article 8 ECHR did not give a 'right to adopt'; R Wintemute, 'France Permitted to Ban Adoptions to Lesbian and Gay Individuals' (2002) 2(2) *ILGA-Europe Newsletter* 4.

3.3 Stage Two — Which Couples are Comparable?

3.3.1 Discrimination on the Grounds of Sexual Orientation

Despite earlier and persistent indications to the contrary from the Commission,[120] it now seems that the ECtHR has in *Da Silva Mouta*,[121] taken a new direction in relation to discrimination on the grounds of sexual orientation in the enjoyment of other Convention rights, explicitly condemning this as 'not acceptable'. The gist of this conclusion is repeated in *Fretté v France*.[122] There is therefore a clear and compelling argument that immigration policies that discriminate against same-sex couples should be seen as contrary to Articles 8 and 14 ECHR together. This argument is vulnerable in two respects. The first is the extent to which it may apply to discrimination against same-sex *couples*. The second is the extent to which policies which discriminate in favour of married couples and against all unmarried couples, regardless of their sexual orientation, can and should be seen to be inherently discriminatory against same-sex couples.

3.3.2 From Individuals to Same-sex Couples?

Given the view of the ECtHR in *Da Silva Mouta*, this conclusion seems inevitable, although some suggest that extending the concept of discrimination from homosexual individuals to same-sex couples may in practice be problematic.[123] It is true that this is directly contrary to several decisions of the ECommHR.[124] However, these cases were never considered by the ECtHR, and the subsequent decision in *Da Silva Mouta*[125] seems to mark a clear break from the previous approach. The extension of *Da Silva Mouta* to cover same-sex couples is a compelling case, and has recently been accepted by the English Court of Appeal and House of Lords in *Ghaidan v Mendoza*.[126] The ECtHR has recently tackled this question in the case of *Karner v Austria*,[127] a complaint that an unmarried same-sex partner could not succeed to his partner's tenancy of their joint home in the

[120] *Kerkhoven & Hinke v Netherlands* Application 15606/89; *S v UK* (n 5); *Roosli v Germany* Application 283185/95 85 DR 149 and the immigration cases discussed above (n 99).
[121] Above (n 16).
[122] Above (n 17).
[123] N Bamforth, 'Same-sex Partnerships and Arguments of Justice' in R Wintemute and M Andenas (eds), *Legal Recognition of Same-sex Partnerships* (Hart Publishing, Oxford, 2001); M Bell, *Anti-Discrimination Law and the European Union*, (OUP, Oxford, 2002) 22, suggesting that the ECJ may have acknowledged or accepted the principle of non-discrmination on the grounds of sexual orientation but not in relation to same-sex partnerhsips.
[124] Above (n 99).
[125] Above (n 16).
[126] Above (n 18).
[127] Above (n 18).

same way that the survivor of an opposite-sex couple could. The Court declared that there was a violation of Article 14 together with respect for the home (Article 8). This analysis could proceed on one of two bases. It could be said that the protection of the traditional (heterosexual and perhaps married) family is no longer an acceptable and reasonable justification for discriminatory treatment (at least for discrimination against same-sex couples who cannot marry). Alternatively, it might be said that this could still in principle be a legitimate aim, but that there must be far greater precision as to why the particular kind of protection should be reserved for the traditional family. *Karner* certainly suggests that although not ruled out altogether as a potential justification, in so far as the 'protection of the traditional family' is concerned the margin of appreciation will not be that generous when same-sex cohabitants are denied benefits that would be available to similar opposite-sex couples.[128] *Karner* is certainly a groundbreaking case and to be welcomed. It indicates that same-sex couples will certainly be able to rely on Article 14 where they are denied rights and benefits available to heterosexual cohabiting couples—but it stops short of considering the implications of Article 8 alone of the recognition (or non-recognition) of such partnerships, other interferences with private life that might be involved in cases involving same-sex couples, or indeed the question of retention of particular privileges for married couples.

3.3.3 *Favouring Married Couples and Sexual Orientation Discrimination*

A variation on this argument would have to be used however to challenge immigration policies based on the relevant Community law regulations, which do require admission of spouses. This raises the question of whether a 'marriage-only' policy is inherently discriminatory *on the grounds of sexual orientation* against same-sex couples when they cannot legally marry. As we have seen briefly in chapter 1, this argument has been accepted recently by some courts, particularly in South Africa. Logically, it is again a clear and compelling argument. The fact that heterosexual unmarried couples are also excluded from the benefit so the only comparator is the married couple should not affect this claim. The ECHR will soon have an opportunity to consider this question. A case has been

[128] Paras 37–41 of the judgment emphasise that as in the case of sex discrimination, 'particularly serious reasons' are required to justify different treatment on the grounds of sexual orientation, and that although in principle the 'protection of the traditional family' is a permissible state aim which might justify a difference in treatment, *where discrimination on grounds of sex or sexual orientation is concerned* 'the principle of proportionality does not merely require that the measure chosen is in principle suited to the aim sought. It must also be shown that it was necessary to exclude persons living in a homosexual relationship from the scope of s 14 of the Rent Act in order to achieve that aim. The Court cannot see that the Government has advanced any arguments that would allow of such a conclusion' (para 41).

referred from the UK[129] in which a bereavement benefit, available only to the legal spouse of the deceased, was denied to a surviving same-sex partner. The UK government has apparently taken the view that domestic remedies (under the Human Rights Act) have not been exhausted, and the case is delayed pending the outcome of the appeal to the House of Lords in another UK case.[130]

3.3.4 Marital Status — Unmarried Couples

We now turn to consider the application of Article 14 ECHR where married heterosexual couples are privileged over unmarried cohabitants. It is sometimes asserted that marital status is a ground covered by Article 14 ECHR,[131] although this does not reflect the case law accurately. In fact, quite the opposite approach emerges in relation to couples. Many of the relevant cases[132] are concerned with relationships between parents and illegitimate children, not unmarried couples. Certainly the cases involving relationships between parents and children increasingly show discrimination between those born to married and unmarried parents being eliminated.[133] On the other hand, on the few occasions that the ECtHR or ECommHR does tackle the position of unmarried couples directly,[134] it either denies directly the comparability of married and unmarried couples or engages the analysis that protection and promotion of traditional family structures by favouring married couples in particular ways is a proportionate measure in pursuit of a legitimate aim. In the two most recent cases, *Saucedo Gomez v Spain*[135] and *Shackell v UK*,[136] applicants compared themselves to a wife or widow in order to claim financial compensation or a social security benefit. Both complaints were declared inadmissible.

[129] *MW v UK, Application 11313/02*. See Liberty newsletter, Casenotes, Summer 2002. Thanks to Rob Wintemute for drawing my attention to this case.
[130] *R (Hooper) v Secretary of State for Work and Pensions* [2003] EWCA Civ 813 [2003] 3 All ER 673, a case involving widowers' pensions and the provisions of the Human Rights Act requiring legislation to be read in so far as it is possible to do so to comply with Convention rights.
[131] Particularly Clayton and Tomlinson (n 9) para 17.98. The point is also mentioned at paras 17.122 and 17.133 albeit in the context of cases in which different treatment had been held to be justified.
[132] *Marckx v Belgium* (n 4); *McMichael v UK* Series A No 308 (1995) 20 EHRR 205; *Smallwood v UK* Application 23928/94 (1998) 27 EHRR CD 155; *Inze* Application 34406/97 1 feb 2000, *Vermeire* Application 34406/97 1 feb 2000, *Mazurek* Application 12849/87 29 Nov 1991.
[133] Pintens concludes that nearly all discrimination in heritance has been eliminated in this respect, citing *Marckx, Inze v Austria, Vermeire* and *Mazurek*—W Pintens, 'Europeanisation of Family Law' in K Boele-Woelki (ed), *Perspectives for the Unification and Harmonisation of Family Law in Europe* (Intersentia, Antwerp, 2003) 3 at 18.
[134] *Lindsay v UK* Application 11089/94; *Saucedo Gomez v Spain* Application 33784/97; *Shackell v UK* Application 45851/99.
[135] Above (n 134).
[136] Above (n 134).

Saucedo Gomez[137] concerned the complaint of a woman who had been refused financial compensation and allocation of the joint residence she had previously occupied with her partner before the relationship had broken down.[138] She was refused this because the couple had not been married.[139] It was held that the different treatment of cohabitants and spouses pursued a legitimate aim and had a reasonable and objective justification—the protection of the 'traditional family'. This is interesting because this phrase is used in connection not with children born outside marriage, or a same-sex relationship, but with longstanding heterosexual cohabitants. This certainly indicates that the likely response to the question above (whether the unmarried couple *has to be* assimilated to the married couple, or whether this is just *permissible*) is that it is *permitted* rather than *required*. However due to the tendency, discussed below, to run together the tests of justifiability and comparability, it is not entirely clear whether the case is to be read as a denial of any suggestion (such as in *Lindsay*) that married and unmarried couples are in comparable positions under Article 14 ECHR,[140] or an illustration that, even if they are comparable, the justification of 'protection of the traditional family' is still open as a legitimate aim or reasonable and objective justification.

Shackell[141] is an even more unequivocal rejection of the idea that the ECtHR might interpret the Convention as requiring a general principle of equality between married and unmarried couples. It concerned the complaint of a surviving unmarried partner that she was not entitled to a widow's benefit as she would have been had she been married to her partner. In rejecting the claim, the ECtHR makes three points. Its first point is to note and approve the conclusion of the ECommHR in *Lindsay*.[142] It notes that although 16 years have passed:

> ... Marriage remains an institution which is widely accepted as conferring a particular status on those who enter it. The situation of the applicant is therefore not comparable to that of the widow.

[137] Above (n 134).
[138] She had been married previously. When her subsequent relationship started, she could not have married her new partner as Spanish law did not allow for divorce. However, as the ECtHR points out, the couple remained together for 10 years after Spain introduced provision for divorce, and did not marry.
[139] One of the courts hearing the case rejected her claim on different grounds after examining its substance under the laws applicable to divorced couples and concluding that she had no claim. This reasoning however was rejected by the Appeal Court, and it is accepted by the ECtHR that her claim was rejected because she was not married.
[140] Whether for a particular purpose or generally.
[141] Above (n 134).
[142] Above (n 134). Although it cites this, inaccurately, as a case in which an unmarried couple tried to compare themselves to a married couple when in fact it was the married couple complaining of unequal treatment and seeking to compare themselves to an unmarried couple. Nothing however turns on this point.

It then goes onto state that differential treatment is only prohibited under Article 14 ECHR if it does not pursue a legitimate aim, or if there is not a reasonable relationship of proportionality between the means employed and the aim pursued. In both of these areas it asserts that the Contracting States 'enjoy a certain margin of appreciation.' It finds both of these satisfied in the present case:

> The promotion of marriage, by way of limited benefits for surviving spouses, cannot be said to exceed the margin of appreciation afforded to the respondent Government.

3.3.5 Running Together Comparability and Justifications

These two cases illustrate the confusing tendency in the ECHR jurisprudence to conflate two related but conceptually separate questions. Whether the alleged comparator is truly in an analogous or comparable situation is one question, but whether any distinction or different treatment pursues a legitimate aim and/or can be said to be objectively justified is another. Unfortunately, the ECtHR does not always draw the distinction between these two issues as clearly as it might.[143] Van Dijk and Van Hoof are critical of this, suggesting that 'if the comparability test is skipped or merged into the third element—the justification test—the danger arises that the interests protected and/or the goals envisaged in the provisions embodying equality become underexposed,'[144] and Forder shares this view.[145]

On the other hand, it can also be suggested that too rigid separation of the search for a comparator and the question of justification itself has its dangers. This is because the issue of comparability is not to be considered *in abstracto* (is there any difference?) but in the concrete situation of the case (is there any *relevant* difference, or are the two situations '*relevantly*' similar?). Given this approach to comparability, although the convergence of the comparability and justification tests will have serious consequences, an over simplistic approach to the separation of the two is also problematic. This is particularly so if the comparability of two situations arises in a case where the public interest pursued is strong (such as national security, public order, or child protection) or where the practical detriment to the individual or couple is, relatively speaking, limited (such as, within

[143] Livingstone (n 117) 30 and P Van Dijk and G Van Hoof, *Theory and Practice of the European Convention on Human Rights* (Kluwer, The Hague, 1998) 718 ff. Also in the context of the relevance of Article 14 in family law issues, Forder (n 117).

[144] They point in particular to the *Belgian Linguistics* case, and to *Dudgeon* (n 13) and *Abdulaziz* (n 2) to illustrate this point.

[145] Forder (n 117) 43.

limits, tax assessments). There is a risk that the justification of different treatment on a particular ground for one purpose (when the countervailing interest is strong, and/or the detriment limited in practical terms) will spread beyond what should be a limited situation. It may later be seen to justify different treatment on the same grounds where the countervailing interest is weaker and/or the detriment is more serious. This can be seen, for example, when the ECtHR moves smoothly from the assertion that it is permissible to withhold the 'special protection' of housing, tax or pension law to the conclusion that *immigration policies* denying entry to same-sex partners are also justified. It also gives rise to the risk that a decision such as *Lindsay*[146] will be generalised and could be taken to mean that married and unmarried couples are not comparable in any situation. This makes it all the more crucial to articulate clearly the different stages of the test involved. To the comments of Van Dijk and Van Hoof and Forder, I would therefore add that it is indeed important to articulate the comparability test clearly, but also to do so in a way which at least takes into account the possibility that situations may be comparable for some purposes but not for others.[147]

Unfortunately, the ECtHR does not always use such an analysis. The cases are not consistent. Sometimes there are declarations of comparability in general terms that make no mention of the purpose for which the comparison is made.[148] Sometimes, in contrast, the purpose for which the comparison is made is mentioned clearly. For example, in *Kerkhoven,*[149] the comments of the ECtHR denying comparability of same-sex and opposite-sex relationships seem confined to the matter of parental authority over children. In *H v Norway,*[150] the comparability of mother and father of an unborn child is denied—'In relation to the termination of a pregnancy and the proceedings and decisions concerning this situation, the Commission does not find that the applicant was placed in an analogous situation to the mother.' This analysis is striking. The difference between a man and a woman—who would normally be seen to be in comparable situations requiring weighty reasons to justify different treatment—is dismissed on the basis that *for this purpose* (connected to pregnancy and its termination) the mother and father are not in comparable situations. It is thus imperative that the analysis of the distinction between married and unmarried couples proceeds in the most transparent and open way, with close attention to the purpose for which comparison is made.

146 Above (n 134).
147 Van Dijk and Van Hoof do themselves also make this point.
148 Such as is suggested by the comment in *Lindsay* (n 134) and possibly *Marckx* (n 4).
149 Above (n 120).
150 *H v Norway* Application 17004/90 (1992) 73 DR 155.

3.3.6 *Comparability for Immigration Law Purposes?*

We must now turn to consider the question of comparability of different couples for the purposes of immigration rights. The crucial question should be this: is the distinction between the couple that are married and the couple that are not (or the same-sex couple, or the registered partners) *on its own* a rational and acceptable one on which to base the denial of residence rights for a partner? I would argue that they are indeed in comparable situations for this purpose, and that marital or other civil status of the partnership is not on its own a rational and acceptable distinction to deny the couple the opportunity to live together in the host state.

Is this view supported by anything in the ECtHR jurisprudence? *Abdulaziz,*[151] *Marckx,*[152] and the subsequent line of same-sex immigration rights cases are the closest one can get. With reference first to *Abdulaziz,* it will be recalled that this case differentiates—although perhaps unsoundly —between sex (which was not an acceptable ground on which to deny family reunification rights) and birth in the country (which was). If what is being looked for is some apparently objective way of judging the strength of an individual's connection with the host state, the precise traditional or non-traditional nature of the partnership seems inadequate. Family status could be said to be closer to the criterion of sex than birth in the country.

It is certainly true that the same-sex couple cases seem to contradict this, but they can in fact be distinguished on the following basis, and in fact used to glean some support for the comparability of different kinds of families in immigration law. The approach of the ECommHR in these cases rests largely (if not perhaps exclusively) on the assumption that the same-sex couple do not have 'family life' together. It is *for this reason,* we are told that the ECommHR concludes that they cannot be equated to those who are treated as having family relationships for the purposes of family reunification rights in domestic immigration law. Let us assume however that the ECtHR eventually accepts that the same-sex couple may enjoy family life, or indeed that the relevant couple is opposite-sex, as such couples can in principle have 'family life' together under Article 8 ECHR. Although the reasoning employed by the ECommHR is negative,[153] and therefore the argument is less strong than if the reasoning were positive in nature, it is certainly possible to suggest that the ECommHR is, at

[151] Above (n 2).
[152] Above (n 4).
[153] The reasoning proceeds that the same-sex couple (X) are not family (Y) therefore Z (comparability) cannot be. This of course does not necessarily lead to the conclusion that if X (or another couple) are in fact family (Y) then Z (comparability) can be, let alone that it must necessarily be.

least implicitly, accepting that if a couple *have* family life together then they *could* (and perhaps should) be compared to those couples treated as families in domestic immigration law.

3.3.7 Registered Partnerships

Moving on to consider the question of registered partnerships, any remarks are speculative. In so far as some registered partnership laws are clearly intended to mirror marriage as closely as possible for same-sex couples, the concept of sexual orientation discrimination should clearly settle the question in favour of comparability. Other forms of registered partnership status are less clearly comparable to marriage, but, as I have indicated above, the question should not be seen purely in the abstract but should be anchored in the purpose for which comparability is sought. If this is the case, then there seems no reason to deny comparability for the purposes of immigration law. This is all the more so if the argument relating to comparability of unmarried cohabiting couples advanced above is accepted.

3.4 Stage Three — Justification and Proportionality

3.4.1 The 'Special Protection' Analysis

A number of cases[154] suggest a distinction between discrimination on the grounds of family status (between traditional and non-traditional families) in matters that 'impede and thwart' the normal development of family life[155] and discrimination on such grounds in matters of 'special protection'.[156] On those occasions where the comparability of different kinds of family relationships is accepted, this goes hand-in-hand with an analysis based on 'special protection' to blunt the possible impact of the comparability conclusion. The use of a 'special protection' analysis only has meaning, and can only be supported, if it is combined with a proper distinction between those matters which may properly be termed 'special protection' and those which may not. If this distinction is not properly articulated and maintained, then the comparability of different kinds of families and couples is merely empty rhetoric. The Commission has in the

[154] *Marckx* (n 4); *Lindsay* (n 134); *S v UK* Application (n 5); *Saucedo Gomez* (n 134) and the same-sex immigration cases discussed above (n 14).
[155] This is possibly in itself a breach of Art 8 ECHR but is also according to *Marckx* (n 4) a breach of Arts 8 and 14 ECHR together.
[156] This is permissible. This concept is introduced in *S v UK* (n 5) and used, although not developed conceptually in any significant way, in later cases.

past turned to this analysis in some immigration cases, so we must now consider the concept, and its application to immigration laws, in more detail.

3.4.2 The Use of 'Special Protection' in Immigration Cases

Is the move from treating housing protection or tax law as 'special protection' to treating family reunification in the same way justified? Linguistically, there is an obvious argument that the right of a couple to live together in the same country, even if not necessarily *inherent* in the very essence of the concept of 'respect' for family life (at least not, according to the Court, to the exent of construing Article 8 alone to require admission of immediate family as a general principle pursuant to the choice of the family's residence) it cannot really be described as 'special protection' (thus discrimination in the enjoyment of family life is not permitted between different forms of family life). It is protection without which the couple could be severely prejudiced, to the extent of imperilling the very continued existence of the ongoing family relationship. This is less obviously the case when the couple seeks the application of a particular category of tax assessment, pension or inheritance regime.

Turning to the case law, this argument becomes all the more compelling when it is considered how important cohabitation is to a couple and to their normal 'family' life. If the couple are not married, the cohabitation becomes a crucial part of the inquiry as to the stability and duration of the relationship and therefore whether the couple are seen to have 'family life' pursuant to Article 8 ECHR. Being such a fundamental and indeed constitutive element of family life, it cannot be right to talk of the couple seeking 'special' protection when they seek to maintain the joint home they have set up or to migrate together to another state. This is so even if we talk of private life in the context of a same-sex couple. Of course cohabitation is not constitutive of all private relationships in the same way as it is central (even though not strictly indispensable) to the establishment of a 'family' relationship between opposite-sex cohabiting partners. But the 'private' relationship in question between same-sex cohabiting partners can and should be seen in this way. Any analysis that fails to accommodate this kind of distinction between different kinds of private relationships seems inadequate.

The existing case law also provides further support for this. We might examine these cases to see if there is any further elaboration of the concept of 'special protection' that might assist. Although there is no positive definition of 'special protection', the implicit contrast with what is *not* special protection is instructive. We might also consider the one other situation in which the ECtHR has considered discrimination in the context of immigration rights (*Abdulaziz*)[157] which might say something about the permissible reasons for discrimination in this context. Turning finally to examine the ECommHR admissibility decisions which actually adopt the 'special protection' reasoning in the context of same-sex couples, these seem insufficiently reasoned and unconvincing. The only contrary indications come from the cases on polygamy. I shall now address these points more fully.

3.4.3 Back to Basics — What is 'Special Protection'?

In *Marckx*, the ECtHR indicates that it,

> … Recognises that the support and encouragement of the traditional family is in itself legitimate or even praiseworthy. However, in the achievement of this end recourse must not be had to measures which whose object or result is, as in the present case, to prejudice the 'illegitimate family'. The members of the 'illegitimate' family enjoy the guarantees of Article 8 on an equal footing with the members of the traditional family'.[158]

It is of course true that the provisions in *Marckx* were held to violate Article 8 ECHR independently of Article 14 ECHR, whereas the denial of immigration rights to spouses in the pursuance of the State's chosen immigration policy is not necessarily in itself a violation of Article 8 ECHR. It could be suggested that the comments in *Marckx* are merely intended to indicate that protection of Article 8 ECHR is enjoyed by the couple, and that Article 14 ECHR is only relevant to require non-discrimination and equal treatment when Article 8 ECHR is violated anyway. This would make the reference to Article 14 ECHR superfluous and unnecessary, and is contrary to later cases of the ECtHR stressing that an independent violation of another Article of the Convention is not necessary for Article 14 ECHR to be applicable.[159]

However, the case does suggest a helpful dichotomy between measures which impede or thwart the very existence of family life and those which merely provide special or additional or limited assistance to particular families without prejudicing the existence of and ongoing normal family relationships within others. It is of course the case that this does sanction the differential treatment of some families and relationships over others, and some might find this objectionable. However, it is highly unlikely that the ECtHR will abandon the possibility of permitting *some* distinctions to remain between married and unmarried families. Nor is it the task of this book to explore in any detail whether it should or not, and

[157] Above (n 2).
[158] *Marckx* (n 4) para 40.
[159] Van Dijk and Van Hoof (n 143) 725.

I am not going to argue that the ECtHR should abandon an approach that permits a degree of 'special protection' for 'traditional families'. It should be recalled that the role of the ECtHR is not to determine every issue of controversial social policy that comes before it, but to set a floor of rights beyond which Contracting States should not fall. It would seem quite appropriate, and in my view preferable to any other solution, for it to indicate that Contracting States are free, if they so wish, to determine that certain traditional family forms may be given 'special protection' or 'particular assistance' but that they cannot without clear and specific justification take measures that 'impede or thwart' the normal development of the family life of 'non-traditional' families which depart from this preferred norm. In taking this view I am aware that some criticise the 'hierarchy' of family forms and dispute the privileged status of marriage. Nevertheless, the argument that the State has a legitimate interest in establishing and maintaining a legal framework for committed long-term relationships (both heterosexual and homosexual, whether this involves same-sex marriage or some kind of civil union or registered partnership) and as a consequence reserving some particular rights to couples entering into these mutual long-term social and legal commitments, is at the very least a plausible one. It would, in my view, be illegitimate for the ECtHR to prevent states from taking this view and from maintaining *some degree* of particular protection for marriage or similar registered same-sex partnerships. Any decision to the contrary (ie, general equality of all cohabiting couples in most or all areas of law) should be taken by each state after democratic debate leading to legislation, or by judicial decision in national courts. Imposition of such a view from outside by the ECtHR would be inappropriate.

Nevertheless, the emergence of a proper distinction between permissible 'special protection' and other impermissible measures is vital to the continued credibility of this analysis. The approach adopted in *Marckx*[160] strikes a good balance in principle and seems a helpful starting point if this 'special protection' analysis is to be used properly and convincingly. The only help that comes from the later cases of *Simpson*[161] and *Roosli*[162] (concerning succession to tenancies by the tenant's deceased partner) is the additional comment that 'there is no reason why a High Contracting Party should not afford particular assistance to families.' This seems to be essentially a paraphrasing of the existing concept of 'special protection' and takes us no further.

If this is applied to immigration rights—if one considers whether the refusal of immigration rights to the non-traditional family is something

[160] Above (n 4).
[161] *S v UK* (n 5).
[162] *Roosli v Germany* (n 120).

that prejudices that family, or even prejudices it *unduly*, in the way the ECtHR explains is unwarranted pursuant to Article 14 ECHR—the answer would surely be in the affirmative. If there is one thing that can clearly be said to thwart and impede the normal family life of a couple and/or their minor children, it is being *forced* to live apart. Indeed, in one of the cases in which the ECommHR considers the position of a same-sex couple, with a child, it points out that the measures in question, preventing joint parental authority, do not prevent the family living together.[163] Even though this predates the last of the immigration cases, this approach certainly casts doubt on the use of the 'special protection' analysis in immigration law. A comparison with *Marckx* on the facts is also instructive—if the failure there to create an automatic legal recognition of a child born to an unmarried mother thwarts the development of normal family life, the immigration law that prevents the parent and child, or the couple, living together in the same country must surely do so.

3.4.4 The Adoption of the 'Special Protection' Analysis in Immigration Cases

We should also examine the particular case in which the ECommHR first makes this move to examine in what way it justifies (or not) the use of the 'special protection' analysis in the situation of immigration law. Unfortunately, this gets us no further. In the crucial case, *WJ & DP*,[164] the ECommHR merely repeats its assertion that 'special protection' may be reserved for the traditional family, and adopts it to deal with the case under consideration. There is no inquiry into the nature of 'special protection' or to consider whether there is any difference between housing law and immigration law.[165] The two later cases are no more satisfactory. In *C & LM*[166] it asserts that it 'finds no element of discrimination, contrary to Article 14, in such a policy, given the special protection to be afforded to the traditional family.' In *ZB* it finds that 'the difference in treatment pursued the legitimate aim of protecting family-based relationships (including relationships outside marriage) in a manner proportionate to the achievement of that aim.' None of these cases defend these assertions convincingly and they do not deal adequately with the substance of the argument made above and suggested by the applicants in *WJ & DP*[167]—ie, that immigration rights are different from succession to a tenancy on the death of a partner, and cannot properly be described as 'special protection'.

163 *Kerkhoven* (n 120).
164 Above (n 14).
165 The Applicants had argued that no comparison could be made between the housing law in *S v UK* and the deportation issues being considered in their case.
166 Above (n 14).
167 Above (n 14).

3.4.5 Abdulaziz *and Discrimination in Family Reunification*

Abdulaziz[168] also lends some support to this view. It will be recalled that the ECtHR held that sex discrimination in family reunification rights was not justified. It might be suggested that discriminating on the basis of the whether the couple conform to the pattern of what the State sees as the 'traditional' family, can and should be seen in the same way. In response to this it might be suggested that the ECtHR did not uphold all the claims of discrimination. The claim that the foreign national individual with leave to remain in the UK did not have to be treated in the same way as one connected with the UK by birth was accepted. The ECtHR admits that,

> a person who has been settled in a country for several years may also have formed close ties with it, even if she was not born there. Nevertheless there are in general persuasive social reasons for giving special treatment to those whose link with a country stems from birth within it. The difference in treatment must therefore be regarded as having an objective and reasonable justification and, in particular, its results have not been shown to transgress the principle of proportionality.[169]

This approach has been criticised and been argued to rest on flawed and insufficient reasoning.[170] These criticisms seem well-founded. It is not at all clear why being connected with the UK by birth (which, as Van Dijk and Van Hoof point out, is rather a blunt instrument to determine who has the closest connection with the country) rather than by long-term residence, justifies the admission of the spouse of one group rather than the other. The ECtHR merely asserts that this is so without adequate reasoning. Any attempt to justify different family reunification rules on the grounds of the legal status of the relationship alone seems similarly contestable and arguably inadequate.

3.4.6 *The Polygamy Cases*

The only existing cases that might be seen to contradict the analysis above are those related to polygamous marriages.[171] The ECommHR does seem to accept that the fact that polygamy is contrary to public policy in the host state may lead to the conclusion that it is not *obliged* to recognise polygamous marriages for immigration purposes by admitting more than one spouse. There is little discussion of the question of discrimination

[168] Above (n 2).
[169] Para 88.
[170] Van Dijk and Van Hoof (n 143). The ECtHR moves from the assertion that 'in general there are pressing social reasons for giving special treatment to those whose link with a country stems from birth within it' to the assertion that this justifies the distinction made in the UK immigration law, without analysing whether or not these general reasons are valid grounds on which to deny or restrict family reunification rights.
[171] Above (n 37).

between different forms of family life. Admittedly these cases might present something of a difficulty, but they are not conclusive either way. In any event, even if it is assumed that these cases suggest that the ECtHR considers family reunification to be a type of 'special protection' which may be denied to polygamous wives, there are certainly reasons for thinking that same-sex marriages and other conjugal partnerships may be distinguished from polygamy, raising different policy concerns and issues.[172]

3.5 Conclusion on Articles 8 and 14 Together

The possibility of maintaining marriage-only immigration policies under Articles 8 and 14 ECHR together seems to turn on the use of a 'special protection' analysis. If this is used, and immigration rights are viewed as 'special protection' then these policies would seem permissible, except perhaps in relation to same-sex couples. The matter has not yet been considered by the ECtHR itself but this analysis has been used by the ECommHR in cases involving same-sex couples. However, it would be a grave mistake for the ECtHR to proceed any further with this analysis. If this is the case then a far more specific justification of such policies must be brought forward. I shall address this more fully in chapter 7.

CONCLUSIONS OF CHAPTER THREE

Articles 8 and 14 ECHR have significance for family reunification policies. Currently, the case law leaves considerable doubt whether the ECHR requires admission of all cohabiting partners. However, this case law has some significant weaknesses, and in some respects, there are new trends emerging which might indicate that the ECtHR may be moving away from some previously long-held positions. There is at least some chance that this argument might succeed, particularly in relation to legislation disadvantaging same-sex couples, building on recent Article 14 Jurisprudence. Nevertheless, given the complex problems involved, if Community law follows closely the existing pattern of ECtHR case law instead of engaging in proactive development along its own lines, the prospects are at best indifferent at the present time. It will therefore be important to address the case in favour of the adoption of a distinctive Community law concept of respect for family and private life in immigration law and equal treatment in its enjoyment. It is to this that I now turn in chapter 4.

[172] See the literature cited at ch 1 n 16 above. See also S Starr and L Brilmayer, 'Family Separation as a Violation of International law' (2003) *21 Berkeley J Int Law 213*, discussing the recent French policy to deny residence to more than one wife and taking the view that in itself it is not per se objectionable but only becomes so in its retrospective application to those already resident in France.

4

The ECHR in Community Law

INTRODUCTION

THIS CHAPTER ADDRESSES the case for the development of a distinctive Community law interpretation of fundamental rights in the context of family reunification. In particular, it focuses on the right to family life in Article 8 ECHR together with a brief discussion of discrimination in its enjoyment in conjunction with Article 14. The question of different prohibited grounds of discrimination is addressed in more detail in chapter 5. The question will be approached in four stages:

1. It will first (part 1) be necessary to establish that Community law in general and Community migration law in particular must comply with fundamental rights, and that respect for family and private life and non-discrimination in its enjoyment, also protected by the ECHR, are among these protected rights. These are not contentious propositions, either factually or normatively, and will be dealt with briefly.
2. In the light of the ECtHR jurisprudence outlined in chapter 3, it will be crucial to demonstrate that Community law can break free from the constraints of the ECtHR jurisprudence (part 2). The existing attitude of the ECJ to the interpretation of ECHR rights will be addressed. Reference will also be made to the potential impact of the Charter of Fundamental Rights on this question. This part will highlight the ECtHR interpretation of the fundamental rights contained in the EHCR as a minimum rather than a maximum standard for the ECJ.
3. The next task (part 3) is to address the reasons why Community law should not be bound by ECtHR interpretations in this particular context. Specific weaknesses in the context of Community law will be addressed, suggesting compelling reasons for abandoning the ECtHR approach and developing a distinctive 'Community law' interpretation.
4. Finally, (part 4) the extent to which the Community legislative institutions and the ECJ are currently receptive to such a development will be addressed.

PART ONE — FUNDAMENTAL RIGHTS — COMMUNITY LAW AND THE ECHR[1]

1.1 Historical Background

The EC Treaty itself contained no provisions dealing with fundamental rights. This can be explained in two somewhat different ways.[2] One suggestion is the wish of the Member States not to jeopardise the success of the entire project by what might have been seen by some as excessive ambitions in the field of human rights, after the failure of early plans for a 'European Political Community'. The other is that it might not have been at all obvious to those drafting the Treaty that there was any real need for human rights protection in what was primarily an economic and trade treaty.

1.2 Changing Attitude of the ECJ

The attitude of the ECJ has undergone, on any view, a significant change since its earliest days. It initially resisted any attempt to suggest that principles of fundamental rights were protected by Community law, in early cases such as *Stork*,[3] *Geitling*,[4] and *Sgarlata*.[5] This may have been prompted by caution in respect of arguments based on principles derived primarily from national legal systems at a time when it was in the process of developing its vision of Community law as a 'new legal order of International Law.'[6] This concern, however, soon began to point in the opposite direction, as the goodwill and co-operation of national courts was crucial in turning the ECJ's vision into reality.[7] This might have been jeopardised if the ECJ was seen to ignore or brush aside lightly national courts' concerns about fundamental rights, particularly those protected by national constitutions.

The ECJ eventually took a different approach, in a line of cases beginning with *Stauder*.[8] It gave its interpretation of the Regulation in question,

[1] There is a vast literature on this subject. General discussions this can be found in P Craig and G de Búrca, *EU Law* (3rd edn, OUP, Oxford, 2002) ch 8; L Betten and N Grief, *EU Law and Human Rights* (Longman, London, 1998); P Alston (ed), *The EU and Human Rights* (OUP, Oxford, 1999); N Neuwahl and A Rosas (eds), *The European Union and Human Rights* (Kluwer, The Hague, 1995).
[2] Craig and de Búrca (n 1) 318–19.
[3] Case 1/58 *Stork v High Authority* [1959] ECR 17.
[4] Case 36/59 *Geitling v High Authority* [1960] ER 423.
[5] Case 40/64 *Sgarlata & ors v Commission* [1965] ECR 215.
[6] Case 26/62 *Van Gend en Loos v Nederlandse Administratie der Belastingen* [1963] ECR 1.
[7] On this development and its subsequent acceptance by national authorities see K Alter, *Establishing the Supremacy of Community Law* (OUP, Oxford, 2002).
[8] Case 29/69 *Stauder v City of Ulm* [1969] ECR 419.

adding rather cryptically that 'interpreted in this way the provision at issue contains nothing capable of prejudicing the fundamental human rights enshrined in the general principles of Community law and protected by the Court.' It avoided having to decide whether the relevant provision violated principles of Community law, by way of a 'compatible interpretation', while at the same time, and for the first time, indicating that this might in theory be possible. It then faced some rather more sensitive cases, in which it was less easy to dismiss the potential conflict between fundamental rights protected under national constitutions and Community law. In these cases, most notably *Internationale Handelsgesellshaft*,[9] the ECJ embarked on significant development of its fundamental rights jurisprudence. It became established that the breach of fundamental rights protected by the Community was a ground for annulment of Community action. This principle is well established, and the ECJ has stressed that respect for fundamental rights, as they are protected by Community law, is a condition of lawfulness of Community acts, including secondary legislation.

1.3 Member States and Community Fundamental Rights Law

The ECJ has also established that Member States may be bound by the same Community law principles of fundamental rights. It began by asserting jurisdiction to examine Member State acts for compatibility with fundamental rights protected by Community law when they were implementing Community law.[10] It then extended its jurisdiction even further. It first adopted an exclusionary approach—that when the Member State was acting *outside* the sphere of Community law, it would have *no jurisdiction* to review its acts for compliance with Community law fundamental rights.[11] This then developed into an inclusionary approach—that Member State acts *within* the scope of Community law *may be reviewed* for compliance with Community law fundamental rights.[12]

[9] Cases 51–54/71 *Internationale Handelsgesellshaft* [1971] ECR 1107.
[10] Cases of this nature include Case 36/75 *Rutili* [1975] ECR 1219; Case 222/84 *Johnston v CC RUC* [1986] ECR 1651; Case 249/86 *Commission v Germany: Re Housing of Migrant Workers* [1989] ECR 1263; Case 63/83 *R v Kent Kirk* [1984] ECR 2689; and Case 5/88 *Wachauf v Germany* [1989] ECR 2609.
[11] Case C-60 and 61/84 *Cinéthèque* [1985] ECR 2605; Case 12/86 *Demirel* [1987] ECR 3719.
[12] Case C-260/89 *ERT*, and Case C-386/95 *Familiapress* [1997] I-3689, effectively reversing its stance in *Cinéthèque* above. The ECJ and national courts have continued this line of reasoning, including in *First City Trading* [1997] 1 CMLR 150; Case C-2/92 *R v MAFF Ex p Bostock* [1994] ECR I-955; Case C-292/97 *Karlsson*. See also the Opinions of AG Geelhoed in Case C-313/99 *Mulligan & ors v MAFF* (12 July 2001), and AG Mishco in Cases C-20/00 and C-64/00 *Brooker Aquaculture & Hydro Seafood v The Scottish Ministers* (20 September 2001). For cases in which matters have been considered to be outside the scope of Community Law, Case C-144/95 *Maurin* and Case C-299/95 *Kremzow v Austria* [1997] ECR I-2629.

Exactly how far this extends remains somewhat vague and contentious.[13] However, the ECJ has indicated that this includes the situation where a Member State derogates from Community law rules or fundamental freedoms. This applies whether the derogation is by way of direct reliance on Treaty Articles providing for the possibility of such derogation, or by way of judicially developed concepts of 'mandatory requirements' or imperative reasons of public interest.[14]

It has been suggested that the wording of the Charter of Fundamental Rights may muddy even further these already somewhat obscure waters.[15] As De Witte points out, the addressees of the Charter in Article 51 are said to include the Member States ... 'only when they are implementing Union Law.'[16] This seems narrower than the existing position under Community law that Member States are bound by Community principles of fundamental rights when they are acting within the scope of Community law, including when they take autonomous, ie independent, national law measures which have the effect of restricting one of the fundamental freedoms of Community law.[17] De Witte suggests that the wording of the Charter might cast some doubt on the future of this latter line of reasoning. However, it has to be emphasised that this remains speculation. There is, as yet, no sign from the ECJ of any willingness to retreat from these cases because of the Charter.[18] It is however interesting to note the explanation of this Article,[19] which does not seem to express any intention to *depart from* or *narrow* the scope of Member States' obligations to respect fundamental rights. It again is ambiguous, as De Búrca points out, referring both to a vague and broad concept of Member States acting 'in the context of Community law' and to 'implementing Community rules',[20] the latter not seemingly reflecting the full extent of the existing jurisprudence.

However, this debate has little relevance for this book. Nothing in the Charter would alter the fact that the Community and its legislation are bound to comply with Community law principles of fundamental rights. If it is determined by the ECJ that principles of respect for family life

[13] G De Búrca, 'Fundamental Rights and the Reach of EC Law' (1993) 13 *OJLS* 283; J Temple Lang, 'The Sphere in Which MS are Obliged to Comply with the General Principles of Law and Community Fundamental Rights Principles' [1991] *LIEI* 23.
[14] *ERT*, *Familiapress* (n 12).
[15] B De Witte, 'The Legal Status of the Charter: Vital Question or Non-issue?' (2001) 8 *MJ*; G De Búrca, 'The Drafting of the Charter of Fundamental Rights (2001) *ELRev* 126. Cf Menendez, 'Chartering Europe: The Charter of Fundamental Rights of the EU' Arena Working Paper, *http://www.arena.uio.no/publications/wp01_13htm*.
[16] For a discussion of the development of this precise formulation, De Búrca (n 15).
[17] De Witte (n 15).
[18] *Brooker Aquaculture*, *Mulligan* (n 12), and most recently and strikingly, Case C-60/00 *Carpenter v SSHD* [2002] 2 CMLR 64 all take this approach.
[19] In the Explanatory Memorandum published with the text of the Charter.
[20] Taken from *Karlsson* (n 12).

require or support an interpretation of the relevant Regulations that would grant residence rights to the cohabiting partner in question, the Member State would obviously be bound by that interpretation. If such an interpretation is not possible, but it is determined that the Regulations as they stand are in breach of such superior principles, they will to that extent be invalid. It would then be necessary for them to be altered by the Community legislature. However, in the meantime, Member States would also be affected by such a ruling. It would seem inappropriate, even unlawful, for them to maintain in force and to seek to enforce, to the extent of that invalidity, the invalid Regulations or national laws based on them.[21] If the objection were one of unequal treatment in the enjoyment of family life, the Member State would be required to grant the same treatment and benefits. If the objection were the interference with family and private life regardless of discrimination, the Member State could not rely on its own legislation that interfered with family and private life in the same way.

If, however, it were thought that the Regulation could not be interpreted to grant residence rights to the partner in question, and if it were not held to be invalid for breach of fundamental rights, the Member State would retain a *power* to grant rights to such partners, but it would not be under any *duty* in Community law to exercise that power in any particular way. The only contrary argument would then be that that the individual has a directly effective right that could be relied upon against the Member State to create such an obligation. I shall address this in chapter 6.

1.4 Endorsement by other Community institutions

The ECJ has not been the only actor in this arena. Endorsement of the general proposition that Community law and the Community institutions should respect fundamental rights has come over the years from the Community institutions themselves.[22] With the Treaties of Maastricht and Amsterdam, this 'soft' approval of the developments of the ECJ moved to more explicit 'hard' approval.[23] Critical in this process were the insertion of Article F in the Treaty on European Union at Maastricht, and its development into Articles 6 and 7 TEU at Amsterdam. Yet the Community still lacked its own 'Bill of Rights'. There has been pressure

[21] This would seem to be in breach of the obligation under Article 10 EC. On this obligation, E Guild, *Immigration Law in the European Community* (Kluwer, The Hague, 2001) 32, and more generally the writings of J Temple Lang, including 'Community Constitutional Law: Article 5 [10] EEC Treaty' (1990) 27 *CMLRev* 645.

[22] Most notably a Joint Declaration by the Parliament, Council and Commission in 1977 [1977] OJ C103/1.

[23] Craig and De Búrca (n 1).

for some time from various quarters for action. Various options have been proposed—(1) that the Community should develop a more coherent and systematic policy on fundamental rights; (2) that it should accede to the ECHR, or incorporate it into the Community Treaties, and (3) that it should develop a specific Community Bill of Rights. Accession to the ECHR was considered by the ECJ in its Opinion 2/94.[24] It was held that the Community lacked competence to accede to the Convention and that a Treaty amendment would be necessary to enable it to do so. Subsequent events (in particular the drafting of the Charter of Fundamental Rights) have perhaps made this debate on the possibility of accession to the Convention less important than it was, although the debate remains a live one.[25]

The eventual course most closely approximates the third option, with some progress on the first, and the second now a real prospect if the Constitutional Treaty agreed in June 2004 is ratified. In 1999, the European Council[26] decided to establish a Charter of Fundamental Rights and subsequently[27] commissioned a drafting body (subsequently and confusingly renamed the 'Convention') to consult and to draw up such a document.[28] Although drawing much inspiration from the ECHR, the Charter that finally emerged is far from a simple copy of it. It contains some modifications and different ways of expressing ECHR Rights, as well as significant additions of a number of issues not mentioned in the ECHR at all.

The Charter raises many interesting questions, and has given rise to much discussion.[29] The instructions to the drafting body were to prepare it (the Charter) 'as if' it were to be legally binding at some stage, although at the time of drafting the precise legal status of the document that would result had not been determined.[30] Some Member States were opposed to

[24] *Opinion 2/94* [1996] ECR I-1759.

[25] There are some who see the Charter as a step on the way to the ultimate accession of the Community to the ECHR, while others regard it more negatively as a distraction from that aim.

[26] In Cologne, June 1999.

[27] In Tampere, October 1999.

[28] On the drafting process, generally De Búrca (n 15), and G Braibant, *La Charte des Droits Fundamentaux de l'Union Europèene* (Éditions du Seuil, Paris, 2001).

[29] De Búrca (n 15), Braibant (n 28); K Feuss (ed), *The EU Charter of Fundamental Rights* (Federal Trust, London, 2000), and the volume of the *Maastricht Journal of European and Comparative Law* dedicated entirely to the Charter, (2001) 8(1) *MJ;* P Eckhout, 'The EU Charter of Fundamental Rights and the Federal Question' (2002) *CMLRev* 945. On the Charter in the ECJ see J Morijn, 'Judicial Reference to the EU Fundamental Rights Charter: First Experiences and Possible Prospects' (online, *www.europa.eu.int/futurum/documents/other/oth000602_en.pdf*), and generally on its future legal status, House of Lords European Union Select Committee 6th Report of 2002/3 *The Future Status of the European Union Charter of Fundamental Rights* (HMSO, London, 2003).

[30] The Presidency Conclusions in Cologne envisaged the process in two stages. First, the Charter would be 'proclaimed' by the Institutions and then 'it will have to be considered whether, and if so, how, the Charter should be integrated into the Treaties'. See de Búrca (n 15) on the different aims and ambitions of those involved in the drafting process, and

the idea that it would become legally binding, whereas others felt that this was inevitable.[31] Once the document had been finalised, the issue of its legal status was conveniently fudged. The Community institutions made a 'solemn declaration' of the Charter at the Nice summit in December 2000, but it was clear that this was an interim measure and that further discussion of the matter would follow. This compromise has prompted much debate both about the future of the Charter and its current and future legal status and effect. One British politician (the then Minister for Europe, Keith Vaz) compared the Charter to the Beano (a well known British children's comic magazine) in its potential legal effect before the Court of Justice.[32] The debate has many aspects and is bound to be a continuing one. It is part of the larger agenda of discussion on the future of the structure of the Union and its activities in advance of the 2004 IGC: the Convention has recommended incorporation in its Draft Constutional Treaty, although ratification of the text agreed in the summer of 2004 remains to be completed.

1.5 Community Migration Law and Fundamental Rights

It is, however, clear that Community law on migration is not exempt from the general Community law obligation of respect for fundamental rights. It is also clear that the fundamental rights which Community law protects include respect for family and private life, the same right enshrined in Article 8 ECHR. This has been repeated several times by the ECJ,[33] and so this in itself is not a particularly controversial statement. The consequence of this is, of course, that Community legislation on migration, immigration and family reunification in particular—and Member State implementation of it—must comply with the requirements of respect for family and private life.[34] Several cases emphasise this point, including

Commission *Communication On the Legal Nature of the Charter of Fundamental Rights of the European Union* COM(2000) 644.

[31] Discussion of this in the House of Lords European Union Select Committee, 8th Report of 1999/2000 *The EU Charter of Fundamental Rights* (HMSO, 2000).

[32] A comment made by K Vaz to reporters in Biarritz in October 2000, BBC News website, *http.news.bbc.co.uk*, 'Blair Plays Down EU Rights Charter' 13 October 2000.

[33] Cases in E Guild and G Lesieur, *The ECJ on the ECHR, Who said What, When?* (Kluwer, The Hague, 1998) ch 7.

[34] K Lundstrom, 'Family Life and the Freedom of Movement of Workers in the European Union' (1996) 10 *IJLPF* 250. On the limitations of this in practice and the problems with the current state of Community law; N Blake, 'Family Life in Community Law: the Limits of Freedom and Dignity' in E Guild (ed), *The Legal Framework and Social Consequences of Free Movement of Persons in the European Union* (Kluwer, The Hague, 1999), also T Hervey, 'A Gendered Perspective on the Right to Family Life in European Community Law' in N Neuwahl and A Rosas (eds) (n 1); L Woods, 'Family Rights in the EU: Disadvantaging the Disadvantaged?' (1999) 11 *CFLQ* 17.

Commission v Germany,[35] *Demirel*,[36] and *Eyup*,[37] as well as the recent Opinions in *Baumbast*,[38] *MRAX*[39] and *Orfanopoulos*[40] and the case of *Carpenter*.[41] A recent striking example of this is the use of these principles by the Parliament to challenge various provisions of the Family Reunification Directive on the basis of incompatibility with the right to family life.[42] It is also clear that the Community's legislation and the interpretation and application of the Treaty on this—as all other matters—must in principle comply with the concept of equal treatment. This includes (but is not confined to) the particular articulation of this concept found in Article 14 ECHR.[43] The application of equal treatment to Community migration law and residence rights has not been expressly considered by the ECJ,[44] but it follows naturally from these previous cases.

1.6 The Charter Revisited

The argument being presented is not, therefore, that the Charter might be used to suggest the inclusion into Community law of a right that has not yet been recognised, or the recognition for the first time of the legally binding nature of a particular right. On the contrary, it can only reinforce what is already established. The Charter contains several obvious similarities to the text of the ECHR itself, particularly in relation to the Articles of the Convention that are of interest in this book. In particular, Article 7 of the Charter declares that 'Everyone has the right to respect for his or her private and family life, home and communications.' This echoes Article 8 ECHR,[45] although without the specific limitation provision contained in Article 8.[46] As regards discrimination, Article 21 of the Charter states more clearly and explicitly than the ECHR[47] that discrimination on the

[35] *Commission v Germany: Re Housing of Migrant Workers* (n 10).
[36] *Demirel* Case (n 11).
[37] *Eyup v Landesgeschaftsstelle des Arbeitsmarktservice Vorarlberg* Case C-65/98 [2000] ECR I-4747.
[38] *Baumbast & R v SSHD* Case C-413/99 Opinion of AG Geelhoed of 5 July 2001.
[39] *MRAX v Belgian State* Case C-459/99 Opinion of AG Stix-Hackl of 13 September 2001.
[40] Cases C-482/01 and C-493/01 *Orfanopoulos*. Opinion of AG Stix-Hackl of 11 September 2003.
[41] *Carpenter* (n 18).
[42] *European Parliament v Council* Case C-540/03 [2004] OJ C47/21.
[43] The Community law concept of equal treatment is arguably wider than that found in Art 14 of the ECHR. I shall return to that later, in ch 5.
[44] As it has been by the ECtHR, *Abdulaziz, Cabales & Balkandali v UK* Series A No 94 (1985) 7 EHRR 471.
[45] Indeed, Arts 8 of the Convention and 7 of the Charter are listed among those 'corresponding' rights in the Explanatory Memorandum.
[46] The provisions of Art 52 fulfil this function in the Charter.
[47] Arts 21 and 14 are not listed in the list of corresponding rights in the Explanatory Memorandum.

grounds of sexual orientation is prohibited. This is an independent right and applies generally, not just to the enjoyment of other Charter rights, as does Article 14 ECHR. These provisions, as well as the provisions of Article 52(3) of the Charter,[48] reinforce the link between the Charter and the ECHR, and emphasise the relevance of the ECHR as an obvious starting point for consideration of the meaning and scope of these particular rights in Community law.

Other noteworthy provisions of the Charter include Article 33 ('The family shall enjoy legal, social and economic protection') and, in cases where children are involved, Article 24 ('In all actions relating to children, whether taken by public authorities or private institutions, the child's best interests must be a primary consideration,' and 'Every child shall have the right to maintain on a regular basis a personal relationship and direct contact with both his or her parents, unless that is contrary to his or her interests'). However, these seem of little relevance to the present discussion. Given the presence of Article 7 (respect for family and private life) in the Charter, it is not likely that Article 33 will add much, except persuasive force in favour of interpretations giving greater protection to the family. Article 24 could be of importance to the situation of couples with children, whether or not the relationship between the two adults is still ongoing. However, my main argument in this book rests on the position of the couple as such.

However, as we have seen in chapter 3, the ECHR—at least as it is applied by the ECtHR—does not necessarily seem to *require* the law to develop in the way that I am advocating here. The only possible exception to this is sexual orientation discrimination, the prohibition of which now arguably extends to same-sex relationships and couples and to their enjoyment of family reunification rights. The crucial question is the status of the already established ECtHR interpretations of these rights. In particular we must examine whether there is sustainable argument that these interpretations of EHCR rights are in any way binding on the ECJ so as to prevent the development of an autonomous *and more protective* interpretation of these rights in Community law. The Charter may have some relevance to this issue, and it is on this that I shall focus, concentrating particularly on the meaning of Article 8 of the ECHR (independently and in conjunction with Article 14 ECHR) in the context of immigration law, leaving detailed consideration of the status of the principle of equal treatment and its application to discrimination on the grounds of sexual orientation to a later chapter.

[48] To which I shall return below.

PART TWO — ECtHR JURISPRUDENCE IN THE ECJ

A. Prior to the Charter

The relationship between the ECtHR and the ECJ is a complex and ambiguous one. There is a general respect for established ECtHR jurisprudence, but a reluctance to admit any obligation to follow it. There are many cases in which the ECJ has considered the ECHR,[49] often turning to it as a source of inspiration to clarify the rights protected by Community law and their meaning and scope. Reference to ECtHR jurisprudence, however, is less common. Discussion of the case law is most often found in AG's Opinions, although the ECJ has now made reference to it in several cases.[50] The ECJ does not however see itself as being bound by ECtHR case law, even where it accepts that the right in question is protected by Community law. This position is articulated in AG's Opinions, although there is no indication that the ECJ would adopt any radically different approach. On several occasions differences of opinion have arisen between the ECtHR and the ECJ, both in the direction of providing greater protection and lesser protection. Most or all of these cases, however, involve one of two situations. Either there was no direct case law from ECtHR at the time of the ECJ decision and the ECtHR subsequently adopted a different view when it had the chance to consider the matter,[51] or the ECJ was perhaps unaware of and did not expressly cite ECtHR jurisprudence.[52] Direct and explicit departure from *existing established* ECtHR case law in ECJ judgments is far rarer, indeed practically non-existent. The two cases closest to this are *Emesa Sugar*[53] and *Limburgse Vinyl Maatschappij NV* (the *PVC Cartel* case).[54] However, these two cases, as I will discuss below, have unusual features. *Carpenter*[55] is another case

[49] Case C-36/75 *Rutili* (n 10) is the first such case, but there have been many since. For a collection of these cases, E Guild and G Lesieur (n 33).

[50] D Spielmann, 'Human Rights Caselaw in the Strasbourg and Luxembourg Courts: Conflicts, Inconsistencies, and Complementaries' in Alston (ed) (n 1). Most recently see S Peers, 'The European Court of Justice and the European Court of Human Rights: Comparative Approaches' in E Orucu (ed), *Judicial Comparativism in Human Rights Cases* (BIICL, 2003); S Peers, 'Human Rights Jurisprudence of the European Court of Justice' (2002) 2 *HRLRev* 211.

[51] As in Case 374/87 *Orkem v Commission* [1989] ECR 3283, which came before *Funke v France* Series A No 256-A (1993) 16 EHRR 297 in the ECtHR and Case 46/87 *Hoescht* [1987] ECR 1549 (followed in Case 85/87 *Dow Benelux* [1989] ECR 3137, and Case 97-99/87 *Dow Chemical Ibérica v Commission* [1989] ECR 3165), which came before the case of *Niemietz v Germany* Series A No 251-B (1992) 16 EHRR 97 in the ECtHR.

[52] The cases cited by Spielmann (n 50) where the ECJ has gone beyond ECtHR interpretation might be given as examples of this. Case 257/85 *Dufay v European Parliament* [1987] ECR 1561; Case 22/84 *Johnston v CC RUC* (n 10), compared with ECtHR case law including *Neigel v France* Application 18725/ 91 1997-II 399; *Lombardo v Italy* ECHR (1992) Series A Vol 249-B, and *Massa v Italy* ECHR (1993) Series A Vol 265-B.

[53] Case C-17/98 *Emesa Sugar (Free zone) v Aruba* Order of 4 Feb 2000.

[54] Case T-305 et al *Limburgse Vinyl Maatschappij NV v Commission* [1999] ECR II-931 on appeal to the ECJ Case C-344/99P and C-238/99P.

[55] Above (n 18).

that may be seen in this light, but as it is so central to the discussion (in that it involves residence rights of a spouse under Article 8 ECHR) I shall deal with it separately later.

2.1 Community Law Autonomy and Conflicting Intepretations

There are many statements from the ECJ emphasising its reluctance to be bound by intepretations of the ECHR given by the ECtHR. One of the seminal and often quoted articulations of this position is that of AG Darmon in *Orkem*,[56] who comments as follows:

> ... I must not fail to remind the Court that, according to its case law, the existence in Community Law of fundamental rights drawn from the European Convention on Human Rights does not derive from the wholly straightforward application of that instrument as interpreted by the Strasbourg authorities. In its judgment in Nold confirmed in Hauer, the Court stated that, in the discharge of its duty to safeguard the fundamental rights which form an integral part of Community Law, 'international treaties for the protection of human rights on which the member-states have collaborated or of which they are signatories can supply guidelines which should be followed within the framework of Community Law.'
>
> The most authoritative commentators on the decisions of this Court also emphasise that the Court's position regarding the European Convention on Human Rights consists in most cases 'in using it merely as a reference,' even though it 'goes as far as possible in that direction' and that, by so doing, it develops 'directly or indirectly its own case law interpreting the Convention.' This Court may therefore adopt, with respect to provisions of the Convention, an interpretation which does not coincide exactly with that given by the Strasbourg authorities, in particular the European Court of Human Rights. It is not bound, in so far as it does not have systematically to take into account, as regards fundamental rights under Community Law, the interpretation of the Convention given by the Strasbourg authorities. It seems to me that, a fortiori, the Court is even less bound in the present case, since no authorised interpretation of the Convention has been given showing that administrative infringements of competition law give rise to the application of Article 6(2) and (3), or that those provisions make available, in such matters, the right not to give evidence against oneself.

The ECJ did not make any comment either way on this view. Support for this as the general position in Community law has come in a number of other cases, in particular from AG's Opinions.[57] For illustrative purposes,

[56] Above (n 51), paras 139, 140.

[57] The cases are too numerous to mention individually, but see Guild and Lesieur (n 33), also Spielmann (n 50) above; R Lawson, 'Confusion and Conflict? Diverging Interpretations of the European Convention on Human Rights in Luxembourg and Strasbourg' in R Lawson and M de Bloijs (eds), *The Dynamics of the Protection of Human Rights in Europe: Essays in Honour of H Schermers* (1994) vol iii, 219, and N Foster, 'The European Court of Justice and the European Convention for the Protection of Human Rights' (1987) 8 *HRLJ* 245.

three particular instances in which the ECJ may be open to departure from ECtHR jurisprudence may be identified.

2.1.1 *Community Law providing Greater Protection*

In *Mutsch*,[58] the right to use a particular language in criminal proceedings was in question, and the right to a fair trial under Article 6 ECHR was considered. It was suggested that the obligation of the host state under Community law would be fulfilled by providing an interpreter, as would be the case under the ECHR.[59] However, the AG rejects this view. He notes that the ECJ has drawn inspiration from the ECHR as a source of common minimum standards, but also emphasises that 'it is not contrary to the European Convention on Human Rights to grant more extensive protection to individual rights.' The fact that the ECHR would simply require an interpreter does not mean that Community law cannot, through the provisions of Article 7(2) of Regulation 1612/68,[60] require a higher standard of protection. This approach is repeated by AG Geelhoed in *Baumbast*.[61] He considers that the ECHR would not require the granting of a right of residence to *both* parents of the children concerned,[62] but only after having found another basis in Community law for the right of residence of the second parent in his own right, rather than as father of the children.[63] In both of these cases the additional protection granted by Community law came not from a distinctive 'Community law' interpretation of fundamental rights, but from other provisions of Community law. *MRAX*[64] may be seen as another similar case, the ECJ resolving the case using Community law alone, without reference to the ECHR, and reaching conclusions that seem distinctly more protective of individual rights than Article 8 ECHR as currently interpreted in the ECtHR.

2.1.2 *Distinguishing ECtHR Case Law*

In *Emesa Sugar*[65] the applicants had received and read the AG's Opinion and sought to make further representations to the ECJ. This request was

[58] *Mutsch* Case 137/84 [1985] ECR 2681.
[59] Opinion of AG Lenz [1986] 1 CMLR 659.
[60] Which requires that workers be granted equal treatment in respect of 'social and tax advantages'. It was concluded, both by the Court *and* the Advocate General, that the right to use a particular language *that was granted to nationals or residents* was a social advantage, also subsequently Case C-274/96 *Bickel & Franz* [1998] ECR I-7637.
[61] Above (n 38).
[62] Para 124–5.
[63] Para 122.
[64] Above (n 39).
[65] Above (n 53).

initially refused because the rules of procedure made no provision for such a course of action and the applicants request was then considered by the ECJ itself. The applicants cited several cases from the ECHR[66] to suggest that the refusal of an opportunity to comment on a document such as the AG's Opinion was a breach of Article 6 ECHR (right to a fair trial). These cases however were dealing with domestic legal systems. They did not consider the particular factual and legal position and role of the AG in the ECJ's proceedings. The ECJ considered the authorities of the ECtHR briefly, but ultimately dismissed them. It commented that,

> ...having regard to both the organic and functional link between the Advocate General and the Court, referred to in paragraphs 10 to 15 of this order, the aforesaid case law of the European Court of Human Rights does not appear to be transposable to the Opinion of the Court's Advocate General.

This is a clear indication of willingness on the part of the ECJ to examine the particular institutional structure of the Community, and to reject as inappropriate particular conclusions of the ECtHR.

There are three points that should be noted about this case before proceeding. First, it is clearly of some concern to see the ECJ depart from the views of the ECtHR not in the direction of increased protection for the individual, but in the opposite direction. However, if the ECJ is indeed not bound to respect ECtHR interpretation as a *minimum* standard, it can hardly be bound to do so as a *maximum* standard. Second, although the ECJ subsequently followed its approach in *Emesa Sugar* in refusing to allow the parties to submit observations on the AG's Opinion in the case of *Kaba*,[67] this decision has subsequently been criticised by the referring tribunal,[68] as well as being subject to critical academic comment.[69] A further reference to the ECJ was made to clarify this point although the complaint was ultimately rejected.[70] The final point is that the particular circumstances making the ECJ reluctant to transpose ECtHR case law into Community law are factual and administrative. It is not anything inherent in the nature of Community law or its underlying foundational

[66] *Lobo Machado v Portugal* (20 Feb 1996 1996-I 195); *Vermeulen v Belgium* (20 Feb 1996 1996-I, 224); *Van Orshoven v Belgium* (25 June 1997 1997-III, 1040); *JJ v Netherlands* (27 March 1998 1998-II, 604); *KDB v Netherlands* (27 March 1998 1998-II, 621).

[67] Case C-356/98 *Arben Kaba v SSHD* [2001] ECR I-2623.

[68] *Arben Kaba v SSHD* Appeal No TH/00476/97, Decision of December 2000. Transcript on file with author.

[69] Annotations by R Lawson (2000) 37 *CMLRev* 983; Benoit-Romer, 'L'affaire *Emesa Sugar*' (2001) *CDE* 403, and D Spielmann (2000) *RTDH* 581.

[70] The case was referred back to the ECJ a second time, *Arben Kaba v SSHD (No 2)* Case C-466/00. The concern of the Tribunal was that the Court of Justice had underestimated the differences between the Advocate General and the Procureur General, and had overlooked some relevant case law of the ECtHR. AG Ruiz-Jarabo Colomer rejected the argument based on Art 6 ECHR as did the Court of Justice.

legal principles that the ECJ perceives as problematic. It is primarily[71] the administrative structure of the ECJ and the role of the AG which (according to the ECJ) differ *in fact* from the situations in the relevant ECHR cases.[72] As Beaumont notes,[73] this seems more like a case of skilful, if not particularly convincing, distinguishing of the ECtHR approach than an outright rejection of it. My argument is somewhat different, resting not on the administrative and factual background of a particular Community institution, but on foundational *legal* principles of Community law. Nevertheless, the order in *Emesa Sugar* is a welcome confirmation that, as Speilmann had suggested,[74] the ECJ can and will reject particular ECtHR interpretations of ECHR rights if it considers them to be inappropriate for the particular context of Community law.

2.1.3 *Reluctance to Change Course: The* PVC Cartel *Case, and* Mannesman

The *PVC Cartel* case,[75] and *Mannesman*[76] seem to take further and entrench somewhat the divergence between the ECJ and the ECtHR that emerged following the judgments of the ECtHR in *Niemetz v Germany* and *Funke v France*, alluded to briefly above. It might have been thought[77] that the subsequent divergence would prompt a rethink of the approach in *Hoescht* and *Orkem*, and that if an opportunity arose to redirect its approach in the light of the subsequent case law of the ECtHR, the ECJ might well be willing to take it. Such an opportunity has recently come before the Court of First Instance (CFI) twice, both of which are now on appeal to the ECJ. However, the CFI did not take it, and the AG's Opinion in the appeal follows the same approach. There are two different issues—that of the interpretation of Article 8 ECHR put forward by the ECJ in *Hoescht*, and that of the interpretation of Article 6 ECHR put forward by the ECJ in *Orkem*. The reluctance to change course is combined with another example of the ECJ's willingness to distinguish ECtHR jurisprudence in order to justify sticking to its previous view and not expressly overruling its own previous decisions. Nevertheless, this tendency should not be overestimated. On appeal to the ECJ, the tendency to stick to the

[71] The Court does mention the 'special constraints inherent in the Community Judicial procedure.'

[72] A somewhat similar approach can be seen in the Opinion of AG Jacobs in Case C-270/99P *Z v European Parliament*.

[73] P Beaumont, 'Human Rights: Some Recent Developments and their Impact on Convergence and Divergence of Law in Europe' in P Beaumont et al (eds), *Convergence and Divergence in European Public Law* (Hart Publishing, Oxford, 2001).

[74] 'Moreover, it is submitted that in very specific areas such as competition law, the protective standard might vary in the light of policy considerations specific to the European Community legal order.'

[75] Case T-305/94 *Limburgse Mvinyl Maatschappij v Commission* [1999] ECR II-931.

[76] Case T-112/98 *Mannesman-Röhrenwerke v Commission*.

[77] Lawson (n 57) 247.

previous view is less marked,[78] and more recently, the ECJ has confirmed more clearly that:[79]

> For the purposes of determining the scope of that principle in relation to the protection of business premises, regard must be had to the case-law of the European Court of Human Rights subsequent to the judgment in *Hoechst* ....

This is welcome and not entirely unexpected. It seems inevitable that, if the ECHR—and the ECtHR's interpretation of it—is to be seen as having value (even if simply persuasive rather than binding and as a minimum standard) it must also be recognised that it is a living instrument the understanding and interpretation of which is not static but changes over time.

2.1.4 Conclusion

These cases show that the ECJ's willingness to follow the ECtHR does have its limits, and divergent interpretations should certainly not be ruled out, although it may at least be said that coherent and convincing reasons for departure from ECtHR jurisprudence would be required before any explicit divergent interpretation may be expected.

2.2 General Respect for ECtHR Jurisprudence

Nevertheless, Spielmann sounds a warning note and encourages the reader not to overestimate the extent of the trend discussed above:

> Not taking into account Strasbourg case law because there was none, or because the ECJ inadvertently believed that there was none, should thus not lead to an over-estimation of inconsistency, and there is good reason to believe that the Luxembourg Court would not adopt conflicting solutions to the problems at stake if there were relevant case law from Strasbourg.[80]

If the ECJ guards the principle of its autonomous interpretation of Community law fundamental rights jealously, it also recognises the persuasive authority of the ECtHR and does accept that the wisest course is to exercise this autonomy and independence with some restraint. Extra-judicial comments also confirm the general willingness in practice of ECJ Judges to respect ECtHR jurisprudence.[81] AG Opinions containing references to ECtHR jurisprudence as well as to the text of the ECHR are too numerous to mention individually.[82]

[78] Case C-238/99P *Limburgse Vinyl Maatschappij v Commission* Judgment, para 236–80.
[79] Case C-94/00 *Roquette Frères SA v Directeur Général de la Concurrence*, para 29.
[80] Above (n 50), 770.
[81] For example Spielmann, *ibid*, referring to a speech of Judge Moitinho de Almeida at the ECtHR (1997) 7 *Bulletin des Droits de l'Homme* 280.
[82] See the cases in Guild and Lesieur (n 33).

Turning from AG's Opinions to ECJ judgments, the cases are fewer. Spielmann[83] refers to four cases: *P v S*,[84] *Criminal proceedings against X*,[85] *Familiapress*,[86] and *Grant*.[87] However, not all these contain specific use of the ECtHR case law to elucidate the content of an ECHR right.[88] There are other more recent cases, however, in which the ECJ has referred to ECtHR jurisprudence.[89] *Baustahlgewbe*,[90] *Krombach*,[91] *Connolly*[92] and *Van Der Wal*[93] in the ECJ can now be cited in this regard, as well as the *PVC Cartel*[94] case, *Roquette Frères*[95] and *Carpenter*.[96] It certainly seems not only that the ECJ is now willing to refer to the ECHR itself, but that it shows a growing trend to make explicit reference to ECtHR jurisprudence to help elaborate the meaning of a particular ECHR right if it finds it helpful.

Nevertheless, it remains the case that in none of these cases has there been any departure from the fundamental position articulated by AG Darmon in *Orkem* quoted above. The adherence to existing ECtHR jurisprudence is, strictly speaking, a matter of choice and respect rather than of legal obligation. *Emesa Sugar* and the *PVC Cartel* case are exceptions rather than the rule[97] in the ECJ attitude to ECtHR jurisprudence. Beyond this, a consistent and coherent explanation for the ECJ's approach is, Speilmann suggests, 'very difficult to provide'.[98] Doubtless the likelihood of divergence will depend on the volume and longevity of the case law being departed from, and the force of the reasons being put forward for departure—in particular, whether there are any reasons *specific to the nature or context of Community law* that might give force to the suggestion of a distinctively 'Communitaire' interpretation of a particular right.

2.3 Analysis and Application

Much is made in the literature of the possibility, or even the reality, of divergent interpretations of ECHR rights by the ECJ and ECtHR, and whether or not this phenomenon is problematic.[99] It is true that such

[83] Above (n 50).
[84] Case C-13/94 *P v S & Cornwall CC* [1996] ECR I-2143.
[85] Case C-129/95 *Criminal Proceedings against X* [1996] ECR I-6609.
[86] Above (n 12).
[87] Case C-249/96 *Grant v Southwest Trains* [1998] ECR I-0621.
[88] In truth, only the *X* and *Familiapress* cases really do this.
[89] Peers (n 50).
[90] Case C-185/99P *Baustahlgewebe GmbH v Commission* [1998] ECR I-8411 para 29.
[91] Case C-7/98 *Krombach v Bamberski* [2000] ECR I-1935.
[92] Case C-274/99P *Connolly v Commission*.
[93] Case C-174 and 189/98P *Netherlands v Van der Wal*.
[94] Above (n 54).
[95] Above (n 79).
[96] Above (n 18).
[97] Lawson (n 69) 990.
[98] Spielmann (n 50) 776.
[99] Discussions in the literature (n 57).

divergences might be problematic, particularly in cases in which, for example, two individuals were both suggesting that their (different, and conflicting) rights were infringed. Likewise, a clear and unambiguous departure from ECtHR interpretation in favour of a less protective interpretation of a particular right would seem problematic. It would certainly leave the ECJ open to criticism, and could leave the Member State with an unenviable dilemma as to which to follow, if the two were truly incompatible.[100]

Yet this book involves neither of these situations. Immigration law disputes are clearly between the individual and the State. There is no question of another individual's right (privacy, family life, freedom of expression) being infringed by *granting* residence. The only issue is whether there has been undue infringement either of the State's general capacity under international law to control the entry and residence of foreign nationals, or of its ability to use that right as an instrument to pursue particular *general* aims and policies. The choice is a stark one between a more limited standard of protection under the ECtHR interpretation, or a greater level of protection under a Community law interpretation. The countervailing interest pointing towards a narrower interpretation is not another conflicting individual right, but the more amorphous and general concepts of public policy and the general interest.

In this context, the words of AG Jacobs writing extrajudicially in 1994 are apt:

> There is no reason why national courts or the Court of Justice should not apply a higher standard, based on a more far-reaching interpretation of the Convention, or on national provisions or indeed on other international human rights instruments. To accept this view is not to question the pre-eminent status of the Convention but merely to recognise the obvious, that its role is necessarily limited, however important.[101]

[100] In some situations, of course, the two interpretations would be divergent but not strictly speaking incompatible, in that compliance with one would not be incompatible with compliance with the other. Member States in their own actions would be bound by the greater obligations under the Convention, but their position in respect of acts of the Community itself is a more complex matter, *Matthews v UK* Application 2433/94 (1999) 28 EHRR; I Canor, 'Primus Inter Pares: Who is the Ultimate Guardian of Fundamental Rights in Europe?' (2000) 25 *ELRev* 3, and R Harmsen, 'National Responsibility for European Community Acts under the European Convention on Human Rights' (2001) 7 *EPL* 625. The case of *Guérin Automobiles* Application 51717/99 was held inadmissible on another point, but there are also two cases pending before the ECtHR, seeking to make the 15 Member States collectively responsible for the acts of Community institutions: *Senator Lines* Application 56672/00 (memorandum of the applicants to the Court is reproduced at (2000) 21 *HRLJ* 112, now declared inadmissible) and *Lenz* Application 38837/97.

[101] F Jacobs, 'European Community Law and the European Convention on Human Rights' in D Curtin and T Heukels (eds), *Institutional Dynamics of European Integration* (Martinus Nijhoff, Dordrecht, 1994) 219 at 227.

A House of Commons library research paper also echoes this view,[102] asking rhetorically whether, even if there is a risk of divergent interpretations, this is necessarily a bad thing. There is generally little concern expressed about the possibility of the ECJ providing greater protection by a more generous interpretation of a particular right.

This view seems commendable and it is the approach that I intend to adopt. Disagreements may persist as to the extent of any obligation on the ECJ to respect ECtHR interpretation as a minimum standard. However, the question becomes entirely different when the possibility of the provision of a higher standard of protection is in issue, and there is no direct conflict with any other individual right. It would be a grave mistake to see the ECHR, and ECtHR jurisprudence interpreting it, as anything other than a minimum standard, not least because the Contracting States are not bound by ECtHR jurisprudence as anything more than a minimum level of protection: nothing prevents national law from adopting a more generous and protective interpretation of particular rights,[103] and nothing should prevent Community law, and the ECJ as the final authority on its interpretation, from doing so.

B. The Potential Impact of the Charter

Article 52(3) of the Charter states:

> In so far as this Charter contains rights which correspond to rights guaranteed by the Convention for the Protection of Human Rights and Fundamental Freedoms, the meaning and scope of those rights shall be the same as those laid down by the said Convention. This provision shall not prevent Union law providing more extensive protection.

The Charter itself makes no reference to ECtHR case law, but the preamble to it does. The accompanying Explanatory Memorandum also refers to it, stating that the 'meaning and scope' of the guaranteed rights are determined not only by the text [of the ECHR and the protocols to it], but by the case law of the ECtHR and of the ECJ. From this, it may be suggested that ECtHR case law is to be taken as a concrete minimum level of protection, not just a useful guideline from which the ECJ may depart at will.[104] But this says little about whether the ECJ both *can* and *should* depart from the view of the ECtHR and adopt a *more extensive interpretation* of the right in question.

[102] House of Commons Library Research Paper 00/32, *The EU Charter of Fundamental Rights*.
[103] Spielmann (n 50).
[104] A Herringa and L Verhey, 'The EU Charter: Text and Structure' (2001) 8 *MJ* 11; also J Liisberg, 'Does the EU Charter of Fundamental Rights Threaten the Supremacy of Community Law?' (2001) 38 *CMLRev* 1171 emphasising the status of the ECHR as a *minimum* standard.

The final part of Article 52(3) is of central importance, stating that 'this provision shall not prevent Union law providing more extensive protection.'[105] This would certainly prevent any argument that EU legislation could not grant more generous rights than would be required under the ECtHR interpretation of Article 8 ECHR. Indeed, such a suggestion seems so absurd that it can hardly have been the intention for this part of Article 52 to guard against this argument. So perhaps we must conclude that, if it is not there to prevent this, it must have *some additional or other* significance? The most obvious alternative significance to attach to it would be that the 'more extensive protection' that Union law may still provide *may* indeed be by interpretation of a Convention/Charter right by the ECJ. This is certainly a plausible interpretation of the last sentence of Article 52(3) taken alone. However, the approach becomes less clear in the light of the preceding sentence ('the meaning and scope shall be *the same as*,' not '*at least the same as*' or '*similar to*') and the explicit reference (at least in the Explanatory Memorandum and Preamble) to ECtHR case law. As McCrudden points out,[106] the Charter is a fundamentally ambiguous document, and this matter is no exception. Seemingly, either Article 52(3)b is present to guard against a wholly unsustainable argument, or the text of Article 52(3) read as a whole is inherently contradictory. Neither is a particularly satisfactory solution, but if a choice is necessary, the first seems preferable.

2.4 The Drafting Process

During the process of drafting the Charter this issue was the subject of much discussion.[107] There were divergent views, with the UK opposed to the Charter having any legal force, but insistent that the meaning and scope of the rights should be tied to the ECHR and ECtHR interpretations. Other representatives, notably the Spanish and Italian, but also the French, were more insistent on the autonomy (or *autonomía*) of the Charter as an EU document that should not be constrained by ECtHR interpretations.[108] At one stage a draft was produced which seemed to suggest that

[105] This is also repeated in the explanatory memorandum.

[106] C McCrudden, 'The Future of the EU Charter' in *Europe 2004 —Le Grand Débat*.

[107] I am grateful to Professor Jacqueline Dutheil de la Rochère for discussing the drafting process with me and giving me some first-hand insights into the discussions that took place. See also P Lemmens, 'The Relation between the Charter of Fundamental Rights of the European Union and the European Convention on Human Rights—Substantive Aspects' (2001) 8 *MJ* 49.

[108] Discussion with Professor Jacqueline Dutheil de la Rochère, March 2002, also the discussion of the drafting process in Liisberg (n 104). Liisberg points out that the discussions about the ECHR and ECtHR jurisprudence originally arose in relation to Art 53, but this point was subsequently moved to Art 52(3) of the Charter.

the Convention (and presumably therefore also the ECtHR case law) would not be a 'minimum' standard, but would be 'the' standard, unless departed from in the Charter.[109] The final version, however, seems less conclusive. It has to be regarded as an open question,[110] and the process of drafting, even if admissible as an aid to interpretation, does not resolve the ambiguity. Indeed, it simply confirms the impression that the Charter provisions here, as elsewhere, were the result of a search for compromise, and for forms of expression that leave some crucial and divisive issues unresolved.

2.5 The Commission Communication

The Commission Communication on the legal nature of the Charter of Fundamental Rights[111] states:

> **Respect for the Autonomy of Union Law:** it is also important that the Charter be incorporated harmoniously into the Union legal system and that its underlying legal principles be respected. This applies in particular to the autonomy of the Community legal order in relation to international law and the national law of the Member States; the Charter is drafted in such a way as to respect that autonomy. In particular, the explicit recognition by the last sentence of Article 52(3) is perfectly satisfactory: there is nothing to preclude Union law from giving more extensive protection than the European Convention.
>
> **The relationship between the Charter and the European Convention for the protection of Human Rights and Fundamental Freedoms**: the risk of disparity between the rights and freedoms secured by the European Convention and those set forth in the Charter, and the risk of the case law of the Luxembourg and Strasbourg courts diverging, was carefully analysed when the Charter was being prepared. The solutions adopted by Article 52(3) of the Charter are entirely satisfactory; there was the same broad consensus on them as on the other provisions of the draft, and the Council of Europe observers in the Convention also supported them: the rights set forth in the Charter correspond in their meaning and scope to the rights already secured in the European Convention, without prejudice to the autonomy of Union law. The risk of the case law diverging should therefore be removed…

With respect, this seems an inadequate analysis. Autonomy and the risk of divergence are inseparable, as autonomy may sometimes require not just a risk of, but actual divergence. If any risk of divergence is removed, whatever autonomy the ECJ has would be unacceptably limited to the situation where the ECtHR has not yet ruled. If this were to prevent a

[109] Lemmens (n 107) 52.
[110] Lemmens (n 107); J Dutheil de la Rochère, 'Droits de L'Homme: la Charte des Droits Fundamentaux et Au-delà' in *Europe 2004—Le Grand Débat*.
[111] Above (n 30).

more protective interpretation, it would be particularly troubling in the situation where the more limited interpretation of the rights put forward by the ECtHR is arguably inconsistent with certain foundational principles of Community law. This is exactly the argument that I shall advance below. The Commission seems to be putting the best face on a deliberate ambiguity arising from remaining divergences of opinion.

2.6 Other Provisions of the Charter

Most importantly, Article 45 of the Charter recognises the EU citizen's right to 'move and reside freely within the territory of the Member States', repeating the rights contained in the EC Treaty.[112] It could therefore be said that the other provisions of the Charter (and the suitability of ECtHR jurisprudence) do indeed have to be read in the light of this fundamental freedom. In this respect, the comments of the AG in *Hautala*[113] may be relevant. I shall return to consider this Opinion in more detail, but for now it is sufficient to note that it considers the effect of recognition in the Charter that a right is fundamental, and the effect of this on the interpretation of the right.

Article 52 also provides that,

> Any limitation on the exercise of the rights and freedoms recognised by this Charter must be provided for by law and respect the essence of those rights and freedoms. Subject to the principle of proportionality, limitations may be made only if they are necessary and genuinely meet objectives of general interest recognised by the Union or the need to protect rights and freedoms of others.

This raises in acute form the complex question of whether refusal of settlement for unmarried partners respects the 'essence' of the rights and freedoms contained in the Charter provisions of Article 7 and 45, and whether the Charter and EU law can or should, if faced with the issue of unmarried partners' migration rights, take a narrower approach to the extent of permissible limitations on the Charter rights than does the ECtHR in relation to ECHR rights. Herringa and Verhey note that, in so far as it deals with derogations from or limitations on Charter/ Convention rights, this provision may go further than ECtHR case law. This is particularly so in as far as it talks of respecting the 'essence' of the rights. They comment that,

> Although this approach is also well known in Strasbourg case law and has been used by the Court in several cases, it cannot be said that the 'essence

[112] Most importantly and symbolically now contained in Art 18 EC, but also Arts 39, 43 and 49 EC.

[113] Case C-353/99 *Heidi Hautala & others v Council* Opinion of AG Léger of 10 July 2001.

> doctrine' forms a coherent and consistent part of the Strasbourg law as far as the application of the limitation clause is concerned. In this respect the Charter could make a valuable contribution to the further development of this doctrine.[114]

As the right of couples to live together is accepted in principle to be part of the right to family and private life in the ECtHR (albeit one that can be restricted and interfered with), this different approach to *limitations* on the rights contained in the Charter could be significant. I shall return to this point later in chapter 7.

2.7 The Charter in the ECJ

The Commission has suggested that the ECJ itself would, in effect, turn the Charter into a legally binding or 'mandatory' document. It is however too early to say whether and to what extent this will happen. Early indications are, perhaps unsurprisingly, that AGs[115] and indeed the CFI and ECJ itself[116] are treading a fine line between respecting the wish not to make the Charter a legally binding document (yet), while still acknowledging the obvious point that it represents a statement of values and a collection of rights agreed by all the Member States and the Community institutions which cannot be ignored in the ECJ's task of identifying those fundamental rights that are included in the general principles of Community law.

In any event, as we have seen already, the existing and already established place of fundamental rights in Community migration law means that the significance of the Charter itself is unlikely to influence or require the introduction by the ECJ of entirely new rights relevant to this book into Community law. It is the effect, if any, that it may have on the ECJ's attitude to ECtHR jurisprudence in its interpretation of existing rights that will be crucial.

[114] Above (n 104).

[115] Reference has been made to the Charter in a growing number of cases, including *Hautala* (n 113); Case T-112/98 *Mannesman-Röhrenwerke v Commission* (n 76); Case C-173/99 *BECTU*; Cases C-122 and 125/99P *D & Sweden v Council* [2001] ECR I-4319. Less extensive references, sometimes simply in footnotes, are also contained in the Opinions in Case C-340/99 *TNT Traco*; Case C-270/99 *Z v European Parliament* (n 72); Case C-49/00 *Commission v Italy*; Case C-377/98 *Netherlands v Council*; Case C-413/99 *Baumbast* (n 38); Case C-309/99 *Wouters*; Case C-313/99 *Mulligan & Ors v MAFF* (n 12); Case C-160/00 *Neilsson*; Case C-60/00 *Carpenter* (n 18); Case C-459/99 *MRAX v Belgian State* (n 39); Case 64/00 *Brooker Aquaculture* (n 12); Case C-210/00 *Kaserei*; Case C-208/00 *Uberseering*.

[116] Case T-54/99 *Max.mobil.Telekommunikation Service GmbH v Commission*, CFI Judgment of 30 January 2002 is the first case in which any reference is made to it in a CFI Judgment, also Case T-177/01 *Jego-Quere v Commission* [2002] 2 CMLR 41.

Of most interest here are comments of AG Léger in *Hautala*,[117] concerning the *interpretation* and status of Charter rights. Although he emphasises that the intention of those who drew up the Charter not to make it legally binding 'should not be overlooked', he does recognise that the Charter cannot be ignored. He states that it 'is intended to constitute a privileged instrument for identifying fundamental rights. It is a source of guidance as to the true nature of the Community rules of positive law.' First, he concludes that the Charter may be useful in determining the group of 'fundamental' rights, as distinct from other rights. He then goes on, having identified the right of access to documents as being a fundamental one, to consider the consequence of this. He says that the lack of binding legal status of the Charter 'should not, however, cause us to overlook the fundamental nature of that right', which

> ...confers on that right a quality which should provide guidance as for its interpretation. I consider that where it is decided that a right should be classified as a fundamental right, the authorities responsible for applying it are under a strict requirement to give it the wide interpretation demanded by its true nature.[118]

Consequently, he considers, that the right of access to documents cannot be restricted to documents, as opposed to the information in the documents and thus that it includes a right of *partial* access to documents. He then interprets Decision 93/731 in this light, concluding that it 'does not prohibit' partial access to documents and that the CFI was right to say that the Council was required to consider whether partial access should be granted.

These and other similar comments[119] certainly add weight to the suggestion that the ECJ might in time use the Charter to support its conclusion that a departure from ECtHR case law was warranted in favour of a wider interpretation of a particular right. This could be particularly so if this were seen to be required by, or consistent with, another right in the Charter but not in the ECHR,[120] or by a different approach to the permissible extent of limitations on these rights.[121] However, it does have to be conceded that none of the cases yet takes the ECJ into the territory into which it is suggested here that it should venture; namely, express rejection of an interpretation of a particular right already established by the ECtHR.

[117] Opinion, paras 77–87.
[118] Para 86.
[119] A similar approach can be discerned in the Opinion of Advocate General Tizzano in *BECTU* (n 115).
[120] That is, the right to move and reside freely throughout the territory of the Member States, Art 45 of the Charter and Art 18 EC.
[121] Art 52.

It is certainly possible that the Charter may contribute to the continuation and entrenchment of the already existing possibility of divergent approaches in the ECtHR and the ECJ. As Lawson suggests, 'This is quite acceptable as long as the ECJ applies higher standards than the ECtHR, as the Convention only intends to lay down common *minimum* standards.'[122] Nothing in the Charter or in the current judicial attitude to it alters the fundamental tenability of the proposition that the ECJ remains free to depart from ECtHR interpretation of ECHR rights in adopting and developing more generous and protective interpretations of these rights in Community law. Nor do the recent moves toward incorporation of the Charter and EU accession to the ECHR in the Constitutional Treaty agreed in 2004 (but not yet ratified) seem to fundamentally challenge these propositions.

2.8 ECtHR Jurisprudence in the ECJ since the Charter

One case of crucial significance for Article 8 ECHR, *Carpenter*,[123] has been decided by the ECJ since the adoption of the Charter, in which the ECJ refers briefly to ECtHR jurisprudence but develops what is arguably a distinctly greater level of protection. The case concerns precisely the issues of family life and immigration law that are central to this chapter, and I shall discuss it in greater detail later. However, it should be noted at this stage that this development is very low key and subtle, leaving the impression that the ECJ had either misunderstood the ECtHR jurisprudence and thus the extent of its departure from it, or wished to conceal or minimise the degree of divergence, and there is no reference to the Charter itself.

PART THREE — WEAKNESSES OF THE ECtHR CASE LAW IN COMMUNITY LAW

Having concluded that there is nothing in principle to preclude the ECJ from departing from ECtHR jurisprudence and adopting the kind of approach that I have proposed to family and private life and equal treatment in its enjoyment, it still remains to persuade it to do so in this particular situation.

3.1 Article 8 Jurisprudence

As we have seen in chapter 2, there are some crucial assumptions underlying the case law of the ECtHR, which drive it towards a limited

[122] Above (n 69), 990.
[123] Above (n 18).

review of Contracting States' policies and decisions in the field of immigration:

1 The ECHR itself does not give an individual a right to travel to or reside in another Contracting State.
2 The ECHR does not protect the individual's private and family life to the extent of giving a prima facie right to choose where to conduct that family life or private relationship. There is no *general* obligation on the Contracting State to respect that choice by authorising family reunification of non-national family members.
3 In particular, the real possibility of family life being conducted elsewhere will often be relevant. The ECtHR has until now been reluctant to accept that there has been a violation of Article 8 ECHR if the family can reasonably be expected to set up home or continue living together elsewhere.
4 The economic interests of the host state may be a legitimate concern of the authorities, both when determining general immigration policy and determining how rigidly to adhere to it when an applicant seeks to demonstrate 'exceptional circumstances'.

Replicating these statements replacing 'the ECHR' with 'Community law and Member States in implementing Community law and/or derogating from it' seems problematic.[124] I shall return in a later chapter to examine these issues in more detail, but for the present time I shall outline the main objections to adopting in Community law an approach which relies on these assumptions.

The first assumption is simply wrong. The EC Treaty of course *does* give the individual EU citizen a right to 'move and reside freely throughout the territory of the Member States.'[125] However, the obvious response to this is that, at best, this only places the migrant EU citizen, in respect of a host Member State, in the same position as the national of a Contracting State under the ECHR, or of an immigrant lawfully settled and resident there. As we have seen, this in itself does not *automatically* (or even in a *general* way) require the Contracting State to respect the choice of matrimonial or family residence by permitting settlement of a non-national spouse or other family member. Yet the EU citizen may indeed be in a better position than the national under the ECHR, as the right to reside and be economically active in a host state is well protected under Community law, more so than under the ECHR.

The second assumption can also be questioned in the Community law context, both in relation to secondary legislation and by reference to general principles. The importance of the right of the migrant to be

[124] See also Lundstrom (n 34).
[125] Art 18 EC.

accompanied by immediate family members, and on favourable terms, is recognised by the Community institutions. No Member State national has ever had a right of residence granted, clarified or confirmed by secondary legislation[126] without provision for some kind of family reunification[127] being included. As regards immediate members of the family such as spouse, minor child, or perhaps unmarried partner, principles of Community law inherent in the Treaty itself can also arguably be used to assert a right of residence.[128] In particular, concepts of obstacles to the exercise of fundamental freedoms and indirect nationality discrimination may be useful. If this is so, then the policy of refusing family reunification rights to non (hetereosexually) married couples must be justified.

The third related point, that the real possibility of family life being conducted elsewhere will often persuade the ECtHR that there has been no breach of Article 8 ECHR, seems difficult to reconcile with basic principles of Community law in relation to EU citizens, which are based on precisely the opposite assumption. Choice, and *effective* freedom to exercise that choice[129] is the cornerstone of Community law on free movement, whether of goods, persons, establishment or services. The fact that a product has one, or even more, Member State market(s) in which it *can* lawfully be sold does not provide any justification for refusing to protect its access to another Member State market. The fact that an Italian or German national could work, reside and/or continue his or her family life in Italy or Germany is no reason why he or she should be prevented from choosing do so elsewhere in the Community. Free movement law assumes that borders should be eliminated as far as possible and that buyers and sellers of goods and services, and individual EU citizens contemplating a change of job or residence, should as far as possible be able to chose freely whether to remain in one state, or to migrate across the Community's internal borders. In the particular context of immigration law in respect of Member State nationals Guild[130] shows the evolution of Community law into a system where the individual's choice is central:

> The Community, in developing its immigration law, consistently removed from the Member State Authorities the power to decide who to admit. Instead the process was transformed into one increasingly characterised by the power of the individual to choose.[131]

[126] Council Regulation 1612/68 of 15 October 1968 on the Freedom of Movement for Workers within the Community [1968/9] OJ Sp Ed (II) 475, Directives 73/148, 90/364, 90/365, 93/96.
[127] Which always includes at least the spouse and minor children.
[128] Chs 5 and 6, and E Guild, 'Free Movement and Same-sex Relationships: Existing Law and Article 13 EC' in R Wintemute and M Andenas (eds), *Legal Recognition of Same-sex Partnerships* (Hart Publishing, Oxford, 2001).
[129] Not just legal rights subjected to conditions making them unattractive and unreasonable to exercise in practice.
[130] Above (n 21), especially chs 1 and 2.
[131] Above (n 130), 13–14.

> ...a direct legal relationship is created with the EC. On the basis of that relationship the individual is entitled to make choices irrespective of the wishes of the Member States. If the Member State wishes to interfere with the individual's choice it must justify that interference within the parameters of its legal relationship with the Community in accordance with the Community's rules regarding the individual's rights.[132]

Thus it is argued that this kind of reasoning—advancing the possibility of regrouping elsewhere to deny the state's obligations to admit family members—should be regarded with the greatest scepticism in Community law.[133]

Finally, economic justifications for measures which restrict the fundamental freedoms of Community law are generally not permitted, or at the very least are regarded with great suspicion. If it is accepted that immigration restrictions on certain immediate family members are potential infringements of fundamental freedoms protected by EC law, then this should apply here also. At the very least, any obstacle to migration should be subject to the Community law principle of proportionality. This means that any obstacle must pursue a legitimate aim, and go no further than is necessary. The principle of proportionality could be used to suggest that the imposition of a reasonable requirement of sufficient means is all that should be imposed on families of migrants if the objection to their presence is economic.[134]

3.2 Article 14 Jurisprudence

The main problem with the ECtHR case law on Article 14 ECHR again centres on the crucial role of migration and free movement in Community law. We have seen in chapter 3 that the ECommHR has seemingly expressed the view that immigration rights for (same-sex) cohabiting couples fall within the class of 'special protection' that a Contracting State *may* under the ECHR reserve for 'traditional' families. These comments appear in the context of same-sex couples, but it seems likely that the Contracting State wishing to preserve such benefits exclusively for married opposite-sex couples could and would raise the same point. I have already suggested that this approach is vulnerable to criticism, even in the ECHR context. Given that the cohabitation of the couple is central to,

[132] *Ibid*, 36.
[133] It may be admitted that, so long as Community law preserves the possiblity for migrants—and in particular long-term migrants—to be expelled this kind of argument should be permissible to enhance the protection of the migrant against expulsion on the basis that it would be unreasonable to expect the family to regroup elsewhere. There may indeed be a useful function for such an argument, but it should be strictly limited to those circumstances.
[134] There is a hint of this in the Opinion of AG Stix-Hackl in *Carpenter* (n 18).

indeed in a real way constitutive of, the 'family' relationship between them, it seems inappropriate to classify this as 'special protection' that may be reserved for the 'traditional' family. For the same reasons as set out above, relating to the centrality of migration and choice to Community law, the same comments can be made, but with even greater force, in relation to the use of this analysis in Community law.

3.3 Conclusion

More attention should therefore be given to developing a distinctive understanding of 'respect for private and family life' and equal treatment in its enjoyment in the particular context of Community migration law. In the context of Community law, respecting family and private life should be recognised as entailing a prima facie obligation to respect the family's choice of residence by authorising reunification of close TCN family members who would normally expect to live together in the same household. This applies at least to spouses, minor dependent children and cohabiting partners. The concept that immigration rights of cohabiting partners are properly seen as 'special protection' which can be withheld from 'non-traditional' families is also inappropriate. If this is so, then Article 14 ECHR, in the context of Community law, would require equal treatment in the enjoyment of family reunification rights for all couples, regardless of their formal legal status and/or sexual orientation, unless a more specific and convincing justification than granting 'special protection' to the 'traditional' family can be advanced for such a policy.

PART FOUR — A DISTINCTIVE COMMUNITY LAW APPROACH?

In this section I shall review briefly the current prospects for the development of such an understanding of Articles 8 and 14 ECHR in Community law.

4.1 Community Institutions

It has been seen in chapter 2 that a consolidatory Directive has just been agreed on the residence rights of all EU citizens,[135] as well as a Directive to provide for family reunification rights of certain legally resident

[135] Proposal for a European Parliament and Council Directive on the Right of Citizens of the Union and their Family Members to Move and Reside Freely Throughout the Territory of the Member States COM(2001) 257 [2001] OJ C270/150.

TCNs.[136] These Proposals presented ideal opportunities to rethink the scope of the definition of 'family member' as they moved towards completion. Nevertheless, the issue is deeply divisive and no consensus emerged—on the contrary, what emerged was a pragmatic and disappointing compromise. Although there was some recognition of the need to review the situation, and the open discussion of the problems involved is certainly to be welcomed, the Commission and certain Member States were determined to maintain a strong degree of Member State autonomy over this issue in the final legislation. In any event, it is not clear that even those in the legislative process advocating a more liberal family reunification regime *in respect of partners* along the lines proposed in this book were doing do so clearly on the basis of *fundamental rights obligations* rather than on the basis of political consensus for action beyond what fundamental rights might *legally require*.[137] In this respect it is interesting to note that the EP stopped short of challenging the narrow definition of partnership in its case concerning the Famly Reunification Directive, including in its challenge only certain provisions permitting restrictions relating to the entry of children and delays in applications and granting of permits. In the process of reaching political agreement on a text of a Directive this is perhaps understandable, in order to avoid sceptical Member States feeling that their position is being forced too hard. But these arguments, if they are convincing, can and should be advanced to encourage political agreement.

4.2 The ECJ

Although the ECJ has sometimes been distinctly activist in protecting individuals' rights, the signs that it might be willing to embrace the arguments put forward here are at best ambivalent.

4.2.1 Protection of De Facto Family Life

The issue of 'de facto' family life and whether the ECJ will recognise and protect the 'functional family' rather than the 'legal family' will be an

[136] Amended Proposal for a Council Directive on the Right to Family Reunification COM(2002) 225 [2002] OJ C203/136, also Arts 2 and 6 of the Proposal for Directive on the Qualification and Status of Third Country Nationals and Stateless Persons as Refugees COM(2001) 510 [2002] OJ C51/325.

[137] The only exception to this may be the issue of sexual orientation discrimination. However, even then the argument that action might be *required* to the extent of making the legislation vulnerable to a successful legal challenge does not seem to be widespread or strongly put.

important one.[138] On the question of the definition of the family, the case of *Eyup*[139] may be significant. The case involved a Turkish couple, who had been married, divorced, and remarried some years later but had in the meantime continued cohabiting and had four children. AG La Pergola refers with apparent approval to the ECtHR case law relating to 'de facto' family life and accepts an unmarried partner as a family member.[140] The ECJ, although it falls short of accepting that unmarried couples generally can be members of each other's family[141] and enjoy family life that Community law can and will protect, seemingly accepts that the provisions of Decision 1/80[142] is intended to protect 'de facto' family unity.[143] But one should be cautious and realistic. The Judgment says nothing about Article 14 ECHR and equal treatment of married and unmarried couples, and is a long way from a conclusive statement that Community law would be willing to protect family reunification rights of unmarried partners generally.[144]

4.2.2 Sexual Orientation Discrimination

The judgment in *Grant*[145] (in which it was held that it was not sex discrimination under Article 119 (now Article 141) to deny a 'spousal' employment benefit to a same-sex partner) has been criticised in relation to its attitude to sexual orientation discrimination and same-sex couples.[146] There are reasons for thinking that the attitude to sexual orientation

[138] Arguing in favour of acceptance of 'de facto' family life by the ECJ following the ECtHR, *inter alia* K Lundstrom (n 34), Blake (n 34), and H Stalford, 'Concepts of the Family under EU Law: Lessons from the ECHR' (2002) 16 *IJLPF* 410.
[139] *Eyup* (n 37).
[140] Paras 18 and 23.
[141] A fortiori, this case does not mean that married and unmarried couples need be treated equally, nor that the obligation to 'facilitate' entry in Art 10(2) of Reg 1612/68 creates directly effective rights, nor that the immigration rights of unmarried opposite-sex couples could be protected in some other way if it is decided that it does not.
[142] Decision 1/80 Concerning the Rights of Turkish workers.
[143] Para 34.
[144] The subsequent case C-407/99 *Pathminidevi* (a case similar to *Eyup* concerning the situation of unmarried partners more generally, without the added circumstance that the couple had been married both before and after the period of non-marital cohabitation) was removed from the Court registry.
[145] Above (n 87).
[146] There has been an extensive literature on *Grant*, including, inter alia, N Bamforth, 'Sexual Orientation After *Grant v Southwest Trains*' (2000) 63 *MLR* 694; '*Grant v Southwest Trains*: Some Comparative Observations' (1999) 2 *CYELS* 125; M Bell, 'Shifting Conceptions of Sexual Discrimination at the Court of Justice' (1999) 5 *ELJ* 63; C Barnard, 'Some Are More Equal Than Others: The Decision of the Court of Justice in *Grant v Southwest Trains*' (1998) *CYELS* 147; C Stychin '*Grant*-ing Rights: the Politics of Rights, Sexuality and European Union' (2000) 51 *NILQ* 251; A Koppelman, 'The Miscegenation Analogy in Europe, or, Lisa Grant Meets Adolf Hitler' in R Wintemute and M Andenas (eds), *Legal Recognition of Same-sex Partnership* .

discrimination, freed from the constraints of having to fit within the limits of a prohibition on sex discrimination, should now be different. However, the more recent case of *D & Sweden*[147] demonstrates the persistence of the ECJ's traditional and conservative attitudes on this matter. It was held that a couple with a registered partnership under Swedish law were neither 'married' nor entitled to treatment equal to a married couple in the context of a family benefit payable to Council staff officials.[148] Even if *Da Silva Mouta*[149] and *Karner* do indicate a new approach in the ECtHR, and a willingness to classify as suspect discrimination against same-sex couples and eventually to reconsider the exclusion of same-sex relationships from the ambit of 'family life', it seems unlikely that the ECJ would be enthusiastic about taking a lead on this in advance of further clear indications from the ECtHR. I shall return to discuss this more fully in chapter 5.

4.2.3 *Immigration Law*

On the obligations of Member States under Article 8 ECHR in relation to immigration law, there are three important recent cases. AG Geelhoed in *Baumbast*[150] considers the relationship between the ECHR and Community law. He does accept that Community law may, using its own principles, be able to grant rights of residence which 'do justice to' the right to respect for family and private life under Article 8 ECHR, even if, as interpreted by the ECtHR, it might not require the particular right of residence in question to be recognised. Having considered that Community law can protect the right of the mother to reside in the UK in order to care for the children, he considers that the right of the second parent is not required under the ECHR or the equivalent protection in Community law, and seeks an alternative basis for the right of the father to reside in the UK. It is of course welcome that he finally concludes that Community law can and should protect his right of residence on other grounds. In discussing this, however, he specifically cites, with approval, the ECtHR principle that the obligation to 'respect' the individual's private and family life does not impose a general obligation to respect the choice of family residence by authorising family reunion in its territory.[151] As discussed above, this assumption seems contrary to the Community law concept of free movement of persons, at least if applied to immediate family members that might be expected to live in the same household as the migrant, such as spouse, partner, or minor child.

147 Cases C-122 and 125/99P *D & Sweden v Council* (n 115).
148 I shall return to this in ch 5.
149 *Da Silva v Portugal* Application 33290/96 (2001) 31 EHRR 47, previously discussed in ch 3.
150 Above (n 38).
151 Para 58–64, 124 and 125.

Linked to this is the apparent approval of the view that the alternative options available to the Baumbast family may be relevant *not just under the Convention but also in Community law*. He notes that,

> ... there are real alternatives available to the Baumbast family in order to be able to live in a family relationship, for example by the family following the father in his occupational activities or by establishing itself in Germany. I refer in that connection to the case law of the European Court of Human Rights to the effect that Article 8 cannot be considered to impose on a State a general obligation to respect immigrants' choice of the country of their matrimonial residence and to authorise family reunion in its territory.[152]
> Finally, I refer to the right to respect for family and private life, which is enshrined in Article 8 of the ECHR. Community legislation on rights of residence, and in particular Regulation 1612/68, adequately observes Article 8 ECHR since the worker's right of residence is also applicable to members of his family. Applied to the Baumbast case that would not be otherwise if the Court were to form the view that under Community law Mr Baumbast has no right to remain in the United Kingdom.[153]

Certainly, providing residence right for spouses and children ensures compliance in this respect with Article 8 ECHR. What is worrying about *this* particular comment, however, is its complacency, for two reasons. The first is the tacit assumption that unmarried partners are not relevant 'family' members which underlies the assertion that Community law is ECHR-compliant because family members are included. Of course this question was not in issue in *Baumbast*, and the position of 'non-traditional' couples may not have crossed his mind at all. Indeed further, as we have seen, this view may be right. Nevertheless, it is expressed with unmerited finality and certainty. The second is that it misunderstands the scope of Article 8 ECHR, in so far as it may protect the right of *both* parents. AG Geelhoed is surely not right to say that, just because *one* parent has a right of residence that would enable the child to remain and be educated in the host state, Article 8 ECHR would not and could not protect the right of the other parent. Without prejudging the issue, suffice it to say that Article 8 ECHR is clearly *capable* of protecting the rights of *both* parents. The UK *might* have been in breach of Article 8 ECHR if it had confirmed the rights of the children and mother to remain in the UK, but not allowed the father to retain his residence status.[154] In particular, the existing stable settlement of the family in the UK might tip the balance in favour of

[152] Para 125.
[153] Para 124.
[154] In this respect, cases can be cited in which the ECtHR has both found and denied breaches of Art 8 ECHR in refusing settlement of or deporting a second parent, or child. See the literature cited in ch 3 n 31.

Mr Baumbast, and there are no considerations such as infringements of immigration law or criminal convictions.

The Opinion in *Baumbast* is certainly welcome in its general approach and the result it recommends. However, if it is scrutinised closely, specifically in relation to its attitude to the ECHR and ECtHR jurisprudence, it is of serious concern. It demonstrates an unwillingness to question critically the transposability of ECtHR case law on immigration to the unique legal situation of Community law. The subsequent judgment does not pursue the point concerning Article 8 ECHR. If the approach in the Opinion of AG Geelhoed on this specific issue is indeed to be seen as an isolated view which will not be pursued further this would be welcome.

The Opinions in the two other cases, *MRAX*[155] and *Carpenter*,[156] also contain references to the interaction between residence rights (and family reunification rights in particular) in Community law and Article 8 ECHR. In *Carpenter*, a Phillipine national sought to use the Community law rights of her husband to protect her own right of residence in the UK. The main difficulty was to establish that the case was not a purely internal situation.[157] It was argued that, since the husband provided services in other Member States, he (and hence also his wife) could benefit from Community law rights. Thus, it was argued, the refusal of a residence permit because the wife had been an illegal overstayer at the time of the marriage would not be permissible under Community law.[158] *MRAX* concerned the lawfulness of various Belgian policies concerning entry, expulsion, and admission of spouses of migrant Community nationals.[159] These two cases are of course distinguishable from the situation in question in this book in one crucial way. The question was not whether they were family members, or (certainly in *MRAX* although the question does arise in *Carpenter*) entitled to a residence permit if they were, but whether the rules in question were a justified restriction on that right. Nevertheless, they are of interest in that they consider the approach of Community law to the protection of family reunification and the Opinions[160] at least contain some interesting observations on the protection of family life in Community immigration/migration law.

There are two positive aspects of these Opinions. First, AG Stix-Hackl accepts in principle that the refusal of the residence permit is an interference

[155] Above (n 39).
[156] Above (n 18).
[157] Cases 35 and 36/82 *Morson & Jhanjhan v Netherlands* [1982] ECR 3723, and Cases C-64 and 65/96 *Uecker & Jaquet v Land Nordrhein-Westfalen* [1997] ECR I-3171.
[158] She could however have applied for revocation of the deportation order and leave to enter as the applicant's wife, so the situation would not be permanent.
[159] (1) refusal of entry at border without visa, (2) unlawful entry followed by a subsequent marriage to an EU Member State national, and (3) lawful entry followed by the expiry of visa.
[160] Written by the same AG, Christine Stix-Hackl, and delivered on the same day.

with family life.[161] She starts from the premise that the refusal of a residence permit for the spouse of an EU citizen interferes with the right to respect for family life.[162] She also accepts that exceptions to this right have to be narrowly construed.[163] These aspects of the Opinions are welcome, but are far from a clear acceptance that there should be a distinctive *Community law* concept of respect for family life, differing from that outlined by the ECtHR in imposing a general obligation to respect the family's choice of residence by admitting, at least, the spouse/partner and minor children. Second, in discussing the extent to which the right under Article 8 ECHR may be limited, there is a *hint* that Article 8 ECHR in its entirety (and presumably by implication the ECtHR case law) may not be appropriate for Community law. She indicates that 'of the aims mentioned in Article 8(2) of the Convention, the protection of public order will generally be a possible one.'[164] Are we to imply from this that some or all of the *other* aims set out in Article 8(2) are perhaps *not* permissible in principle under Community law? I have indeed argued that economic justifications should be regarded with scepticism, and that the readiness of the ECtHR to accept limitations on the right of families to choose the location of their residence is inappropriate for Community law, but the extent to which AG Stix-Hackl would agree is unclear.

There are however also some difficulties with these Opinions, and some aspects of them remain troubling. The AG does not explicitly cast doubt on the approach in *Abdulaziz*,[165] which she cites with apparent approval. It will be recalled that I have suggested that this approach needs to be treated with great caution in the Community law context. However, even more worrying than this is the following comment in *Carpenter*:

> In such an analysis of proportionality, it must be examined in particular whether it is proportionate that Mrs Carpenter may only apply for leave from abroad ... It would also have to be examined whether, if Mrs Carpenter were to stay in the Philippines, it would be reasonable for Mr Carpenter—possibly with his children—to live in the Philippines and be economically active there.[166]

This comes perilously close to an acceptance of the ECtHR view that the obligation of the State under Article 8 ECHR may be curtailed by the reasonable prospect of the family being able to settle elsewhere.[167] As I have

[161] *MRAX* (n 39) paras 61ff, 65, 92. *Carpenter* (n 18) para 86.
[162] This approach is ambiguous. It does not seem an *entirely* accurate picture of the ECtHR approach, but equally there is no indication of a conscious departure from it.
[163] *MRAX* (n 39) para 68, *Carpenter* (n 18) para 88.
[164] Para 97.
[165] *Abdulaziz, Cabales & Balkandali v UK* Series A No 94 (1985) 7 EHRR 471.
[166] *Carpenter* (n 18) para 91.
[167] It is not clear that she intends to suggest that the measure *is in fact proportionate*. It is of course correct that the referring court is to determine the proportionality of a measure in

indicated, this seems a flawed analysis in a Community law context, and it is regrettable that she did not suggest giving guidance of this nature to the referring court.

The final Opinion that requires comment is that of AG Geelhoed in *Akrich*.[168] It seems from the outset distinctly unsatisfactory, and hard to reconcile with the generous approach of the Court in *Carpenter* and *MRAX*. In brief, the facts are that the couple (one British, one TCN) moved to Ireland with a view to returning to the UK, complete with Community law rights under *Surinder Singh*. AG Geelhoed accepts that this is not an abuse of rights. However, his solution to the problem is not without its own difficulties. He considers that the UK, and any other Member State, is entitled to apply its *own immigration law* to a TCN family member who has not yet been admitted under the immigration law of any Member State. In this way he radically restricts the application of the provisions of Regulation 1612/68 and other similar provisions of Community secondary law providing for family reunification. There is also brief reference to Article 8 ECHR in the Opinion and the Judgment, but exactly how this fits with the denial of Community law protection through Regulation 1612/68 is not clear and although *Carpenter* is referred to, there is little detailed discussion about the content of the Article 8 ECHR right and the circumstances in which it might constrain Member States immigration laws and policies.

These Opinions are intriguing. They contain interesting and important discussion of the relationship between the ECHR and Community law on family reunification. There is an unsurprising general respect for ECtHR jurisprudence and certainly no express disapproval of it. However, there are also some interesting suggestions that open up the possibility of divergences between the ECtHR and the ECJ. They may act as a catalyst to encourage more detailed and systematic scrutiny of the question, but they certainly do not provide a clear answer to it. The judgment in *MRAX* takes the approach alluded to briefly above,[169] providing distinctly greater protection for the individual's rights than would be the case in existing ECtHR jurisprudence, but doing so on the basis of Community legislation and without reference to the ECHR or to ECtHR jurisprudence. The subsequent judgment in *Carpenter* is more significant and merits more detailed scrutiny.

practice. However, the ECJ must give sufficient guidance, and has in the past done so, eg Case C-169/91 *Stoke on Trent v B&Q* [1992] ECR I-6635 (Sunday trading rules), and Case C-178/94 *Dillenkoffer v Germany* [1996] ECR-I 4845; Case C-5/94 *Ex P Hedley Lomas* [1996] ECR I-2553 regarding the requirement of a 'sufficiently serious breach' of Community law in the context of state liability. It would have been quite possible, and arguably appropriate, for the AG to indicate more clearly a definitive conclusion on proportionality.

[168] Case C-109/01 *Akrich v SSHD*.
[169] Section 2.1.1.

4.2.4 *The* Carpenter *Judgment*

The ECJ[170] considered that the applicant's husband was able to demonstrate a link to Community law by reliance directly on Article 49 EC (the deportation was an obstacle to the exercise of the right—see chapter 5), but not on Directive 74/183 EC. This meant that she was not obviously able to rely directly on the provisions of Directive 64/221[171] to prevent her deportation. The ECJ was therefore faced with a slightly more complex question as to whether the deportation was a permissible (ie, justifiable and proportionate) infringement of her husband's rights. It comes to a very interesting—and welcome—conclusion. It is difficult to overstate the significance of this judgment, and it seems helpful to set out the relevant section (paras 40–5) in full:

> 40 A Member State may invoke reasons of public interest to justify a national measure which is likely to obstruct the exercise of the freedom to provide services only if that measure is compatible with the fundamental rights whose observance the Court ensures …
>
> 41 The decision to deport Mrs Carpenter constitutes an interference with the exercise by Mr Carpenter of his right to respect for his family life within the meaning of Article 8 of the Convention …
>
> 42 Even though no right of an alien to enter or to reside in a particular country is as such guaranteed by the Convention, the removal of a person from a country where close members of his family are living may amount to an infringement of the right to respect for family life as guaranteed by Article 8(1) of the Convention. Such an interference will infringe the Convention if it dos not meet the requirements of paragraph 2 of that Article, that is unless it is 'in accordance with the law', motivated by one or more legitimate aims under that paragraph and 'necessary in a democratic society', that is to say justified by a pressing social need and, in particular, proportionate to the legitimate aim pursued (see, in particular, *Boultif v Switzerland*, no 54273/00 …).
>
> 43 A decision to deport Mrs Carpenter, taken in circumstances such as those in the main proceedings, does not strike a fair balance between the competing interests, that is, on the one hand, the right of Mr Carpenter to respect for his family life, and, on the other hand, the maintenance of public order and public safety.
>
> 44 Although, in the main proceedings, Mrs Carpenter's spouse has infringed the immigration laws of the United Kingdom by not leaving the country prior to the expiry of her leave to remain as a visitor, her conduct, since her arrival in the United Kingdom in September 1994, as not been the subject of any other complaint that could give cause to fear

[170] Departing on this particular point from the reasoning of AG Stix-Hackl.

[171] Council Directive 64/221 of 25 February 1964 on the Coordination of Special Measures Concerning the Movement and Residence of Foreign Nationals which are Justified on Grounds of Public Policy, Public Security or Public Health [1963/64] OJ (Sp Ed) 117.

> that she might in the future constitute a danger to public safety. Moreover it is clear that Mr and Mrs Carpenter's marriage, which was celebrated in the United Kingdom in 1996, is genuine and that Mrs Carpenter continues to lead a true family life there, in particular by looking after her husband's children from a previous marriage.
>
> 45 In those circumstances, the decision to deport Mrs Carpenter constitutes an infringement which is not proportionate to the objective pursued.

It is interesting to see the ECJ engage in such specific scrutiny of a Member State policy under the ECHR and determine an ECHR question so directly. It is even more striking to see it *in fact* reaching quite a different conclusion[172] from either the ECtHR or the UK courts.[173] This is all the more surprising given that this explicit link to Article 8 ECHR is made, yet there is no conscious effort to move towards a distinctive 'Community' understanding of the proportionality and justifiability of interferences with Article 8 ECHR rights by deportation of family members.

The facts that the ECJ seems to consider of central significance are that she is not a danger to the public order or security of the host state (the only complaint against her being her infringement of immigration rules), and that her marriage and family life are genuine—yet neither of these points would in themselves in the ECtHR *necessarily* justify the conclusion that the enforcement of immigration regulations in question would be incompatible with Article 8 ECHR. Certainly, the ECtHR approach to such matters may be on an 'upward curve' and may be heading in this direction—but the ECJ's approach seems to go further than the ECtHR would at present. Indeed the potential weaknesses of Article 8 ECHR in this respect may explain why the applicants pursued what might be regarded as a somewhat tenuous link to Community law in the ECJ rather than using the ECHR directly. As Acierno points out, the HRA was not yet in force at the time when the case was referred, and this might have made taking the ECHR point a more difficult and prolonged process, which may also have had some influence on the legal strategy employed.

[172] Peers seems less convinced that the approach is a radically different or autonomous one—see S Peers (n 50). Acierno considers that the issue of a disproportionate breach of fundamental rights is clear: S Acierno, 'The Carpenter Judgment: Fundamental Rights and the Limits of the Community Legal Order' (2003) 28 *ELRev* 398. It will be clear that I cannot agree with such a statement—it may be arguable and one may wish it to be so, but to suggest that the disproportionality of the interference—*judged by Strasbourg standards*—is clear seems unwarranted at the present time. Perhaps Acierno herself is influenced by precisely the same *Commaunitaire* concepts of proportionality in respect of family reunification cases that seem to lie at the root of the Court's reasoning. It remains to be seen whether the view put forward here is widely shared.

[173] Discussion of the policy guidance DP3/96, above in ch 3.

Yet the ECJ gives no indication of even being aware of departing from or extending the ECtHR approach, let alone explaining and/or justifying it. It is difficult to avoid the conclusion that the ECJ was, at least to some extent, influenced by its usual approach to the deportation of migrant EU citizens and their families under Directive 64/221. Paragraph 44 is particularly revealing in the way in which the ECJ mentions the absence of any particular proven danger to public order or safety of Mrs Carpenter, even if she has overstayed in breach of the immigration laws. This is very reminiscent of the individualistic approach to expulsion found in Directive 64/221, and in *MRAX*. It fails to address explicitly the policy concerns underlying DP3/96,[174] about the orderly and proper control of immigration (a 'firmer, faster, and fairer immigration control'),[175] and fairness between applicants who abide by the rules and apply for entry from abroad and those who do not and try to find an easier route to settlement despite their irregular immigration status. Such reasons and general policies are in principle acceptable under the ECHR,[176] even if it is necessary to consider the facts of each case to deal with situations of exceptional hardship, whereas they would not be permitted under Community law.[177] This view, that the ECJ is heavily influenced by the individualistic approach in Directive 64/221, is supported by the fact that the only ECtHR case cited is *Boultif v Switzerland*,[178] involving a public order deportation and refusal of re-admission rather than infringement of immigration law and the need to maintain the fairness and integrity of immigration policies and procedures. The other possible influence on a decision such as *Carpenter* is, of course, the wish of the ECJ, in appropriate cases, to enhance its standing as a human rights court and to demonstrate that it is perfectly capable of understanding the issues involved and protecting human rights, even perhaps to a greater extent than Strasbourg. It may be that this had some influence, but clearly it is difficult, if not impossible, to tell what influences judgments in particular cases. Moreover, if the ECJ was wishing to send such a message (of its competence as a human rights court) the rather subtle nature of the judgment and the omission to make any express reference to the point means that it is certainly not as strong a message as it might otherwise have been.

It is not clear whether and to what extent this will lead to the kind of distinctive Community law interpretation of respect for family and

[174] Aired eg in *Ex Parte Hashim* CO/2052/99 unreported 12 June 2000 Lexis transcript; *Ex p Mahmood* [2001] 1 WLR 840; *McCollum v SSHD* [2001] EWHC Admin 40 [2001] Admin Ct Digest 58; *Ex p Isiko* [2001] Imm AR 291.

[175] *Ex p Isiko* (n 174).

[176] The only judicial opinion to the contrary appears in the judgment of Hidden J in *Ex p Isiko* (unreported judgment, Lexis transcript) which was overturned in the Court of Appeal (n 174).

[177] Cf the views of AG Geelhoed in *Akrich*, (n 168) above.

[178] Ch 3 above.

private life in immigration law for which I have argued. In this respect it is perhaps significant that the ECJ in the somewhat similar case of *MRAX*,[179] only very shortly after *Carpenter*,[180] chose not to pursue the AG's suggestion that Article 8 ECHR was relevant. It resolved the case by coming to the same conclusion on the basis of Community law legislation and principles alone. AG Stix-Hackl in the recent opinion in *Orfanopoulos*[181] does embark on a significant discussion of Article 8 ECHR and in particular seems to suggest an autonomous ECJ interpretation of Article 8 in the *Carpenter* case,[182] although elsewhere in her Opinion she notes, apparently without criticism, the view that the reasonable possibility to live together elsewhere (in the Member State of origin of the expelled migrant) may be relevant in assessing compatibility of any expulsion with the ECHR.[183] There is no doubt that *Carpenter* is a judgment of significance in the field of judicial protection of fundamental rights in the EU, but the full extent of its future implications remains to be seen.

CONCLUSIONS OF CHAPTER FOUR

This chapter has explored in some detail the place of fundamental rights in Community law, and the particular relevance of the ECHR Convention and ECtHR jurisprudence. The ECHR retains a particular importance as a source of fundamental rights in Community law, but the ECJ is not legally bound by the interpretations of ECHR rights given by the ECtHR, particularly when the interpretation in question is incompatible with basic principles of the Community legal order. The Charter of

179 Above (n 39).

180 Above (n 18).

181 Cases C-482/01 and C-493/01 *Orfanopoulos*.

182 Para 56. In relation to the objection that the expulsion order under German law did not directly prejudice the applicants because it was possible to remain in the territory by applying for 'tolerance' she suggests that 'without embarking upon an assessment of the decisions of the ECHR based on French law relating to aliens, it suffices in this connection *to refer to this Court's own interpretation of the term "interference"* (emphasis added) within the meaning of Art 8 of the European Convention.' According to the Court's Judgment in *Carpenter* there can be such interference where there is a mere decision to make a deportation order. Even though the Court refers expressly only to a 'decision to deport,' the main proceedings related to a 'decision to make a deportation order.' Therefore, there can be an interference even where the deportation order itself has not yet been made, let alone executed. It is not clear here whether she considers that this is filling a gap in relation to a question not yet decided in Strasbrourg or whether she considers this is Community law providing greater protection.

183 Para 61. Although she does not criticise this line of reasoning openly, perhaps this may be explained and defended by the fact that the case is one of expulsion—it might be argued that it ought to be permissible to take into account the unreasonableness of regrouping elsewhere in order to enhance the migrant's protection against expulsion. This argument was noted briefly above as one situation where it might be acceptable to maintain such reasoning in Community law.

Fundamental Rights adds a new dimension to this debate, but does not seem to alter this basic position. There is nothing to prevent the ECJ or the Community's legislative institutions developing a distinctive Community law understanding of what respect for family and private life and non-discrimination in its enjoyment require in the context of immigration law. I have argued that it should do so because the ECtHR and EC law assumptions (at least in the case of EU Citizens) concerning migration are fundamentally different, almost to the extent of being diametrically opposed to each other. This makes the transposition of ECtHR case law in this area into EC law dubious and potentially highly problematic, particularly in relation to close immediate family members such as dependent children and partners/spouses who would normally be expected to share the same household as the primary migrant.

The most recent AGs Opinions and judgments from the ECJ are ambiguous on this point. The Opinions of AG Geelhoed in *Baumbast*[184] and AG Stix-Hackl in *Carpenter*[185] in particular seem problematic, and *Akrich* even more so. The judgment in *Carpenter* may be a crucial turning point, indicating a willingness to depart from established ECtHR jurisprudence. However, the ECJ gives no explanation of, or even indication of being aware of, its departure from the ECtHR approach to Article 8 ECHR, and the long-term significance of this judgment is unclear.

[184] Above (n 38).
[185] Above (n 18).

5

Community Law Principles of Discrimination

THIS CHAPTER WILL focus on the principle of non-discrimination, or equal treatment, in Community law, and its possible application to the problem being considered in this book. Part 1 will focus on the Community law prohibition of discrimination on the grounds of nationality within the material scope of the Treaty. I will include in this analysis general arguments based on indirect discrimination,[1] as well as a specific consideration of a 'mutual recognition' approach. Part 2 will approach the question in a somewhat different way. We have already seen that Article 14 ECHR prohibits discrimination on certain grounds in the enjoyment of other Convention rights, and we have considered its application to the question at hand in this book. However, the Community's 'general principles of law' contain a freestanding and independent principle of non-discrimination. There are two crucial points to note about this Community law principle. First, it is *not* necessarily confined to discrimination in the enjoyment of specific ECHR rights, as Article 14 ECHR currently is. It is a general principle that Community law, whatever rights and obligations it creates for individuals, traders, and enterprises, should treat comparable situations equally, in the absence of objective justification for different treatment. Second, it is not confined to the grounds covered by Article 14 ECHR (even though the grounds in Article 14 are not themselves exhaustive) but applies wherever there are two situations that are comparable for the purpose in question. This more general freestanding principle of non-discrimination or equal treatment in Community law, its current state of development and application, and its possible relevance for this book, will be the subject of part 2.

PART ONE — INDIRECT NATIONALITY DISCRIMINATION AND DUAL REGULATION

Section 1 will introduce the principle of nationality discrimination in Community law. Section 2 will then consider the applicability of the

[1] I shall move directly to consider indirect discrimination on the grounds of nationality, as the prohibition of direct discrimination on the grounds of nationality requires little consideration.

general principle of equal treatment on the basis of nationality to the immigration rights of unmarried TCN partners. Section 3 will consider the possibility of viewing this situation as one requiring the mutual recognition of the residence rights of a partner in order to avoid imposing a dual regulatory burden on the migrant. I consider this here because it has its origins in and close connections with the principle of indirect nationality discrimination.

1.1 Introduction

1.1.1 The Origin of the Principle of Equal Treatment on the Grounds of Nationality

This principle has its origins in the Treaty itself, as well as being elaborated in secondary legislation. Articles 12 and 39 EC are central to this field of Community law, although Article 12 EC makes it clear that the *general* prohibition of nationality discrimination applies only where there is no *specific* provision, such as Articles 39 EC and 7(2) of Regulation 1612/68. This prohibition of discrimination, or entitlement to equal treatment, applies *within the scope of the Treaty.*

1.1.2 Personal and Material Scope of the Treaty

The ECJ distinguishes between the *personal* and *material* scope of the Treaty. In order for the *individual* concerned to rely on the entitlement to equal treatment, he or she must show that they come within the *personal scope of the Treaty*. Originally restricted to workers and those otherwise economically active, this now embraces any lawfully resident, migrant EU citizen.[2] TCNs are excluded from this guarantee of equal treatment. The protection of Community law persists once the individual returns to their state of origin after exercising free movement rights,[3] and the ECJ has recently determined[4] that the individual resident in his state of origin but providing services in other Member States as a 'significant' part of his/her business is also within the scope of Community law. These are both exceptions to the general principle that the individual resident in

[2] Case C-85/96 *Martínez Sala v Friestaat Bayern* [1998] ECR I-2691; Case C-184/99 *Grzelczyk v Centre Public d'Aide Sociale d'Ottignies/Louvain-La-Neuve* [2001] ECR I-6193.
[3] Case C-370/90 *Ex p Surinder Singh* [1992] ECR I-4265; Case 115/78 *Knoors v Secretary of State for Economic Affairs* [1979] ECR 399; Case C-18/95 *Terhoeve v Inspecteur van de Belastingdienst Particulieren/Ondernemingen Buitenland* [1999] ECR I-345; Case C-135/99 *Elsen v Bundesversicherungsanstalt fur Angestellte* [2000] ECR I-10409; Case C-224/98 *D'Hoop v Office National de l'emploi* [2002] 3 CMLR 12.
[4] Case C-60/00 *Carpenter v SSHD* [2002] 2 CMLR 64.

his/her state of origin is generally excluded from the scope of this equal treatment guarantee.[5]

It must also be established that the benefit is within the *material* scope of the Treaty. As regards workers, this includes all 'social and tax advantages' pursuant to Regulation 1612/68, Article 7(2). This has been given a wide interpretation.[6] In 1979, in *Ministère Public v Even*,[7] the ECJ establishes that social advantages are,

> Advantages which, whether or not linked to a contract of employment, are generally granted to workers primarily because of their objective status as workers or by virtue of the mere fact of their residence on the national territory and the extension of which to workers who are nationals of other Member States therefore seems suitable to facilitate their mobility within the Community.

Analogies are drawn between this and the scope of the Treaty for those economically active in a self-employed capacity, and also (although not clearly) for those individuals who are lawfully resident EU citizens. It may indeed be that the material scope of Article 7(2) of Regulation 1612/68 has now been extended by judicial activism,[8] in the cases of *Martínez Sala*[9] and *Grzelczyk*.[10] In both of these cases, the Court readily concludes that a worker's 'social advantage' is also within the material scope of the Treaty generally for the purposes of equal treatment of a non-working migrant EU citizen. The alternative reading of *Grzelczyk* is hardly less generous, mandating equal treatment in the grant of a benefit if to do so would 'enhance' the exercise of the fundamental freedoms in the Treaty.[11]

Subsequent cases continue this trend. *Garcia Avello*[12] confirms that the opportunity for a child to carry a surname formed in accordance with the traditions of another Member State is within the material scope of the Treaty. The Opinion in *Ninni-Orasche*[13] and the recent judgment in *Collins*[14] also fit into this trend on their treatment of access to financial benefits.

[5] Cases 35 and 36/82 *Morson & Jhanjhan v Netherlands* [1982] ECR 3723, Cases C-64 and 65/96 *Uecker & Jaquet v Land Nordrhein-Westfalen* [1997] ECR I-3171.

[6] R Allen, 'Equal Treatment Social Advantages and Obstacles: In Search of Coherence in Freedom and Dignity' in E Guild (ed), *The Legal Framework and Social Consequences of the Free Movement of Persons in the European Union* (Kluwer, The Hague, 1999).

[7] Case 207/78 *Ministère Public v Even* [1979] ECR 2091 para 22.

[8] A Iliopoulou and H Toner, Annotation of *Grzelczyk* (2002) 39 *CMLRev* 609. See also A Castro Oliveira, 'Workers and Other Persons: Step by Step from Movement to Citizenship – Caselaw 1995–2001' (2002) 39 *CMLRev* 77. For a critical view of *Martínez Sala* see C Toumschat, Annotation of *Martínez Sala* (2000) 37 *CMLRev* 449.

[9] *Martínez Sala* (n 2).

[10] *Grzelczyk* (n 2).

[11] Iliopoulou and Toner (n 8).

[12] Case C-148/02 *Garcia Avello*.

[13] Case C-413/02 *Ninni-Orasche*.

[14] Case C-138/02 *Collins*.

1.1.3 The Concept of Indirect Nationality Discrimination

It is clear that the prohibition on discrimination on the grounds of nationality extends beyond formal equality or direct discrimination to embrace indirect discrimination also. The ECJ provides the following explanation in *O'Flynn*:

> Unless objectively justified and proportionate to its aim, a provision of national law must be regarded as indirectly discriminatory if it is intrinsically liable to affect migrant workers more than national workers and if there is a consequent risk that it will place the former at a particular disadvantage.[15]

And in *Kaba*:

> The Court has consistently held that the equal treatment rule laid down in Article 48 of the Treaty and in Article 7 of Regulation No 1612/68 prohibits not only overt discrimination by reason of Nationality but also all covert forms of discrimination which, by the application of other distinguishing criteria, lead in fact to the same result (see, inter alia, Case C-57/96 *Meints* [1997] ECR 1-6689, paragraph 44).[16]

Clearly, in contrast to the situation prevailing in Community sex discrimination law[17] the actual proof of an effect on migrant workers is not required—a risk or intrinsic liability that such an effect will occur is enough. Given this, it is not surprising to hear AG Lenz in *O'Flynn* state that once discrimination is shown, it is not necessary to show any real effect on the movement of or economic activity of the migrant—the fact of different treatment or differential impact is enough.

The ECJ in *O'Flynn* also describes several particular situations where indirect discrimination may be found:

1. Where a measure although applicable irrespective of nationality affects essentially migrant workers.
2. Where the great majority of those affected are migrant workers.
3. Where a measure is indistinctly applicable but can more easily be satisfied by national workers than by migrant workers.
4. Where there is a risk that the measure may operate to the particular detriment of migrant workers.

[15] Case 237/94 *O'Flynn v Chief Adjudication Officer* [1996] ECR I-2617 para 20.
[16] Case C-356/98 *Arben Kaba v SSHD* [2001] ECR I-2623.
[17] See AG Lenz in *O'Flynn*, para 27.

This certainly makes clear that indirect nationality discrimination is capable of bearing a wide meaning.[18] However, as Guild notes, it remains the case that,

> Discrimination is a notoriously difficult concept to pin down in law. All too often situations are inherently different and inherently the same depending on the point of view from which one is looking at them.[19]

The rather contentious outcomes of *Grant* (same-sex and opposite-sex couples apparently not comparable, even if this comment was arguably *obiter* and made in the specfic context of sex discrimination), *D & Sweden v Council* (registered partnership not comparable to marriage) and *Kaba (I) and (II)* (position of nationals or those settled permanently not comparable to migrant workers) well illustrate this point.

1.1.4 *The Case of* Reed

Reed[20] is a very pertinent example of this principle in action. Dutch law permitted settlement of unmarried partners of permanent residents. It was held that, although not a spouse entitled to settlement under Article 10(1) of Regulation 1612/68, the unmarried partner's residence permit was a 'social advantage' pursuant to Article 7(2) of Regulation 1612/68. It therefore had to be granted without discrimination on the grounds of nationality, and extended to all migrant EU workers.[21] As we have seen[22] this applies not only to workers but also to all migrant EU Citizens.

1.1.5 *How Far can a Discrimination Analysis Go?*

Beyond this however, it is generally thought that the principle of non-discrimination on the grounds of nationality does not require a Member State to recognise residence rights for unmarried partners of migrant EU Citizens if they do not already do so in domestic law.[23] It is this assumption that I shall now examine and challenge in more detail. I shall approach this in two different ways.

[18] See on this Davies, ch 5.
[19] E Guild, *Immigration Law in the European Community* (Kluwer, The Hague, 2001) 45.
[20] Case 59/85 *Netherlands v Reed* [1986] ECR 1283.
[21] The concept of indirect nationality discrimination is used to conclude that the requirement of permanent residence status, not automatically granted to EU workers, was discriminatory. Cf *Arben Kaba* (n 16), referred again to the ECJ, *Arben Kaba v SSHD (No 2)* Case C-466/00.
[22] See discussion in ch 2.
[23] This is implicit in the generally accepted exposition of the current situation that spouses are entitled to residence but unmarried partners are not unless the host state already grants such rights to its own nationals in domestic law.

1 Is the requirement for an unmarried partner to have an independent residence permit for the host state in his/her own right, indirectly discriminatory against the Community migrant because he or she is more likely to have a relationship with a TCN lacking such a permit?
2 If a Member State national has a relationship with a TCN who is lawfully resident in another Member State, could this give rise to a sustainable argument that the host state to which the couple wish to move ought to recognise the lawful residence of the partner on the basis of mutual recognition or the general prohibition of dual regulatory burdens? I deal with that here because this principle is closely related to indirect nationality discrimination, the origin of the underlying principle being that goods lawfully sold or professionals qualified in one Member State should in principle not have to comply with *two* systems of regulation, as this would put them at a disadvantage vis-à-vis domestic goods or professionals.

1.2 Immigration Rules as Indirect Discrimination Against Migrants?

1.2.1 The Problem — Lack of a Comparator?

One problem is immediately obvious. We are by definition facing a situation in which there is no national law permitting settlement of unmarried partners. There is no such benefit for anyone and it is therefore difficult to find a comparator for the migrant. This is precisely why principles that go beyond requiring equality with nationals of the host state may be helpful. A somewhat similar problem with a lack of a comparator has arisen in the context of sex discrimination and pregnancy. This was eventually resolved by an approach which accepted that pregnancy discrimination, being unique to women, was indeed sex discrimination without the need for a male comparator.[24] However, one may doubt whether the situation of unmarried partners cannot be solved this way. Cohabitation with an unmarried partner is certainly not unique to any one nationality group.[25] It might be possible to point to different rates of unmarried cohabitation in different Member States, but it seems doubtful that this in itself would assist an applicant. In relation to same-sex marriage and registered partnership recognised under the law of one Member State but not another, the argument for indirect nationality discrimination may be stronger; as the main focus here is to identify principles that would apply to all couples I will not pursue this argument in detail here.

[24] See eg P Craig and G de Búrca, *EU Law* (3rd edn, OUP, Oxford, 2002) 899.
[25] There might perhaps be a stronger argument from nationality discrimination if a registered partnership or same-sex marriage moved from one state to another which refused to recognise it.

1.2.2 *Two Alternative Analyses*

This brings us back to the point made by Guild. Discrimination, like beauty, is often in the eye of the beholder. Alternative analyses certainly can be offered, and may lead to very different conclusions. These three questions would be asked, to which different answers might be given:

1. What is the benefit sought by the applicant?
2. What is the condition imposed or requirement that must be met in order for this benefit to be obtained?
3. Is this requirement more easily satisfied by one group than another?

Considering our present problem, we might suggest the following two analyses:

Analysis One

- The benefit is being able to cohabit with one's partner, both being lawfully resident in the same host Member State.
- The requirement is that the TCN partner must seek and acquire legal residence rights. As this is not available on the basis of the unmarried relationship, the partner must seek residency in his or her own right.
- This requirement is in practice likely to fall most heavily on migrants as they are more likely to have relationships with individuals settled in their country of origin or last residence. The national (or permanent settled resident) is more likely to have a relationship with an individual who already has at least temporary permission to reside in the host state.

This analysis would demonstrate that the requirement to seek residence rights for a TCN partner in his or her own right was likely to have a greater and more significant impact on migrants than on nationals of Member States who do not migrate.

Analysis Two

- The benefit is cohabitation with the partner.
- Community law *does* indeed allow settlement of cohabiting partners as such. The requirement is simply that the couple marry.
- This requirement is no more difficult for a migrant to satisfy than for a host state national, does not work particularly to the detriment of migrants, and therefore not discriminatory on the grounds of nationality. This might be argued to discriminate against same-sex partnerships as they generally cannot marry, but we shall leave that aside for the present.

There would be two crucial points, if such a question were to appear before the ECJ. The first seems somewhat more problematic than the second.

1.2.3 *First Question — Choice of Analysis*

The first preliminary question would be a choice between two different perspectives on this problem set out above, either of which seems possible in terms of logic. It is rather the outcome of adopting the first approach that might raise the main concerns as to its legitimacy. The one obvious difference is that the second approach regards the State's imposition of a marriage requirement as legitimate, whereas the first protects the couple's choice to remain unmarried.

Would Community law accept that insisting on marriage was legitimate and/or that the free choice to remain unmarried was the source of the couple's problem? Looking at *O'Flynn*,[26] this seems doubtful, although not out of the question. AG Lenz[27] specifically rejects the suggestion that the choice of the applicant (to have his son's funeral in Ireland, which was therefore ineligible for the funeral benefit) meant that his claim must fail. He also asserts directly that the fact that persons in the applicant's situation follow customary or cultural requirements is irrelevant.[28] This is not quite the same as our question here—whether an otherwise discriminatory requirement (to seek independent residence rights for the partner) may be saved by an alternative option (marriage, thus acquiring residence for a partner) defined by or imposed for customary or cultural reasons by a state wishing to preserve and privilege the unique status of heterosexual marriage for cultural, traditional and/or religious reasons. Turning to examine the question from the point of view of choice, *O'Flynn* is rather more helpful. In this case it emerges clearly that the choice of the individual to have the funeral of the family member abroad must be protected. In fact, the ECJ goes so far as to say that migrant workers above all 'may, on the death of a member of the family, *have to arrange* (emphasis added) for burial in another Member State, in view of the links which the members of such a family generally maintain with their state of origin.' Despite the ECJ's use of language implying *obligation*, it seems quite clear that it was indeed protecting the *choice* of Mr O'Flynn to have the body of his son buried in Ireland. This fits well with the liberal, individualistic, empowering ethos of Community free movement law. As we have seen,[29] Community law clearly protects the

[26] Above (n 15).
[27] Opinion para 28.
[28] Presumably this reference to custom and culture made by the UK government refers to the habit of returning to the home state for a family funeral.
[29] See ch 4 above, referring to E Guild (n 21).

choice of the individual to live and work in another Member State, and *O'Flynn* seems to suggest that other family-related choices linked to this and consequent upon it will also be protected, as does the more recent case of *Garcia Avello*. It is less immediately obvious that this would necessarily include the individual's right to choose to remain unmarried for the time being by opting for the first analysis presented above rather than the second. It would seem to be presupposing at an early stage the (il)legitimacy of a requirement (marriage before a partner may enter) which is at the centre of the dispute. The ECJ has often been criticised for its traditional attitude to the family[30] and one may be sceptical as to whether a choice to remain unmarried is something that it would be quick to protect. Nevertheless, set against this are more recent indications that it may be willing to recognise and protect at least heterosexual 'de facto' family life.[31] The best that can be said is that it is a possible although not certain outcome.

1.2.4 *Second Question — the Meaning of Indirect Nationality Discrimination*

The second question is the interpretation of the final part of analysis one, if that is chosen. What exactly is meant by a measure that discriminates against other Member State nationals? Could this concept assist our hypothetical migrant couple?

O'Flynn has been referred to subsequently on a number of occasions,[32] and this approach may be taken to represent the current view taken in Community law of what is indirect nationality discrimination. It may be instructive to consider the facts of *O'Flynn*, and other situations in which the territoriality of a measure has been considered. The benefit concerned was a funeral benefit which was paid only in respect of funerals held in the UK. The applicant arranged a funeral for his deceased son in Ireland (the country of origin and nationality of the applicant) and was refused a funeral allowance in respect of this because the funeral took place outside the UK. AG Lenz suggests:

> The decisive question is in my opinion whether it is more probable for nationals of other Member States than for nationals of the United Kingdom that they or their relatives will be buried in another Member State. The question must be answered in the affirmative.[33]

[30] See, inter alia, C McGlynn, 'The Europeanisation of Family Law' (2001) 13 *CFLQ* 35; C McGlynn 'A Family Law for the European Union?' in J Shaw (ed), *Social Law and Policy in an Evolving EU* (Hart Publishing, Oxford, 2001). H Stalford, 'Concepts of the Family under EU Law: Lessons from the ECHR' (2002) 16 *IJLPF* 410.

[31] Case C-65/98 *Eyup v Landesgeschaftsstelle des Arbeitsmarktservice Vorarlberg* [2000] ECR I-4747.

[32] Case C-212/99 *Commission v Italy*; Case C-195/98 *Österreichischer Gewerkschaftsbund*; Case C-124/99 *Borawitz*; Case C-102/99 *Kocak*; Case C-274/96 *Bickel & Franz* [1998] ECR I-7637; Case C-15/96 *Schöning-Koubetopoulou* [1998] ECR I-47; Case C-57/96 *Meints* [1997] ECR I-6689.

[33] Para 16.

The ECJ in its judgment takes a similar view, considering simply that:

> It is, above all the migrant worker who may, on the death of a member of the family, have to arrange for burial in another Member State, in view of the links which the members of such a family generally maintain with their state of origin.[34]

Assuming the benefit sought by the migrant is cohabitation in the host state with their TCN partner, and that the condition that has to be satisfied in order to acquire it, is that the partner already has or acquires independent residence rights in the host state, the approach taken in *O'Flynn* would seem to suggest a positive outcome for the migrant couple. The requirement would be more likely to be satisfied by nationals of the host state, as they are more likely to have relationships with those (including TCNs) resident there. The arriving migrant is by contrast more likely to have a relationship with those (including TCNs) settled in the country of origin or last residence. Thus, the migrant with a TCN unmarried partner will be disadvantaged as the partner may have to seek an independent residence permit. Proof that there is an effect on a substantially greater proportion of migrant workers is not necessary, it is sufficient that the measure 'is liable' to have such an effect. It could easily be suggested that this is the case, adapting the terminology used in *O'Flynn*, that 'it is above all the migrant worker who will find himself in the position of seeking residence for a TCN partner without residence rights in the host state.' Alternatively, that it is 'more probable that the migrant will have a relationship with a TCN having residence rights in another Member State but not in the Host State.'[35]

1.2.5 Conclusions

Although deeply rooted in Community law, the principle of discrimination on the grounds of nationality seems to have significant shortcomings

[34] Para 22.

[35] See also G Davies, *Nationality Discrimination and Free Movement Law* (PhD Thesis, Groningen, 2002), 184, published as *Nationality Discrimination in the European Internal Market* (Kluwer, The Hague, 2003), suggesting that nationals and migrants are not in comparable positions as regards family reunification. This has to be so where (as there is sometimes with unmarried partners) there is no provision for family settlement, but it is rather more difficult to see why this is so where there are particular family immigration rules that *do allow for settlement*. Davies statement that 'were the rule simply to be that migrants had the same rights to bring their family as nationals do under national law, migrants would of course be much worse off—because their starting point is different' seems to overstate the case somewhat. Admittedly this would often have been the case initially when non-working spouses of the same Member State nationality as the worker did not have independent rights of residence dependent on means (which could be provided by the worker), and principles of mutual recognition would require admission of spouses admitted to one Member State.

as a conceptual tool to justify the imposition of any general obligation to permit settlement of cohabiting partners. It does not seem the most convincing way to deal with the situation, or the most likely to be adopted, if the ECJ considers the *outcome* (ie, securing residence rights for all partners) to be within the legitimate bounds of its judicial and constitutional role. The main weakness is that the concept of discrimination is inherently uncertain and flexible. On one view the arguments seem convincing, but there is an obvious alternative analysis, which would readily permit the conclusion that settlement of a partner is indeed permitted subject to the entirely nationality-neutral requirement of marriage. This would leave same-sex couples as the principal beneficiaries of this approach, as they cannot at present marry in most Member States.

1.3 Dual Regulatory Burdens and the Concept of Mutual Recognition

A slightly different spin might be put on this kind of argument in relation to those who are already resident with their TCN partner in one Member State. It could be said that the individual whose unmarried partner has a residence permit in one Member State should, in principle, be able to transfer that legal residence status to another Member State.[36] To prevent him or her from doing so would be to subject the migrant EU citizen's right of residence to a dual regulatory burden, in relation to the important condition of 'de facto' family unity. Instead of simply complying with the immigration rules in one state, the migrant is disadvantaged in having to comply with a second set of immigration rules in order to exercise his or right of residence there together with a TCN partner. The approach suggested in *Akrich*[37] underlines this logic in relation to married partners (emphasising the obstacle to migration that faces the couple who *lose* their right to cohabit by moving to another Member State, thus focusing on the right to transfer legal residence of the TCN spouse to accompany the primary migrant) but it can certainly be extended beyond this.

1.3.1 The Origins of This Principle

The hostility of Community law to dual regulatory burdens leading to the logic of mutual recognition has its origins in the case law of the ECJ

However, it is difficult to see that the migrant begins from an entirely different position from the non-migrant host state national where admission is sought for a TCN spouse without residence rights anywhere in the EU directly from a third country.

[36] I deliberately leave aside the question of mutual recognition of marriages and registered partnerships—Introduction.

[37] Case C-109/01 *Akrich v SSHD.*

relating to free movement of goods, in the seminal *Cassis de Dijon* case.[38] Yet it has developed significantly since then, both in its judicial application in the field of free movement of goods and persons, and through legislation.[39]

1.3.2 Its Applicability to Partners' Residence Rights

The logical underpinnings of this approach seem more solid than the approach above focused simply on indirect nationality discrimination. However, the argument being made here is rather different from the classic case of mutual recognition of professional qualifications or health and safety, or other technical standards in the case of goods. It is less obvious here that there is some characteristic or professional qualification, certification or authorisation granted to an individual *Member State national*, business, trader, or goods, for which recognition is sought abroad. The authorisation to reside is granted to the TCN who at present has no general right to transfer it to another Member State. This would have to be linked to the primary migrant EU citizen. It is still not certain that it would succeed and there are some significant drawbacks.

Perhaps the clearest precedents in favour of applying such an approach to questions relating to the legal status of TCNs are *Rush Portuguesa*[40] and *Vander Elst*.[41] The applicants had been awarded construction contracts in France. The question then arose as to whether France could impose its own domestic legislation[42] requiring work permits on the TCN workers employed by the enterprises in the Member State where they were established. In both cases it was held that this would infringe the right to provide services. Since these cases, action has been taken to give legislative effect to this.[43] These cases show most clearly the concept of dual burdens and mutual recognition of work and/or residence permits obtained in one state being used to break down barriers to economic market access for those wishing to provide cross-border services, although they do also contain elements of an obstacles analysis. It could be argued that this is

[38] Case 120/78 *Rewe-Zentrale AG v Bundesmonopolverwaltung für Branntwein (Cassis de Dijon)* [1979] ECR 649. See the discussion in ch 5 .

[39] See generally K Armstrong, 'Mutual Recognition' in C Barnard and J Scott, *The Law of the Single European Market* (Hart Publishing, Oxford, 2002).

[40] Case C-113/89 *Rush Portuguesa v Office National d'Immigration* [1990] ECR I-1417.

[41] Case C-43/93 *Vander Elst v Office des Migrations Internationales* [1994] ECR I-3803.

[42] In *Vander Elst* the Moroccan workers had been given visas. However, it is generally taken that the principle in these cases would require the host state to grant visas under its immigration legislation as well as work permits.

[43] Amended Proposal for a European Parliament and Council Directive on the Posting of Workers who are Third Country Nationals for the Purposes of Cross-Border Service Provision COM(1999) 0003 [1999] OJ C67/12, revised by COM (2000) 271. See now the Commission's Proposal for a Directive of the European Parliament and of the Council on the Provision of Services in the Internal Market.

similar to the situation we are concerned with in which an individual wishes to transfer the legal residence of his or her TCN partner from one Member State to another. There are, however, three questions that remain.

1.3.3 *Acquiring Long-term Residence?*

The principle in *Vander Elst* has not yet explicitly been extended beyond the freedom to provide services to include the enterprise or individual wishing to post workers (even temporarily) as part of the exercise of the more settled and permanent freedom of establishment.[44] In any event, it is likely that only enterprises wishing to deploy staff on a temporary basis will benefit.[45] Using this general principle to establish a potentially permanent or at least open-ended right of residence for a cohabiting partner would certainly be a major extension of its current scope.

1.3.4 *Mutual Recognition of What?*

The concept is based on mutual recognition of an *existing relationship*. It is therefore confined to those who are already employed by the enterprise.[46] There is an obvious analogy in the context of partners' rights that a stable ongoing relationship would be necessary. This is of course not problematic, as my assumption is that the relationship in question already exists and has a degree of stability. The greater difficulty in contemplating the implications of these cases for our problem is this—what is it that would have to be recognised?

1. Is it merely the fact that the individuals live together as two lawful residents? Or is it only *residence specifically sought and granted in capacity as an unmarried partner* that could be transferred?
2. Is it only *permanent* residence status that could be transferred from one state to another—or could a temporary lawful residence permit suffice?

1.3.5 *Beyond the Boundaries of the EU?*

The final question is how far this idea can stretch beyond the boundaries of the EU. *Vander Elst* and much of the mutual recognition case law

[44] Could the enterprise post the TCN worker, even temporarily, to a permanent establishment in another Member State rather than just to complete one specific contract?
[45] The judgments in *Vander Elst* (n 41) and *Rush Portuguesa* (n 40) both emphasise that the workers being posted are not seeking to join the regular labour market of the host state.
[46] For criticisms of this, see S Peers, 'Indirect Rights for Third Country National Service Providers Confirmed' (1995) 20 *ELRev* 303.

concerns mobility from one Member State to another.[47] The problems of recognition of residence outside the EU would be far greater, and could mean that those who have lived together *outside* the EU could be excluded.

1.3.6 *Towards a Legislative Solution Based on Mutual Recognition?*

Legislative strategies have always played an important part in ensuring the operation of the mutual recognition principle. Here, as in other areas, a legislative strategy might be more likely to succeed than any individual challenge through court action, and would be necessary for the long-term success of this approach. For the reasons we have seen above, however, even a legislative strategy explicitly based on the concept of mutual recognition of residence rights of TCN partners has its drawbacks in that political agreement might be difficult to reach.[48]

A legislative approach that is more likely to succeed is a more general strategy to include lawfully resident TCNs within the scope of guarantees of free movement contained in the Treaty, allowing them to follow their partners around the EU. TCNs have in practice been excluded from the concept of 'workers of the Member States'[49] and the consequent guarantees of free movement, equal treatment, and now the ability to strike down non-discriminatory obstacles to the fundamental freedoms.[50] The introduction of EU citizenship in the Maastricht Treaty only served to highlight and exacerbate this problem. It extended (initially symbolically, and increasingly now actually) the rights of Member State nationals while doing nothing for the many long-term resident TCNs, except to introduce the language of citizenship which is potentially as exclusionary of 'outsiders' as it is inclusionary, identity-building, and equalising in relation to 'insiders'. Progress in addressing this issue has been made since then, but slowly.

There is a Proposal[51] that deals with the ability of TCNs to move freely around the EU on a short-term basis (less than three months). This

[47] There is emerging case law on recognition of qualifications obtained by Member State nationals in third countries, although these are dealt with in a different way, and less generously, than qualifications obtained in a Member State. On this generally see Armstrong (n 39) and C Barnard, *The Substantive Law of the EU: The Four Freedoms* (OUP, Oxford, 2004).

[48] Note the difficulties that arose with the interaction of the the Family Reunification Directive and the Long Term Residents Directive, and the compromise that although a LTR can normally take family members who have been admnitted to the first state with them to the second state of residence this does not apply to unmarried partners who must wait for their own autonomous LTR status to *guarantee* a right to move to the second state. See ch 2.

[49] Case 238/83 *Meade* [1984] ECR 2631. See H Staples *The Legal Status of Third Country Nationals in the European Union* (Kluwer, The Hague, 1999) 35 and E Guild (n 19) 22–3.

[50] Case C-230/97 *Criminal Proceedings against Awoyemi* [1998] ECR I-6781.

[51] Proposal for a Council Directive relating to the Conditions in which Third Country Nationals shall have the Freedom to Travel in the Territory of Member Sates for a Period Not Exceeding Three Months COM (2001) 388 [2001] OJ C270/244.

however does not assist in the consideration of our problem, as the question being addressed is residence rather than short-term travel. The suggestion that TCNs should be able to transfer established permanent residence from one Member State to another is a different matter, and if anything perhaps more difficult for Member States to accept.

Despite this sensitivity, a Proposal to regulate the rights of long term-resident TCNs[52] was published in 2001 and finally agreed in 2003.[53] It provides[54] a 'long term resident' (LTR) status for TCNs after five years. It also, and crucially for these purposes of this discussion, provides for a right of residence for periods over three months in another Member State, subject to means or economic activity.[55] Thus once the LTR status is acquired, the individual would be enabled easily to transfer his/her residence to follow his/her EU citizen partner. This would clearly be a significant and welcome step forward. It would provide a practical solution to the difficulties faced by some couples, and in some respects would be of greater benefit to the individual TCN than one based purely on the partnership. The partner would, from the beginning, be protected in his or her own right rather than being dependent on the relationship until autonomous residence status was obtained (whether under national law or Community law), and the enactment of the new Directive is a welcome step in the right direction. However, it is by no means a comprehensive or adequate solution. It would as currently drafted only apply to those TCNs who have been resident in a Member State for five years, and would not assist those EU citizens resident with their partners outside the EU.

1.3.7 Conclusion

The concept of mutual recognition and presumptive prohibition of dual regulation seems a somewhat more convincing approach than simple indirect discrimination to justify intervention and the imposition of a general obligation to permit settlement of partners who are already resident elsewhere in the EU. The legitimacy of such an approach also seems relatively secure in principle. However, certain problems remain, and any resulting solution is likely to be limited. The practical difficulties facing migrant bi-national couples will be mitigated by the Directive on long-term resident TCNs, but it is far from a comprehensive solution.

[52] Proposal for a Council Directive concerning the Status of Third Country Nationals who are Long Term Residents COM(2001) 127 [2001] OJ C240/79.
[53] Council Directive 2003/109/EC of 25 November 2003 Concerning the Status of Third Country Nationals who are Long Term Residents [2004] OJ L16/44.
[54] Art 5(1).
[55] Art 16.

PART TWO — THE GENERAL PRINCIPLE OF EQUAL TREATMENT IN EC LAW

Introduction

The principle of equal treatment in EC law however, is of wider application than simply to discrimination on the grounds of (Member State) nationality. The concept also appears in much more abstract and general terms, asserting that similar situations, and similarly situated individuals, must be treated equally. Section 1 will examine the origins of this principle, and section 2 will examine its current scope and application to questions of sexual orientation and family status, primarily with reference to the case of *D & Sweden v Council*.[56]

2.1 Legislative Origins and Judicial Development

2.1.1 *Treaty Articles and Secondary Legislation*

As well as the prohibition of discrimination on the grounds of nationality, the Treaty began with Article 119 (now 141) EEC ensuring that men and women receive equal pay, and contained the principle that the Common Agricultural Policy should 'exclude any discrimination between producers and consumers within the Community' (Article 40 now 34 EC). The Community legislature and ECJ have developed these basic Treaty Articles, elaborating the meaning of discrimination and equal treatment in these three particular contexts.[57]

2.1.2 *Judicial Development*

In the 1990s, there has been much academic discussion concerning the extent to which the principle of equal treatment of equal situations has managed to free itself of the particular situations (commercial and agricultural policy, nationality and sex discrimination) in which it has been most visible and most often found. It has certainly been accepted that these instances are but specific examples of the general principle that comparable situations must be treated equally.[58] However, this kind of

[56] Cases C-122 and 125/99P *D & Sweden v Council* [2001] ECR I-4319.
[57] See A Dashwood and S O'Leary (eds), *The Principle of Equal Treatment in EC Law* (Sweet & Maxwell, London, 1997); G More 'The Principle of Equal Treatment—From Market Unifier to Fundamental Right' in P Craig and G de Búrca (eds), *The Evolution of EU Law* (OUP, Oxford, 1999) and T Tridimas, *The General Principles of EC Law* (OUP, Oxford, 1999).
[58] The Court has confirmed that the specific instances of discrimination discussed above are examples of a general principle of equal treatment of equal situations. See eg Case C-292/97

general statement still leaves considerable uncertainty. Prohibited grounds of discrimination and questions of comparability of different situations are highly contested political questions, and they remain unresolved by such general sweeping statements. The question of the application of the principle of equal treatment to different forms of family life, registered partnerships and different relationships remains.

Two leading cases that are often cited are *P v S*,[59] and *Grant v Southwest Trains*.[60] These are often presented as representing different approaches, *P v S* being hailed as the possible beginnings of a 'new constitutional approach' to equal treatment, *Grant* often criticised both for its approach to sex discrimination, and for failing to live up to the 'new constitutional approach' to equality and to sex discrimination in particular said to be implicit in *P v S*.[61] It is true that *P v S* and *Grant* both contain indications from which general statements about the place of the principle of equal treatment in Community law may be derived.[62] It is however crucial to the understanding of these cases, and their significance, to appreciate the background against which they were decided and the *particular* questions that were being addressed.

The crucial point is that, although admittedly some comments are made in terms that are of broader application, *both cases are primarily if not exclusively about sex discrimination*. *P v S* involved the case of a transsexual claiming protection from dismissal on the grounds of sex, pursuant to Article 5(1) of Directive 76/207.[63] This claim succeded. *Grant* involved the equal pay claim under Article 141 EC and Directive 75/117[64] of an employee of Southwest Trains for a free travel pass for her same-sex partner. This claim failed. It will be immediately obvious that the fundamental question posed in these cases is one of the scope and reach of

Karlsson, and Case C-442/00 *Rodriguez Caballero*. Case T-160/97 *Gevaert v Commission* and Case T-224/97 *Martínez de Peral Cagigal v Commission* repeat this in the context of staff cases. Cases concerning discrimination against free movers suggest that the guarantee of equal treatment inherent in EU citizenship extends beyond even indirect nationality discrimination to prohibit discrimination on the grounds of migration—see *D'Hoop* (n 3).

[59] Case C-13/94 *P v S & Cornwall CC* [1996] ECR I-2143.

[60] Case C-249/96 *Grant v Southwest Trains* [1998] ECR I-0621.

[61] C Barnard, '*P v S* – Kite Flying or a New Constitutional Approach?' in A Dashwood and S O'Leary (n 57); A Koppelman,'The Miscegenation Analogy in Europe, or, Lisa Grant Meets Adolf Hitler' in R Wintemute and M Andenas (eds), *Legal Recognition of Same-sex Partnerships* (Hart Publishing, Oxford, 2001); N Bamforth, 'Sexual Orientation After *Grant v Southwest Trains*' (2000) 63 *MLR* 694.

[62] *Grant* (n 60) para 35; *P v S* (n 59) paras 18–21.

[63] Council Directive 76/207 EEC of 9 February 1976 on the Implementation of the Principle of Equal Treatment for Men and Women as Regards Access to Employment,Vocational Training and Promotion, and Working Conditions [1976] OJ L39/40.

[64] Council Directive 75/117 EEC of 10 February 1975 on the Approximation of the Laws of the Member States Relating to the Application of the Principle of Equal Pay for Men and Women.

Community sex discrimination law. This is made clear from the Opinion of AG Elmer in *Grant*, who notes that:

> The questions referred to the Court must therefore be answered on the basis of Article 119 of the Treaty alone. Since the above Directives supplement and develop the basic principle of equal treatment contained in Article 119 of the Treaty, the Court's caselaw concerning those directives is nevertheless of great importance in this case.[65]

Whatever comments might have been made about general principles of equal treatment in Community law were therefore not necessary for the case to be decided, and must therefore be seen as, at best tangential, if not wholly irrelevant to the outcome of the case.

Approaching this from a different angle, it is instructive to ask whether a general principle of equal treatment of equal situations in EC law applicable to transsexuals or homosexuals would or could have assisted P, or Lisa Grant. The answer has to be that this is unlikely, *unless this could have been used as an argument in favour of a particular interpretation of sex discrimination.*[66] Such a principle could no doubt assist a Community staff official, an individual with some other complaint directly addressed against a Community institution, an individual seeking to assert a right to equal treatment against a Member State implementing or acting within the scope of Community law. It could also be used to challenge (as I will suggest below) a provision of Community law that discriminates against same-sex couples. But this is far from giving a directly effective right to challenge transgender or sexual orientation discrimination by Southwest Trains or Cornwall County Council as employers, if these cannot also and simultaneously be regarded as discrimination on the grounds of sex. The most recent case of *D & Sweden*[67] is entirely different. A general principle of equal treatment would and could in that case have resulted in the applicant asserting a direct right to the benefit that he had been denied. The existence, scope and application to same-sex couples and registered partnerships of any general independent, freestanding Community law obligation of equal treatment therefore assumes far more central importance in *D v Sweden* than it could ever have had in *P v S* or *Grant*.

[65] Para 12.

[66] There is of course an argument to that effect, in that the comparison between a male and female both involved in same-sex relationships changes not only the sex of the applicant but *also* the sex of the partner. See R Wintemute, 'Recognising New Kinds of Direct Sex Discrimination: Transsexualism, Sexual Orientation and Dress Codes' (1997) 60 *MLR* 334; A Koppelman, (n 61), although it is not universally accepted. See in particular the judicial consideration of the question in *Grant v Southwest Trains* (n 60) and *MacDonald v Ministry of Defence* [2003] UKHL 34, [2004] 1 All ER 339 and amongst others cited by Koppelman, eg J Gardner, 'On the grounds of her sex(uality)' (1998) 18 *OJLS* 167.

[67] Above (n 56).

2.1.3 Further Legislative Development

Subsequently, changes were made in the Treaty of Amsterdam. The principle of equality between men and women was given a somewhat higher profile, as it was inserted into Article 2 EC as a task of the Community. The EC Treaty now also confers competence on the Community through Article 13 EC to enact measures to combat discrimination within the scope of application of Community law on a number of other grounds[68] including sexual orientation. This competence has now been exercised in two Directives:[69] one to combat discrimination on the grounds of racial or ethnic origin across a wide range of situations,[70] the other designed specifically to combat discrimination in employment (thus not relevant to immigration law) but on a wide range of grounds, including sexual orientation.[71]

2.1.4 The Charter of Fundamental Rights

The Charter of Fundamental Rights reinforces the place of equality as a fundamental value of EC law and also lends significant support to its application to combat discrimination on the grounds of sexual orientation. It declares that:

> Any discrimination based on any ground such as sex, race, colour, ethnic or social origin, genetic features, language, religion or belief, political or any other opinion, membership of a national minority, property, birth, disability, age or sexual orientation shall be prohibited.

It is worth recalling at this stage two points about the Charter that have been made previously in chapter 3. It is not (yet) legally binding, but AGs and the CFI have begun to make reference to it. It applies to the Institutions of the Union and to Member States when they are implementing Union law, but it does not create any new power or task for the Community or Union.

[68] K Hailbronner, *Immigration and Asylum Law and Policy of the European Union* (Kluwer, The Hague, 2001) 193 suggests that this provision would not provide a legal basis to enact residence rights for non-marital partners. I consider that this is possible in relation to same-sex couples—but the question is academic. The Treaty confers competence through the other Treaty Articles to ensure free movement of persons and now in Title IV Art 63(3) EC to enact legislation conferring residence rights on TCNs, either as family members of EU citizens or lawfully resident TCNs. The question is not the existence of competence but whether and how to exercise it. It is also to be noted that the procedure under Art 13 is different from that under Art 18 EC, requiring unanimity.

[69] On the development of Art 13 EC at Amsterdam and its subsequent use, see M Bell *Anti-Discrimination Law and the European Union* (OUP, Oxford, 2002).

[70] Council Directive 2000/43 of 29 June 2000 Implementing the Principle of Equal Treatment between Persons Irrespective of Racial or Ethnic Origin [2000] OJ L180/22.

[71] Council Directive 2000/78 of 27 November 2000 Establishing a General Framework for Equal Treatment in Employment and Occupation [2000] OJ L303/16.

2.2 Application to Sexual Orientation and Family Status

As we have seen, the crucial question is the extent to which the ECJ has developed the concept that like should be treated alike into a generally applicable *legally binding* principle of Community law that could be used to suggest, for example, the following:

1 That married and unmarried couples should be treated equally.
2 That registered partnerships are entitled to treatment equal to that accorded to married couples.
3 That homosexual individuals or same-sex partnerships are entitled to treatment equal to that accorded to heterosexual individuals or opposite-sex partnerships.

The case of *D & Sweden v Council* is central to these questions and will be the focus of my discussion.

2.2.1 D & Sweden — *Introductory Remarks*

D, a staff official of the Council, applied for 'household allowance'[72] on the basis of his registered partnership with his (male) partner under Swedish law. He was denied the benefit on the basis that he had to be treated as a single unmarried man and thus not entitled to the allowance. He challenged this refusal, and the case was heard by the CFI. The decision in this case will have fundamental implications in relation to the inquiry that is central to this book, both in relation to the attempt to include registered partnerships within the meaning of the word 'spouse' in Community law, and in relation to the application of the general principle of equal treatment.

2.2.2 CFI Judgment

The CFI rejected the contention that a party to a registered partnership, ought *either* to be seen as 'married' within the meaning of this Regulation, *or* at least to be entitled to treatment equal to that granted to a married official.[73] It considered various submissions on behalf of the applicant,

[72] The Staff Regulations of Officials and Conditions of Employment of Other Servants of the European Communities (now amended by Regulation 781/98 [1998] OJ L113/4) provides in Art 1(2) of Annexe VII that the following are entitled to a family allowance:
A married official.
An official who is widowed, divorced, legally separated, or single, who has one or more dependent children as provided in Art 2(2) and (3).
By special and reasoned decision of the 'authority invested with power of nomination,' taken on the basis of supporting documentation/documentary proof, who, although not meeting the criteria in (a) and (b) above, nevertheless has assumed family responsibilities.
[73] Case T-264/97 *D & Sweden v Council*. G Scappuci, 'Court of First Instance Refused to Recognise Swedish Registered Partnership Rights and Duties' (2000) *EPL* 355.

including allegations of the violation of the principle of equal treatment,[74] a breach the principle of the *'unicité'* (integrity) of civil status, a manifest error of assessment[75] of Article 8 ECHR,[76] and a breach of Article 119 EC (now Article 141), guaranteeing equal pay for men and women. All these were rejected, including the arguments that the Council was obliged *in its capacity as employer* to treat a registered partnership in the same way as a marriage. An appeal was lodged against this decision and the case proceeded to the ECJ.

2.2.3 *ECJ Judgment*

The ECJ's judgment confirmed the AG's rejection of the appeal. The ECJ joined the AG in concluding that the term 'spouse' could not be interpreted to include the applicant's partner, as the term referred to a married couple. The judgment differs from the AG in its analysis of discrimination. It clearly points out[77] that it is not the sex of the partner or sexual orientation of the couple that is the cause of the refusal of the family allowance and the alleged discrimination, but 'the legal nature of the ties between the official and the partner,' whereas AG Mischo focuses on the question of sexual orientation discrimination, using *Grant*[78] to reject this claim. Having pointed out the nature of the distinction that is being made, the next step in the ECJ's analysis is consideration of the question of whether this distinction, *between couples registered in different ways*, ie *the legal nature of the ties between the official and the partner*, infringes the Community law principle of equal treatment.[79] It makes three points:

1. In considering this point it 'cannot disregard' the view prevailing in the Community as a whole.
2. There is a 'great diversity' of laws and an 'absence of general assimilation' of marriage and other forms of statutory partnership.
3. In such circumstances 'it cannot be held' that the Swedish registered partners are comparable, for the purposes of applying the Staff Regulations, to a married couple.

Given the clear conclusion reached by the ECJ in relation to one of the strongest cases—the Swedish/Nordic model of registered partnership,

[74] Paras 22–34.
[75] Paras 35–7.
[76] Paras 38–41.
[77] Para 47.
[78] Above (n 60).
[79] It is therefore slightly odd to see the same-sex nature of the couple repeated in paras 48 and 50. The ECJ as well as the AG seem to assume that registered partnerships are exclusively for same-sex couples.

containing a presumption of equality with marriage in the domestic legislation, the question of whether other kinds of registered partnership can claim equal treatment with marriage is also clearly settled in the negative. Four particular points may be made to highlight the difficulties with this judgment.[80]

2.2.4 *Analysis 1 — What Kind of Discrimination?*

As we have seen, the ECJ and the AG take different views of the kind of discrimination involved—reaching different conclusions as to whether the case involves discrimination on the grounds of sexual orientation or on the basis of the legal nature of the partnership. In fact, both are correct. It is disingenuous to claim that it is not the sex of D's partner or his sexual orientation that is relevant. If D had been heterosexual and his partner female he would not have been allowed to enter a registered partnership but would have married instead. The ECJ is therefore wrong to dismiss this claim.[81] However, the AG's claim that this case is one of sexual orientation discrimination alone seems equally flawed. As well as distinguishing couples on the basis of sexual orientation the approach of the Council also, and perhaps primarily, distinguishes between different legal forms of partnership. There is also a more practical difficulty. AG Mishco assumes that all registered partnerships are of same-sex couples (and also that all marriages are between men and women). This is true of the Swedish registered partnerships, but has been seen in chapter 1, it is not universally the case. Given that registered partnerships are not exclusively same-sex, and that now marriage is no longer exclusively opposite-sex, his approach is overly simplistic and narrow.

2.2.5 *Analysis 2 — Comparability of Marriage and Registered Partnerships*

The ECJ rejects the comparability of the different kinds of partnership with marriage despite the admission[82] that under Swedish law, and other legal systems, there are close similarities between registered partnerships and marriage. It is conceded that some registered partnerships have effects the same as or comparable to those of marriage.[83] It is also noted

[80] For a less critical commentary see the note by E Ellis (2002) 39(1) *CMLRev* 151.
[81] Perhaps the reason for the ECJ's rejection of this analysis is not too difficult to discern. Given the precarious and unconvincing nature of the AG's rejection of any prohibition on sexual orientation discrimination, particularly in the light of the equality provision of the Charter of Fundamental Rights, the ECJ might have been seeking a way to dismiss the case without having to address sexual orientation discrimination—which might well have made it rather more difficult to dismiss the case.
[82] Para 33.
[83] Para 35.

that (in the submission of the Council) although registered partnerships do not exist in all countries, where they do they are 'regarded as equivalent *only as regards its effects and subject to exceptions*' (my emphasis).[84] It is indeed difficult to see how this assists the Council. It is self-evident that the registered partnership is not formally a marriage. To deny the possibly equal treatment of the two institutions on that basis alone is an overly formal and narrow understanding of the nature of the principle of equal treatment. Once this is accepted, the similarities between registered partnerships and marriages cannot be dismissed so lightly. It is difficult to imagine what other kind of similarity the Council is expecting to encounter before conceding the principle of equal treatment would apply, other than an *exact* correspondence of legal consequences or even recognition of same-sex marriage. The approach to equality taken by the Council and endorsed by the ECJ is disturbingly formalistic, ignoring the substantive similarities in the legal effects and social function of these two institutions. This attitude seems to flow from a wish (perhaps understandable) to come to a single solution to deal with all registered partnerships.

The only other point made by the Council that might carry any weight is that the similarities with marriage in legal effect are 'subject to exceptions'. This is indeed something that might rightly lead to the conclusion that the situations should not be treated equally. But these 'exceptions' are not specified. The Council merely asserts that exceptions exist without examining them in detail or addressing the important question of whether they are significant enough and sufficiently strongly related to the *purpose for which recognition is sought* to justify a difference in treatment. We have seen already the limited nature of the exceptions to the basic principle that the Nordic registered partnerships are equal to marriage. There is nothing in the Swedish law to sustain the suggestion that for the purposes of a household allowance, the two are not comparable. Again, however, given the inherent weaknesses of this line of reasoning it is perhaps unsurprising that the ECJ contents itself with generalities, referring also to the position in other Member States, rather than exploring in any detail the clear and obvious functional comparability of the two institutions in Swedish law.

2.2.6 *Analysis 3 — One Solution or Several?*

One of the concerns that underlies this judgment seems to be a leaning towards a single solution that can be applied to all registered partnerships. Given what we have seen earlier in chapter 1 regarding the variety of legislation in the Member States, is this wise? Of the two basic models of partnership available (strong, 'marriage-like' for same-sex couples and

[84] Para 31.

weaker 'marriage-lite', often for all couples) the claim to equal treatment is much stronger in the first instance. Should an arrangement like the French PACS, German Life Partnership or Belgian statutory cohabitation, which dilute the rights and obligations of marriage in some significant ways and are clearly functionally and substantively distinct from marriage, be entitled to equal treatment? This surely depends on the context in which the claim arises, and a general answer asserting an obligation of equal treatment in all circumstances is arguably not warranted.[85] However, the ECJ uses this argument to deny what should be a clear and compelling case for equal treatment of a partnership that *is* clearly functionally and substantively close enough to marriage to merit equal treatment. This calls into question the approach of the ECJ seeking a single solution regarding equal treatment for all registered partnerships. Although this may be a laudable and attractive aim, it seems that the current diversity of legislation renders it unattainable. In this case the success of one group (the 'strong' Nordic partnerships) may have to come at the expense of another (those 'weaker' registered partnerships lacking a fundamental starting point of comparability to marriage). Given the choice between an approach which accepts equal treatment for some and one that accepts equal treatment for none, the approach accepting equal treatment for some is clearly more advantageous. But it is also more logically compelling and consistent with the basic principle that civil status is primarily an issue for national law and thus comparability should also be decided with reference to national law.

2.2.7 *Analysis 4 — A Critique of the Constitutional Legitimacy of the Court's Approach*

The ECJ's approach can also be criticised from the point of view of constitutional legitimacy.[86] The question of equality is of course one of Comunity law, but the nature of D's civil status as a registered partner can only be determined by reference to Swedish law. In paragraphs 49–51 however the ECJ looks far more widely throughout the Community. It notes that there is a great diversity of laws and *because of this* it cannot accept that the partnership is comparable to marriage. In doing so, it deprives the individuals in Swedish and other similar registered partnerships of the protection and the clear comparability with marriage that the legislators clearly intended to confer on them. Given that the issue of civil status is primarily for the Member States, and given the strong concept of

[85] I would, however, argue that if what is at stake is the immigration rights of the couple the two should be treated as comparable. All of these partnerships indicate and recognise a wish to live a common life to some degree. Immigration rights if the couple are to travel to another Member State are a necessary part of this.

[86] See E Caracciolo di Torella and E Reid, 'The Changing Shape of the European Family and Fundamental Rights' (2002) 27 *ELRev* 80.

comparability contained in the Swedish registered partnership law, this is disappointing.

2.2.8 *Can the Judgment be Distinguished?*

The only possible comfort to others in similar situations is that the judgment does suggest that the denial of equal treatment *might* be confined to the situation of a staff official seeking a family benefit for the purposes of the Staff Regulations.[87] It does not explicitly make a *general and universal ruling* that for all purposes and in all circumstances Community law will not require registered partners to be treated in the same way as married couples. But this is little comfort indeed. Unless there is a significant change in the attitude of the ECJ, this precedent will pose a serious difficulty to any other couple in a registered partnership seeking to suggest on the basis of Community law that it should be *treated as* equivalent to marriage. It is also perhaps significant that it was not in fact a Member State that was defending the case, and it was a Community Regulation dealing with thc situation of Community staff that was challenged. Thus, the same difficulties of the proper respect for the autonomy of Member States over family law and relationships and the way these are recognised and regulated by its domestic law arguably do not arise. Where the administrative action or legislation of a Member State, or for example the terms of a Community Regulation which requires a Member State to admit a partner are in question, these issues would come more sharply into focus. If the ECJ is unwilling to force the *Community institutions* to recognise the equivalence of marriages and registered partnerships in its dealings with its own staff, it seems that much less likely to do so when the autonomy of a *Member State* over its family law or concepts of partnerships and civil status is perceived to be threatened in a more direct way.

Another possibility is that the ECJ might recognise at some stage in the future that the legal position in national law throughout the Member State had developed in such a way as to enable it to conclude that the registered partnership ought to be treated in the same way as marriage. The judgment does seem to be inherently time-limited, speaking of the views prevailing as a whole in the Member States, implicitly at the present time. Nevertheless, the prospects of this happening are slim. The ECJ implicitly envisages a significant degree of convergence between the laws of the Member States before it would accept the equivalence of marriage and registered partnerships. An instructive comparison may be its acceptance (first in *P v S* and more clearly now following in *KB*[88] following the ECtHR lead in *Goodwin v UK*)[89] that there is a significant consensus on

[87] Para 51.
[88] Case C-117/01 *KB v NHS Pensions Agency*.
[89] *Goodwin v UK* Application 28957/95 (2002) 35 EHRR 18.

permitting transsexuals to marry in their assumed gender. Only two states did not, and will now have to change their laws to comply with the ECtHR ruling. The survey in chapter 1 has shown the diversity of national laws, and this seems unlikely to change in the near future. Of particular note has to be the effect of the accession of the new Member States in 2004, which will 'dilute' what consensus there currently is on non-marital and same-sex registered partnerships. In any event, if this degree of convergence did ever occur, the matter would be far more easily settled by Community legislation agreed by all.

Finally, the question of sexual orientation discrimination might be of some assistance. As I have indicated above this is a convincing analysis and might be of some use in suggesting a different outcome in future cases concerning registered partners, particularly in the light of the clear provisions in the EU Charter. I shall address this in section 2.2.10 below. However, the problematic nature of a direct reversal and overturning of the ECJ's clear conclusion that the case did not involve discrimination on the grounds of sexual orientation (rather than a clear acceptance that it did but that such discrimination was not unlawful) should not be underestimated.[90] And although it might assist all same-sex couples where they cannot marry, and might assist those who do enter into marriages or registered partnerships (and as we have seen, perhaps only some of these), it would not necessarily help all couples and provides a less than comprehensive solution.

2.2.9 *The Implications of the Judgment in* D & Sweden *for Unmarried Cohabitants*

The position of the prohibition of sexual orientation discrimination as a legally binding principle of Community law remains unclear. If the ruling is to be taken as a precedent for the future attitude of the ECJ, same-sex cohabiting couples cannot claim with any confidence that their relationships are to be granted treatment equal to that of similar opposite-sex couples. AG Mischo, drawing on *Grant* directly rejects the suggestion, and the ECJ is scarcely more positive on the matter. Mark Bell is rather more positive about this part of the ECJ's reasoning, implying that it recognised the concept of discrimination on the grounds of sexual orientation,[91] even if its application to same-sex couples remains unclear. I am not convinced

[90] The ECJ does sometimes depart or overturn previous judgments—eg Cases C-267 and 268/91 *Criminal Proceedings against Keck & Mithouard* [1993] ECR I-6097, and the *Café Hag* cases (I) and (II)—Case 192/73 *Van Zuylen Freres SA v HAG AG* [1974] ECR 731 and Case 10/89 *Cnl-Sucal NV SA v Hag GF AG* [1990] ECR I-3711. But these occasions are indeed rare.

[91] Bell (n 69) 22, 'While the Court of Justice has recently recognised the principle of equal treatment irrespective of sexual orientation [reference to *D & Sweden*] its application to discrimination against same-sex partnerships remains controversial.'

by this. I have no doubt that the principle should be recognised, and the recent ECtHR jurisprudence[92] and the equality provisions in the EU Charter provide all the political legitimacy that might be required for the ECJ to develop its general principle of equality in this way with confidence (see further 2.2.10 below). But is Bell right that it has done so in *D & Sweden*, simply remaining unconvinced about the question of partnerships? The particular passage in the judgment (paragraph 47) does indeed mention discrimination on the grounds of sexual orientation, but seems merely to be an acknowledgment of the argument made. It does not explicitly or implicitly confirm that it forms any part of Community law, merely rejects its application in the particular case. This could be seen as an implicit acceptance that, if it was a case of sexual orientation discrimination, this would assist the applicants. However, this seems an overly optimistic reading of what is in my view a deeply ambiguous statement, and I remain unconvinced by Bell's suggestion that the ECJ has finally accepted that this principle is part of Community law. [93] In any event even if such a principle is recognised, as Bell notes the application to same-sex partnerships may not be recognised immediately, and the question of reserving rights for married couples remains contentious.[94]

As to unmarried and unregistered opposite-sex couples, there are no specific implications, as the case deals exclusively with the situation of those who (a) have registered their partnership and (b) according to the AG, all same-sex couples.

2.2.10 Postscript — Sexual Orientation Discrmination, the ECHR, and the Charter of Fundamental Rights

As indicated above, perhaps the most attractive argument would be to suggest that, in the light of the Court of Human Rights rulings in *Da Silva Mouta*[95] and *Karner*,[96] and the Charter of Fundamental Rights, discrimination on the grounds of sexual orientation in the enjoyment of Community law rights must now be regarded as contrary to Community law. The most recent judicial pronouncement on this question is somewhat ambiguous—AG Ruiz-Jarabo Colomer in *KB*[97] suggesting that it is inevitable that Community law will develop in the direction of some recognition of functional 'de facto' family life. Nonetheless, alongside this he expresses doubt

[92] Discussed in ch 3 above.
[93] If indeed this is what he means, it may be that I am reading too much into his statement.
[94] It is notable that in the Framework Equality Directive (n 71), the first to mention sexual orientation discrimination, the Recital 22 (although not the text of the Directive iteslf) states that it is 'without prejudice to national laws on marital status and the benefits dependent thereon.'
[95] *Da Silva Mouta v Portugal* Application 33290/96 (2001) 312 EHRR 47.
[96] *Karner v Austria* Application 40016/98.
[97] *KB* (n 88) para 63.

about whether the time is right for that development, and considers that it is ultimately unnecessary to decide the matter for the resolution of the case at hand. The ECJ also declines to proceed along that direction, confining its remarks to the particular situation in question, that of a transsexual unable to contract a valid marriage in breach of the ECHR consequent upon the ruling in *Goodwin v UK*. It would be welcome for the ECJ to proceed along these lines and to reconsider its previous attitude to these questions. Indeed it will become increasingly necessary to do so if potentially embarrassing conflicts with the ECHR are to be avoided in the light of *Karner v Austria*. This might well prove helpful for those couples encountering discrimination between unmarried same-sex and opposite-sex cohabitants, particularly in the implementation of the new Directive. However, although the trend in the ECtHR case law gives some cause for optimism, several cautionary comments may be made. In particular, it is not yet clear whether preservation of particular benefits for married couples in comparison with all unmarried couples is sexual orienatation discrimination[98] and the status of registered partnership has not yet been considered in the ECtHR. It may therefore be expected that until these questions are resolved it may be, as McGlynn suggests, premature to expect the ECJ to provide more extensive protection than the ECtHR has already established.[99]

2.3 Conclusion

The approach taken in *D & Sweden* is flawed and unsustainable, and will only look more and more dated, inappropriate, and out of line with the diversity of Member States laws and practices, and with the requirements of the ECHR as interpreted by the jurisprudence of the ECtHR. It is certainly to be hoped that the approach in this case will quickly be left behind. However, the unwillingness of the legislative institutions to accept the consequences of the principle of non-discrimination on the grounds of sexual orientation, and to assimilate registered partnerships to marriages in the drafting of recent immigration legislation,[100] is an indication that this attitude persists.

[98] There are comments in the *KB* case which suggest that this argument would be met with some secepticism: paras 28 & 29, denying that this should be sex discrimination and citing *D & Sweden*.
[99] C McGlynn, 'Challenging the European Harmonisation of Family Law: Perspectives on "the Family"' in K Boele-Woelki (ed), *Perspectives for the Unification and Harmonisation of Family Law in Europe* (Intersentia, Antwerp, 2003) and C McGlynn, 'Families and the Charter of Fundamental Rights: Progressive Change or Entrenching the Status Quo?' (2001) 26 *ELRev* 582.
[100] See ch 2.

CONCLUSIONS OF CHAPTER FIVE

The principle of equality is fundamental to Community law, but its practical application is problematic. It is arguable that indirect discrimination on the grounds of nationality or mutual recognition might assist, but these principles do have their limitations and seem less convincing and more difficult to sustain than the arguments based on non-discriminatory obstacles considered in chapter 6.

As to the application of the general principle of equal treatment to assert comparability between same-sex and opposite-sex couples, or between marriage and the strongest form of registered partnerships found in the Nordic countries, these arguments seem conceptually sound but are undoubtedly deeply contested in Community law at present. They will be difficult to sustain after the decision in *D & Sweden* unless there is a significant change of attitude in the ECJ. The Charter of Fundamental Rights, recent ECHR case law, and the more recent proliferation of registered partnerships in domestic law, might be seen to require a reconsideration of these issues in relation to same-sex couples and registered partners, but one may doubt whether the ECJ is currently willing to make the necessary political choices. It also seems to be seeking a single approach to equal treatment that can be applied to all registered partnerships—this is both unnecessary in the light of the diversity of different forms of partnership, and unhelpful in that it clouds the issues and prevents recognition of equality in the strongest and clearest cases. Moving beyond these arguments to assert that heterosexual cohabitants ought to be treated in the same way as married couples even for the limited purpose of immigration law also seems problematic.

6

A Non-discriminatory Obstacle?

INTRODUCTION

THIS CHAPTER DEALS with EC law relating to free movement—particularly relating to the free movement of workers and other persons—in order then to consider its application to 'marriage-only' immigration laws.[1]

It has been clear for a long time that the Treaty provisions on free movement[2] are capable of conferring directly effective rights on individuals. An administrative or legislative measure directly prohibiting entry to and residence of an EU citizen in another Member State is a violation of these provisions, and can be saved only by recourse to derogations expressly permitted by the Treaty.[3] A similar view would be taken of a measure which denies access to a particular job or profession purely on the grounds of nationality.[4] This can be saved only by recourse to Article 39(4) EC dealing with employment in the public service[5] or the similar (but perhaps slightly broader) exceptions dealing with the self-employed in Article 55 EC. The ECJ has extended the right to equal treatment from measures which discriminate expressly, to include also those which discriminate indirectly. Indirect discrimination is found where a measure subjects the individual to a requirement which, although applied to all, affects migrant workers or individuals from another Member State in an unequal way,[6] although such measures may be be justified by imperative reasons of public interest. It may, however, be that the measure applies the same rules to all Member State nationals, migrant or not, and cannot

[1] This chapter develops some ideas first presented in H Toner, 'Immigration Rights of Unmarried Partners as Obstacles to Free Movement under Community Law' (2001) 15 *IANL* 207 and see further, 'Non-discriminatory obstacles to the free movement of persons' *YEL* (forthcoming) which draws heavily on the materials and analysis in this chapter. I am grateful to Catherine Barnard for commenting on an early draft, and I have benefited greatly from having sight of some draft chapters of her forthcoming book on Substantive EU Law.

[2] Arts 28 (Goods), 39 (Workers), 43 (Establishment) and 49 (Services) of the EC Treaty.

[3] Case 41/74 *Van Duyn v Home Office* [1974] ECR 1337.

[4] Art 39(2) EC, Council Regulation 1612/68 of 15 October 1968 on the Freedom of Movement for Workers within the Community [1968/9] OJ Sp Ed (II) 475.

[5] N Beenen, *Citizenship and Access to Public Service Employment* (Europa Publishing, Groningen, 2001).

[6] On indirect nationality discrimination see Case C-237/94 *O'Flynn v Chief Adjudication Officer* [1996] ECR I-2617, discussed in ch 5.

truly be said to have a more burdensome, indirectly discriminatory effect on nationals of other Member States. As we have seen, the suggestion that 'marriage-only' family reunification policies discriminate in law or in fact on the basis of nationality against the migrant is, at the very least, problematic. An analysis based on obstacles or restrictions on the fundamental Treaty freedoms may well be more attractive. TCNs have been excluded from the benefit of these provisions and cannot rely on them directly themselves,[7] but it is certainly possible that they may be interpreted in such a way that the TCN might benefit from the right of residence if he or she is a close family member such as spouse, partner or child of a Community migrant exercising these rights. This chapter will address this suggestion and argue that this is a logical conclusion of the ECJ's current approach. The major implication of this analysis is that it may enable the individual to have more choice over the definition of the 'family member' entitled to accompany him/her to a new host state, and thus offers a potentially powerful tool with which to bypass the restrictive secondary legislation[8] or now an interpretative tool to point in favour of a broad interpretation of the obligation to 'facilitate' in the new Directive.

I shall first consider the general nature of 'obstacles', examining the development of this jurisprudence and its place in Community law generally. This is one of the more complex and obscure areas of Community law jurisprudence, and the reader should be aware of this at the outset. However, for present purposes this concept may be described as a measure which is incompatible with the Treaty freedoms (in the absence of objective justification) *otherwise than because of direct or indirect nationality discrimination*. Part 1 will outline the development of the concept in the case law relating to goods in Article 28 EC, as it is impossible to understand fully the development of the case law on the free movement of persons, establishment and services without this background. Parts 2 and 3 will examine the adoption and elaboration of the concept of a 'non-discriminatory obstacle' in the context of free movement of persons (including workers, establishment, and services). Part 4 will consider the possible implications of this approach for those EU citizens who are not economically active, pursuant to Article 18 EC, and Part 5 will consider the implications of this discussion to the question of immigration rights of partners.

PART ONE — THE FREE MOVEMENT OF GOODS

Article 28 EC provides that 'Quantitative restrictions on imports and measures having equivalent effect shall be prohibited between the

[7] Eg Case C-230/97 *Criminal Proceedings against Awoyemi* [1998] ECR I-6781.
[8] E Guild, 'Free Movement and Same-sex Relationships: Existing Law and Article 13 EC' in R Wintemute and M Andenas (eds), *Legal Recognition of Same-sex Partnerships* (Hart Publishing, Oxford, 2001) also suggests this approach.

Member States.' The ECJ's jurisprudence on this issue has a long history and has provoked much comment and discussion,[9] the crucial issue being the meaning of a 'measure having equivalent effect' to a quantitative restriction on imports.

1.1 *Dassonville* and *Cassis*

The classic definition of a 'measure having equivalent effect' is found in *Dassonville*:[10]

> All trading rules enacted by Member States which are capable of hindering, directly or indirectly, actually or potentially, intra-Community trade are to be considered as measures having equivalent effect to Quantitative Restrictions.[11]

If applied widely, this is clearly a very generous interpretation capable of applying to a wide range of trading rules. The ECJ first had occasion to consider situations involving directly discriminatory or distinctly applicable measures,[12] and made it clear that they were infringements of Article 28 EC that could only be saved by recourse to the provisions of the Treaty in Article 30 EC. It then addressed the issue of indirectly discriminatory or indistinctly applicable measures, which are applied to all goods but have an unequal effect on imported goods over domestically produced goods,[13] essentially by subjecting them to the burden of complying with regulation in two markets instead of just one. Rules of this nature typically include those relating to the content, packaging or labelling of a product. In the seminal *Cassis de Dijon* case[14] the ECJ ruled

[9] Recent discussions include S Weatherill, 'After *Keck*: Some Thoughts on How to Clarify the Clarification' (1996) 33 *CMLRev* 885; S Weatherill, 'Recent Caselaw Concerning the Free Movement of Goods' (1999) 36 *CMLRev* 51; P Oliver, 'Some Further Reflections on the Scope of Articles 28–10 EC' (1999) 36 *CMLRev* 783; J Weiler, 'Text and Context in the Free Movement of Goods' in P Craig and G De Búrca (eds), *The Evolution of EU Law* (OUP, Oxford, 1999); M Jarvis, *The Application of EC Law by National Courts: The Free Movement of Goods* (OUP, Oxford, 1998); J Snell, *Goods and Services in EC Law* (OUP, Oxford, 2002); C Barnard, 'Fitting the Remaining Pieces into the Goods and Services Jigsaw' (2001) 26 *ELRev* 35; N Nic Shiubhne, 'The Free Movement of Goods and Article 28 EC: An Evolving Framework' 27 (2002) *ELRev* 408.

[10] Case 8/74 *Procureur du Roi v Dassonville* [1974] ECR 837.

[11] Para 5. See also the previous Dir 70/50 [1970] OJ L3/29.

[12] The measure in *Dassonville* (n 10) itself was arguably of this nature, although the reasoning goes beyond this.

[13] Which it is assumed will primarily be made for the domestic market and therefore comply with the necessary technical standards.

[14] Case 120/78 *Rewe-Zentrale AG v Bundesmonopolverwaltung für Branntwein* [1979] ECR 649.

that such measures would be in breach of Article 28 EC unless justified by 'mandatory requirements of public interest,' invoking the principle of mutual recognition,[15] or as Weiler describes it 'functional parallelism.'[16] These two central cases, *Dassonville* and *Cassis* (in very simplistic terms) may be seen to typify different approaches to the regulation of the internal market.[17] *Dassonville* in its widest interpretation may be seen as an approach based on deregulation, intrinsically suspicious of national regulation and viewing this as a temporary measure pending Community harmonisation, whereas *Cassis* may be seen as an approach based on mutual recognition, accepting the intrinsic legitimacy of national regulation. The reasoning in *Cassis* and the kind of rule in question there are best seen as discrimination of a sort, albeit indirect, as they impose a *dual burden* on imports. The reasoning in *Dassonville,* however, without the explicit focus on recognition of products already lawfully sold abroad, is at least potentially wider. It offers the possibility, if given a robust interpretation, of applying Article 28 EC to all kinds of market regulation measures, even those which impose equal burdens on domestic and foreign goods merely by regulating the environment in which trading takes place.

In the late 1980s and early 1990s, the ECJ had to consider such 'equal burden' measures in the light of Article 28 EC. It was argued that discrimination in law or fact was not necessary, so long as the total volume of sales of imported goods might be affected by the measure. Measures prohibiting Sunday trading (*Torfaen*)[18] and regulating the distribution of videos for a period of time after their release at the cinema (*Cinéthèque*)[19] were challenged as 'measures having equivalent effect.' The ECJ held that such measures were capable of falling within the scope of Article 28 EC, and therefore that justification was required. This was a clear indication that a non-discriminatory barrier to market access through such regulatory rules was (presumptively) prohibited. The result of this was generally accepted to be both chaotic uncertainty and an unacceptable proliferation of opportunities for traders to challenge rules that had very little to do with cross border trade. A 'general right to trade' was being pursued through Article 28 EC, and it was argued by some that this was not a proper use of Community law. The ECJ and national courts also became engaged in adjudicating on the lawfulness of what were increasingly delicate social choices far removed from any intention to regulate,

[15] ie, that a product lawfully sold in one Member State may be sold elsewhere in the Community in the absence of imperative requirements of the public interest justifying the maintenance of the rule.

[16] Weiler (n 9).

[17] N Bernard, *Multilevel Governance in the European Union* (Kluwer, The Hague, 2002) ch 2.

[18] Case 145/88 *Torfaen BC v B&Q* [1989] ECR 3851.

[19] Cases C-60 and 61/84 *Cinéthèque* [1985] ECR 2605.

and any significant effect on, interstate trade, raising problematic questions of proportionality, illustrated by the Sunday trading cases.[20]

1.2 *Keck* and 'Selling Arrangements'

In *Keck*,[21] a case involving French regulations preventing retail resale at a loss, the ECJ consciously and deliberately changed course. It effectively narrowed the scope of application of Article 28 EC and 'exploded the idea that there might be a general right to trade that could be vindicated through Article 28.'[22] It drew a distinction between 'certain selling arrangements', and other measures, generally known as 'product rules'. It determined that the former, 'selling arrangements', were to be regarded as falling outside the scope of Article 28 EC if they apply to all traders operating in the territory and if they affect equally in law and in fact the marketing of domestic products and imported products.[23] This was because, according to the ECJ, such measures were 'not by their nature liable to affect interstate trade.'[24] Thus, if a rule was a selling arrangement rather than a product rule, the search was on again for discriminatory effect (unequal application in law or in fact) before a rule would be seen as an infringement of Article 28 EC. 'Product rules' however would continue to be governed by the principle in *Cassis* based on mutual recognition. The ECJ thus distanced itself from its previous view, but its solution was not without criticism. It has been suggested that *Keck* was overly formalistic, and that a test based more explicitly on market access should be adopted.[25] It should however also be noted that some writers question the utility of this alternative approach on the basis of its vagueness. In particular, it has been suggested that distinguishing between identifying barriers to market access and merely measuring an impact on the volume of sales could be problematic.[26]

[20] There were a number of cases in the UK and France in which justifications were canvassed, usually with success but not always. Eventually the question of justification was referred to the Court of Justice a second time and in Case C-169/91 *Stoke on Trent v B&Q* [1992] ECR 6635 the ECJ accepted that Sunday trading measures were justified. See the detailed discussion in Jarvis (n 9) 195-227.
[21] Cases C-267 and C-268/91 *Criminal Proceedings against Keck & Mithouard* [1993] ECR I-6097.
[22] Weatherill '*After Keck*' (n 9).
[23] Para 16.
[24] Para 17.
[25] Weatherill '*After Keck*' (n 9) and AG Jacobs, particularly in Case C-412/93 *Societe d'Importation Edouard Leclerc-Siplec v TF1 Publicité SA* [1995] ECR I-179, have been two of the most high profile advocates of this approach.
[26] P Craig and G de Búrca, *EU Law* (2nd edn, OUP, Oxford, 1998) 624–5. See further on this G Davies, *Nationality Discrimination and Free Movement Law* (PhD Thesis, Groningen, 2002), ch 6.3, 139ff. Published as *Nationality Discrimination in the European Internal Market* (Kluwer, The Hague, 2003).

1.3 The Emergence of a 'Market Access' Approach in ECJ Case Law?

Keck has been followed and applied 'with enthusiasm',[27] if at times (and particularly in more recent cases, perhaps indicating an increasing sophistication and refinement of the ECJ's approach) with a welcome degree of flexibility,[28] and a 'relatively light touch where it considers market access to be materially threatened.'[29] This flexibility has led to the emergence of academic literature more supportive of *Keck* as now applied, as the best compromise possible in the circumstances. One of the significant features of recent case law prompting this has been the ECJ moving some way towards the adoption of a 'market access' analysis. In particular, it had been observed that advertising restrictions or prohibitions might pose significant obstacles to market access even if they applied equally to all manufacturers.[30] The ECJ has recently shown itself willing to take note of these concerns and has recognised the potential and actual effects of restrictive advertising rules on cross-border market access—first leaving the question of unequal impact to the referring court in *De Agostini*,[31] and then deciding the question itself in *Gourmet International*.[32] *Gourmet* may be significant because of its suggestion[33] that entirely non-discriminatory measures precluding market access may be within the scope of Article 28 EC—even though on the facts it asserts that the national measure in question affects imported goods unequally in fact. *Heimdeinst*[34] (concerning a prohibition of selling groceries on rounds unless the trader had a permanent establishment in the same or a neighbouring municipality) is another case in which a market access analysis gains a foothold in the ECJ's reasoning. The ECJ there, however, still seems to indicate that where market access is not *precluded*, a greater impact on imported goods will be necessary before Article 28 EC bites on the national measure.[35] While it is true that market access is now a more significant part of the ECJ's analysis in these recent cases, it still follows

[27] Barnard (n 9) 42.

[28] Some have noted in particular that the Court is increasingly willing to find an unequal effect in fact, even if not in law, if the measure has a significant effect on access to the market of imported products (this analysis is particularly important in the area of advertising restrictions) particularly Oliver (n 9) and P Koutrakos, 'On Groceries, Alcohol and Olive Oil: More on Free Movement of Goods after *Keck*' (2001) 26 *ELRev* 391.

[29] AG Fennelly in Case C-190/98 *Volker Graf v Filzmoser Maschinenbau GmbH* [2000] ECR I-493, para 20.

[30] Particularly Weatherill and AG Jacobs in *Leclerc-Siplec* (n 25).

[31] Cases C-34-36/95 *Konsumantenombudsmannen v De Agostini* [1997] ECR I-3843.

[32] Case C-305/98 *Konsumantenombudsmannen v Gourmet International* [2001] ECR I-1795.

[33] Para 18. It is only a suggestion, however, and is not entirely clear.

[34] Case C-254/98 *Schutzverband gegen unlauteren Werttwerb v TK Heimdienst Sass GmbH* [2000] ECR I-15.

[35] Para 29.

the basic *Keck* formula and looks for and finds a different impact in fact on market access of imported goods from other Member States.[36] It is true that at some point such assertions may appear increasingly artificial, but they are still made, and the ECJ has not yet moved towards a pure and explicit market access test.[37]

PART TWO — OBSTACLES TO THE FREE MOVEMENT OF PERSONS — INTRODUCTION

Similar issues have arisen relating to the free movement of workers and persons generally, although there are differences both in the texts of the Treaty Articles and in the solution reached by the ECJ.[38] It has had to deal both with measures that are directly and indirectly discriminatory, and those that are equally applicable and not indirectly discriminatory, although in truth it is not always easy to distinguish these from each other.[39] It is in the area of non-discriminatory barriers to the exercise of the Treaty freedoms that the ECJ's approach has differed from that in relation to goods. As Barnard explains:

[36] Maduro cites other cases such as *Franzen* which arguably are more consistent with a 'market-access' approach but this still does not seem deeply embedded in the Court's current Art 28 case law—M Maduro, 'Harmony and Dissonance in Free Movement' (2001) 4 *CYELS* 315.

[37] For a view that sees rather more convergence than this, see Craig and De Búrca, and Barnard.

[38] The development of the Court jurisprudence on these Treaty Articles has been the subject of much comment. Generally G Marenco, 'The Notion of a Restriction on the Freedom of Establishment and Provision of Services in the Case Law of the Court' (1991) 11 *YEL* 110; C Costello, 'Market Access All Areas—the Treatment of Non-discriminatory Barriers to the Free Movement of Workers' (2000) 27 *LIEI* 267; C Barnard (n 9); E Guild, *Immigration Law in the European Community* (Kluwer, The Hague, 2001) ch 2; D O'Keefe and A Bavasso, 'Four Freedoms, One Market and National Competence—in Search of a Dividing Line' in D O'Keefe (ed), Liber Amicorum Lord Slynn (Kluwer, The Hague, 2000); N Bernard, 'Discrimination and Free Movement in EC Law' (1996) 45 *ICLQ* 83; C Hilson, 'Discrimination in Community Free Movement Law' (1999) 24 *ELRev* 445; L Daniele, 'Non Discriminatory Restrictions to the Free Movement of Persons' (1997) 22 *ELRev* 191; E Johnson and D O'Keefe, 'From Discrimination to Obstacles to Free Movement—Recent Developments Concerning the Free Movement of Workers 1989–1994' (1994) 31 *CMLRev* 1313; A Castro Oliviera, 'Workers and Other Persons: Step by Step from Movement to Citizenship—Caselaw 1995–2001' (2002) 39 *CMLRev* 77; D Martin, 'Discriminations, Entraves et Obstacles: Trois Concepts en Quête d'Identité' (1999) *CDE* 260 and 561; A Biondi, 'In and Out of the Internal Market—Recent Developments on the Principle of Free Movement' (1999/2000) 19 *YEL* 469 and S O'Leary, 'The Free Movement of Persons and Services' in P Craig and G de Búrca (eds), *The Evolution of EU law* (OUP, Oxford, 1999).

[39] Eg Case C-19/92 *Dieter Kraus v Land Baden-Würtemberg* [1993] ECR I-1663 is a case that is often suggested to be a possible instance of indirect discrimination, but the judgment clearly indicates that discrimination is not necessary to find an infringement of the Treaty. Case C-55/94 *Reinhard Gebhard v Consiglio dell'Ordine degli Avocati e Procuratori di Milano* [1995] ECR I-4165 is another case that might be seen in this light.

> …the requirement of differential impact on access to the market is not found in the context of persons: non-discriminatory measures breach the relevant Treaty provision unless justified where they 'substantially impede access to the market (or at times the lower standard of liable to hinder or make less attractive the exercise of fundamental freedoms guaranteed by the Treaty').[40]

To the extent that this is the case, it will immediately be apparent that this raises issues similar to those with which the ECJ had to grapple in the context of Article 28 EC immediately prior to *Keck*. How far will Community law reach in to the general regulatory competence of Member States in pursuing the Community's interest in free movement and market integration? Does such a broad and sweeping statement on its own (ie, that any measure that precludes or substantially impedes access to the market, or even more radically, any measure that hinders or makes less attractive the exercise of the rights) strike an adequate balance between free movement and market integration and general Member State regulatory competence? If it does not, how may it be supplemented or further refined to achieve such a balance?[41]

Crucial cases which establish this expansive approach to free movement of persons include *Kraus*[42] (recognition of a postgraduate degree title obtained in another Member State); *Gebhard*[43] (affiliation to Bar Council); *Alpine Investments*[44] (a ban on cold-calling to acquire new clients outside the Member State of establishment), and most famously *Bosman*[45] (football transfer fees). Most recently the same approach seems to be emerging in the context of residence rights of family members, in *Baumbast*[46] (parent) and *Carpenter*[47] (spouse). All of these national measures were held to be Treaty infringing[48] obstacles requiring justification, without any clear recourse to nationality discrimination. Contrasted with this are other—fewer—cases which seem to limit the concept, or at least pointing out that its application has limits. *Volker Graf*[49] is the leading ECJ case of this nature, denying that a rule precluding a termination payment

[40] Barnard (n 9).
[41] Many of these questions are touched upon in the literature cited (n 38) above and also very helpfully in the Opinion of AG Fennelly in (n 29).
[42] Above (n 39).
[43] Above (n 39).
[44] Case C-384/93 *Alpine Investments BV v Minister van Financien* [1995] ECR I-1141.
[45] Case C-415/93 *Union Royale Belge des Societes de Football Association v Bosman* [1995] ECR I-4921.
[46] Case C-413/99 *Baumbast & R v SSHD*.
[47] Case C-60/00 *Carpenter v SSHD* [2002] 2 CMLR 64.
[48] Except *Baumbast* (n 46) where the protected Community right was derived from secondary legislation.
[49] *Graf* (n 29).

to an employee who resigned to move to a job in another Member State was a Treaty-infringing restriction on the employee's right under Article 39 EC. It is clear from these cases that the ECJ has, for now, definitively moved away, in language if not in reality, from a rigid insistence that the Treaty can only control measures which involve some kind of overt or covert discrimination on the grounds of nationality. Therefore, I do not intend to defend normatively that basic proposition in any detail, nor to argue extensively for or against a return to a stricter discrimination analysis of these Treaty freedoms. It suffices to note that the comments of those such as Weatherill and Jacobs (that a barrier to market access is still a barrier to market access even in the absence of discrimination) apply equally here, yet some such as Davies still argue that 'Discrimination is better than Market Access.'[50] However, the parameters of the application of Articles 39, 43 and 49 EC are still unclear, and of course the impact of EU citizenship and the right contained in Article 18 EC is still emerging.[51] It is these questions that remain unresolved and still open to dispute which be the focus of this discussion.

There seem to be three important questions to address:

1 If the non-discriminatory nature of a measure is not a barrier to the application of these Treaty Articles, are there any other preconditions? In other words, *what kind of non-discriminatory obstacles* to the exercise of the fundamental freedoms will be Treaty infringing 'restrictions'? Particular attention will be focused on the issues of the directness and significance of the effect on the exercise of the Treaty freedoms. This will be addressed in part 3.
2 Can this approach be extended beyond national regulations which are related to or impinge upon economic market participation? In other words, can the right to *reside* be treated in the same way as the right to *work* or to exercise an *economic activity*? This could be described as an extension of the material scope of this approach. This will be addressed in part 4.
3 Can this approach be extended not just in its material scope for workers away from professional regulations and like rules, but in its personal scope for those who do not participate in the market, but who are enjoying or exercising their rights of residence under Article 18 EC? This will be addressed in part 5.

[50] This is the title of a chapter in his PhD thesis and book: Davies (n 26).
[51] Spaventa considers the cases moving beyond discrimination in the free movement of persons and suggests viewing this development in the context of EU Citizenship—E Spaventa, 'From *Gebhard to Carpenter*: Towards a (non-economic) European Constitution' (2004) *CMLRev* (forthcoming).

PART THREE — WHAT KIND OF OBSTACLE?

3.1 Introduction

As Costello suggests, 'a key issue which warrants clarification is to what extent market access must be affected in order to trigger the application of Article 39.'[52] Two key questions seem to remain. The first is the significance of the measure—is it only non-discriminatory restrictions which preclude or prevent access to the market or exercise of the fundamental freedom which will be Treaty-infringing obstacles, or does the Treaty extend further to embrace restrictions which in some way hinder, impede or make less attractive the exercise of the fundamental freedom? The second is the role of directness of the effect of the measure. To the extent that it is possible to distinguish between measures which have direct and indirect effects on market access or exercise of the fundamental freedom, can a measure that cannot truly be said to have a *direct* effect on market access or the exercise of the Treaty rights ever be seen to be an obstacle? [53] Finally, do these two dimensions interact in any way, with a less significant impact on the exercise of the fundamental freedom required if the measure has a direct effect, and vice versa?

It should be noted at the outset that these two questions may be related, because of the duality of the rights contained in the Treaty Articles: as well as giving the individual a right to work, provide services, or establish a business, they also protect the individual's right to reside in the host state in order to do so. A measure which directly and/or substantially affects the individual's right of residence may also, although rather more indirectly, affect his or her right to pursue the economic activity in question. This is particularly important in considering family reunification laws as the absence of the family may more easily be seen as an obstacle to the residence rather than the economic activity of the primary migrant.

3.2 A Brief Look at the Case Law

There seem to be two approaches in the ECJ to determination of whether a national measure is a Treaty-infringing obstacle. The first, I shall call this a '*special categories*' approach, identifies specific recurring patterns of

[52] Costello (n 38). The AGs' Opinions in *Graf* (n 29) and Case C-225/97 *Pfeiffer Großhandel GmbH v Lowa Warenhandel GmbH* [1999] ECR I-2835 in particular bring out the necessity for such a control mechanism.

[53] I do not distinguish sharply between these. As Barnard suggests, in the area of free movement of persons the distinction seems difficult to maintain. Moreover, many of the cases talk about exercise of the freedoms as much as access to the labour market. See particularly *Carpenter* (n 47).

behaviour of Member States which are deemed to be incompatible with the Treaty freedoms, without relying on a direct or indirect nationality discrimination analysis. The main feature of these cases is that they do so *without* detailed analysis in abstract general terms of direct and/or substantial restrictions on the right in question.

3.2.1 Specific Categories

The categories that have been identified by the Court are the following:

1. Because they discriminate against those who are exercising or have exercised their free Treaty rights.[54]
2. Related to these, although not entirely identical, are cases in which the Court concludes that measures, not discriminatory on the grounds of nationality, which penalise or make more difficult the provision of cross-border services than similar services provided entirely within the State.[55]
3. Because they deny rights of secondary establishment[56]—the right to have more than one place of business.
4. Because they impose a requirement of establishment on all who wish to provide services or otherwise[57] deny the right to provide services.
5. Because they are a disproportionate use of a permission granted by Community law to impose a measure that does restrict the freedoms.[58]

3.2.2 A More General Approach

The other approach that is sometimes taken is simply to consider in general terms whether the measure directly and/or substantially hinders,

[54] Cases of this nature include Case 154/87 *Rijksinstituut voor de Sociale Verzekering der Zelfstandigen (RSVZ) v Heinrich Wolf* [1988] ECR 3897; Case 143/87 *Stanton v Institute National d'Assurances Sociales pour Travailleurs Independants (INASTI)* [1988] ECR 3877; Case C-18/95 *Terhoeve v Inspecteur van de Belastingdienst Particulieren/Ondernemingen Buitenland* [1999] ECR I-345; Case C-135/99 *Elsen v Bundesversicherungsanstalt fur Angestellte* [2000] ECR I-10409 and most recently Case C-224/98 *D'Hoop v Office National de l'emploi* [2002] 3 CMLR 12 although *D'Hoop seems to* concentrate on migration discrimination as such rather than an obstacles analysis.

[55] Case C-381/93 *Commission v France* [1994] ECR I-5145.

[56] Cases of this kind include Case 107/83 *Order des Avcocats au Barreau de Paris v Klopp* [1983] ECR 2971 and most recently in the EFTA Court, Case E-4/00 *Johann Brändle* [2001] 2 CMLR 52.

[57] In Case C-147/86 *Panhellinios Syndesmos Idioktition Frontistirion Xenon Glosson-PALSO v Greece (Syndesmos)* [1989] ECR 4111 by imposing an employment contract on all qualified tourist guides who wished to carry out that activity in Greece. This prevented them from working in a self-employed, 'service providing' capacity.

[58] Case 118/75 *Italy v Watson & Belmann* [1976] ECR 1185; Case 16/78 *Amtsgericht Reutlingen v Choquet* [1979] ECR 2293.

makes less attractive or restricts the fundamental freedom. *Bosman*,[59] *Graf*,[60] *Gebhard*,[61] *Kraus*,[62] and *Carpenter*,[63] are leading cases of this kind. As we have seen requirements to affiliate to professional bodies (*Gebhard*), football transfer fees (*Bosman*), recognition of a postgraduate academic degree (*Kraus*), and residence rights for close family members (*Baumbast* and *Carpenter*) have all been regarded as obstacles.

Cases of the kind mentioned above may employ an 'inclusionary' analysis (ie, the Court examines the measure, and declares that its effects are such that it is an infringement of the Treaty requiring justification) or an 'exclusionary' analysis, concluding that the effects are not enough (too remote, uncertain, indirect, insignificant) to bring the measure within the scope of the scrutiny of the Treaty.[64] The 'inclusionary' analysis of the effects of measures on the exercise of the Treaty freedoms seems to proceed in two directions. The first is directness (or remoteness) and the second is the perceptibility (or significance) of the effect.[65] Although these two dimensions do seem to be recognised by the ECJ there is little discussion or clarity about the difference between them and what combination of directness and significance of effect will suffice to engage the application of the Treaty. I will suggest below that distinguishing more clearly between the directness and significance of the effect of the measure is a crucial and helpful step in forming a coherent and rational analysis of the scope of these Treaty Articles.

3.3 Evaluating the Court's Approach — What is an Obstacle?

3.3.1 Other Literature

The orthodox view, if there can be said to be one, is that the most obvious kind of measure that will infringe these Treaty Articles is one which directly excludes the exercise of the right concerned. There is less agreement as to whether measures which do not *preclude* the exercise of the right may be classed as Treaty infringing obstacles. Barnard suggests[66]

[59] Above (n 45).
[60] Above (n 29).
[61] Above (n 39).
[62] Above (n 39).
[63] Above (n 47).
[64] Sometimes an exclusionary analysis of this nature is suggested to the Court and rejected. The acceptance of the exclusionary approach is most evident in *Graf* (n 29).
[65] The final one is certainty, but this seems to be used in a negative way in the Court's *exclusionary* analysis cases, so I shall postpone my discussion of that until a later stage.
[66] Barnard (n 9).

that precluding market access is not strictly necessary, but that the ECJ looks for a 'direct and substantial' effect. AG Fennelly in *Graf* suggests that only neutral measures which have an effect akin to exclusion will be considered to be relevant obstacles. Arnull, Wyatt and Dashwood[67] suggest that there may be a distinction between measures affecting access to or taking up of economic activities and those concerning the conditions under which they are exercised. Castro Oliviera[68] suggests two types of obstacles cases—those involving discrimination against free movers and those involving other restrictions, although he admits that one might question what constitutes a sufficient restriction. Most, however, would accept that the concept remains uncertain.[69]

3.3.2 *An Alternative Suggestion*

My own suggestion[70] is that on a very simple level, the test may be described as one of whether the obstacle is *direct OR significant*, rather than whether it is *direct AND significant*—subject to an additional qualification that measures may be seen as too indirect or too insignificant to be Treaty infringing obstacles. The cases considering measures of this kind are therefore best understood as falling into three basic categories:

1. First, measures presenting a direct obstacle to the exercise of the freedom: in which case the effect need only be perceptible rather than significant/substantial/exclusionary (if it is not it cannot be described as an obstacle to the exercise of the fundamental freedom).
2. Second, measures presenting an exclusionary, significant, or substantial obstacle to the exercise of the freedom: in which case the obstacle need not be direct.

   It should of course be noted immediately that measures may satisfy *both* approaches above and pose a *direct and substantial* obstacle to the exercise of the fundamental freedoms. In that case clearly there will be an infringing obstacle, but it may be that the ECJ finds it unnecessary to explore both of these dimensions and will satisfy itself with a conclusion that the measure 'directly affects' access to the labour market, or sometimes that it

[67] *Wyatt & Dashwood's European Union Law* (4th edn, Sweet & Maxwell, London, 2000) 409–12. After *Carpenter*, this seems difficult to maintain.
[68] Castro Oliviera (n 38) 90.
[69] See in particular Costello (n 38) and Biondi (n 38).
[70] I do not intend to defend this in extensive detail, as the elaboration of a precise definition of what is an obstacle is not the aim of this chapter. I am mainly concerned here to elaborate and explain the concept sufficiently to show that national laws refusing settlement of partners fall within the definition.

precludes or makes the exercise of the right 'impossible' without considering both.

3 Third, as a final residual category, those measures whose effect cannot be classified in either of the above ways may be excluded, no issue of Treaty infringement arising. In particular, those measures whose effect on the exercise of the right are both indirect and merely perceptible (rather than significant) are not obstacles.

3.3.3 Why this Approach?

This approach has not yet been explicitly adopted by the ECJ, and indeed has been almost directly rejected by the English Court of Appeal.[71] Nevertheless, it seems consistent with much if not all of the ECJ jurisprudence. It has the benefit of making sense of an otherwise disparate and confusing set of decisions. In particular, it offers some explanation for otherwise problematic discrepancies and inconsistencies in the way the ECJ expresses the degree of interference and/or directness that is necessary to trigger the application of these Treaty Articles.[72] The main criticism that may be levelled at this approach is that it is too complex, but it seems no more so than is necessary to make sense both of the ECJ case law and to accommodate the inherent complexity that arises if one wishes to permit the directness and significance of the obstacle to interact, and if one wishes to move beyond a vague and ultimately not very helpful statement that some rules (which ones?) are sufficiently closely connected to the process of market integration to require justification whereas others (again, which ones?) are not. It also has several virtues at a normative level. First, it has the benefit of catching and subjecting to the control of Community law all national measures which have an effect on the exercise of the freedoms which is direct or substantial, without catching any measures whose effect is *both* indirect *and* merely arguable or perceptible without being substantial or significant. It therefore strikes a reasonable and workable balance between the Community interest in free exercise of these rights, and general Member State regulatory competence. It also has the benefit of rationalising and giving effect to what may be an instinctive but not yet fully articulated tendency to balance the degree of directness

[71] *Ex p Professional Contractors Group Ltd* [2001] EWCA Civ 1945 [2002] I CMLR 46, concerning carrier sanctions on those found transporting illegal immigrants, and *Ex p International Transport Roth* [2002] EWCA Civ 158 [2002] 1 CMLR 52, concerning tax rules implemented prevent tax avoidance by individuals setting sham independent contractor status, both seem to reject this approach.

[72] Barnard's comment above (n 40). I would explain this by suggesting that when the Court insists that the obstacle must substantially impede market access or exercise of the right, it is talking in the context of *indirect* obstacles, whereas when it insists only that the measure 'hinders or makes less attractive' the exercise of the right it is dealing with measures whose effect is more *direct*.

and significance of the effects of the measure—which arguably produces the inconsistencies alluded to above in the degree of interference with the protected Treaty right required by the ECJ before it will intervene and conclude that the measure is a Treaty-infringing 'obstacle'.

There are two points to be made about this approach. The first is that the concept may well go beyond the paradigmatic and most obvious case of measures which preclude the exercise of the right altogether. This is because I consider that both the reasoning of the ECJ and the situations in which it uses 'obstacles' jurisprudence justify this.[73] This is however merely a matter of emphasis as other writers (including Barnard) also admit readily that the concept of a Treaty infringing obstacle is not *necessarily* confined to those measures which exclude the exercise of the right.

The second is that it is not simply a 'de minimis' test. In this respect, it is helpful to distinguish between effects on the exercise of the right that are more than merely minimal, and those that are significant or substantial. Although some see the new case law as introducing something akin to a 'de minimis' test—and that may be what *Graf* does—the approach here is capable of, and indeed is intended to, extend further than this. It is intended to indicate that not only those measures that can be dismissed as *de minimis* may be excluded, but those measures (whose effects are indirect) whose effects might pass such a test but could not be described as substantial can also be excluded.

This may best be illustrated in relation to measures that are significant (but not exclusionary) but cannot be described as direct. My view is that these measures are quite possibly included, although Barnard seems less convinced that this is the case. The clearest cases which demonstrate this kind of measure being classed as an obstacle are *Vander Elst*[74] and *Kraus*.[75] In *Vander Elst*, the measure concerned was a prohibition on a firm established in another Member State from using TCN employees without gaining authorisation and work permits for them. It was held that this measure was indeed an infringement of the Treaty, without expliclity relying on nationality discrimination.[76] Even though obtaining the authorisation would have involved a significant delay, and perhaps the case is closer to an outright prohibition in practice than a mere administrative hindrance,

[73] For example, the Court in *Bosman* (n 45) does not mention the significance or exclusionary effect of the measure, in *Gebhard* (n 39) it simply mentions measures that 'hinder or make less attractive' the exercise of the right and in several cases, such as *Kraus* (n 39), Case C-43/93 *Vander Elst v Office des Migrations Internationales* [1994] ECR I-3803; *Alpine Investments* (n 44), *Terhoeve* (n 54) and most recently *Carpenter* (n 47) an obstacles analysis is used in cases where the argument that the national measure made the exercise of the right impossible might be difficult to sustain.

[74] Above (n 73).

[75] Above (n 39).

[76] The judgment is somewhat ambiguous in that it is difficult to tell whether it is an obstacles analysis or discrimination that eventually persuades the ECJ.

it still seems difficult to suggest that this totally precluded the applicant's business from carrying out the contract. The possibility remained of using workers already authorised to work in France. In *Kraus*, the German applicant returned from the UK to Germany with his Edinburgh University LLM degree. He was not permitted to use this title without authorisation, and this requirement was held to be an obstacle. Again the measure cannot really be described as a direct or exclusionary hindrance to his professional activity. The postgraduate academic title is helpful to, and may enhance, the lawyer's career but lack of it does not preclude him from exercising the activity, and it seems difficult to describe its effect as direct.[77] Another clear example of this trend seems to be the recent decision in *Carpenter*.[78] It is of central importance so it merits a fuller discussion.

3.4 *Carpenter* — A Problematic Case?[79]

This case will already be familiar from the discussion in previous chapters, but it is central both to the evolving concept of what is an 'obstacle' to a fundamental freedom and to the possibility of viewing residence rights of family members as obstacles, so it also deserves close attention here.

Mr Carpenter was resident in his state of origin, the United Kingdom. There, he ran a business:

> ... selling advertising space in medical and scientific journals and offering various administrative and publishing services to the editors of those journals. The business is established in the UK, where the publishers of the journals for which he sells advertising space are based. A significant proportion of the business is conducted with advertisers established in other Member States of the European Community. Mr Carpenter travels to other Member States for the purposes of his business.[80]

Mrs Carpenter, a Phillipine national had overstayed her visitor's visa, and therefore her immigration status was irregular. She had married Mr Carpenter during this time. She applied for leave to remain on the basis of her marriage, but pursuant to the published policy guidance,

[77] AG Fennelly in *Graf* (n 29) suggests that this measure may not be direct in the strict sense but is so closely bound up with the activity that it may be treated in the same way. Perhaps the only economic activity that would be directly affected by this would be academic employment.
[78] Above (n 47).
[79] See further H Toner, Annotation of *Carpenter* (2003) 5 *EJML* 163.
[80] Judgment para 14.

DP3/96, this was refused. She was expected to return to the Phillipines to apply for entry clearance.[81]

AG Stix-Hackl considers that the situation *is* covered by Community law because Mr Carpenter is providing services in other Member States. She also considers that this gives Mrs Carpenter a right of residence as his spouse, regardless of whether or nor her presence in the host state, including her contribution to the care of his children, actively assists him in his business. However, she bases this clearly on the secondary legislation[82] and explicitly rejects the conclusion that the right of residence for the TCN spouse may be based directly on the right of the Member State national under the Treaty.[83] The ECJ however takes a different view, rejecting the application of Directive 71/148,[84] but accepting that the deportation of Mrs Carpenter may be an obstacle to the exercise of Mr Carpenter's right under Article 49.[85] It is ambiguous as to whether the active contribution to the service provision of Mrs Carpenter's childcare and other household tasks is of importance to the decision.[86] Neither the ECJ nor AG Stix-Hackl analyse the situation as one involving discrimination on the grounds of nationality.[87] The ECJ concludes:

> 38 In that context it should be remembered that the Community legislature has recognised the importance of ensuring the protection of family life of a national of the Member State in order to eliminate obstacles to the exercise of the fundamental freedoms guaranteed by the Treaty…
>
> 39 It is clear that the separation of Mr and Mrs Carpenter would be detrimental to their family life and, therefore, to the conditions under which Mr Carpenter exercises a fundamental freedom. That freedom could not be fully effective if Mr Carpenter were to be deterred from exercising it by obstacles raised in his country of origin to the entry and residence of his spouse.

[81] These rules apply irrespective of nationality. They apply equally to all foreign spouses of all settled residents (including UK nationals such as Mr Carpenter) although not to Community migrants. However, if the conclusion is reached that the couple's situation is indeed covered by Community law, there would arguably be direct discrimination on the basis of nationality as Mr and Mrs Carpenter were subjected to regulations that would not normally apply to migrant EU citizens.

[82] Council Directive 1973/148 of 21 May 1973 on the Abolition of Restrictions on Movement and Residence within the Community for Nationals of Member States with regard to Establishment and the Provision of Services [1973] OJ L172/14. Opinion para 101.

[83] Paras 33–41.

[84] Paras 35 and 36.

[85] Paras 37–9.

[86] The AG considers this point and concludes that this is not necessary, but the ECJ does not address the question directly, particularly at the point where it considers the concept of an obstacle and whether the deportation is one.

[87] As I have noted above (n 81) a nationality discrimination analysis might be possible, but is not pursued by the ECJ.

> 40 A Member State may invoke reasons of public interest to justify a national measure which is likely to obstruct the exercise of the freedom to provide services only if that measure is compatible with the fundamental rights whose observance the Court ensures (see, to that effect, *ERT* and *Familapress*).
>
> [The Court then goes on to consider whether the deportation is an infringement of Article 8 ECHR and concludes that it is].

What may be deduced from this as to the nature of an 'obstacle' that will infringe Treaty rights? Merely that it is something that 'is detrimental to the conditions under which [the individual] exercises a fundamental freedom,' that it makes the freedom 'not fully effective' by deterring its exercise, or that it is 'likely to obstruct the exercise of that freedom.' This is all the more remarkable as it concerns the situation of the *exporting* state rather than the state in which or to which the services are provided.

Four objections may be made. First, the reliance on *Singh*[88] is questionable, as that case was arguably not about the denial of residence rights *as such* but the denial of equal access to the residence rights under Community law to which other migrant Community law nationals were entitled in the UK, and to which the Singhs had been entitled in Germany.[89] Secondly, the judgment seems hopelessly lacking in reasoning, making virtually no reference to the crucial cases on obstacles to justify its decision, and offering little normative defence of its conclusion. This brings us to the third objection. It does nothing to clarify the already uncertain terrain of 'obstacles' jurisprudence. It merely adds to the confusion, while at the same time adding what seems to be a new, and possibly significantly more liberal test which is at odds with some of its previous conclusions. It seems a wasted opportunity. Finally, although it may be an excellent and helpful precedent for immigration law, it arguably sets the standard for an 'obstacle' too low and therefore in the long run may be unhelpful. The reasoning is potentially deeply problematic, seemingly venturing into territory where it should not go—accepting the existence of a restriction without requiring (or even mentioning) either a direct or substantial effect on the exercise of the Treaty right. This is all the more regrettable

[88] Case C-370/90 *Ex p Surinder Singh* [1992] ECR I-4265.

[89] *Singh* (n 88) itself (paras 19 and 20) is at best ambiguous as to whether the obstacle is the refusal of residence of the wife or the fact that the rules in force in the UK are less generous than those in Community law to which the family had been entitled in Germany. It can of course now be argued after *Carpenter* that the measure in *Singh* was an obstacle in two respects—both that it discriminated against free movers *and* that the measure itself (refusal of residence to a spouse) was a Treaty-infringing obstacle in its own right regardless of this discrimination issue. But to treat *Singh* itself as authority for the second proposition seems unwarranted.

as there is no shortage of more sound reasoning to lead to the same conclusion. In particular:

1 It could easily be argued that the absence of the wife, although indirect, would have significant (or even exclusionary) effects on the right to provide services from the host state.[90] It is therefore regrettable that the ECJ confined itself to observing merely that the measure had 'detrimental effects' on the 'conditions under which Mr Carpenter exercised' his Treaty rights.
2 Alternatively, given that Community law may also protect the individual's right to *reside* as well as to be economically active, the case could be looked at in this way—either under Article 49 EC or perhaps more plausibly under Article 18 EC since Mr Carpenter is no longer in a purely internal situation.[91] In that case, a *direct* restriction on the right of residence of Mr Carpenter could be more plausible, on the basis that Community law can and should regard the choice to live with a spouse as directly related to and inherent in the choice to move and reside oneself. Even if this is not accepted however, the significance of the obstacle can hardly be understated. Enforced separation of the family, even if not permanent, cannot be regarded as an insignificant obstacle to residence in a particular location, whereas the connection to provision of services in other Member States is less obvious.
3 It might even be argued that the right to have a resident spouse could have a direct effect on the *economic* right to provide services (and/or by analogy, where the other Treaty freedoms are concerned, work or establishment).[92] This is rather less convincing, and seems to stretch the concept of directness too far. It is also unnecessary given the foregoing discussion of other means to reach the same result.

In retrospect, what will be the significance of *Carpenter*? It is possible that in the future the ECJ will take it at face value and follow it, and that it will

[90] The incentive to take the whole family elsewhere (for example to relocate to the nearest and only English-speaking EU Member State, Ireland, or to travel to the Philippines while the immigration issue was resolved) would be significant. In either case, the disruption to the business would be significant. If the family had to separate even temporarily, leaving Mr Carpenter with his children in the UK, this could also be a significant disruption to Mr Carpenter's ability to pursue his business activities, if Mrs Carpenter usually frees him from much of the daily burden of childcare.

[91] The freedom to provide services normally gives rise to a right of residence in the state in which the services are provided or received. Nevertheless, in Mr Carpenter's situation if he is providing cross-border services from the UK there is no reason why his right to reside in the UK in order to do so cannot be protected.

[92] This was suggested explicitly in *Carpenter*, as the referring Court asked whether there was any significance to be attached to the fact that the assumption of childcare responsibilities by the wife was of direct assistance to the economic activities of the husband. AG Stix-Hackl considered that a response to this was unnecessary, and the Court does not specifically mention it.

become as significant in the law of free movement of persons as *Dassonville, Cassis, Torfaen* or *Cinéthèque* in the free movement of goods. This would be problematic and should not be pursued. Once this analysis is rejected, much depends on the extent to which the ECJ is prepared to see the right of *residence* act as an anchor for the application of the doctrine of non-discriminatory obstacles. If it is, then *Carpenter* is arguably one of those cases that can properly be seen as both a direct and significant obstacle to the exercise of the freedom. If not, and it is considered that only the economic acticity is relevant, the the case becomes more problematic but is best seen as one which is an indirect but still significant obstacle to the economic right to provide services. In this light, the outcome is perhaps less convincing but may still be defended.

3.5 Conclusion — What Kind of Effect is Required?

It is certainly welcome that the ECJ has begun to grapple with this thorny issue. The possibility of abusive claims being made under these Articles is just as great as it was under Article 28 EC immediately prior to *Keck*.[93] Once the possibility of non-discriminatory obstacles is accepted in principle, some kind of limiting principle is clearly necessary. *Graf*[94] (challenging dismissal compensation denied when the employee leaves voluntarily) and *Ex p Professional Contractors Group*[95] (challenging tax regulations intended to combat the use of 'artificial' service provision companies by those who are in reality in the position of employees) are certainly cases in which the claim could be seen as abusive, and in which any limiting principle ought to apply to reject the application of the Treaty to these particular national measures. But equally it is difficult to argue with Costello[96] and Biondi[97] when they suggest that far more clarity is required in this matter. This is all the more important when there begin to be cases in national courts, such as *Hoverspeed*[98] and *International Transport Roth*[99] (concerning carrier sanctions on cross-border freight carriers) and *McCollum*[100] (residence rights of a TCN same-sex partner) where the possible effect on the exercise of the fundamental freedoms seems rather more convincing and yet the claim that these apparently

[93] Above (n 9).
[94] Above (n 29).
[95] Above (n 71).
[96] Above (n 38).
[97] Above (n 38).
[98] *Ex p Hoverspeed* [1999] Eu LR 595.
[99] Above (n 71).
[100] *McCollum v SSHD* [2001] EWHC Admin 40 [2001] Admin Ct Digest 58. This conclusion may be doubtful after *Carpenter*, and the point was not dealt with in the judgment.

non-discriminatory measures might infringe Community law is either rejected or not addressed, without any reference to the ECJ to clarify the point.

Some commentators start from the assumption that the Treaty will strike at measures which preclude the exercise of the fundamental freedoms, and go on to consider the extent to which measures which do not do so but nevertheless have a direct and significant effect on the protected rights may also be obstacles. I have suggested a slightly different analysis which seeks either (1) a sufficiently direct obstacle (in which case the obstacle must simply have a perceptible effect), or (2) a sufficiently obstructive, possibly exclusionary, effect (in which case the directness of the obstacle is not an issue). To this it may be added that some measures may qualify under *both* approaches—if they are both direct and exclusionary or significant. This makes sense both as a descriptive analysis of a diverse and sometimes confused set of cases, and as a normative suggestion as to how best to balance the Community interest in controlling national measures which obstruct the fundamental freedoms and the national interest in maintaining their general residual regulatory autonomy. The utility of this analysis may be seen vividly in *Carpenter*,[101] in which this kind of reasoning is not employed. As a consequence, although the ECJ arguably reaches a defensible conclusion on the facts, the reasoning is inadequate and likely to prove problematic in future.

PART FOUR — AN OBSTACLE TO WHAT FREEDOM?

It is now necessary to turn to examine the place of residence rights and Citizenship in this jurisprudence. A notable aspect of many of the judgments discussed above is that they are often explicitly *market-based*, access to the labour market, or to professional or economic activity of some kind being crucial. This is understandable as these rights have always been central to EC law. Where then do measures that affect the right to *reside* rather than the economic activity stand? This is particularly crucial for this discussion, as immigration rights of partners might be said to be one such measure, affecting neither the qualification for, taking up or pursuit of any economic or professional activity. They primarily affect the right of *residence*, and could thereby be argued to fall outside the scope of the principle behind the cases discussed above, if applied only to the economic Treaty rights. I will first deal with this point in terms of the 'economic freedom' articles, and then consider the relevance of Article 18 EC.

[101] Above (n 47).

4.1 The 'Economic Freedom' Articles

The centrality of economic activities in the above cases is hardly surprising since the measures concerned affected not the *residence* of any individual in a host Member State, but the exercise of an economic activity or profession there.[102] This is one aspect of the freedoms—the freedom while resident (or even, whether or not one is resident) to pursue economic activities. But these freedoms also have another aspect—the right to enter and stay in the host state in order to do so. Prohibitions[103] or other unreasonable administrative restrictions[104] on the residence of workers, or other economically active or self-sufficient EU citizens, are generally not permissible. If this is so, then just as non-discriminatory obstacles which *directly and/or substantially hinder or preclude access to the labour market* are contrary to these Treaty Articles unless justified, so should be non-discriminatory obstacles which *directly and/or substantially hinder or preclude the settlement and residence of the individual* in the Host State. When talking about a 'direct or substantial hindrance' to a fundamental freedom, the duality of these Treaty Articles must be recognised. They do not simply protect inter-state access to markets (for goods, services, employees) but also incidentally and consequentially protect the migrant EU citizen's right of residence.

An example of this kind of logic in action can clearly be seen in *Raulin*,[105] where ECJ clearly states that the *right of access to vocational training on equal terms* (old Articles 7 and 128) can be the basis of a (temporary) right of residence for the individual who has been admitted to a course. *Antonissen* may also be seen to support this in the way it provides a (temporary) right of residence for workseekers. *Terhoeve*[106] is a further example involving a challenge to social security law under which a Dutch worker was assessed separately (and therefore less advantageously as he was subject to two maximum contributions rather than one) for social insurance in respect of two periods of residence in the UK and in the Netherlands in the same tax year. This would not have happened if he had remained living in the Netherlands but worked in another Member State. It was therefore arguably *not* as closely connected with access to employment as the provisions in *Bosman*[107] and *Graf*.[108] Much more so than these other cases, the additional social security contributions were an obstacle to a change of *residence* rather than the exercise of any *economic*

[102] *Kraus* (n 39) *Bosman* (n 45) *Gebhard* (n 39) *Graf* (n 29).
[103] *Van Duyn* (n 3).
[104] *Watson and Belmann* (n 58).
[105] Case C-357/89 *Raulin v Minister van Onderwijsen Wetenschappen* [1992] ECR I-1027. AG's Opinion, para 18, judgment paras 30–40.
[106] *Terhoeve* (n 54).
[107] Above (n 45).
[108] Above (n 29).

activity. The outcome in *Carpenter*[109] may also be seen to support this view, as the right to have a residence permit for the spouse seems to be something that would affect the right of residence rather than the activity of service provision itself.

4.2 Citizenship and Article 18 EC

A more fundamental point can be made. Against the argument above, it might be maintained that the right of *residence* is implicit rather than explicit in the economic freedoms and that the secondary legislation relating to workers and establishment does not fundamentally alter this. This is not really persuasive in relation to Article 39 EC given the terms of Article 39(3)c providing a right to stay in the host state, but perhaps a little more so in relation to Articles 43 and 49 EC which do not explicitly mention residence. There might therefore be some remaining scepticism about the extension of the concept of non-discriminatory obstacles being extended from the economic aspects of these Treaty Articles. And, as we have seen, the connection between family reunification and economic activity is less clear and convincing than that between family reunification and the residence of the principal migrant. However, there have been significant legal developments in the last decade, which have introduced wider residence rights for EU citizens: the importance of Article 18 EC and the specific rights of residence in secondary law for all EU citizens[110] need not be repeated.

The future use of Article 18 EC to found an unlimited right of residence, or to challenge the existing limitations on other rights of residence, remains uncertain. However, the recent groundbreaking case of *Baumbast*[111] invites the reader to consider Article 18 EC in a new light, and to leave behind some of the caution and scepticism which for so long characterised much commentary on the legal nature of EU citizenship. The judgment confirms that Article 18 EC does have direct effect and creates an enforceable right of residence.[112] Although this right remains 'subject to the limitations and conditions laid down in this Treaty and the measures adopted to give it effect' the ECJ makes it clear that these limitations and conditions will be subject to judicial scrutiny, and in particular that they must be proportionate.[113]

[109] Above (n 47).
[110] Council Directive 1993/96 of 29 October 1993 on the Right of Residence for Students [1993] OJ L317/59; Council Directive 90/364 of 28 June 1990 on the Right of Residence [1990] OJ L180/26; Council Directive 90/365 of 28 June 1990 on the Right of Residence for Employees and Those who Have Ceased their Occupational Activity [1990] OJ L180/28.
[111] Above (n 46).
[112] Paras 84, 86.
[113] Para 91.

The suggestion that the lack of emergency medical cover could be a legitimate and proportionate reason to deny residence to an individual who was otherwise fully insured in Germany and economically self-sufficient by working outside the EU, was rejected by the ECJ. As well as this right of residence that may be actively asserted against the host state, even those EU citizens who do not comply with reasonable and justified requirements imposed on the Article 18 EC right but are nevertheless lawfully resident under national law as Martínez Sala was, enjoy the status of EU citizen and the consequent right to equal treatment under Article 12 EC.[114]

If this is so, then in the same way as the right in Article 39 EC has moved from ensuring equal treatment to embracing certain non-discriminatory obstacles, so the right in Article 18 EC, already seen in *Martínez Sala* to require 'equal treatment within the material scope of the Treaty,' ought also to be at least capable of a similar application to strike down certain non-discriminatory measures affecting residence. There are two sources of judicial support for this approach. First, from the 'obstacles' cases themselves. Some of these cases confine their statements to the particular Treaty freedom in question, whether Article 39, 43, or 49 EC.[115] But others, particularly *Kraus*[116] and *Gebhard*,[117] suggest that the same approach can be taken to any of the fundamental freedoms contained in the Treaty. The exclusion from this principle of the fundamental freedom to reside throughout the territory of the Member State would have to be explained and justified. Secondly, this may be supported by reference to the cases in which Article 18 EC is treated in the same way as the other Treaty Articles for the purposes of providing a link to Article 12 EC and equal treatment on the basis of nationality within the material scope of the Treaty. AG Cosmas' Opinion in *Wijsenbeek*[118] is a forceful articulation of this position, considering that it might require the abolition of obstacles to the exercise of the right to *move* freely throughout the territory of the Member State such as passport controls, even though he ultimately considered such measures to be justified. The ECJ was equivocal on the matter although it did not reject it completely. Most clearly, *Baumbast*[119] is another powerful indication of the 'mainstreaming' of the Article 18 EC right of residence, and in the way the children's claim to have the company of a parent carer is treated, provides further support for the suggestion that Article 18 might be used to nullify certain unjustififed non-discriminatory obstacles to its exercise.

[114] Case C-85/96 *Martínez Sala v Friestaat Bayern* [1998] ECR I-2692.
[115] Eg, *Bosman* (n 45).
[116] Above (n 39).
[117] Above (n 39).
[118] Case C-378/97 *Criminal Proceedings against Wijsenbeek* [1999] ECR I-6207.
[119] Above (n 46).

Indeed, there are signs that the ECJ is moving in this direction. In precisely the cases where this might be expected (ie, in the 'discrimination against free movers' cases, which often deal with tax, social security and welfare benefits rules law, which arguably affect *residence* rather than cases concerning professional rules affecting the *economic activity* itself), it seems increasingly willing to take a global view and declare the measure an obstacle to all of these Treaty Articles together, or incompatible with Community law generally. The recent case of *D'Hoop* exemplifies this trend,[120] even though the ECJ's analysis of discrimination against free movers seems to be more focused on migration discrimination as such rather than on an analysis based on obstacles.[121] There is therefore a strong case that the application of the principles of non-discriminatory obstacles to Treaty freedoms may also apply to Article 18 EC. The most striking comments, however have come recently from AG Jacobs in *Pusa*.[122] The case involved a Finnish pensioner resident in Sweden who objected that more was deducted from his pension for payment of a debt than would have been if he had been resident in Finland (tax paid was not automatically taken into account for those resident abroad). Here (although arguably he need not have done so as the case could be resolved by principles of indirect discrimination—discrimination on the basis of residence often being treated in Community law as indirect nationality discrimination) Jacobs makes his views on the matter quite clear. Again, it is helpful to set out the relevant passage in full:

> 20 Furthermore, freedom of movement was originally guaranteed by a prohibition of discrimination on grounds of nationality but there has been a progressive extension of that freedom in the Court's case-law so that non-discriminatory restrictions are also precluded. Article 39 EC, which explicitly secures freedom of movement for workers through 'the abolition of discrimination based on nationality,' has been interpreted as precluding also certain non-discriminatory measures. And the wording of Article 18, for its part, is clearly not limited to a prohibition of discrimination; paragraph 1 simply sets out the right of a citizen of the Union to move and reside freely within the territory of the Member States, subject only to any limitations or conditions laid down in the Treaty or implementing measures.
>
> 21 It is also clear that freedom of movement entails more than simply the abolition of restrictions on a person's right to enter, reside in or leave a Member State. Such freedom cannot be assured unless all measures of any kind which impose an unjustified burden on those exercising it are also abolished. Whatever the context in which it may arise—including

[120] Above (n 54).
[121] H Toner and A Iliopoulou, Annotation of *D'Hoop* (2003) 28 *ELRev* 389.
[122] C-224/02, Opinion of AG Jacobs of 20 November 2003.

> leaving or returning to the Home Member State, or residing or moving elsewhere in the Union—no such burden may be imposed.
>
> 22 The conclusion—which is consistent with and complementary to the Court's judgments in *D'Hoop* and *Baumbast*—must thus be that, subject to the limits set out in Article 18 itself, no unjustified burden may be imposed on any citizen of the European Union seeking to exercise the right to freedom of movement or residence. Provided that such a burden can be shown, it is immaterial whether the burden affects nationals of other Member States more significantly than those of the State imposing it.

The significance of this can hardly be understated. It is a clear statement of the mainstreaming of Article 18 and a clear willingness to accept that, in respect of whatever doctrine of non-discriminatory obstacles is adopted, it may apply in relation to this Article. It will be seen from the above that I consider this logical and—unless one rejects the idea of non-discriminatory obstacles altogether and prefers a discrimination approach to these Treaty Articles—not in itself inherently problematic or undesirable. However, a note of caution must be sounded here, although not in relation to the basic principle of whether Article 18 is capable of reaching beyond discrimination but to the way Jacobs articulates *what kind of non-discriminatory measures may breach Article 18 EC*. One lesson should be clear from the pre-*Keck* case law, that a non-discriminatory obstacles approach must, if it is to be used, be combined with an approach that is sufficiently capable of containing this principle to avoid the possibility of abusive claims and to protect adequately Member State autonomy in areas where there is little connection with cross-border trade or movement of persons. Jacob's approach arguably fails to put in place any realistic control mechanism—other than the willingness of the Judge in question (in the National Court or the ECJ in its advisory capacity) to see a burden and the possibility of justifying the measure. It is therefore perhaps to be welcomed that the recent ECJ judgment in the case does not follow this line of reasoning.

4.3 Obstacles and the Material Scope of the Treaty

The proposition being advanced would stand as follows:

> Any measure which has a direct or substantial/exclusionary effect on the right of residence contained in Articles 18, 39, 43 and 49 is incompatible with the Treaty unless objectively justified by imperative reasons of public interest.

This would depend on differentiating these (non-discriminatory) obstacles from 'social advantages' or benefits that are within the material scope of the Treaty for the purposes of Article 12 EC and therefore must not be subject to nationality discrimination but lawful if implemented without discrimination. The critical differences would of course be *either* directness of effect on the residence right, or the fact that the measure goes beyond *hindering or making less attractive* the exercise of the right to having a *significant, substantial, or exclusionary effect* (making it impossible to exercise the right).

A good example of how to distinguish between measures falling within the scope of the equal treatment guarantee and 'obstacles' to residence may be provided by comparing the benefit in *Martínez Sala*[123] itself with those measures which *have* been considered to be obstacles. *Martínez Sala* concerned a child-raising benefit, the refusal of which could 'hinder or make less attractive' the right of residence of the mother, and indeed the child. But it does not directly impede or block access to the right of residence right in the same way as the provisions in *Bosman*[124] or *Gebhard*[125] directly affected access to the employment or professional services market. Nor is it easily described as making the exercise of the right impossible or even a significant obstacle to the exercise of the right. Thus this should not be seen as a Treaty-infringing non-discriminatory obstacle. However, because it does in a broad sense 'hinder or make less attractive the exercise of' the right, it is within the material scope of the Treaty for the purposes of equality of access and the prohibition of *nationality discrimination* against migrants, linking Articles 12 and 18 EC together. This contrast again demonstrates the difficulties with the reasoning in *Carpenter*.[126] If one considers whether the refusal of a child-raising benefit has a 'detrimental effect on the conditions under which Ms Martínez Sala exercised her right' under Article 18 EC, it seems artificial to deny that this would be the case. This emphasises the concern that the ECJ in *Carpenter*, referring merely to 'detrimental effect on the conditions under which the freedom is exercised,' is setting the standard for an 'obstacle' too low and embarking on a course that will, if followed, blur the distinction between obstacles and the material scope of the Treaty for the purposes of Article 12 EC.

4.4 Are There Any Objections to This Approach?

It could be said that the statements in *Bosman*,[127] *Gebhard*,[128] and *Graf*[129] about measures that hinder, preclude etc the right to exercise the economic activity, are intended by implication to exclude the possibility of using

[123] Above (n 114).
[124] Above (n 45).
[125] Above (n 39).
[126] Above (n 47).
[127] Above (n 45).
[128] Above (n 39).
[129] Above (n 29).

such an approach in relation to the fundamental freedom of residence. However, this seems an unnecessary implication, particularly in the light of the comment in *Gebhard* which makes no distinction between the different fundamental freedoms. There is nothing in this judgment to indicate that the freedom to reside is to be treated in any different way.

It might be suggested that if Community law controlled measures that interfered with the right to *reside* as well as the right to *work* or to exercise another economic activity, this might be by its nature far more sensitive and less easy to control. It is arguably more likely to lead to the ECJ and national courts being called upon to adjudicate upon sensitive issues of social policy. The response to this is twofold. First, that it is simply impossible to draw a rigid line between the right to work and the right to *reside in order to work*. It therefore has to be accepted that the rights of residence of those who are economically active may already be protected by the concept of non-discriminatory obstacles. In that case, it makes no sense to exclude from this possible protection those EU citizens who are not economically active but are exercising their rights under Article 18 EC. Secondly, it may be asserted that it is quite possible to keep this principle within reasonable bounds, even if applied to residence. The concept of a direct, significant or exclusionary measure would be susceptible to a robust and sufficiently controlled application. It must also be recalled that the finding that a measure is an 'obstacle' is not the end of the process, as the host state will always be able to rely on justifications for such measures. The ECJ, however, if it takes such a step, should take care to ensure that these concepts are used appropriately to avoid a repeat of the *Sunday Trading* and *Keck* cases.

4.5 Conclusion

It seems sufficiently supported by authority, logic, and the policy of building the internal market and ensuring effective free movement to suggest that a national measure which has a *direct or substantial or possibly exclusionary effect* on the exercise of the fundamental freedoms guaranteed by the Treaty is prima facie in breach of it, and requires justification. This in itself seems well-established now in relation to the economic freedoms although the precise definition of an obstacle remains somewhat elusive. The missing link that has not yet been made here is the detachment of this line of reasoning from the economic freedoms and its extension to the fundamental freedom of residence. This detachment has taken place in relation to the guarantee of equal treatment pursuant to Article 12 EC, and could and should take place in the field of non-discriminatory obstacles. As long as there is a sufficiently robust approach to the concepts of direct or substantial/exclusionary effect to ensure the containment of this principle within reasonable bounds, the difficulties that gave rise to the need for the ruling in *Keck*[130] can be avoided. *Graf*[131] seems a modest step in this direction, although *Carpenter*[132] undermines this, in its reasoning if not the result, and AG Jacobs takes a similar approach in *Pusa*. Further clarification would be welcome.

PART FIVE — APPLICATION TO PARTNERS' IMMIGRATION RIGHTS

We must now consider the application of these general principles to immigration laws:

1. If the test is a measure that impedes the right of residence *in such a way as to have effects akin to exclusion*, would this be satisfied? The individual may well not wish to move without his/her partner, and it might well be seen as unreasonable to expect this. It is likely that this test would be satisfied.
2. If the test is a measure which directly and/or substantially impedes the exercise of the right of residence, there is a very strong case that it would be satisfied.
3. If (contrary to the above suggestion) the lower standard of 'hinder or make less attractive' is chosen without any suggestion of necessity for a substantial or direct effect, then the matter becomes even clearer. It seems unquestionable that it would do so.
4. If the inquiry is restricted to the impact of a national measure on the right to engage in economic activities, immigration laws might be too remote. Yet even here the question seems open. The inability to live in another Member State could indeed be a measure that has effects akin to exclusion from the employment market there—precisely why Articles 39 EC et al provide not only for access to employment, but to residence rights for the worker. If so, a measure having effects akin to exclusion from the right of residence can and should be treated in the same way, as having effects akin to exclusion from the employment market.

I shall now examine some of the most relevant cases dealing with immigration and partnership rights to ascertain if there is anything in them that confirms or rebuts these suggestions, or gives any indication of the current attitude that may be expected from the ECJ.

[130] Above (n 21).
[131] Above (n 29).
[132] Above (n 47).

This question, linked to an allegation of interference with private and family life, was raised recently in the English High Court in the case of *McCollum*.[133] The judgment contains little detailed analysis of the point, and it is rejected without sustained consideration, the judgment focusing largely if not exclusively on the interpretation of Regulation 1612/68. The case was appealed but settled during the appeal hearing and unfortunately not referred to the ECJ in the case, so for now the question remains hypothetical.

Reed[134] and *D & Sweden v Council*[135] are two of the most obvious and high profile ECJ cases relating to non-marital partners, but neither is helpful. In *Reed* an unmarried partner's settlement was a 'social advantage' that had to be granted on equal terms to Community migrant workers if it were granted to the host state's own nationals—but there was no suggestion that the unmarried partner could have any right to accompany the Community migrant if the domestic law of the Host State did not already provide for this in some way. However, the case predates the development of the 'obstacles' analysis in the ECJ, and is primarily concerned with the concept of equal treatment in the enjoyment of social advantages. To suggest that a partner's immigration right may be a social advantage does not discount the possibility that its denial or absence may also be a non-discriminatory obstacle. *D & Sweden* concerned the recognition of a Swedish registered partnership for the purposes of an employment benefit normally granted to a spouse. The question of whether this was a breach of Article 39 EC was not raised in the CFI and thus the ECJ refused to consider the point in any detail on appeal. In any event, the cases are also distinguishable in that the benefit denied was not a residence permit for the partner, but an employment-related family allowance from the employer. The ultimate result, according to Bell, was that the couple returned to Sweden. The denial of a residence permit for the partner seems an even more convincing obstacle to migration and movement, and could certainly be treated differently even if there had been a clear indication that the refusal of employment benefit did not infringe Article 39 EC on its own.[136]

MRAX[137] involved a challenge to various provisions of Belgian immigration law which resulted in spouses of migrant EU Citizens being denied entry or deported. It is assumed throughout that the individuals in question can prove their identity and family link to the migrant EU

[133] Above (n 100).
[134] Case 59/85 *Netherlands v Reed* [1986] ECR 1283.
[135] Cases C-122 and 125/99P *D & Sweden v Council* [2001] ECR I-4319.
[136] Bell, however, considers that the facts of *D & Sweden* case would fall 'comfortably within the definition of an obstacle given by the Court in *Bosman*'—M Bell, *Anti-Discrimination Law and the European Union* (OUP, Oxford, 2002) 102.
[137] Case C-459/99 *MRAX v Belgian State*.

citizen—they are therefore in the classic position of migrant's spouses with rights under secondary legislation. There was therefore no need to consider whether and to what extent the Treaty gives rise directly to residence rights for spouses or other family members without reliance on secondary legislation. *Baumbast*[138] is interesting as it suggests that the child, otherwise unable to reside in order to complete his/her education, may be able to rely on Community law to assert a right of residence for a TCN parent/carer. This is certainly interesting, but whether the residence of a TCN partner would be treated in the same way (as making the residence of the other partner *impossible* without it) might be doubtful.

Yet again *Carpenter*[139] is crucial. The approach of AG Stix-Hackl denying that Article 49 EC (and by implication probably the other free movement Treaty Articles) gives rise to a residence right for a close family member is problematic. It is difficult to reconcile with the view in in *Baumbast* which seems preferable,[140] and the ECJ rightly rejected it. There is arguably some residual uncertainty about whether the childcare provision provided by Mrs Carpenter and the practical assistance that this provided to Mr Carpenter in conducting his business abroad was important to the ECJ's reasoning (this question was raised by the referring court). However, the better view is that the deportation of his spouse was sufficient in itself to affect the conditions under which he provided services. Thus we may conclude from *Carpenter* that the refusal of settlement of a spouse to anyone exercising Treaty rights is an obstacle to the exercise of those rights and presumptively incompatible with the Treaty.

Regarding those who are not married, there is little in *Carpenter* to suggest whether the same analysis would be employed in relation to other partners. The only indication that might favour this kind of interpretation is the reference to 'family life', which might be taken to refer to the 'traditional' family as accepted in EC law (ie, above all spouse and minor dependent children). Yet the ECJ has indicated some willingness to follow the lead of the ECtHR in recognising a wider concept of the family,[141] and this might give some hope of a wider application. Further, the refusal to authorise residence of a registered partner or cohabitee would, to the primary migrant, be just as detrimental to the conditions of residence, work or establishment in the host state. The seemingly subjective reasoning employed in *Carpenter* certainly gives the individual a powerful tool enabling a challenge to an overly restrictive definition of the family and

[138] Above (n 46).
[139] Above (n 47).
[140] That the children entitled to remain pursuant to Reg 1612/68 to complete their education could not be deprived of the company and care of their TCN parent as this would make the exercise of their right impossible in practice.
[141] Case C-65/98 *Eyup v Landesgeschaftsstelle des Arbeitsmarktservice Vorarlberg* [2000] ECR I-4747.

opens up the possibility of some degree of individual choice of the family member to be admitted. In this respect, it is instructive to compare *Carpenter* with *Rattigan*,[142] a case similar to *Abdulaziz*[143] involving sex discrimination in family reunification rights decided under the Constitution of Zimbabwe. Because of the lack of constitutional protection against sex discrimination, the Court resorted to the right of the wives to move and reside freely throughout Zimbabwe in order to establish the right of their foreign husbands to stay in the country. However, the judgment places considerable emphasis on the uniting of husband and wife in marriage, and the mutual obligations involved, including an expectation of mutual financial support and cohabitation. This approach might not easily be used to suggest that immigration rights should be extended beyond married couples, although it could perhaps assist registered partners who do have similar mutual obligations. The approach in *Carpenter* is arguably not so clearly tied to marriage and therefore offers greater opportunities to other couples.

CONCLUSIONS OF CHAPTER SIX

This chapter has explored the concept of an obstacle to the exercise of the fundamental freedoms under the Treaty. We have seen that certain non-discriminatory obstacles to the exercise of the fundamental freedoms may be nullified if not justified. Although the current state of the law is unclear, it has been suggested that the obstacles which may trigger the application of these Articles in the context of the free movement of persons are those that are either direct and/or significant (possibly exclusionary) obstructions to the exercise of the right. It has also been suggested that the right to reside in the Host State, whether under Articles 18, 39, 43, or 49 EC should also be subject to this principle. The main objection in principle to this approach is that it might be excessively intrusive into areas of social policy rightly reserved for the Member States. Certainly care is needed, but I have argued that limits on this principle may be emerging along with the principle itself and indeed that more attention should be paid to these limits. It might even be argued that the concept of 'significantly obstructive measures' is or should be confined to those which have the *effect of exclusion* from the exercise of the right, or perhaps putting it another way, those measures that make it impossible in practice for the individual to exercise that right. Even if this is the case, a measure preventing settlement of a cohabiting partner fulfils this definition and should be seen as a restriction on the exercise of these Treaty rights.

[142] *Rattigan v Chief Immigration Officer Zimbabwe* 1995 SA 182.
[143] *Abdulaziz, Cabales & Balkandali v UK* Series A No 94 (1985) 7 EHRR 471.

Although not part of the early jurisprudence on 'obstacles', there is an emerging trend of recent case law supporting this analysis by employing the idea of obstacles to the exercise of Community law rights in the context of immigration rights of family members. *Baumbast*[144] and *Carpenter*[145] are the first two leading cases of this kind, but more may be expected.[146] There is thus now good reason to think that an immigration case involving a cohabiting partner could be argued to be a non-discriminatory obstacle to one or more of the fundamental freedoms. Although the outcome is not certain, it is to be hoped that the approach in *McCollum*,[147] which did not really address these issues properly, would not be repeated in the ECJ.

[144] Above (n 46).
[145] Above (n 47).
[146] *Chen & Zhu*, referred to as Case C-200/02 [2002] OJ C180/12 is a follow-up to *Baumbast* raising similar issues. AG Tizzano in his Opinion of 18/05/04 suggests similarly that the mother may remain to care for her infant child.
[147] Above (n 100).

7

Justifications for Married-Partners-Only Immigration Policies

INTRODUCTION

THUS FAR I have suggested that marriage-only immigration policies are prima facie violations of principles discussed in chapters 3–6, whether maintained by the individual Member State or the Community. The next stage in the analysis, addressed in this chapter, is to examine whether and how the maintenance of such a policy might be justified.

Part 1 will deal with the situation under the ECHR, and consider the way Community law does and should approach these same fundamental rights issues. I have already discussed this in chapter 3, and in some respects this will be a brief review of what I have set out there, but focusing specifically on the concepts of justification and proportionality. It will then be necessary to address the question with specific reference to Community law. Part 2 will discuss generally the approach to interference with protected rights in Community law. There may be a distinction between 'moral' or 'principled' justifications and 'pragmatic' or 'practical' reasons, and this classification will be used to address the particular question at hand in more detail. Part 3 will examine whether and to what extent Member States' particular traditions and views on marriage and family life might justify the maintenance of such a policy. Part 4 will address the question from a slightly different angle, examining briefly the pragmatic or practical reasons why a marriage-only policy might be seen to be necessary or justified to maintain a properly functioning system of immigration law.

It is however crucial at this stage to set out the limits of the argument being addressed here. It is argued that a Member State must have *some* policy presumptively permitting as of right the immigration and settlement of a partner regardless of gender and/or legal status of the partnership. However, nothing that I have presented so far would preclude the Community or individual Member States formulating the exact boundaries of these rules. Indeed such rules would be vital to make any scheme workable. The rules should be modelled as far as possible on those relating to marriage, in particular where registered partnerships are involved, but some further comments may also be made:

1 One important issue is the question of proof of the relationship. Rules identifying which couples in stable de facto relationships could benefit would be necessary. For example, the current rules in force in the UK whereby a two-year relationship is necessary seem permissible. The previous rules required a four-year relationship: this seems more doubtful and somewhat harsh,[1] but is not so manifestly disproportionate as to be dismissed out of hand. Member States examining applications could develop and maintain rules and practices intended to verify that the relationship is genuine. Issues of respect for privacy certainly arise, and unreasonable intrusions into privacy should be avoided. But such intrusions as are necessary and proportionate to verify the relationship would be permissible.
2 Whether cohabitation should be strictly necessary as a part of this inquiry is a delicate question. Rejecting the application of a couple purely because they do not have a common home[2] would seem disproportionate if in the circumstances other proof of the stability of the relationship was provided. Beyond this, an element of discretion would clearly be permissible in drawing up rules or guidelines to deal with such cases.
3 The continued residence of the non-national partner after the death of the other partner or the breakup of the relationship is not addressed here. The individual would no longer be permitted to stay as a partner, but long-term residence in the host state should always be respected. Any model of long-term residence adopted elsewhere in Community law should be taken as a minimum,[3] but equality with married couples (in so far as this is more generous)[4] would also be appropriate, and indeed necessary if the arguments relating to equality with married couples were accepted as the conceptual basis of action.

[1] Note the brief discussion in *Ex parte Hashim* (CO/2052/99 12 June 2000 Lexis transcript) concerning whether the requirement of four years might be disproportionate and a violation of Art 8 EHCR. It was not ultimately necessary to decide the question as the regulations had changed.
[2] Particularly if this is for pressing reasons such as different locations of employment of difficulties with immigration law outside the EU.
[3] Council Directive 2003/109/EC of 25 November 2003 Concerning the Status of Third Country Nationals who are Long Term Residents [2004] OJ L16/44 enacts a period of five years.
[4] The Proposal for a European Parliament and Council Directive on the Right of Citizens of the Union and their Family Members to Move and Reside Freely Throughout the Territory of the Member States COM(2001) 257 [2001] OJ C270/150 would grant a permanent residence status after four years to family members, Art 14(1) but this has been extended to five years in the final agreed text of the Directive.

4 This book primarily considers residence rights of partners, and deliberately avoids making a more general analysis of the treatment of different kinds of families central to the discussion. There is however one other right that seems so central that it would accompany the right to residence—partners should also be permitted to work.

5 As regards expulsion, the protection of Directive 64/221[5] can and should be extended by analogy. If there are genuine objections to the individual's presence on the basis of personal conduct they should be permitted, and the provisions of Directive 64/221 or any subsequent replacement for it provide the best model to follow in this respect.

It is against this background that the question of justification comes to be considered. I am primarily concerned with the fundamental question of whether any objections could be seen to be sufficiently cogent and persuasive to justify a *complete failure to offer any immigration rights beyond married couples*, rather than to offer a comprehensive solution to all the possible questions. This final chapter is more about raising questions and outlining the contours of the debate rather than providing definintive answers.

PART ONE — THE ECHR: MARGIN OF APPRECIATION AND PROPORTIONALITY

I have previously discussed the position under the ECHR. I do not intend to repeat this discussion here, merely to highlight the most important issues. It has been accepted for some time that the concept of respect for family and private life may *in principle* protect the individual against the use of immigration laws to exclude or deport family members.[6] However, the right under Article 8 ECHR is inherently limited. As we have seen in chapter 3, the ECtHR takes a deferential approach, leaving a generous margin of appreciation to the Contracting States in such matters, especially in admission cases. Although there have not been any cases specifically considering the question of entry and settlement rights for heterosexual unmarried couples, several cases have been decided in relation to spouses, children and parents, and same-sex couples. If the issue falls to be decided purely under the principles as articulated and applied by the ECtHR, the likelihood of success under Article 8 ECHR alone in

[5] Council Directive 64/221 of 25 February 1964 on the Coordination of Special Measures Concerning the Movement and Residence of Foreign Nationals which are Justified on Grounds of Public Policy, Public Security or Public Health [1963/64] OJ (Sp Ed) 117.

[6] *Abdulaziz, Cabales & Balkandali v UK* Series A No 94 (1985) 7 EHRR 471.

challenging a married-partners only immigration policy seems at best indifferent.

After *Da Silva Mouta*[7] and *Karner*[8] It seems highly arguable that the ECHR now prohibits immigration policies which deny a lawfully resident and settled individual any possibility of applying for settlement for a long term same-sex partner. This argument is strongest where same-sex and opposite-sex unmarried couples are treated differently (as in *Karner* itself), where the ECtHR indicates that convincing and weighty reasons will have to be given for such distinctions. The extent to which the ECtHR will use Articles 8 and 14 ECHR to protect same-sex couples against the sexual oreintation discrimination inherent in various 'marriage-only' policies remains to be seen. *Karner* may also mean that same-sex registered partnerships (particularly those following the 'strong' model and starting from a presumption of equality in domestic law) might be able to claim equality with married heterosexual couples. Community law should follow this lead.

On the other hand, the compatibility with Articles 8 and 14 ECHR together of policies which privilege spouses over unmarried heterosexual partners is more finely balanced. Much depends on the continuing use by the ECtHR of two concepts. The first, that 'traditional families' may be given 'special protection', seems well settled. It is unlikely that the ECtHR would abandon this concept, and I do not argue here that it should. The second is the use of this kind of reasoning in the context of immigration law. The ECtHR itself has not had the opportunity to consider this, although the ECommHR has used this reasoning in the past. I have suggested that this is highly suspect. It is possible that the ECtHR would not accept the proposition that immigration rights were 'special protection' that could be reserved for the 'traditional' married couple—and such an approach would be welcome. If so, the Contracting State would have to bring forward more pressing and convincing specific justifications for maintaining a married partners only policy for heterosexual couples.

It has been argued that the approach currently taken by the ECtHR is unhelpful and inappropriate for Community law. This applies to the concepts of justification used, as much as to the basic principles of whether Article 8 ECHR imposes a general obligation to admit non-national family members in some cases. In particular, although the ECtHR has been reluctant to suggest that refusal of entry of even the closest non-national family members does not respect the 'essence' of the Article 8 ECHR right to the extent of imposing a general obligation to admit family members, this kind of argument might fare better in Community law with the added protection of the right of the primary migrant to move and reside freely

[7] *Da Silva Mouta v Portugal* Application 33290/96 (2001) 31 EHRR 47.
[8] *Karner v Austria* Application 40016/98.

throughout the Community. The decision in *Carpenter*[9] may be a move in the direction of a more generous approach to Article 8 ECHR rights in the ECJ, in particular an emphasis on individual conduct such as is found in Directive 64/221. However, the judgment is somewhat opaque and it remains to be seen whether this will develop into a distinctive Community law approach.

PART TWO — COMMUNITY LAW AND PROPORTIONALITY GENERALLY

Academic commentators generally content themselves with brief consideration of this issue, pointing out that there may be reasons for thinking that the current 'marriage-only' immigration policy requires justification, but that the question of whether or not such justification might be successfully advanced is another question altogether.[10]

2.1 Different Approaches to Justification

As a preliminary point, it must be noted that there are two possible approaches to justification. If the individual *is entitled to residence rights as a family member under secondary legislation* then individual justifications would be required to exclude them, pursuant to the Directive 64/221.[11] No such justification would be found, as it has to be based on individual conduct,[12] which must be a 'genuine and sufficiently serious threat to one of the fundamental interests of society.'[13] Inter alia, this implies that the Member State concerned takes effective, repressive measures of some kind to combat the behaviour concerned among its own citizens.[14] This would make it very difficult for the Member States concerned to refuse residence to the partner simply because of the nature of the relationship or its legal recognition, or the fact of non-marital cohabitation. On the other hand, a different approach would be necessary if the Member State was trying to justify the particular way it defines the family for the purposes of immigration law. In that case, the question is not whether to deny rights to someone who is already presumptively entitled to residence.

[9] Case C-60/00 *Carpenter v SSHD* [2002] 2 CMLR 64.
[10] See eg, D Martin, 'Discriminations, Entraves et Obstacles: Trois Concepts en Quête d'Identité' (1999) *CDE* 260 and 561, 590.
[11] Above (n 5).
[12] *Ibid*, Art 3(1).
[13] Case 30/77 *R v Bouchereau* [1978] ECR 1999; Cases 115 and 16/81 *Adoui & Cornuaille v Belgium* [1982] ECR 1665; Case C-348/96 *Criminal Proceedings against Calfa* [1999] ECR I-11 and Case C-268/99 *Jany v Staatssecretaris van Justitie* [2001] ECR I-8615.
[14] Although criminal penalties and imprisonment are not necessarily required.

It is how to define the categories of those who are so entitled as family members—and this surely admits of a rather wider scope for the Member State to defend and justify its policy.

There are a number of statements from the ECJ that clarify the approach to the permissibility of justifications for measures that are either *indirectly discriminatory* on the grounds of nationality or are nevertheless *obstacles to free movement*. For example, the ECJ in *Gebhard* states:

> It follows however from the Court's caselaw that national measures liable to hinder or make less attractive the exercise of the fundamental freedoms guaranteed by the Treaty of Rome must be applied in a non-discriminatory manner, must be justified by imperative requirements in the public interest, must be suitable for attaining the objective which they pursue and must not go beyond what is necessary in order to attain that objective.[15]

It is clear from this a sophisticated balancing act must performed. The heart of this will be the test of proportionality.

2.2 The Principle of Proportionality in Community Law — Introduction

Much will depend on the application of the principle of proportionality. For clarity, I shall separate the proportionality test into four stages, while noting briefly that some courts sometimes ignore or sideline some of the stages or run them together:

1. Identifying the aim involved and ascertaining whether it is a legitimate one.
2. Determining whether the aim is suitable for achieving the end pursued.
3. Determining whether it goes beyond what is necessary to achieve the aim.[16]
4. Determining whether, even if these first requirements are satisfied, the interference with the protected right is disproportionate given the aim. This is sometimes referreed to as 'true proportionality'.

As Jarvis notes, the outcome may be influenced by the emphasis put on the different limbs of the test.[17]

[15] Case C-55/94 *Reinhard Gebhard v Consiglio dell'ordine degli Avocati e Procuratori di Milano* [1995] ECR I-4165, para 37.
[16] An analysis of alternative means less disruptive to free movement is required here.
[17] M Jarvis, *The Application of EC Law by National Courts: The Free Movement of Goods* (OUP, Oxford, 1998) 203–4, 211.

The principle of proportionality is one of the central principles of Community law. It raises complex issues, and there is an extensive literature on it.[18] But because of its complexities there are rarely any straightforward answers. Bermann notes:

> No one who has seriously studied the proportionality cases involving Community measures seems very comfortable drawing general conclusions on the basis of which firm predictions may be drawn—either as to the terms in which and the level of scrutiny with which the Court will apply the proportionality principle in any given case or as to the probable outcome. Tridimas expresses the apparent consensus in remarking that 'far from dictating a uniform test, proportionality is a flexible principle which is used in different contexts to protect different interests and entails varying degrees of scrutiny. It is by its nature flexible and open-textured.' Eimiliou tends to agree.[19]

With this in mind, the first task is to outline different factors that may influence the operation of proportionality—while bearing in mind that this inquiry is by its very nature open-textured, flexible, and rather more about raising questions than providing definitive answers to them.

2.3 Factors Influencing how Proportionality is Applied

This is one of the questions that occupies much of the literature on the subject. One of the first considerations is whether the act being challenged is one of the Community or of the Member States. Generally, it is thought that Member State acts may be more carefully scrutinised than those of the Community.[20] Yet even where Community acts are challenged, although there are cases involving policy decisions under the CAP in which a very wide margin of discretion is left,[21] there are others in which issues of fundamental rights[22] or harsh penalties[23] are involved in which a rather more searching degree of scrutiny is applied.

[18] See eg, G De Búrca 'The Principle of Proportionality and its Application in EC law' (1993) 13 *YEL* 105; E Ellis (ed), *The Principle of Proportionality in the Laws of Europe* (Hart Publishing, Oxford, 1999); N Emiliou, *The Principle of Proportionality in European Law: a Comparative Study* (Kluwer, The Hague, 1996); T Tridimas, *The General Principles of EC Law* (OUP, Oxford, 1999) chs 3 and 4, and P Craig and G de Búrca, *EU Law* (3rd edn, OUP, Oxford, 2002) ch 7.
[19] F Bermann, 'Proportionality and Subsidiarity' in C Barnard and J Scott (eds), *The Law of the Single European Market* (Hart Publishing, Oxford, 2002).
[20] De Búrca (n 18), Tridimas (n 18).
[21] Case 331/88 *R v MAFF Ex p FEDESA* [1990] ECR I-4023; Case T-30/99 *Bocchi Food Trade International v Commission* [2001] ECR II-943. The measures taken were not 'manifestly inappropriate' and even though they caused harm to the applicants they were not overturned by the ECJ.
[22] Case 4/73 *Nold v Commission* [1975] ECR 985.
[23] Eg, situations where deposits are forfeited.

Turning to acts of the Member States, a similar picture of somewhat contradictory decisions emerges. These cases often involve situations where Member States interfere with Treaty rights protected under Community law and it is therefore not surprising to see the Community interest being pursued and quite searching scrutiny being applied. Beyond the consensus that these measures are scrutinised somewhat more carefully, Craig and de Búrca offer four suggestions[24] to which I add another two:

1 The intensity of review has tended to increase over time.[25]
2 The ECJ will be more searching when it suspects covert protectionism.[26] To this may be added that inconsistencies in treatment of various situations having the effect, albeit unintended, of perpetuating national traditions or protecting national markets may also be condemned by the ECJ.[27]
3 The subject matter will be relevant. Craig and de Búrca suggest that health concerns may be given a considerable leeway in the absence of clear scientific information and where a genuine doubt remains.[28] To this may be added that likewise, in matters of morality and public policy the ECJ may consider a wide margin of discretion to be appropriate.[29] On the other hand, it will understandably be anxious to protect individuals against serious and intrusive infringements of basic Community Treaty rights and perhaps also where fundamental rights are involved.[30] These two inclinations towards different intensities of review cannot always be easily reconciled. Indeed the question of partners' immigration rights at issue here is precisely of this nature, with immigration sovereignty of states and dictates of policy in relation to the concept of the family in each Member State

[24] Craig and de Búrca (n 18) 378–9.
[25] Contrast Case 41/74 *Van Duyn v Home Office* [1974] ECR 1337 with *Adoui & Cournouaille* (n 13).
[26] The *French Turkeys* case Case 40/82 *Commission v UK* [1982] ECR 2793 is often quoted as an example of this.
[27] Examples of this might be the *Cassis de Dijon* case Case 120/78 *Rewe-Zentrale AG v Bundesmonopolverwaltung für Branntwein* [1979] ECR 649, and the *German Beer* case Case 178/84 *Commission v Germany: Re Purity Requirements for Beer* [1987] ECR 1227 and other cases in which the ECJ is swift to condemn measures which may have the effect of crystallising existing national consumption and purchasing habits.
[28] Craig and de Búrca (n 18) 379.
[29] Eg, Case C-159/90 *Society for the Protection of Unborn Children (Ireland) Ltd (SPUC) v Grogan* [1991] ECR I-4685 involved the clash between the right to life of the unborn and the freedom of expression of student unions to provide information about abortion services abroad. It is often suggested that the ECJ was influenced to find that there was no interference with protected Treaty rights in order to avoid this delicate balancing act.
[30] Eg, Case C-60/00 *Carpenter* (n 9) where Art 8 ECHR was used to establish that the interference with Mr Carpenter's rights under Art 49 EC was unjustified.

clashing with the rights to free movement and family life of the couple.

4 The ECJ will sometimes send the question back to the Member Sate court to determine—although this is not always accompanied by guidance pointing towards a less strict standard of scrutiny.

5 Some suggest that the concepts of indirect discrimination and non-discriminatory obstacles can and/or should be treated differently in terms of justification and proportionality.[31] The case for so doing rather depends on the concept of 'obstacle' that is employed.[32] I do not intend to pursue this in great detail but simply to note that it might be part of the larger picture affecting the balance of justification and intensity of scrutiny employed in the proportionality inquiry.

6 Dougan[33] and Tridimas[34] note there is certainly authority that in considering the principle of equality the ECJ may be influenced by the necessity for integration and harmonisation to proceed by degrees. Particularly where partial harmonisation permits the maintenance of divergences among existing national laws, this may be accepted as a justification for the different treatment of different situations.[35]

2.4 Conclusions

The principle of proportionality is a concept that is fundamental and central to Community law. It is however as vague and flexible as it is important. Without reference to the particular issues involved, the discussion remains abstract and not altogether helpful. I shall therefore now turn to examine the issues raised by a state which wishes to maintain a married couples only immigration policy (1) on the grounds of public morality, tradition and protecting or preserving the preferred 'traditional' (ie married and heterosexual) form of family life and (2) on practical grounds, to maintain an orderly system of immigration law.

[31] J-Y Carlier, 'La Libre Circulation des Personnes dans l'Union Européenne' (1999) *Journal des Tribunaux* (Droit Européen) 56, 59–60.

[32] If a broad and inclusive (perhaps over inclusive) concept of obstacle is employed then such a difference (as suggested by Carlier n 31) might be attractive, whereas if a more restrictive concept of obstacle is employed then treating the question of justification in the same way as indirect discrimination becomes less problematic.

[33] M Dougan, 'The Workseeker as Citizen' (2001) 4 *CYELS* 1503.

[34] Above (n 18).

[35] This however collapses into circular self-justificatory reasoning if the diversity of national laws itself is used to justify the indefinite retention of this diversity.

PART THREE — MORAL REASONS

3.1 Introduction

Member States' freedom to derogate from Community free movement law in order to maintain particular moral or ethical policy choices and traditions[36] has always been a sensitive issue, and this particular point is no different.

At the outset, the following analysis is offered:

1. I wish to cohabit in the host state with my partner. My partner is lawfully resident there independently—as a national, EU citizen, or TCN with an independent residence permit. The state takes no action to prohibit or actively penalise this although it may give me and my family certain 'special protections' if I marry.
2. I wish to cohabit in the host state with my TCN partner who has no residence permit. The state says, 'marry or you cannot cohabit here,' and uses its immigration laws to enforce this.

Given that all Member States adopt position (1), is position (2) justified? The crucial point will be to what extent the principle (outlined most clearly in Directive 64/221 and the cases in which this has been interpreted and applied) that conduct which the state does not repress or take effective measures against among its own nationals cannot justify expelling a migrant or taking other measures to interfere with the Treaty rights—can and will be transferred to the present situation.

3.2 Justifying Expulsions and Refusals of Residence under Directive 64/221

3.2.1 General Principles

Directive 64/221 and the ECJ jurisprudence elaborating it[37] clearly requires the conduct of the individual concerned to be a sufficiently serious threat to one of the fundamental interests of society before expulsion will be permissible. It also states that the host state should take 'effective and repressive measures' to combat the conduct in question under its own law in relation to its own nationals if its claim that the conduct is contrary to

[36] See generally, E Steyger, *National Traditions and European Community Law* (Dartmouth, Aldershot, 1997).

[37] Above (n 11 and 13). See also Craig and de Búrca (n 18) ch 19, and E Guild, 'Security of Residence and Expulsion of Foreigners: European Community Law' in E Guild and P Minderhoud (eds), *Security of Residence and Expulsion: Protection of Aliens in Europe* (Kluwer, The Hague, 2001).

public policy to the extent of justifying expulsion of a non-national protected by Community law is to be accepted.

The main reason that this concept has developed is to enable a balance to be struck between the interests of the Member States and the interests of the individual in the particular legal situation concerned. *Nationals* may not be excluded or expelled from their own state—but migrants may be, and are. This is of course inherently discriminatory. The ECJ is not willing to say that this discrimination in itself is unlawful. It is an inevitable consequence of nationality and the fact that the EU is composed of sovereign Member States, and the only way to eliminate it is to create a genuinely permanent residence status. This, the ECJ has refused to do itself, even as a consequence of EU citizenship.[38] It considers this to be a task for the Community legislators—and of course at the time of writing a Proposal has just been agreed which would create just such a permanent status after five years for migrant EU citizens and their families.[39] Even this however has been a tough task, with Member States concerned about losing their ability to remove individuals for public policy and security reasons after this period of time, and securing an amendment to make the 'permanent' status no longer truly permanent. Yet the ECJ remains hostile to double standards and unwilling to permit the use of public policy reasons to justify expulsion of a migrant EU citizen where the same conduct is not dealt with in some effective and repressive way domestically. It has however stopped short of suggesting that criminal sanctions must be applied before expulsion may be contemplated.

The following comments from the recent case of *Jany*[40] illustrate the approach. Polish and Czech window prostitutes in The Netherlands relied on the Association Agreements with these countries,[41] suggesting that they were pursuing self-employed economic activities. A question arose as to whether prostitution could be considered such an activity because it was illegal and/or contrary to public morality. The ECJ concludes that it is indeed a relevant economic activity:

> So far as concerns the immorality of the activity, raised by the referring Court, it must also be borne in mind that, as the Court has already held, it is

[38] *Calfa* (n 13), although a case about expulsion of a transient visitor rather than settled resident and indicating that an automatic lifetime ban is disproprotionate does not suggest a fundamental change in relation to expulsions, nor does case Case C-100/01 *Olazabal*. The more recent Cases C-482/01 and C/493/01 *Orfanopoulos*, provide a more relevant test of the ECJ's attitude as well as the ECJ's judgment, being concerned with long-term residents with families in the host state. However, the Opinion of AG Stix-Hackl stops short of suggesting that long residence may provide a complete defence to expulsion, although it is certainly relevant to an assessment of proportionality.

[39] COM(2001) 257 (n 4).

[40] Above (n 13).

[41] The Europe Agreements with Poland established by Decision 93/743 of 13 December 1993 [1993] OJ L348/1 and with the Czech Republic established by Decision 94/910 of 19 December 1994 [1994] OJ L360/1.

> not for the Court to substitute its own assessment for that of legislatures of the Member States where an allegedly immoral activity is practiced legally (see with regard to abortion, case C-159/90, *SPUC v Grogan*, and with regard to lotteries Case C-275, *Schindler*).
>
> Although the Community does not impose on Member States a uniform scale of values as regards the assessment of conduct which may be considered to be contrary to public policy, conduct may not be considered to be of a sufficiently serious nature to justify restrictions on entry to, or residence within, the territory of a Member State of a national of another Member State where the former Member State does not adopt, with respect to the same conduct on the part of its own nationals repressive measures or other genuine and effective measures intended to combat such conduct (*Adoui & Cournouaille*).[42]

3.2.2 *Application to Partners' Residence Rights*

Applying this approach, the use of immigration law to prevent unmarried couples cohabiting if no 'effective and repressive measures' are taken against unmarried cohabitation under domestic law would clearly be impermissible. It would be difficult to establish that unmarried cohabitation was a sufficiently serious threat to public order to justify exclusion, and the measures that some Member States still maintain to preserve, protect and privilege favoured 'traditional' marriage might be difficult to characterise as sufficiently 'effective and repressive' in relation to other forms of family life. Moreover, the general nature of the rule would be problematic. This is emphasised in the Opinion of AG Stix-Hackl in the recent case of *MRAX*:[43]

> Refusal of a residence permit must be classified as a public order measure. According to Article 3(1) of Directive 64/221, measures taken on such grounds are to be based 'exclusively on the personal conduct of the individual concerned.' A general, abstract national rule, such as that in the Circular at issue in the proceedings, which does not impose an obligation to examine the individual case ie that such factors be taken into account, for example in that it requires a residence permit to be refused generally in the event of unlawful entry, is therefore impermissible.[44]

This approach however remains problematic. There is one serious difficulty alluded to earlier. The provisions of Directive 64/221 are only applicable to individuals who have or claim an established right of residence as EU citizens or recognised their family members under secondary legislation. The use of these strict criteria focusing narrowly on the serious harmful conduct of the individual when seeking to challenge the general

[42] *Jany* (n 13) Para 60.
[43] C-459/99 *MRAX v Belgian State.*
[44] Para 82.

policy of how the family is defined is doubtful. Tempting as it might seem to apply the principles of Directive 64/221 by analogy,[45] this temptation should be resisted. To do so would be to assume at the outset of the analysis the existence of that which the applicant is seeking to establish. It is not a well-founded approach and would in all likelihood be rejected swiftly by any judge or policymaker. The approach of justification that must be adopted here is not that the *individuals* concerned are entitled to residence under Regulation 1612/68[46] and must be refused under Directive 64/221. It is a rather more general justification that the *entire policy concerned in the definition of the family* (exclusion of unmarried couples from Regulation 1612/68 altogether so they never get as far as Directive 64/221) is a justified restriction on Treaty rights. This certainly leaves more latitude for the Member States, but principles of mandatory requirements of public interest and proportionality are still of central importance. It is to this that I shall now turn.

3.3 Justifying Interferences with Treaty Freedoms

3.3.1 Introduction

The basic structure of analysis would be that discussed above. Once a right has been established, one then has to ask whether there is an admissible reason to interfere with it, whether the measure taken is suitable to achieve that aim, whether the interference is proportionate—whether there are other less intrusive measures to achieve the same aim, whether the measure is nonetheless disproportionate to the aim achieved. The question of symmetry or consistency between different but comparable situations is also best considered here (ie, as part of proportionality). It is worth repeating briefly my initial analysis above—that Member States are effectively using immigration laws to prevent and deter unmarried cohabitation among bi-national couples including one TCN, when they take only limited measures to combat such living arrangements among those lawfully resident on its territory.

3.3.2 An Admissible Reason?

There is no doubt that preserving national moral or ethical standards and traditions are in principle admissible to justify directly or indirectly discriminatory measures, and a fortiori obstacles that are not discriminatory on

[45] As I have noted above, it is difficult to escape the conclusion that in considering the position of the applicant in *Carpenter* (n 9) the Court was heavily influenced by the individualistic conduct-oriented approach of Dir 64/221.
[46] Council Regulation 1612/68 of 15 October 1968 on the Freedom of Movement for Workers within the Community [1968/9] OJ Sp Ed (II) 475.

the grounds of nationality but which still have the effect of blocking market access or exercise of the fundamental freedoms. Nevertheless, the task is difficult. Mustill LJ in *WH Smith v Peterborough City Council* articulates the dilemma:

> How is the balance to be struck, given that the conflicting interests are so totally different in kind? How could (say) a desire to keep the Sabbath holy be measured against the free-trade economic premises of the Common Market?
>
> If this is what the *Cassis de Dijon* exception requires, it seems to be that the task would be difficult to the point of impossibility in any but the simplest case, where the balance is to be struck not between two conflicting trade interests, but between Community free trade interests on the one hand, and an elusive national moral, social, or cultural norm on the other.[47]

There is, however, plentiful support for the proposition that the range of such interests that states may legitimately pursue is not closed.[48] The preservation of the 'traditional family' rests squarely on a conservative and traditional view of sexual morality and ethics. At its most blunt, it allies itself with the Vatican, which describes in strong terms the uniqueness of marriage and the intrinsic 'evil' to society of equating de facto relationships, and particularly same-sex relationships, to marriage,[49] and with others influenced by this view.[50] Whether or not one agrees with these views, the question seems first and foremost a matter for national law and not necessarily a collective choice that is intrinsically incompatible with the EC Treaty. Although it is possible to envisage that the ECJ might adopt a sceptical view of the arguments presented in the previous chapters to avoid the necessity for such a decision on proportionality,[51] it is likely that, should the question be addressed, the policy of protecting

[47] *WH Smith Do It All v Peterborough City Council (No 2)* [1991] 1 QB 304, 330.

[48] See most recently for example the acceptance in case C-112/00 *Schmidberger* that freedom of expression of protesters could rightly be balanced against the disruption caused to free movement and also the discussion by AG Stix-Hackl in Case C-36/02 *Omega* (Opinion of 18 March 2004) of whether the principle of respect for human dignity could justify a ban on a laser game involving simulated killing.

[49] Pontifical Council for the Family, Marriage, and 'De Facto' Unions (Vatican, 2000). Available online, *www.vatican.va/roman_curia_20001109_de-facto-unions_en.html*. See further on this 'Considerations Regarding Proposals to Give Legal Recognition to Unions Between Homosexual Persons' (approved by Pope John Paul II on 28 March 2003, dated 3 June 2003, published on 31 July 2003), *http://www.vatican.va/roman_curia/congregations/cfaith/documents/rc_con_cfaith_doc_20030731_homosexual-unions_en.html*.

[50] George, Wardle and Finnis are among those articulating these views: R George and G Bradley, 'Marriage and the Liberal Imagination' (1995) 84 *Geo LJ* 301; R George, *In Defense of Natural Law* (OUP, Oxford, 1999); L Wardle, 'Multiply and Replenish: Considering Same-sex Marriage in the Light of State Interests in Marital Procreation' 24 *Harvard JLPP* 771; J Finnis, 'Law, Morality and Sexual Orientation' (1993–94) 69 *Notre Dame Law Review* 1049; J Finnis, 'The Good of Marriage and the Morality of Sexual Relations: Some Philosophical and Historical Observations' (1997) 42 *Am J Jurisprudence*.

[51] As for example, it arguably did in *SPUC v Grogan* (n 29).

and defending the 'traditional family' would be accepted as a potentially legitimate aim. This is particularly so in the light of the fact that this kind of language is still used by the ECtHR albeit now not in the context of discrimination between opposite-sex and same-sex cohabitants.

3.3.3 *A Suitable Policy to Pursue this Aim?*

If the State wishes to pursue this policy (ie, encouraging traditional family life, and married rather than unmarried cohabitation), a policy of refusing entry to non-national partners who are not married is unlikely to be regarded as an entirely irrational or unsuitable means of achieving this aim. On the other hand, if the purpose was said to be the preservation of the exclusive and heterosexual nature of marriage as the only form of partnership recognition present in the host state to avoid the problems of admitting individuals in registered partnerships or same-sex marriages which the host state does not have, this might seem rather less convincing. The majority of those individuals involved would be couples who were both nationals of the Member States anyway, both having rights of residence that will be unable to be defeated by the fact that the couple are living in a cohabiting/unmarried/same-sex relationship or are parties to a same-sex marriage or registered partnership. Given that this is the case, keeping out the smaller numbers of non-EU nationals involved could never achieve the aim of keeping out same-sex spouses or registered partners completely. Again much depends on the intensity of review applied.

3.3.4 *A Necessary and Proportionate Interference with the Protected Right?*

The more difficult question is whether the policy would be strictly *necessary* to achieve this aim, and whether in any event the results of the policy are *disproportionate* to any benefit achieved in furthering the aim pursued. It will immediately be apparent that these concepts are flexible and the outcome depends on the degree of scrutiny applied by the ECJ or policymaker. If either of these requirements is applied strictly then the argument seems difficult to sustain.

There are a number of ways in which states can and do 'protect the traditional family'—these include tax laws, pension provisions, security of tenure in housing, protection of financial interests on divorce or break-up of the relationship, and issues of parenting and filiation of children. There are therefore a number of ways in which this same aim can be pursued without recourse to measures which have the possible effect of preventing the couple from living together.

There is certainly a strong argument to be made on 'true proportionality' on this point. The rationale underlying Directive 64/221 is that expulsion or refusal of entry of a close family member is the ultimate penalty and one of the most intrusive interferences with protected family life that can be envisaged. Therefore, it must be controlled strictly. Once it is accepted that the 'de facto' family life of the unmarried or same-sex couple may be protected by the Treaty Articles on free movement, the same argument applies, that any measure which prevents the establishment or continuance of the cohabitation in the Member State of choice must be scrutinised most strictly. These measures are only partially saved by the possibility of marriage in some cases, and conceivably by the possibility that family life may be resumed elsewhere than in the chosen Host State. However neither of these seem particularly convincing. The argument that the splitting of the de facto family unit (or indeed parties to registered partnerships or same-sex marriages) is simply too high a price to force the migrant to pay in pursuit of the Host State's moral sensibilities is certainly plausible, and yet one may still pause before resting confident that the argument has been won. The ECJ, and any policymaker, might be reluctant to make such a bold assertion.

3.3.5 *The Requirement of Consistency — A More Attractive Approach?*

It would be possible to strengthen the argument considerably by using a requirement of symmetry or consistency of treatment between similar situations. We have seen that although the ECJ is unwilling to remove the power of Member State to expel individuals, it applies the principle of proportionality in such a way as to require a degree of consistency between the way conduct is treated by Member States dealing with individuals that they can and cannot expel. In this way the policy concerns and moral sensitivities of the Member States are acknowledged but their impact is controlled by Community law. In particular the practice of applying 'double standards' and thereby perpetuating discriminatory and protectionist rules (whether or not conscious or deliberate) may be halted and states may be required to be more open to traditions from other Member States when they manifest themselves in situations involving goods, services or migrants from other Member States. For this reason, it is best seen as a part of the proportionality inquiry. We must now ask where else this kind of approach is found and to what extent it could also be applicable to a proportionality inquiry in the context of family reunification laws, as it may add considerably to the argument.

3.3.6 *Consistency and Symmetry in Article 36 EC*

In the context of goods,[52] the same concern over 'double standards' (using public policy concerns to prevent importation of goods when they are not

[52] For a detailed discussion of the law relating to free movement of goods, including the questions of justifications for restrictions on free movement, see Jarvis (n 17).

the subject of a total prohibition in the host state) has arisen. Two cases in particular are worth comparing—*Henn & Darby*,[53] and *Conegate*.[54] In *Henn & Darby*, the ECJ effectively sanctioned the maintenance of a discriminatory rule under Article 30 EC (previously Article 36 EC). UK law permitted the sale of indecent materials (pornography) and there was a defence permitting the sale of 'obscene' materials if they were of particular artistic or scientific merit. However, the *importation* of both indecent and obscene materials was prohibited. An objection to this legislation was brought under Article 36, and yet the ECJ permitted the legislation to remain:

> A Member State may, in principle, lawfully impose prohibitions on the importation from any other Member State of other articles which are of an indecent or obscene character as understood by its domestic laws and that such a prohibition may lawfully be applied to the whole of its national territory even if, in regard to the field in question, variations exist between the laws in force in the different constituent parts of the Member State concerned.

The crucial point is that the ECJ concluded that 'on a comprehensive view' there was no lawful trade in the goods in question. Therefore, importation could be banned under Article 30. This view has been criticised.[55] The ECJ in more recent cases has taken a rather more robust view of the permissibility of restrictions on trade resting on standards which are not applied consistently to goods within the host state. In *Conegate*[56] it ruled that restrictions on imports of life-size inflatable dolls was not permissible under Article 36 EC because there were no restrictions on manufacturing and marketing such products in the UK. There is some uncertainty about whether and to what extent *Conegate* and *Henn & Darby* are consistent.[57] *Conegate* certainly seems to apply a more rigorous approach, but the Court of Appeal in the UK continued to apply *Henn & Darby* in 1989,[58] and again more recently in 1994[59] and 1998.[60]

These cases all deal with the specific derogation under Article 30 EC—dealing with discriminatory measures, and total bans of importation of particular goods. It is therefore likely that they are more analogous to the situations considered under Directive 64/221 (refusal of admission to an individual who otherwise clearly has a right of residence under Community law) than to the question of the justifiability of immigration policies which exclude certain relationships from the definition of the

[53] Case 34/79 *R v Henn & Darby* [1979] ECR 3795.
[54] Case 121/85 *Conegate v Customs and Excise Commissioners* [1986] ECR 1007.
[55] Jarvis (n 17) 237.
[56] Above (n 54).
[57] See E Steyger, (n 36) 109.
[58] *R v Bow Street Magistrates Court Ex p Noncyp Ltd* [1990] 1 QB 123.
[59] *R v Uxbridge Justices ex p Webb* [1994] 2 CMLR 288.
[60] *Wright v Commissioners of Customs & Excise* [1999] 1 Cr App Rep 69.

'family' and thus from the protection of Directive 64/221. Nevertheless, they do illustrate that the application to particular facts of the general principle (even when refined and expressed in such a way as to ask whether there is or is not a 'lawful trade' in goods) may be far from simple. Much will depend on the assessement of the ECJ or policymaker concerned as to whether there is a lawful trade in goods or whether the measures that the State takes to combat the conduct concerned among individuals such as its own nationals whom it cannot expel are sufficiently effective and repressive.

3.3.7 *Consistency in Mandatory Requirements Cases*

The concept of symmetry and consistency is also found from the earliest stages in this line of reasoning, in *Cassis de Dijon*[61] itself. The point being considered was the necessity for a minimum alcohol content for liqueurs. Paragraphs 10 and 11 of the judgment read as follows:

> As regards the protection of public health the German Government states that the purpose of fixing the minimum alcohol contents by national legislation is to avoid the proliferation of alcoholic beverages on the national market, in particular alcoholic beverages with a low alcohol content, since, in its view, such products may more easily induce a tolerance towards alcohol than more highly alcoholic beverages.
>
> Such considerations are not decisive since the consumer can obtain on the market an extremely wide range of weakly or moderately alcoholic products and furthermore a large proportion of alcoholic beverages with a high alcohol content are freely sold on the German market.

It can clearly be seen that the ECJ is immediately suspicious of a Member State which considers weak alcoholic beverages to be a sufficiently serious threat to public health to justify banning the importation of spirits of this strength (not traditionally made in the host state) while freely permitting both the importation of and sale of other kinds of alcoholic drink of this strength or less. Thus, although the rules were strictly speaking 'indistinctly applicable' (in that they applied to domestically produced goods as well as imported goods) there was clearly a lack of consistency in the way the German rules treated the question of strength of alcohol content—above and beyond the indirect discrimination inherently involved in imposing such product rules on imported products.

A similar conclusion emerges from the *German Beer*[62] case, concerning the German beer purity laws. One of the laws in question would prevent the importation and sale of beer as 'beer' that contained additives.

[61] Above (n 27).
[62] *Commission v Germany* (n 27).

German traditional beermaking enforced on domestic beer manufacturers by the German beer purity laws did not permit such additives at all. One of the justifications advanced by the German government in support of the application of these laws to all imported beers was public heath. Again however, although the rules were formally applicable to all beer producers, there was no public health concern about using the additives concerned in other foods. German law permitted the substances concerned to be used, simply not in beer. There is an extensive discussion of the principle of proportionality in the case generally, but the crucial point here is the ECJ's attitude to the German legislation, which permitted certain additives in other foods and drinks but (purportedly on the grounds of public health) banned their use in beer. The ECJ makes it clear that a blanket prohibition on the sale of beer containing additives is not justified on the grounds of public health. It states in particular that:

> However, it appears from the tables of additives authorised for use in the various foodstuffs submitted by the German government itself that some of the additives authorised in other Member-States for use in the manufacture of beer are also authorised under the German rules, in particular the Regulation on Additives, for use in the manufacture of all, or virtually all, beverages. Mere reference to the potential risks of the ingestion of additives in general and to the fact that beer is a foodstuff consumed in large quantities does not suffice to justify the imposition of stricter rules in the case of beer.[63]

Again, we see clearly the ECJ concluding that the lack of consistency between the German rules permitting additives to be used in other foodstuffs and beverages but not in beer means that the German government's public health justification fails.

3.3.8 Consistency Applied to Family Reunification Rights

Applied to our present case, it could be suggested that the use of immigration law to separate unmarried or same-sex bi-national couples is suspect when domestic law is not used to penalise in an effective and repressive way the conduct of such relationships in the host state by those who live there lawfully. The success of this argument will depend on the degree to which it is accepted that the states do not in fact take effective measures against those who do not marry, or in the language used in the cases on goods, whether there is a 'lawful trade'. Finding the most appropriate language to use in the context of family rights is somewhat difficult, but the concept is clear enough. As has been seen in chapter 1, a variety of different consequences attach to marriage, and a number of

[63] Para 49.

states continue to privilege married couples over others. So, it might well be suggested by a Member State that since it does not in domestic law treat married and unmarried couples equally (and it would in all probability be such a state that was presenting such arguments), it is being entirely consistent in applying this policy to immigration law and should not be required to change this policy. Yet, if one asks not whether the couples are generally treated equally, but whether 'effective and repressive' measures are taken against them or whether the relationships are, to some degree, tolerated and acknowledged in domestic law and practice (as we have seen the ECtHR requires, to some degree) then this seems highly doubtful. The preferred approach, it is suggested, must be that there are no sufficient effective and repressive measures to combat and deter cohabitation and same-sex relationships in domestic law, and that therefore the use of immigration law to achieve the same result by keeping out a long-term partner is not justified.

3.3.9 Conclusions

Applying the principle of proportionality is always a difficult and uncertain task, and never more so than when the aim pursued by the host state is bound up with its own traditions and morals. Such reasons are unlikely to be rejected out of hand by the ECJ, but it is also quite possible that it would avoid an outright determination that the 'true proportionality' requirement has been breached in such a case.[64] Yet on occasions, and particularly when such delicate policy and moral issues are involved, the ECJ may insist on a high degree of consistency of treatment. The pattern of reasoning likely to emerge is not simply whether the protected rights outweigh the State's interest in defining and protecting its concept of the traditional family. The inqury is more likely to be whether it does so *given the degree of recognition and/or toleration already extended to such relationships* in domestic law and practice between lawful residents of the State.

PART FOUR — PRACTICAL REASONS

4.1 Introduction

There are five more mundane and practical concerns that might be brought forward by the host state to justify rejection of a de facto relationships immigration policy. They would all of course have to be considered under the same principles of the Member States relying on 'imperative

[64] Ie, that the protected right simply outweighs the interest pursued by the State.

reasons of public interest' to justify restricting the definition of 'family member' to married partners only discussed above:

1 It is necessary to prevent and detect fraud.
2 It is necessary to ensure that the relationships are lasting and durable.
3 It is necessary for reasons of administrative efficiency in proving relationships.
4 It is necessary to ensure no undue financial burden on the State.
5 It is necessary because there is no more room for immigrants.

4.2 Fraud

The argument that moving away from marriage as the paradigm 'community of life' between a couple would give rise to opportunities for abuse and fraud is sometimes made,[65] but it seems unconvincing. Fraudulent marriages take place already, and there are certainly ways of making sure that relationships (whether marital or not) are checked for fraud.[66] In any event, if minded to evade immigration laws, it would seem far easier to arrange a marriage (or registered partnership) of convenience rather than bring proof of a non-existent relationship, given the strong protection for married couples in Community law.[67] Nothing here would preclude Member States taking reasonable and proportionate measures to verify that such relationships were genuine and to detect fraud, and it is demeaning and disproportionate to stigmatise all unmarried couples as potential perpetrators of fraud against immigration authorities by refusing them all possibility of entry and residence.

4.3 Identifying Enduring and Stable Relationships

This is at the same time hopelessly over-inclusive and under-inclusive. On the one hand, it is over-inclusive in that marriage is no guarantee of long-term stability. This is particularly so where there are strong incentives to marry in order to secure residence rights for a TCN partner in an ongoing relationship that would not otherwise (yet) be formalised into a marriage without this incentive. And on the other, it is under-inclusive in that long-term relationships can and do exist outside marriage. This is

[65] See eg the quote from Taschner, (ch 1).
[66] Community law already accepts this: see Council Resolution 97/C 382/01 on Measures to be Adopted on the Combatting of Marriages of Convenience [1997] OJ C-382/1. See also the brief comments in *Akrich*.
[67] H Stalford, 'Concepts of the Family under EU Law: Lessons from the ECHR' (2002) 16 *IJLPF* 410, 427–8. Stalford notes the current highly formalistic and legal approach to the definition of the family adopted by EC law is also open to fraud and abuse.

particularly so in the situation of same-sex couples who are generally precluded from demonstrating their intended lifelong commitment by marriage, and may be precluded from doing so by entering into *any* kind of legal regulation of their partnership.

A rather more fundamental flaw underlies this reasoning. It relies not simply on the supposition that marriage is an acceptable shorthand way of identifying stable and durable relationships, which is in itself doubtful, but on the supposition that the possibility that the relationship might not *on average* be as stable and durable in the *long term* (perhaps over 5, 10 years or more) justifies the denial of residence permits at the outset when the couple are considering migration. The prospect of the relationship breaking up at some indefinite and undetermined stage in the future does not make the absence of the residence permit *now* any less of an obstacle to migration. The best that could be said is that this might justify the host state wishing to verify periodically the continuance of the relationship—until the partner had a right of residence in his or her own right as a long-term resident. Moreover, this justification makes no sense if applied to registered partnerships which are often the only way in which same-sex couples are able to demonstrate their mutual lifelong commitment in a public and legally recognised way.

4.4 Administrative Efficiency

This is perhaps a more plausible reason. It could be said that there is a considerably greater administrative burden on the State if the unmarried and unregistered couple have to prove their relationship. There might be questions about the propriety of using administrative efficiency to refuse residence rights. It could easily be argued that the detriment to the couple requires very weighty reasons to interfere with the right, and that administrative efficiency is simply not such a weighty reason, particularly when some states operate such systems successfully in relation to unmarried partnerships (and also do not refrain from conducting inquiries into the genuine nature of marriages). The other question is one of proportionality, and it could easily be argued that the splitting of the couple is disproportionate to the administrative burden of verifying the relationship. And yet again this justification makes little sense applied to legally registered partnerships from other States which could be treated in the same way as marriages.

4.5 Financial Burden on the State

This may be at first sight a seemingly plausible reason. It could be thought that the financial burden of additional unmarried partners might be too great, particularly if the couple are not bound by the long-term mutual financial commitments and interdependence of marriage. Yet, once more, if the principle of proportionality is applied, it would seem that there would be alternatives that would be less intrusive in family life—such as requiring financial means or self-sufficiency, at least for a period of time after admission of the partner. This might then engage squarely some rather more delicate questions about the degree to which greater financial requirements could be imposed on unmarried couples than on married couples, given the extremely relaxed requirements of means applied by Community law in the case of Member State workers who wish to bring their families. But there is no doubt that a right of residence subject to financial means (and a right to work to obtain such finances) would be a great deal better than the present situation, and less intrusive and obstructive of the protected rights.

4.6 No More Room for Immigrants

Finally, and perhaps most sensitively, there could be argument advanced that the state was not in any position to receive more immigrants, however self-sufficient they were. This argument could take two forms. First, that the employment market could not provide work for the additional residents. Second, a rather stronger version of this argument might run that there is simply no more room in the country for more residents. This, if sustained by evidence, might be a rather more plausible justification. Yet the EU is currently in the situation of expressing the need to develop an orderly and coherent immigration policy to recruit workers in the medium-term future.[68] If this is the case, then insisting on keeping out unmarried partners cannot be seen as justified. And indeed, if there is limited scope for inward migration, this still begs the question of why married (rather than other) partners should be privileged.

4.7 Conclusion

Although Member States might put up a brave fight on this point and may be able to justify measures to verify the genuine nature of the

[68] See eg the Proposal for a Council Directive on the Conditions of Entry and Residence of Third Country Nationals for the Purpose of Paid Employment and Self-Employed Activity COM(2001) 386. The contours of this remain highly contentious with some Member States particularly Germany insisting on clarification that the new Draft Constitution did not remove the competence of Member States to determine volumes of admissions of TCNs for such purposes. This is hardly surprising as the demographic and employment situation in each Member State may be variable. This variation has been highlighted most recently with the varying responses to the possibility of limiting free movement of Accession State Nationals—many Member States have decided to avail themselves of this option because they fear disruptive effects on their employment markets and exacerbation of existing unemployment, whereas the UK in particular intends to permit workers to enter to fill gaps in the labour market at time of shortage in particular sectors.

relationship, pragmatic and practical reasons for maintaining a strict and inflexible married-partners only immigration policy seem distinctly shaky.

PART FIVE — SPECIFIC ISSUES ARISING FROM THE NEW DIRECTIVES

There are two speficic questions that have to be addressed in the wake of the passage of the two Directives referred to in chapter 2. The first is the extent to which it will be seen to be permissible to maintain a narrower concept of the family in the context of TCNs. This is difficult to predict. It seems contrary to the spirit of the commitment at Tampere to develop rights for TCNs comparable to those of EU citizens—yet challenging with any effectiveness the exclusion and marginalisation of TCNs in Community law has never been easy and this not seem likely to change in the near future. The second is the EU Citizens Directive, and in particular the extent to which the obligation to 'facilitate' entry will be interpreted. As indicated before, a blanket policy of non-admission now seems to be impermissible, and the Directive does indicate that Member States must justify refusing entry to such partners. However, just how restrictive Member States will be permitted to be and whether they will be permitted to bring forward justifications which focus not on the individual situation of the couple (suspicion about or wish to verify the genuine nature of the relationship, suspicion of fraud, the financial situation of the couple, the length of the relationship) but on the general proposition that the host state legal system does not recognise unmarried couples, same-sex relationships or marriages, and that the host society disapproves of such relationships, will be an interesting question.

CONCLUSIONS OF CHAPTER SEVEN

The principle of proportionality is at the heart of this inquiry. The prospect of success under the ECHR alone seem at best indifferent, although better now in relation to same-sex couples. Turning to Community law the prospects are brighter. Although there are a range of reasons that might be brought forward to justify maintaining a marriage partners only immigration policy, there is a strong case to be made—based on the fundamental nature of the migration rights in question and the limited degree to which Member States take effective and repressive measures against unmarried cohabitation in their own territory—that these justifications are insufficient.

8

Conclusions

THIS FINAL CHAPTER will summarise the discussion so far and draw some more general and wide-ranging conclusions, setting the rest of the discussion in a wider context. The main theme that emerges is that this is an area in which certain fundamental tensions exist, the resolution of which will not be simple.

QUESTION 1: MEMBER STATE AUTONOMY IN FAMILY LAW MATTERS AND IMMIGRATION POLICY VS COMMUNITY INTERVENTION

We have seen the initial assumption that Community law arguably cannot and should not attempt to construct a single concept of 'European family law' in the sense of wholesale harmonisation of domestic family law either in relation to concepts of marriage, partnership and cohabitation or the legal incidents thereof. The objections to this are significant. Establishing competence for the Community to do so would be problematic. The closest the Treaty currently comes to this is judicial co-operation in civil matters in Title IV. The emphasis on matters in the field of judicial co-operation in civil matters *having cross-border implications* in Article 65 immediately focuses attention on trans-national recognition of relationships and marriages and recognition of court judgments rather than wholesale harmonisation of domestic family law. The explicit recognition that issues of family law with cross-border implications may legitmately fall within the scope of Community competence in the draft Constitutional Treaty is to be welcomed but again the cross-border element is emphasised. However, the necessity for the proper functioning of the internal market and the cross-border implications would have to be shown, and it may certainly be surmised that, after the recent *Tobacco Advertising* case[1] a rather more robust approach may be taken to the limits of Community competence. An alternative source of competence, but one that might

[1] Case C-376/98 *Germany v Council & Parliament: Re Tobacco Advertising Directive* [2000] 3 CMLR 1175.

only justify measures in relation to EU citizens, would be Articles 40 and 18 EC on the basis of facilitation of the free movement of EU citizens.

The next issue is subsidiarity. Even if competence were established, the necessity and propriety of Community action in this field is arguably limited. It might well be argued with some force that it is far more appropriate for the Member States to retain general competence and control over such issues of family law with limited Community intervention. Finally, the basic pragmatic question of reaching political agreement on this remains. It seems impossible that any such action would secure sufficient agreement for any legislation to be passed under the unanimity procedure in Title IV. If seen as an EU citizenship measure related to free movement under Article 18, the use of QMV would make the task somewhat easier, but still one might doubt whether sufficient support would exist.

And yet I have argued throughout in favour of Community intervention to impose a single concept of the 'family' in this specific area on the basis that immigration rights are so critical for the continuation of normal family life for the couple, that without them the very continuation of the normal relationship of the couple is jeopardised. As I have suggested, these two are not incompatible—recognition of immigration rights is far from a wholesale harmonisation of domestic family law and an issue where the case for Community law intervention is strong. The foregoing discussion has brought to bear a number of basic principles to resolve this tension in the context of immigration law and to suggest both normative and legal arguments in favour of intervention. This concluding chapter will revisit the arguments briefly and explore the implications of pursuing each of them, discussing both the implications for the resolution of the particular problem being addressed in this book, and the wider implications for the resolution of the tension set out above between the autonomy of Member State family law and the pressure for some intervention by the Community. In other words, what do each of these arguments suggest about how far it may be necessary or legitimate for Community law to intervene in family law matters? I will also address the implications of these different arguments from the point of view of those historically marginalised and excluded from Community family reunification rights—TCNs and non-migrant EU citizens. To what exent are the different arguments easily adaptable and able to assist these groups as and when Community law begins to apply to their situation?

The argument in favour of immigration rights may be made from principles of equality or by arguing that there is an inherent right of family reunification for a partner, regardless of whether the current law actually grants residence rights to married couples. The argument may also be made from principles of Community law or from the ECHR and the way Community law applies it. These are two cross-cutting approaches as

Community law and the ECHR each offer both an equality or inherent rights approach.

INHERENT RIGHTS

Family and Private Life

Precedents from the ECtHR are not altogether helpful. In particular the wide margin of appreciation granted in the field of immigration law means that it is far from clear that the ECHR requires admission of non-national non-marital partners. The future implications of Article 8 ECHR for other cross-border situations is also unclear, although it is entirely possible that in the future the ECtHR may be called upon to protect the rights of couples seeking to export some kind of legal recognition, whether marriage or registered partnership, from one state to another. This very vagueness however may operate to the advantage of couples in that there is as yet no established tradition of what Article ECHR 8 may or may not require of Contracting States in relation to these relationships when they cross borders. Thus, there is as yet no particular interpretation or view emerging from the ECtHR that the ECJ or Community policymaker might wish to distance itself from, which might perhaps deter them from embarking on such a course.

The advantage of using this approach is that Community law is free to develop its own approach to respect for family and private life. Immigration of non-national family members is one in which the established ECtHR approach is arguably inadequate for Community law. In relation to migrant EU citizens, Community law starts from an entirely different position from the Convention. The justification for establishing a greater degree of protection in Community law thus seems clear and this approach would not necessitate reliance on equal treatment. However, although equality is argued by some to be the most convincing conceptual argument overall, and pragmatically the most likely to succeed in securing rights for same-sex couples, for reasons that will be discussed shortly, I remain unconvinced that this is the most practical way forward in this particular area of Community law.

The difficulty in suggesting a distinctive Community law approach to ECHR rights is that this might seem politically sensitive. However, sound the conceptual basis of these arguments, persuading the ECJ or Community policymaker to embark on a clear rejection of the ECtHR approach as inadequate might not be easy. The aspects of Community law that make a distinctive Community law approach attractive could also be limited. In so far as they rely on the imperative of securing and facilitating migration of EU citizens, they may not easily be transferred to internal situations or to TCNs who do not benefit from these basic free movement rights. Yet if these difficulties can be overcome, the concept of respect for family life is perhaps more attractive than an approach based purely on obstacles as it would be more easily adaptable to TCNs and internal situations.

Free Movement and Obstacles

The concept of obstacles to the free movement of persons is another approach. It has the advantage of being easily applicable to all couples, regardless of sexual orientation or legal status, and again it avoids the necessity for direct reliance on a principle of equality. An obstacles approach provides a justification for action that is specific to Community law but would avoid the potential sensitivities of developing a particular concept of respect for family and private life that departs from the specific existing ECtHR interpretation. Potential difficulties do indeed exist in elaborating the exact concept of an obstacle to free movement, but these are not insuperable and most importantly, whatever approach is chosen, the question of immigration rights seems in any event to fit quite comfortably within the definition. Moreover, the approach focusing on the effect on the free movement of the individual of the particular national law measure neatly articulates the limits of the Community's legitimate interest in family law. It enables a line to be drawn to identify those questions of family law and civil status which can and should legitimately be regulated by Community law, and those in which the Community interest is much weaker and the argument in favour of Member State autonomy stronger. It may, however, be deeply problematic to rely on such a principle in relation to TCNs—at least until similar rights of free movement are extended to them. The question of internal situations might remain problematic until legislation addressed the situation of non-migrant EU citizens. More fundamentally, however, if used *as a source of directly effective rights against a Member State* this argument may encounter some scepticism from those such as Davies[2] who are not convinced that the Court of Justice should persist in its 'non-discriminatory obstacles' jurisprudence. Particularly if the Court persists with its current approach, seemingly struggling to articulate the proper boundaries of what is or is not an 'obstacle' or 'restriction' this scepticism may have some foundation. However, in the current situation with the obligation to 'facilitate' in the new EU Citizens' Directive, to employ this argument

[2] G Davies, *Nationality Discrimination in the European Internal Market* (Kluwer, The Hague, 2003).

one need not necessarily go so far as to suggest an infringment of directly effective rights. The underlying normative principle—that obstacles to migration should be removed as far as possible including those arising from the wish to settle with non-national family members—could certainly be used to suggest a wide and generous interpretation of this obligation and a narrow interpretation of the permissible reasons to deny entry and settlement.

In relation to the fundamental question of the extent to which this argument would suggest Community law should intervene in Member State family law and policy, there is nothing to suggest that pursuing this approach would lead to a general Community intervention in family law. It might be suggested that various aspects of family law (inability of same-sex couple to marry or to register a partnership for example) would make the exercise of free movement rights less attractive. The concept of 'obstacle', coupled with the justification that general competence over substantive family law remains with the Member States, is arguably quite sufficient to contain this. In particular the adoption of a higher standard than simply a measure that 'hinders or makes less attractive' or being 'detrimental to the conditions under which' the freedom is exercised would go a significant way to meet these concerns. Asking not whether such measures 'hinder or make less attractive' the right but whether they impose a 'direct or significant/exclusionary obstacle' to its exercise would arguably result in a quite different answer to many of these questions. Many details of family law would be covered by the suggestion in *Graf*[3] that the *potential* loss of a *remote or contingent benefit* is not such as to be an obstacle to the Treaty freedoms. Perhaps the most difficult argument to address would be that the inability of the same-sex couple to marry or have a registered partnership under the domestic law of the host state might in itself be an obstacle, even where the state of origin does not recognise partnerships and there is no question of mutual recognition as discussed below. It might indeed be thought that migrating to a state in which there is no possibility of legal protection of the relationship could hinder or make less attractive the exercise of these rights, perhaps in a significant or substantial way. Yet preserving the autonomy of national family law would surely be capable of being an acceptable justification at the present time for this and protect against this kind of intrusion of directly effective *Community law* into such areas—leaving aside other normative arguments in favour of such developments by agreed legislation at some future time.

There is however one area in which the Community interest seems strong and the autonomy of internal domestic family law not fundamentally

[3] Case C-190/98 *Volker Graf v Filzmoser Maschinenbau GmbH* [2000] ECR I-493.

threatened by a degree of Community law intervention. This is the question of transnational recognition of partnerships. The concept of obstacles could easily, and justifiably, be used to suggest that non-recognition of marriages and arguably also of legally registered partnerships from other Member States can and should be subject to justification. This would provide an impetus towards mutual recognition of marriages and registered partnerships between states who have created such institutions, even if the details of any legislative scheme might be challenging and difficult to complete. This does inevitably lead us to consider migrant same-sex marriages. It may be thought that this approach will lead to the Community law imperative of free movement being used to suggest a requirement of recognition of lawful same-sex marriages involving EU citizens. I readily admit that this is the case. Although in the context of this book with its focus on immigration law relating to all non-marital partners, the question of the general status of migrating same-sex marriages is not central and indeed distracts from the real issue, I have no difficulty accepting that the Community law imperative of free movement does indeed make the non-recognition of existing lawful marriages deeply problematic. I would even go so far as to say that I see no particular reason why the directly effective free movement rights could not and should not be used to require a host Member State to bring forward justifications for the refusal to recognise such a marriage that would be subject to the scrutiny of Community law in the ECJ. If a Member State considers that there are good and defensible reasons for non-recognition of such marriages then it will be open to it to make them openly, but there seems a sound argument in favour of requiring such justifications to be brought forward and subjected to scrutiny.

Clearly the most difficult question would be the mobility of an existing registered partnership to a state which does not yet have such a concept in domestic law. Could the autonomy of the Member State not to recognise such partnerships at all still be preserved? This would admittedly be a potential concern for those who did not wish to see Community law infringe on Member State autonomy in this way. And yet I am not convinced that this approach necessarily leads to this conclusion—ie, that Member States would be required to recognise such rights if they did not have them already in domestic law in the sense that their absence could be seen as an obstacle. The concept of an 'obstacle' might be confined to the situation where the host Member State was reluctant to recognise *within the framework of its own existing marriage and partnership law,* migrant couples with partnerships from other states. And even if the very lack of a registered partnership scheme which would permit such mutual recognition could be seen as an obstacle (and admittedly the argument could not be dismissed) the concept of justification should be sufficiently strong to deal with this, as discussed above. Even if it may be suggested that refusal to offer a degree of mutual recognition to 'foreign' marriages and partnerships within the framework of the State's own existing law is unjustified, the argument becomes much less plausible where the State would, in order to do so, have to recognise an institution that had not yet been introduced into domestic law. It may be that the difficulties posed by the absence of a legal regime for same-sex partners may be one reason to favour a degree of harmonisation or unification of family law in Europe[4]—but this is far from suggesting that directly effective principles of Community law require such schemes to be set up forthwith where they do not currently exist.

EQUALITY

Equality in the ECHR

The guarantee of equality contained in Article 14 ECHR is likely to be applicable in the case of immigration rights because of the clear link to family and private life protected by Article 8 EHCR. Following the ECtHR lead in *Karner*,[5] the most convincing case may be made in relation to equal treatment of same-sex couples, initially where the situations of unmarried same-sex and opposite-sex couples are distinguished, but the question of retention of special rights for married couples only (whether or not the state has a registered partnership law) may be more difficult and may take some time to resolve. This is likely to take longer to resolve. As regards unmarried heterosexual couples the arguments are weaker. There is in fact more established case law that would point towards the retention of a degree of margin of appreciation to preserve the special status of marriage than there currently is in relation to same-sex couples. Yet, if these difficulties may be overcome, the use of equality arguments tied to family and private life would be equally applicable to all individuals whose family and private life EU law undertakes to protect in this way by enacting family reunification rights. Thus non-migrant EU citizens and TCNs could quite easily benefit from such arguments when legislation is passed to regulate their situation.

Turning to other questions of family law, it is certainly conceivable that Article 14 ECHR will increasingly be used to press for changes in domestic family law, particularly in relation to same-sex couples. However, given the limited scope of Community law in family law issues and the

[4] See N Dethloff, 'Arguments for the Unification and Harmonisation of Family Law in Europe' in K Boele-Woelki (ed), *Perspectives for the Unification and Harmonisation of Family Law in Europe* (Intersentia, Antwerp, 2003).
[5] *Karner v Austria* Application 40016/98.

fact that these questions have not yet been addressed by the ECtHR, means that the concept of discrimination tied to family life could not easily be seen to suggest further more radical moves than have been suggested in the previous chapters in relation to immigration law. Asserting the necessity for equality if and when the Community's legislation deals with and regulates issues of family law and policy leaves open the question of the degree to which issues of family life will be dealt with at all.

Equal Treatment in Community Law

Community law also has its own concept of equal treatment. Conceptually this seems sound, and again appeals to a deeply-rooted and fundamental normative principle of equality. The basic principle of equality is long established in Community law and—at least in relation to sexual orientation—now has the advantage of the political legitimacy of the Charter of Fundamental Rights and a strong legal imperative for action in the recent ECtHR case law, if a significant and unwelcome difference of opinion is not to emerge between Luxembourg and Strasbourg on this issue. Moreover, it means that the particular benefit concerned cannot be denied to same-sex couples or registered partners from other Member States without denying it to married couples. As Wintemute points out,[6] if an equality argument is used successfully, then the only way that the State may justify the refusal of a particular benefit or recognition to same-sex couples is to withdraw it from all. In this particular case this seems inconceivable. And yet as we have seen (in contrast with some other contexts where partnership rights might seek recognition) there are strong and coherent arguments *in this field of partners immigration* that these 'inherent' rights are protected anyway regardless of discrimination and so this seems to offer only limited advantage here. There are also other difficulties. The first is the inherently political nature of any choice of comparator. The second more pragmatic concern is the current political climate in the Community.

Problems with an Equality Approach in Community Law

As Bamforth points out,[7] asserting the equivalence in the public legal sphere of same-sex and opposite-sex couples, or indeed of different kinds

[6] R Wintemute, *Partnership Rights as Human Rights* (Oxford Amnesty Lecture, 2002, OUP, Oxford, forthcoming).
[7] N Bamforth, 'Same-sex Partnerships and Arguments of Justice' in R Wintemute and M Andenas (eds), *Legal Recognition of Same-sex Partnerships* (Hart Publishing, Oxford, 2001).

of legally registered partnerships, inevitably begs the question *why* such assertions of equivalence and equality should be accepted. There may be more sound conceptual/legal or moral and philosophical normative justifications for the general recognition of same-sex partnerships and indeed for the granting of specific rights to same-sex couples. Bamforth suggests that autonomy/empowerment may be a stronger philosophical basis on which to argue for partnership recognition for same-sex couples than privacy or equality. As we have seen, in this context of immigration rights in Community law, concepts of family and private life and free movement may provide effective alternatives, both as legally enforceable principles, but also as normative principles to legitimate legislative action or indeed broad interpretations of the new Directives, the EU Citzens Directive in particular.

On a purely pragmatic level, the prospects are not that encouraging. Focusing on the *Community law* concept of discrimination, rather than the EHCR, might avoid any lingering sense that standards are being thrust on Community law from the outside rather than being developed internally. And yet as we have seen, the acceptance of equality of same-sex couples and registered partnerships is a deeply divisive issue. The ECJ seems unwilling to move on this point and seems quite frankly hostile to gay rights and to any concept of imposing equality of different kinds of legally recognised partnerships, as demonstrated by *Grant* and *D & Sweden v Council*. Its attitude to unmarried opposite-sex couples has not been tested so far but a similarly conservative approach is entirely plausible. The Community legislature seems to be following in this path, seemingly encouraged by the reticence of the ECJ (I shall return to this point below).

There is also some difficulty in extending this approach beyond assertions of equality for same-sex couples and legally registered partnerships. It must be stressed that the proper limits of equality of different couples—*with regard to marriages or registered partnerships vs unregistered couples of whatever sexual orientation* still have to be worked out. The imperative of equal treatment here is surely less strong than in the situation where the question is purely one of comparability of opposite-sex and same-sex couples where both are married/registered or both simply cohabiting. Indeed, the ECtHR has been reluctant to require equality where relationships between adult partners (rather than parent/child relationships) are involved, and using the principle of equality to secure residence rights for *all cohabiting couples* thus seems to stretch it beyond its current limits. The crucial importance of immigration rights means that an argument might be made for comparability of all couples for *these*

See further N Bamforth, *Sexuality, Morals and Justice: a Theory of Lesbian and Gay Rights Law* (Cassell, London, 1997).

purposes without necessarily undermining the possibility of maintaining special protection for married couples and those in other similar registered partnerships: This should allay fears that equality in this field will inexorably and inevitably lead to Community law being unable to enact provisions containing, or permitting Member States to maintain, particular protection and rights for married (or registered same-sex) couples on every occasion that it ventures into the field of family law where there are pressing transnational cross-border issues to be addressed.

NATIONALITY DISCRIMINATION

This seems a less convincing alternative to the obstacles approach outlined above in securing immigration rights for non-national partners. It seems more complex than the obstacles approach, and unnecessarily so. The only advantage is that it is perhaps rather more securely based in the Treaty and longstanding principles of nationality discrimination than the obstacles approach. The applicability of this concept to TCNs at this time seems just problematic as obstacles, but again this may be overcome if and when the position of TCNs is increasingly assimilated to that of EU citizens.

It does, however, point to one significant issue. As we have seen in chapter 1, there are some Member States in which registration of partnerships is made subject to more stringent conditions for non-nationals than for nationals, and the Belgian same-sex marriage law initially excluded most non-Belgians altogether. The concession that nationals from states which already have a similar concept of registered partnership or same-sex marriage may be treated as nationals of the host state is not good enough. It still leaves the migrant *and resident* EU Citizen from another Member State subject to potentially significant delays and problems. This seems to be a clear case of direct discrimination against migrants in respect of an issue which should clearly be seen as falling within the definition of 'social advantage' or more generally the material scope of the Treaty for the purposes of Article 12 EC. This says nothing about the internal arrangements of Member State family and partnership law—other than that it should not and cannot under Community law treat migrants differently. It will inevitably mean that special treatment for home state nationals should go and that residence or domicile regardless of (Member State) nationality should become the main criterion for eligibility. This concept of opening same-sex marriage or partnership registration to migrant EU citizens (at the very least those who are settled residents) on equal terms with host state nationals is in line with longstanding principles of Community law. Clarification of this point would in my view be welcome, as is the confirmation in January 2004 of the repeal of these restrictions in the Belgian legislation.

Conclusion

There are a number of approaches that can be taken to this issue, several of which seem convincing in themselves conceptually. However, on reviewing them, an approach asserting that these rights belong inherently to all couples rather than building a claim on equality with married couples seems pragmatically more likely to succeed. Turning to the choice between family and private life and obstacles, the arguments are quite finely balanced. The distinctively Community law non-discriminatory obstacles approach might seem the surest and most attractive way to build a claim for residence rights in Community law. It avoids the potential sensitivities of Community law being seen to reject as inadequate particular established ECtHR jurisprudence, and also provides an interesting foundation on which to proceed in contemplating the proper and legitimate response of Community law to the diversity of family law and policy outlined in chapter 1. Yet there are those who remain unconvinced of the legitimacy of the obstacles approach, and the non-discriminatory obstacles approach would not necessarily easily be extended to assist those TCNs covered by the new Directive. The possibility of a distinctive Community law interpretation of family and private life in immigration law is a real one, and builds on a recent progressive trend in Strasbourg jurisprudence. Of course these two arguments can be presented side by side—they are not mutually exclusive but may be used to reinforce each other.

QUESTION 2: TENSION BETWEEN JUDICIAL AND LEGISLATIVE APPROACHES

There is also clearly a tension between the democratic process taking its course, and the task of the Court in protecting basic fundamental rights—whether those of free movement, equality or family and private life. An in-depth discussion of the proper scope and limits of the ECJ's role and a critique or defence of its approach is impossible in the concluding chapter of this book. However, a few comments may be made to highlight the main issues. A forceful articulation of the desirability and indeed the necessity for judicial intervention in the face of social change and outdated legislation comes in the opinion of AG Geelhoed in *Baumbast*.[8] Speaking in the context of the increasing prevalence of family break-up and the increasing possibilities for work and family life to be separated geographically, he emphasises the legitimacy of the ECJ taking a proactive robust view of the application of basic principles of Community law to deal with these situations in order that undesirable lacunae in the

[8] Case C-413/99 *Baumbast & R v SSHD*.

protection of Community law do not develop. Without making specific reference to this, the ECJ adopts the substance of his suggestions. One may agree with him, and this might seem convincing in itself in the absence of any legislative proposals. Yet this alone does not seem enough to address the complexities of the problem. Family immigration rights have been the subject of heated debate in recent legislative proposals. What may be desirable filling of lacunae, if and when where there are no legislative provisions under consideration, might be seen as undesirable and illegitimate intrusion by the judiciary where the political process of putting together legislation has recently been completed without agreement on a particular point.

However, what is most striking on reading the primary materials referred to—documents relating to the legislative process (chapter 2) and cases from the ECJ (particularly those relating to equality) is the vicious circle that seems to be developing to block progress on this issue. In *Grant*[9] it is quite clear that the ECJ considers judicial deference to the legislative process appropriate. It concludes that discrimination on the grounds of sex *is not* in the current state of Community law to be interpreted as including discrimination on the grounds of sexual orientation. It then goes on to add that:

> It should be observed however that the Treaty of Amsterdam provides for the insertion in the EC Treaty of an art 6a which, once the Treaty of Amsterdam comes into force, will allow the EU Council under certain conditions (a unanimous vote on a proposal from the Commission after consulting the European Parliament) to take appropriate action to eliminate various forms of discrimination, including discrimination based on sexual orientation.[10]

In *D & Sweden*[11] a similar view emerges. The Swedish government had, when the Regulation[12] was adopted, suggested the assimilation of registered partnerships with marriages in the Regulation for the purposes of the family allowance and other benefits. This specific suggestion, which would have helped the couple and confirmed the entitlement to the benefit in question, was rejected. The ECJ considers the arguments of the couple and at the suggestion of the Council[13] it comes to the following conclusion:

> Only the legislature can, where appropriate adopt measures to alter that situation, for example by amending the provisions of the Staff Regulations.

[9] Case C-249/96 *Grant v Southwest Trains* [1998] ECR I-0621.
[10] Para 48.
[11] Cases C-122 and 125/99P *D & Sweden v Council* [2001] ECR I-4319.
[12] Staff Regulation 781/98 ([1998] OJ L113/4).
[13] Para 32.

> However, not only has the Community legislature not shown any intention of adopting such measures, it has even (see paragraph 32) ruled out at this stage any idea of other forms of partnership being assimilated to marriage for the purposes of granting the benefits reserved under the Staff Regulations for married officials, choosing instead to maintain the existing arrangements until the various consequences of such assimilation become clear.[14]

Again judicial deference to legislative judgment prevails, if anything more clearly than in *Grant*. The implications of this approach for immigration law are all too obvious given the reluctance of most involved in discussing the two recently agreed Directives to make any significant move on this issue.

The deeply worrying thing is that this caution seems to have been fed into the current legislative process. The Commission officials seem, implicitly if not explicitly, to be relying on the fact that *D & Sweden* and *Grant* do not require any action in this area, despite both the obvious shortcomings in the reasoning in *D & Sweden* and the fact that some issues of critical importance to the question of immigration rights were simply not addressed. Most striking however is the draft Santini report of November 2002:[15]

> Definition of 'spouse': in line with the case law of the Court of Justice, with particular reference to the judgment of 31 May 2001 in D and Kingdom of Sweden against the Council of the European Union, according to the definition generally accepted by the Member State, the term 'marriage' means a union between two persons of the opposite sex.
>
> Unmarried partner: in the same case, the Court of Justice found that 'the fact that, in a limited number of Member States, a registered partnership is assimilated, although incompletely, to marriage cannot have the consequence that, by mere interpretation, persons whose legal status is distinct from that of marriage can be covered by the term "married official" as used in the Staff Regulations.' This means that the situation of an unmarried partner cannot be treated as 'equivalent' to that of a married partner and that national law must be applied to unmarried partners in accordance with the principle of non-discrimination between other Community citizens and the citizens of the Host State.

The use of the judgment in *D & Sweden* to justify the explicit removal of same-sex spouses from the scope of Article 2(2)a (guaranteed entry), continued total neglect of the situation of registered partners, and

[14] Para 38.

[15] Draft Report of the LIBE Committee on the Proposal COM(2001) 257 Document PE319.238, 25 November 2002.

continued discrimination against unmarried partners is disturbing. The ECJ may indeed have been quite clear about its perception of the proper limits of its role in statutory interpretation and the application of the principle of equal treatment to existing legislation. But to suggest, which is what this passage seems to, that this might constrain the Council and Parliament when adopting the new Directive and might provide any reason to justify the position taken is another matter altogether, and seems entirely unjustified. Although the draft report was amended before the LIBE Committee adopted it, the sentiments expressed remain worrying.

Judicial caution is feeding into the legislative process and being used, in some quarters at least, to justify continued legislative conservatism. The danger is then that this may later feed back into yet more cautious judgments in the ECJ when it sees the cautious approach of the legislature and once again feels it appropriate to defer to the legislative process—in particular on questions that the legislature could not settle by agreement. If Community legislation remains conservative and restricted to married couples, any subsequent judicial decision requiring greater residence rights might be as a bold and ambitious one, and one with little legitimacy. However, the fundamental nature of the basic rights involved is a telling point in favour of judicial intervention.[16] The ECJ should not ignore its role in ensuring that the law is observed. The apparent unwillingness of those involved in the legislative process to recognise that a more specific justification is required than simply stating that agreement is impossible at the present time is disappointing and provides another justification for judicial intervention. As it stands, any decision in favour of the current position seems incomplete and ill-reasoned and should arguably not prevent the Court from intervening to ensure that the basic principles of Community law discussed here are observed. The comments of AG Geelhoed in *KB* are somewhat more positive in this respect, indicating that a move towards recognition of 'de facto' relationships for the purposes of immigration law and indeed beyond may be inevitable.

The compromise eventually reached in the EU Citizens' Directive with an obligation to 'facilitate' entry of couples in stable relationships where the obligation to permit entry of the spouse or limited obligation to permit entry of the registered partner does not apply does not alter this conclusion. On the contrary, it gives the ECJ a legislative provision to work with and may make the task of those arguing for an approach such as the one taken throughout this book somewhat easier. The decicison will no doubt be a delicate one, and the inability to agree a clear expression of a clear

[16] For a recent discussion and defence of the legitimacy of the judicial role in upholding basic (especially equality) rights and using a robust standard of scrutiny in doing so, see *Ghaidan v Mendoza* [2002] EWCA Civ 1533 [2002] 4 All ER 1162.

obligation to admit all partners in stable relationships might point in favour of a somewhat limited reading of the obligation to 'facilitate' entry and residence at least to the extent of not interpreting it as a general obligation to admit. Yet it is clear that it must have some meaning, and the elaboration of the term, together with the legal arguments presented here in favour of such an obligation, would make a stronger reading, akin to an obligation to admit, a plausible one. In particular if the couple are legally unable to marry in the country of origin or in the host state (rather than simply being unwilling to do so for whatever reason) it might prove to be of some assistance. It remains to be seen how Member States will interpret this obligation and what the outcome will be if the point is ever taken to the ECJ—as it seems likely will happen at some stage.

Conclusion

Clear legislation would have been the most desirable way to proceed, and the compromise reached is messy and unclear. Legislative and judicial caution seem to be fuelling each other. Consequently, there is a risk that basic principles of Community law will be sidelined and abandoned along the way, getting little or no serious consideration. This is indeed an unenviable dilemma for any court. The new legislation will present an interesting challenge for the Court of Justice and national policymakers implementing it. It is hoped that the ECJ will respond to the challenges that lie ahead in the interpretation and application of the new legislation rather better than it has done in respect of some of these issues in the past.

Bibliography

Books and Papers

ACIERNO, S (2003) 'The Carpenter Judgment: Fundamental Rights and the Limits of the Communtiy Legal Order' 28 *ELRev* 398

ALLEN, R (1999) 'Equal Treatment Social Advantages and Obstacles: In Search of Coherence in Freedom and Dignity' in E Guild (ed) *The Legal Framework and Social Consequences of the Free Movement of Persons in the European Union* (Kluwer, The Hague)

ALSTON, P (ed) (1999) *The EU and Human Rights* (OUP, Oxford)

ALTER, K (2002) *Establishing the Supremacy of Community Law* (OUP, Oxford)

ANDERFUHREN-WAYNE, C (1996) 'Family Unity in Immigration and Refugee Matters' 8 *IJRL*

ANTOKOLSKAIA, M (2003) 'The Harmonisation of Family Law: New and Old Dilemmas' *ERPL* 28

ARMSTRONG, K (2002) 'Mutual Recognition' in C Barnard and J Scott (eds), *The Law of the Single European Market* (Hart Publishing, Oxford)

ARNULL, A, WYATT, D and DASHWOOD, A (2000) *Wyatt & Dashwood's European Union Law*, 4th edn (Sweet & Maxwell, London)

BAMFORTH, N (1997) *Sexuality Morals and Justice: a Theory of Lesbian and Gay Rights Law* (Cassell, London)

—— (1999) '*Grant v Southwest Trains*: Some Comparative Observations' 2 *CYELS* 125

—— (2000) 'Sexual Orientation After *Grant v Southwest Trains*' 63 *MLR* 694

—— (2001) 'Same-sex Partnerships and Arguments of Justice' in R Wintemute and M Andenas (eds), *Legal Recognition of Same-sex Partnerships* (Hart Publishing, Oxford)

BARLOW, A (2001) *Cohabitants and the Law* (Butterworths, London)

BARLOW, A and JAMES, G (2004) 'Regulating Marriage and Cohabitation in 21st Century Britain' 67 *MLR* 143

BARNARD, C (1997) '*P v S* — Kite Flying or a New Constitutional Approach?' in A Dashwood and S O'Leary (eds), *The Principle of Equal Treatment in EC Law* (Sweet & Maxwell, London)

—— (1998) 'Some Are More Equal Than Others: The Decision of the Court of Justice in *Grant v Southwest Trains*' *CYELS* 147

—— (2001) 'Fitting the Remaining Pieces into the Goods and Services Jigsaw' 26 *ELRev* 35

—— (2004) *The Substantive Law of the EU: The Four Freedoms* (OUP, Oxford)

BARRETT, G (2003) 'Family Matters: European Community Law and Third Country National Family Members' 40 *CMLRev* 369

BAUR, F (2001) 'At the End of the Fairy Tale, Will Heidi Stay Single? Same-sex Partnerships in Switzerland' in R Wintemute and M Andenas (eds), *Legal Recognition of Same-sex Partnerships* (Hart Publishing, Oxford)

BBC News reports, BBC News Website, 27/11/2001, 05/02/2002, 31/05/2002 and 24/06/2002
BEAUMONT, P (2001) 'Human Rights: Some Recent Developments and their Impact on Convergence and Divergence of Law in Europe' in P Beaumont et al (eds), *Convergence and Divergence in European Public Law* (Hart Publishing, Oxford)
BEENEN, N (2001) *Citizenship and Access to Public Service Employment* (Europa Publishing, Groningen)
Belgian Federal Ministry of Justice, Press Relases, 22 June 2001, 7 December 2001, January 2002, on Ministry of Justice Website, *http//194.7.188.126/justice/index_fr.htm*
BELL, M (1999) 'Shifting Conceptions of Sexual Discrimination at the Court of Justice' 5 *ELJ* 63
—— (2002) 'We Are Family? Same-sex Partners and EU Migration Law' 9 *MJ* 335
—— (2002) *Anti-Discrimination Law and the European Union* (OUP, Oxford)
BENOIT-ROMER (2002) 'L'affaire *Emesa Sugar*' *CDE* 403
BERMANN, F (2002) 'Proportionality and Subsidiarity' in C Barnard and J Scott (eds), *The Law of the Single European Market* (Hart Publishing, Oxford)
BERNARD, N (1996) 'Discrimination and Free Movement in EC Law' 45 *ICLQ* 83
—— (2002) *Multilevel Governance in the European Union* (Kluwer, The Hague)
BETTEN, L and GRIEF, N (1998) *EU Law and Human Rights* (Longman, London)
BIONDI, A (1999/2000) 'In and Out of the Internal Market — Recent Developments on the Principle of Free Movement' 19 *YEL* 469
BLAKE, N (1999) 'Family Life in Community Law: the Limits of Freedom and Dignity' in E Guild (ed), *The Legal Framework and Social Consequences of Free Movement of Persons in the European Union* (Kluwer, The Hague)
BLAKE, N and HUSSAIN, R (2003) *Immigration Asylum and Human Rights* (OUP/Blackstone, Oxford)
BOELE-WOELKI, K (ed) (2003) *Perspectives for the Unification and Harmonisation of Family Law in Europe* (Intersentia, Antwerp)
BORILLO, D (2001) 'The Pacte Civil de Solidarité in France: Midway between Marriage and Cohabitation' in R Wintemute and M Andenas (eds), *Legal Recognition of Same-sex Partnerships* (Hart Publishing, Oxford)
BRADLEY, D (2001) 'Unmarried Cohabitation in West-European Jurisdictions' (15) *IJLPF* 22
BRAIBANT, G (2001) *La Charte des Droits Fundamentaux de l'Union Européene* (Éditions du Seuil, Paris)
BROWNSTEIN, A (1994) 'Why Same-sex Spouses should be Granted Preferential Immigration Status: Revaluating *Adams v Howerton*' 16 *Loyola LA Int and Comp L J* 763
BRUMBY, E (1999) 'What Is in a Name: Why the European Same-sex Partnership Acts Create a Valid Marital Relationship' 28 *Georgia J Int and Comp Law* 145
Canadian Journal of Family Law (2000) 17(1), Symposia Papers
CANOR, I (2000) 'Primus Inter Pares: Who is the Ultimate Guardian of Fundamental Rights in Europe?' 25 *ELRev* 3
CARACCIOLO DI TORELLA, E and REID, E (2002) 'The Changing Shape of the European Family and Fundamental Rights' 27 *ELRev* 80
CARACCIOLO DI TORELLA, E and MASSELOT, A (2004) 'Under Construction: EU Family Law' 29 *ELRev* 33

CARENS, J (2003) 'Who Should Get In? The Ethics of Immigration Admissions' (17) *Ethics and International Affairs* 95

CAREY, N (2001) 'From Obloquy to Equality: In the Shadow of Abnormal Situations' 20 *YEL* 79

CARLIER, J-Y (1999) 'La Libre Circulation des Personnes dans l'Union Européenne' *Journal des Tribunaux* (Droit Européen) 56

CASTRO OLIVIERA, A (2002) 'Workers and Other Persons: Step by Step from Movement to Citizenship — Caselaw 1995-2001' 39 *CMLRev* 77

CHAMBERS, D (1994) 'Polygamy and Same-sex Marriage' 27(1) *Hofstra Law Review*

CHOLEWINSKI, R (1994) 'Strasbourg's "Hidden Agenda?" The Protection of Second-generation Migrants from Expulsion under Article 8 of the ECHR' 12 *Netherlands Quarterly of International Law*

—— (1994) 'The Protection of the Right of Economic Migrants to Family Reunion in Europe' 43 *ICLQ* 568

—— (1997) *Migrant Workers in International Human Rights Law* (OUP, Oxford)

CLAYTON, R and TOMLINSON, H (2000) *The Law of Human Rights* (OUP, Oxford)

Copenhagen Post, 'The Government's New Immigration and Integration Proposals' 24 Jan 2002

—— 'Spouses Turn Towards Sweden for Residency Hope' 12 July 2002

COSTELLO, C (2000) 'Market Access All Areas — the Treatment of Non-discriminatory Barriers to the Free Movement of Workers' 27 *LIEI* 267

COUROUGE, E (1997) 'Le Respect de la Vie Familiale: des Etrangers et Article 8 CEDH' 13 *Revue Francaise de Droit Administratif* 318

CRAIG, P and DE BÚRCA, G (1998) *EU Law,* 2nd edn (OUP, Oxford)

—— (2002) *EU Law,* 3rd edn (OUP, Oxford)

CRESSWELL, D (1996) *Lesbians, Gay Men, and Canadian Law* (Edward, Montgomery)

CROSSMAN, B and RYDER, B (2001) 'What is Marriage-like Like? The Irrelevance of Conjugality' 18 *CJFL*

CVETIC, G (1987) 'Immigration Cases in Strasbourg: The Right to Family Life under Article 8 ECHR' 36 *ICLQ* 647

D'OLIVIERA, H (2000) 'Freedom of Movement of Spouses and Registered Partners in the European Union' in Siehr, K and Bassedow, J (eds), *Private Law in the International Arena: From National Conflict Rules Towards Harmonization and Unification* (TMC Asser Press,The Hague)

DANIELE, L (1997) 'Non Discriminatory Restrictions to the Free Movement of Persons' 22 *ELRev* 191

DASHWOOD, A and O'Leary, S (eds) (2000) *The Principle of Equal Treatment in EC Law* (Sweet & Maxwell, London)

DAVIES, G (2002) *Nationality Discrimination and Free Movement Law* (PhD Thesis, Groningen)

—— (2003) *Nationality Discrimination in the European Internal Market* (Kluwer, The Hague)

DE BÚRCA, G (1993) 'Fundamental Rights and the Reach of EC Law' 13 *OJLS* 283

—— (1993) 'The Principle of Proportionality and its Application in EC law' 13 *YEL* 105

—— (2001) 'The Drafting of the Charter of Fundamental Rights' *ELRev* 126

DE SCHUTTER, O (1996) 'Le Droit au Regroupement Familial au Croisement des Orders Juridiques Européens' 90 *RDE* 531

DE SCHUTTER, O and Weyembergh, A (2001) '"Statutory Cohabitation" under Belgian Law: A Step towards Same-sex Marriage?' in R Wintemute and M Andenas (eds), *Legal Recognition of Same-sex Partnerships* (Hart Publishing, Oxford 2001)

DE WITTE, B (2001) 'The Legal Status of the Charter: Vital Question or Non-issue?' 8 *MJ*

DETHLOFF, N (2003) 'Arguments for the Unification and Harmonisation of Family Law in Europe' in K Boele-Woelki (ed), *Perspectives for the Unification and Harmonisation of Family Law in Europe* (Intersentia, Antwerp)

DETHLOFF, N (2002) 'Germany — The Registered Partnerships Act of 2001' in A Bainham (ed) *ISFL* 171

DOUGAN, M (2001) 'The Workseeker as Citizen' 4 *CYELS* 1503

DUCLOS, N (1991) 'Some Complicating Thoughts on Same-sex Marriage' 1 *Law & Sexuality* 31

DUFFY, P (1982) 'The Protection of Privacy, Family Life and Other Rights Under Article 8 of the European Convention on Human Rights' 1 *YEL* 191

DUTHEIL DE LA ROCHÈRE, J (2004) 'Droits de L'Homme: la Charte des Droits Fundamentaux et Au-delà' in *Europe 2004 — Le Grand Débat*

ECKHOUT, P (2002) 'The EU Charter of Fundamental Rights and the Federal Question' *CMLRev* 945

Editorial note, [2001] 'The European Picture of Cohabitation' *International Family Law* 168

ELLIS, E (2002) 'Casenote on *De Sweden v Council*' 39(1) *CMLRev* 151

—— (1999) *The Principle of Proportionality in the Laws of Europe* (Hart Publishing, Oxford)

EMILIOU, N (1996) *The Principle of Proportionality in European Law: a Comparative Study* (Kluwer, The Hague)

ERRERA, R [2000] 'Annotation of *Marrousitch*' *PL* 731

ESKRIDGE, W (1996) *The Case for Same-sex Marriage: From Sexual Liberty to Civilised Commitment* (Free Press, New York)

—— (2001) 'The Ideological Structure of the Same-sex Marriage Debate' in R Wintemute and M Andenas (eds), *Legal Recognition of Same-Sex Partnerships* (Hart Publishing, Oxford)

—— (2002) *Equality Practice — Civil Unions and the Future of Gay Rights* (Routledge, New York)

ETTELBRICK, P (1997) 'Since When is Marriage a Path to Liberation?' (Fall 1989) 6 *OUT/LOOK*, reprinted in W Eskridge (ed), *Sexuality Gender and Law* (Foundation Press, Westbury, NY)

European Co-ordination for the Rights of Foreigners to Family Life, press release 17.6.2002, available on website *http://members.aol.com/coordeurop/indexce.html*

Eurostat, *Social Situation in the EU 2001* (Eurostat/European Commission, Brussels)

—— (2001) *Eurostat Yearbook 2002* (Eurostat/European Commission Brussels)

EYER, K (2002) 'Annotation of *Burns v Burns*' 20 *Yale Law and Policy Review* 297

FEUSS, K (ed) (2000) *The EU Charter of Fundamental Rights* (Federal Trust, London)

FINNIS, J (1993–94) 'Law, Morality and Sexual Orientation' 69 *Notre Dame Law Review* 1049

—— (1997) 'The Good of Marriage and the Morality of Sexual Relations: Some Philosophical and Historical Observations' 42 *Am J Jurisprudence*

FORDER, C (1998) 'The Anti-discrimination Principle as an Instrument of Change in Family Law' 45 *NILR* 29

FOSTER, N (1987) 'The European Court of Justice and the European Convention for the Protection of Human Rights' 8 *HRLJ* 245

FOURLANOS, G (1986) *Sovereignty and the Ingress of Aliens* (Almqvist and Wiksell, Stockholm)

FRUEHWALD, S (1999) 'Choice of Law and Same-sex Marriage' 51 *Fla L Rev* 799

GARDNER, J (1998) 'On the grounds of her sex(uality)' 18 *OJLS* 167

GEORGE, R (1999) *In Defense of Natural Law* (OUP, Oxford)

GEORGE, R and BRADLEY, G (1995) 'Marriage and the Liberal Imagination' 84 *Geo LJ* 301

GRAFF, E (1999) *What is Marriage For?* (Beacon Press, Boston)

GROENENDIJK, K et al (eds) (1998) *Security of Residence and Long-term Migrants: A Comparative Study of Law and Practice in European Countries* (Council of Europe, Strasbourg)

GUILD, E (2001) *Immigration Law in the European Community* (Kluwer, The Hague)

—— (2001) 'Free Movement and Same-sex Relationships: Existing Law and Article 13 EC' in R Wintemute and M Andenas (eds), *Legal Recognition of Same-sex Partnerships* (Hart Publishing, Oxford)

—— (2001) 'Security of Residence and Expulsion of Foreigners: European Community Law' in E Guild and P Minderhoud (eds), *Security of Residence and Expulsion: Protection of Aliens in Europe* (Kluwer, The Hague)

GUILD, E and LESIEUR, G (1998) *The ECJ on the ECHR, Who said What, When?* (Kluwer, The Hague)

GUILD, E and HARLOW, C (eds) (2001) *Implementing Amsterdam* (Hart Publishing, Oxford)

GUILD, E and MINDERHOUD, P (eds) (2001) *Security of Residence and Expulsion — Protection of Aliens in Europe* (Kluwer, The Hague)

GUTTMAN, R (1995) 'Discrimination against Own Nationals: a Brief Look at European and German Immigration Law' 9 *INLP* 97

HAILBRONNER, K (2001) *Immigration and Asylum Law and Policy of the European Union* (Kluwer, The Hague)

HAMILTON, C and STANDLEY, K (eds) (1995) *Family Law in Europe* (Butterworths, London)

HARMSEN, R (2001) 'National Responsibility for European Community Acts under the European Convention on Human Rights' 7 *EPL* 625

Harvard Law Review (2003) 'Developments in the Law — the Law of Marriage and Family. II — Inching Down the Aisle: Differing Paths Toward the Legalisation of Same-sex Marriage in the United States and Europe' 116 *Harvard L Rev* 1996

—— (2003) 'Developments in the Law — the Law of Marriage and Family: III — Consitutional Constraints on Interstate Same-sex Marriage Recognition' 116 *Harvard L Rev* 1997

HENRICH, D (1996) 'Family Law Across Frontiers: Facts, Conflicts, Trends' in N Lowe and G Douglas, *Families Across Frontiers* (Martinus Nijhoff, the Hague)

HERRINGA, A and VERHEY, L (2001) 'The EU Charter: Text and Structure' 8 *MJ* 11

HERVEY, T (1995) 'A Gendered Perspective on the Right to Family Life in European Community Law' in N Neuwahl and A Rosas (eds) *The European Union and Human Rights* (Kluwer, The Hague)

HIBBS, M, BERTON, C and BESWICK, J [2001] 'Why Marry?' *Family Law* 197

HILSON, C (1999) 'Discrimination in Community Free Movement Law' 24 *ELRev* 445

House of Commons Library Research Paper 00/32, *The EU Charter of Fundamental Rights*

House of Commons Library Research Paper 02/17, *The Relationships (Civil Registration) Bill and the Civil Partnerships Bill*

House of Lords European Union Select Committee 6th Report of 2002/3 (2003) *The Future Status of the European Union Charter of Fundamental Rights* (HMSO, London)

ILGA-Europe Position Paper on Proposal COM(2001) 257, available on ILGA-Europe website *www.ilga-europe.org*

ILIOPOULOU, A and TONER, H (2002) 'Annotation of *Grzelczyk*' 39 *CMLRev* 609

Immigration Law Practitioners Association, Scoreboard on Proposal COM(2001) 257, available on ILPA website, *www.ilpa.org.uk*

International Journal of Law Policy and the Family (2001) 15(1), Symposia papers

JACOBS, F (1994) 'European Community Law and the European Convention on Human Rights' in D Curtin and T Heukels (eds), *Institutional Dynamics of European Integration* (Martinus Nijhoff, Dordrecht)

JÄNTERÄ-JAREBORG, M (2003) 'Registered Partnerships in Private International Law: the Scandanavian Approach' in K Boele-Woelki and A Fuchs (eds), *Legal Recognition of Same-sex Couples in Europe* (Intersentia, Antwerp)

JARVIS, M (1998) *The Application of EC Law by National Courts: The Free Movement of Goods* (OUP, Oxford)

JAURENA I SALAS, F (2001) 'The Law on Stable Unions of Couples in the Catalonia Autonomous Region of Spain' in R Wintemute and M Andenas (eds), *Legal Recognition of Same-sex Partnerships* (Hart Publishing, Oxford)

JOHNSON, E and O'KEEFE, D (1994) 'From Discrimination to Obstacles to Free Movement — Recent Developments Concerning the Free Movement of Workers 1989–1994' 31 *CMLRev* 1313

JORDAN, F (1968) 'The Federal Divorce Act (1968) and the Constitution' 14 *McGill LJ* 209

Journal of Ethnic and Migration Studies, Special Issue (1998) 24(2)

KHALIQ, U [2001] 'Protocol 12 to the ECHR: A Step Forward or a Step Too Far?' *PL* 457

KIERNAN, K (1999) 'Cohabitation in Western Europe' 96 *Population Trends* 25

—— (2001) 'The Rise of Cohabitation and Childbearing Outside Marriage in Western Europe' 15 *IJLPF* 1

KOPPELMAN, A (1998) 'Same-sex Relationships, Choice of Law, and Public Policy' 76 *Tex L Rev* 921

—— (2001) 'The Miscegenation Analogy in Europe, or, Lisa Grant Meets Adolf Hitler' in R Wintemute and M Andenas (eds), *Legal Recognition of Same-sex Partnerships* (Hart Publishing, Oxford)

Kortmann Committee Commissie Inzake Openstelling van het Burgerlijk voor Personen van Hetzelfde Geslacht — Rapport (Ministry of Justice, The Hague, 1997)

KOUTRAKOS, P (2001) 'On Groceries, Alcohol and Olive Oil: More on Free Movement of Goods after Keck' 26 *ELRev* 391

KRÉMER, P (2002) 'La Marche des Fiertés Homosexuelles sous le Signe de la Vigilance' *Le Monde*, 30 June 2002

LAHAV, G (1997) 'International versus National Constraints in Family-reunification Migration Policy' 3 *Global Governance* 349

LAMBERT, H (1999) 'The European Court of Human Rights and the Right of Refugees and Other Persons in Need of Protection to Family Reunion' 11 *IJRL* 427

Law Commission of Canada (2001) *Beyond Conjugality* (Law Commission of Canada, Ottawa)

LAWSON, R (1994) 'Confusion and Conflict? Diverging Interpretations of the European Convention on Human Rights in Luxembourg and Strasbourg' in R Lawson and M de Bloijs (eds), *The Dynamics of the Protection of Human Rights in Europe: Essays in Honour of H Schermers* Volume iii (Martinus Nijhoff, Dordrecht/Londong)

LAWSON, R (2000), Annotation of Emesa Sugar, 37 *CMLRev* 983

LEMMENS, P (2001) 'The Relation between the Charter of Fundamental Rights of the European Union and the European Convention on Human Rights — Substantive Aspects' 8 *MJ* 49

LEONARD, A (2001) 'Legal Recognition of Same-sex Partnerships under US State or Local Law' in R Wintemute and M Andenas (eds), *Legal Recognition of Same-sex Partnerships* (Hart Publishing, Oxford)

LEWIS, J (2001) 'Debates and Issues Regarding Marriage and Cohabitation in the British and American Literature' 15 *IJLPF* 159

LIISBERG, J (2001) 'Does the EU Charter of Fundamental Rights Threaten the Supremacy of Community Law?' 38 *CMLRev* 1171

LIVINGSTONE, S (1997) 'Article 14 and the Prevention of Discrimination in the European Court of Human Rights' 1 *EHRLR* 463

LOWE, N (2003) 'The Growing Influence of the European Union on International Family Law' *CLP* 439

LUNDSTROM, K (1996) 'Family Life and the Freedom of Movement of Workers in the European Union' 10 *IJLPF* 250

Maastricht Journal of European and Comparative Law, volume of papers on the EU Charter of Fundamental Rights: (2001) 8(1) *MJ*

MADURO, M (2001) 'Harmony and Dissonance in Free Movement' 4 *CYELS* 315

MARENCO, G (1991) 'The Notion of a Restriction on the Freedom of Establishment and Provision of Services in the Case Law of the Court' 11 *YEL* 110

MARTIN, D (1999) 'Discriminations, Entraves et Obstacles: Trois Concepts en Quête d'Identité' *CDE* 260, 561

MARTINY, D (1998) 'Is Unification of Family Law Feasible or even Desirable?' in A Hartkamp et al (eds), *Towards a European Civil Code* (Kluwer, The Hague)

MCCAFFERTY, C (2001) 'General Prohibition on Discrimination: the New Protocol to the Human Rights Convention' (July) *IFL* 78

MCCRUDDEN, C (2004) 'The Future of the EU Charter' in *Europe 2004 — Le Grand Débat*

MCFADDEN, P (1996) 'The Right to Stay' 29 *Vanderbilt Journal of Transnational Law* 1

MCGLYNN, C (2001) 'The Europeanisation of Family Law'13 *CFLQ* 35

—— (2001) 'Famililes and the Charter of Fundamental Rights: Progressive Change or Entrenching the Status Quo?' 26 *ELRev* 582

—— (2001) 'A Family Law for the European Union?' in J Shaw (ed), *Social Law and Policy in an Evolving EU* (Hart Publishing, Oxford)

——(2003) 'Challenging the European Harmonisation of Family Law: Perspectives on "the Family" in K Boele-Woelki (ed), *Perspectives for the Unification and Harmonisation of Family Law in Europe* (Intersentia, Antwerp)

McLeavy, P (2002) 'The Brussels II Regulation: How the European Community has Moved into Family Law' 51 *ICLQ* 883

Maxwell, N (2001) 'Opening Civil Marriages to Same-gender Couples: a Netherlands-United States Comparison' 18 *Arizona Journal of International and Comparative Law* 141

Meilaender, P (2001) *Towards a Theory of Immigration* (Palgrave Macmillan, New York)

Melis, B (2001) *Negotiating Europe's Immigration Frontiers* (Kluwer, The Hague)

Menendez, AJ, 'Chartering Europe: The Charter of Fundamental Rights of the EU' Arena Working Paper, *http://www.arena.uio.no/publications/wp01_13htm*

Merin, Y (2002) *Equality for Same-sex Couples, the Legal Recognition of Gay Partnerships in Europe and the United States* (University of Chicago Press, Chicago)

Moitinho de Almeida, JC, (1997) Speech delivered at the European Court of Human Rights in Strasbourg 7 *Bulletin des Droits de l'Homme* 280

Moon, G [2002] 'European Equality Rights' (April) *Legal Action* 26

——[2002] 'The Draft Discrimination Protocol to the *ECHR*: A Progress Report' 1 *EHRLR* 49

More, G (1999) 'The Principle of Equal Treatment — From Market Unifier to Fundamental Right' in P Craig and G de Búrca (eds), *The Evolution of EU Law* (OUP, Oxford)

Morgan, P (2000) *Marriage-lite: the Rise of Cohabitation* (Institute for the Study of Civil Society, London)

Morijn, J 'Judicial Reference to the EU Fundamental Rights Charter: First Experiences and Possible Prospects' (online, *www.europa.eu.int/futurum/documents/other/oth000602_en.pdf*)

Murphy, J (2002) 'The Recognition of Same-Sex Families in Britain: the Role of Private International Law' 16 *IJLPF* 181

Neuwahl, N and Rosas, A (eds) (1995) *The European Union and Human Rights* (Kluwer, The Hague)

Nic Shiubhne, N (2002) 'The Free Movement of Goods and Article 28 EC: An Evolving Framework' 27 *ELRev* 408

——(2002) 'Free Movement of Persons and the Wholly Internal Rule — Time to Move On?' 39 *CMLRev* 731

Niessen, J and Yongmi, S (eds) (2003) *EU and US Approaches to the Management of Immigration: Comparative Perspectives* (Migration Policy Group, Brussels)

Norrie, K (2000) 'Marriage is for Heterosexuals — May the Rest of us be Spared from It' 12 *CFLQ* 363

O'Hare, U (2001) 'Enhancing European Equality Rights: a New Regional Framework' 8 *MJ* 133

O'Keefe, D and Bavasso, A (2000) 'Four Freedoms, One Market and National Competence — in Search of a Dividing Line' in D O'Keefe (ed), *Liber Amicorum Lord Slynn* (Kluwer, The Hague)

O'Leary, S (1996) *The Evolving Concept of Community Citizenship* (Kluwer, The Hague)

——(1999) 'The Free Movement of Persons and Services' in P Craig and G de Búrca (eds), *The Evolution of EU Law* (OUP, Oxford)

OLIVEIRA PAIS, S [2002] 'De Facto Relationships and Same-sex Relationships in Portugal' *ISFL* 337
OLIVER, P (1999) 'Some Further Reflections on the Scope of Articles 28–10 EC' 36 *CMLRev* 783
PAPADOPOULOU, L (2002) 'In(di)visible Citizens(hip): Same-sex Partners in Euroepan Union Immigration Law' *YEL* 229
PEERS, S (1995) 'Indirect Rights for Third Country National Service Providers Confirmed' 20 *ELRev* 303
——(1996) 'Towards Equality — Actual and Potential Rights of Third Country Nationals in the European Union' 33 *CMLRev* 7
——(2002) 'Human Rights Jurisprudence of the European Court of Justice' 2 *HRLRev* 211
——(2003) 'The European Court of Justice and the European Court of Human Rights: Comparative Approaches' in E Orucu (ed) *Judicial Comparativism in Human Rights Cases* (BIICL)
PEREZ CANOVAS, N (2001) 'Spain: The Heterosexual State Refuses to Disappear' in Wintemute and Andenas (eds), *Legal Recognition of Same-sex Partnerships* (Hart Publishing, Oxford)
PINTENS, W (2003) 'Europeanisation of Family Law' in K Boele-Woelki (eds) *Perspectives for the Unfication and Harmonisation of Family Law in Europe* (Intersentia, Antwerp)
PLENDER, R (1997) *Basic Documents on International Migration Law* (Kluwer, The Hague)
——(1988) *International Migration Law*, 2nd edn (Nijhoff, Dordrecht)
POLIKOFF, N (1993) 'We Will Get What We Ask For: Why Legalising Gay and Lesbian Marriage Will Not "Dismantle the Legal Structure of Gender in Every Marriage"' 79 *Virginia L Rev* 1535
——(2000) 'Recognising Partners but not Parents/Recognising Parents but not Partners. Gay and Lesbian Family Law in Europe and the US' 17 *NY Law School Journal of Human Rights* 711
Pontifical Council for the Family, Marriage, and 'De Facto' Unions (Vatican, 2000). Available online, *www.vatican.va/roman_curia_20001109_de-facto-unions_en.html*
PROBERT, R [2003] 'The Right to Marry and the Impact of the Human Rights Act 1998' *IFL* 29
PROBERT, R and BARLOW, A (2002) 'Displacing Marriage — Diversification and Harmonisation Within Europe' 12 *CFLQ* 153
RICHARDS, C (2002) 'The Legal Recognition of Same-Sex Couples: the French Perspective' 51 *ICLQ* 305
ROGERS, N [2003] 'Immigration and the European Convention on Human Rights: Are New Principles Emerging?' *EHRLR* 53
RUBELLIN-DEVICHI, J (2002) *Des Concubinages — Droit Interne, Droit International, Droit Comparé : Etudes Offertes à Jaqueline Rubellin-Devichi* (Litec, Paris)
SCAPPUCI, G (2000) 'Court of First Instance Refused to Recognise Swedish Registered Partnership Rights and Duties' *EPL* 355
SCHIMMEL, R and Heun, S (2001) 'The Legal Situation of Same-sex Couples in Germany — an Overview' in R Wintemute and M Andenas (eds), *Legal Recognition of Same-sex Partnerships* (Hart Publishing, Oxford)

SEDDON, D (1999) 'Families, Dependants, Relationships' in *A Guide to the Human Rights Act, Butterworths Immigration Law Service, Special Bulletin* (Butterworths, London)

SHERLOCK, A (1999) 'Deportation of Aliens and Article 8 ECHR' 23 *ELRev* 70

SIEHR, K (2003) 'Family Unions in Private International Law' *NILR* 419

SLOANE, A (1997) 'A Rose by Any Other Name: Marriage and the Danish Registered Partnership Act' 5 *Cardozo Journal of International and Comparative Law* 189

SNELL, J (2002) *Goods and Services in EC Law* (OUP, Oxford)

SOHN, L and BUERGENTHAL, T (1992) *The Movement of Persons across Borders* (ASIL, Washington DC)

SPAVENTA, E (2004) 'From *Gebhard* to *Carpenter*: Towards a (non-economic) European Constitution' *CMLRev* (forthcoming)

SPIELMANN, D (1999) 'Human Rights Caselaw in the Strasbourg and Luxembourg Courts: Conflicts, Inconsistencies, and Complementaries' in P Alston (ed), *The EU and Human Rights* (OUP, Oxford)

—— (2000) 'Annotation of *Emesa Sugar*' *RTDH* 581

STALFORD, H 'Concepts of the Family under EU Law: Lessons from the ECHR' 16 *IJLPF* 410

—— (2003) 'Old Problems, New Solutions? — EU Regulation of Cross-National Child Maintenance' 15(3) *CFLQ* 269

—— (2003) 'Regulating Family Life in Post-Amsterdam Europe' 28 *ELRev* 39

STAPLES, H (1999) *The Legal Status of Third Country Nationals in the European Union* (Kluwer, The Hague)

STARMER, K (1999) *European Human Rights Law* (Legal Action Group, London)

—— (2001) 'Positive Obligations under the Convention' in J Jowell and J Cooper (eds), *Understanding Human Rights Principles* (Hart Publishing, Oxford)

STARR, S and BRILMAYER, L (2003) 'Family Separation as a Violation of International law' 21 *Berkeley J Int Law* 213

STEYGER, E (1997) *National Traditions and European Community Law* (Dartmouth, Aldershot)

STOREY, H (1997) 'Right to Family Life and Immigration Case Law at Strasbourg' 39 *ICLQ* 328

STRASSBERG M (1997) 'Distinctions of Form and Substance: Monogamy, Polygamy, and Same-sex Marriage' 75 *NCL Rev* 1501

STRASSER, M (1997) *Legally Wed: Same-sex Marriage and the Constitution* (Cornell University Press, Ithaca)

—— (1999) *The Challenge of Same-sex Marriage* (Praeger, Westport, CT)

—— (2000) 'The Privileges of National Citizenship: On *Saenz*, Same-sex Couples, and the Right to Travel' 52 *Rutgers Law Review* 554

STYCHIN, C (1994) '*Grant*-ing Rights: the Politics of Rights, Sexuality and European Union' 51 *NILQ* 251

SUMNER, I 'Registered Partnerships and Private International Law: Great Britain and the Netherlands Compared' (Conference paper, publication forthcoming)

TASCHNER, H (1993) 'Free Movement of Students, Retired Persons and Other European Citizens — a Difficult Legislative Process' in H Schermers et al (eds), *Free Movement of Persons in Europe* (Martinus Nijhoff Dordrecht)

TEMPLE LANG, J (1990) 'Community Constitutional Law: Article 5 [10] EEC Treaty' 27 *CMLRev* 645

—— [1991] 'The Sphere in Which Member States are Obliged to Comply with the General Principles of Law and Community Fundamental Rights Principles' *LIEI* 23

THORN, K (2003) 'The German Conflict of Laws Rules on Registered Partnership' in K Boele-Woelki and A Fuchs (eds), *Legal Recognition of Same-sex Couples in Europe* (Intersentia, Antwerp)

—— (2003) 'The New German Law on Same-sex Partnerships' in K Boele-Woelke & A Fuchs (eds), *Legal Recognition of Same-sex Couples in Europe* (Intersentia, Antwerp)

TONER, H (2001) 'Immigration Rights of Unmarried Partners as Obstacles to Free Movement under Community Law' 15 *IANL* 207

—— (2003) 'Annotation of *Carpenter*' 5 *EJML* 163

TONER, H and ILIOPOULOU, A (2003) 'Annotation of *D'Hoop*' 28 *ELRev* 389

TOUMSCHAT, C (2000) 'Annotation of *Martínez Sala*' 37 *CMLRev* 449

TRACOL, X (2003) 'The Pacte Civil de Solidarité (PACS)' in K Boele-Woelke and A Fuchs (eds), *Legal Recognition of Same-sex Couples in Europe* (Intersentia, Antwerp)

TRIDIMAS, T (1999) *The General Principles of EC Law* (OUP, Oxford)

VAN DER MEIDE, W (2001) 'Who Guards the Borders of Canada's "Gay" Community' 19 *Windsor Yearbook of Access to Justice* 39

VAN DER VELDE, S (2003) *The EU Right to Family Reunification in the Context of International Human Rights Protection* (PhD Thesis, EUI, Florence)

VAN DIJK, P (2003) 'The Treatment of Homosexuals under the European Convention on Human Rights' in C Waaldijk and A Clapham (eds), *Homosexuality: A European Community Issue* (Martinus, Nijhoff, Dordreecht)

—— (1998) 'Protection of 'Integrated Aliens Against Expulsion under the European Convention' in E Guild and P Minderhoud (eds), *Security of Residence and Expulsion — Protection of Aliens in Europe* (Kluwer, The Hague)

VAN DIJK, P and VAN HOOF, G (1998) *Theory and Practice of the European Convention on Human Rights* (Kluwer, The Hague)

Vatican, 'Considerations Regarding Proposals to Give Legal Recognition to Unions Between Homosexual Persons' (approved by Pope John Paul II on 28 March 2003, dated 3 June 2003, published on 31 July 2003), *http://www.vatican.va/roman_curia/ congregations/cfaith/documents/ rc_con_cfaith_doc_20030731 _homosexual-unions_en.html*

VAZ, K (2000) Comment to reporters, Biarritz, BBC News website, 13 October 2000

VERBEKE, A (2001) 'Perspectives for an International Marital Contract' 8 *MJ* 189

WAALDIJK, C (1993)'The Legal Situation in the Member States' in C Waaldijk and A Clapham (eds), *Homosexuality: A Community Law Issue* (Martinus Nijhoff, The Hague)

—— (2001) 'Small Change: How the Road to Same-sex Marriage Got Paved in the Netherlands' in R Wintemute and M Andenas (eds), *Legal Recognition of Same-sex Partnerships* (Hart Publishing, Oxford)

WAALDIJK, C and CLAPHAM, A (eds) (1993) *Homosexuality: A Community Law Issue* (Martinus Nijhoff, The Hague)

WAITE, L and GALLAGHER, M (1996) *The Case for Marriage* (Broadway Books, New York)

WARDLE, L (1996) 'International Marriage Recognition — A World Dilemma' in N Lowe and G Douglas (eds), *Families Across Frontiers* (Martinus Nijhoff, The Hague)

——(1996) 'Multiply and Replenish: Considering Same-sex Marriage in the Light of State Interests in Marital Procreation' 24 *Harvard JLPP* 771

WEATHERILL, S (1996) 'After *Keck*: Some Thoughts on How to Clarify the Clarification' 33 *CMLRev* 885

——(1999) 'Recent Case-law concerning the Free Movement of Goods' 36 *CMLRev* 51

WEILER, J (1999) 'Text and Context in the Free Movement of Goods' in P Craig and G De Búrca (eds), *The Evolution of EU Law* (OUP, Oxford)

WINTEMUTE, R (1996) *Sexual Orientation and Human Rights* (OUP, Oxford)

——(1997) 'Recognising New Kinds of Direct Sex Discrimination: Transsexualism, Sexual Orientation and Dress Codes' 60 *MLR* 334

——(2001) 'Same-sex Partners and Parents under the Convention' in R Wintemute and M Andenas (eds), *Legal Recognition of Same-sex Partnerships* (Hart Publishing, Oxford)

——(2002) 'France Permitted to Ban Adoptions to Lesbian and Gay Individuals' 2(2) *ILGA-Europe Newsletter* 4

——(forthcoming) 'Partnership Rights as Human Rights' *Oxford Amnesty Lecture, March 2002* (OUP, Oxford)

WINTEMUTE, R and ANDENAS, M (eds) (2001) *Legal Recognition of Same-sex Partnerships* (Hart Publishing, Oxford)

Women & Equality Unit (2003) *Civil Partnership — A Framework for the Legal Recognition of Same-Sex Couples* (Women & Equality Unit/HMSO, London)

WOODS, L (1999) 'Family Rights in the EU: Disadvantaging the Disadvantaged?' 11 *CFLQ* 17

WU, Z (2000) *Cohabitation — an Alternative Form of Family Living* (OUP, Oxford)

Websites

BBC News, *http.news.bbc.co.uk*

Canadian Department of Justice, *http://www.justice.gc.ca*

Canadian Law Commission, *www.lcc.gc.ca*

Commission on European Family Law, *www.law,uu.nl/priv/cefl/*

Copenhagen Post, *http://chpost.periskop.dk/*

Equal Marriage for Same-sex Couples website, *www.samesexmarriage.ca*

European Co-ordination for the rights of foreigners to family life, *http://members.aol.com/coordeurop/indexce.html*

GayLawNews, *www.gaylawnet.com*

Human Rights Campaign, *www.hrc.org*

ILGA-Europe, *www.ilga-europe.org*

Immigration Law Practitioners Association, *www.ilpa.org.uk*

Partners Task Force for Gay and Lesbian Couples, *www.buddybuddy.com*

TUC Gay Lesbian: Bisexual Conference, *www.tuc.org.uk/equality/tuc-5200-fo.cfm*

Official Documents EC

Amended Proposal for a Council Directive on the Right to Family Reunificaiton COM(2000)264 [2000] OJ C62/99

Amended Proposal for a Council Directive on the Right to Family Reunification COM(2002)225 [2002] OJ C203/136
Amended Proposal for a Council Regulation to Amend Regulation 1612/68 COM(90)108 [1990] OJ C119/05
Amended Proposal for a European Parliament and Council Directive on the Posting of Workers who are Third Country Nationals for the Purposes of Cross-Border Service Provision COM(1999)0003
Commission *Communication on Family Policies* COM(1989)363
Commission *Communication on the Application of Directive 64/221* COM(1999)372
Commission *Communication On the Legal Nature of the Charter of Fundamental Rights of the European Union* COM(2000)644
Commission *First Report on Citizenship* COM(1993)710
Commission *Second Report on Citizenship* COM(1997)230
Commission *Third Report on Citizenship* COM(2001)506
Committee of the Regions, Opinion on Proposal COM(2001)257 [2002] OJ C192/17
Committee on Youth, Culture, Education the Media and Sport Report on Proposal COM(1989)275 on the Right of Residence for Students. Document A3-77/89, PE134.304/fin
Conclusions of the European Council, Tampere
Council Document 10572/02
Council Document 13017/01
Council Document 14272/02
Council Document 15380/01
Council Document 5881/03
Council Resolution 97/C 382/01 on Measures to be Adopted on the Combatting of Marriages of Convenience [1997] OJ C-382/1
Council Working Document 10857/02
Council Working Document 11787/02
Decision 93/743 of 13 December 1993 [1993] OJ L348/1
Decision 94/910 of 19 December 1994 [1994] OJ L360/1
Economic and Social Committee, Opinion on Proposal COM(2001)257 [2002] OJ C149/46
Economic and Social Committee, Opinion on the 'Proposal for a Council Directive on the Right to Family Reunification' [2000] OJ C204/40
European Parliament Resolution on Family Policy in the EEC [1983] OJ C184/116
High Level Panel, Report of the High Level Panel on the Free Movement of Persons
House of Lords Select European Union Select Committee, 8th Report of 1999/2000 *The EU Charter of Fundamental Rights* (HMSO 2000)
Joint Declaration by the Parliament, Council and Commission [1977] OJ C103/1
LIBE Committee Draft Report on Proposal COM(2001)257 Document PE319.238, 25 November 2002
LIBE Committee Draft Report on Proposal COM(2002)225 on the Right to Family Reunification, Document PE319.245
LIBE Committee Meeting document, 6 June 2000
LIBE Committee Meeting document, 9 December 2002, PE319.238/47–103
LIBE Committee Report on Proposal COM(1999)638 PE//285892, A5/2000/201

LIBE Committee Report on the Proposal for a Directive on the Right to Family Reuniciation, 13 July 2000, document A5-201/2000, incorporating Opinion of the Legal Affairs and Internal Market Committee

LIBE Committee Working Document of 14 March 2002, Document PE 311.026

Proposal for a Council Directive concerning the Status of Third Country Nationals who are Long Term Residents COM(2001)127 [2001] OJ C240/79

Proposal for a Council Directive on a Right of Residence for Nationals of a Member Sates in the Territory of Another Member State [1979] OJ C207/14

Proposal for a Council Directive on the Conditions of Entry and Residence of Third Country Nationals for the Purpose of Paid Empolyment and Self-Employed Activity COM(2001)386

Proposal for a Council Directive on the Right of Residence for Students, Proposal for a Council Direcctive on the Right of Residence for Employees and Self-Employed Persons who have Ceased Occupational Activity, Proposal for a Council Directive on the Right of Residence COM(1989)275, [1989] OJ C191/2–5

Proposal for a Council Directive relating to the Conditions in which Third Country Nationals shall have the Freedom to Travel in the Territory of Member Sates for a Period Not Exceeding Three Months COM(2001)388 [2001] OJ C270/244

Proposal for a Council Regulation to Amend Regulation 1612/68 COM(1998)394 [1998] OJ C344/9

Proposal for a Council Regulation to Amend Regulation 1612/68 COM(88)815 [1989] OJ C100/06

Proposal for a Directive of the European Parliament and of the Council on the Provision of Services in the Internal Market

Proposal for a European Parliament and Council Directive on the Right of Citizens of the Union and their Family Members to Move and Reside Freely Throughout the Territory of the Member States COM(2001)257 [2001] OJ C270/150

Proposal for Council Directive on the Right to Family Reunification COM(1999) 638 [2000] OJ 116/66

Proposal for Directive on the Qualification and Status of Third Country Nationals and Stateless Persons as Refugees, COM(2001)510 [2002] OJ C51/325

Question E-1829/01 by Lousewies van der Laan, 22 June 2001

Question E-1830/01 by lousewies van der Laan, 12 June 2001

Question E-3211/01 by Kathalijne Buitenweg, 9 November 2001

Question E-3261/01 by Joke Swiebel 13 November 2001

Question P-2438/01 by Kathalijne Buitenweg, 29 August 2001

Reply to Question E-3211/01, 7 Feb 2002, Commissioner Kinnock

Reply to Question E-3261/00, 12 March 2002, Commissioner Vittorino

Reply to Question P-2348/01, 15 October 2001, Commissioner Kinnock

Index